Backstage in Hong Kong

A life with the Philharmonic, Broadway musicals and classical superstars

John Duffus

BLACKSMITH BOOKS

Dedicated with much gratitude and affection to Vennie Ho, Sun Man Tseng, Lee Bo-luen, K. C. Lee, David Rule and all others who provided so much help to me during my career in Hong Kong

---

Backstage in Hong Kong

ISBN 978-988-76749-0-0

Published by Blacksmith Books
Unit 26, 19/F, Block B, Wah Lok Industrial Centre,
37-41 Shan Mei Street, Fo Tan, Hong Kong
Tel: (+852) 2877 7899
www.blacksmithbooks.com

With a ten-year background at the BBC in London and with Scottish Opera, JOHN DUFFUS arrived in Hong Kong in 1979 as the most experienced performing arts manager then to work in the city. He had been appointed the fifth general manager of the Hong Kong Philharmonic Orchestra in as many years. Celebrating its 50th anniversary as a professional ensemble in 2024, it has now developed as the finest in Asia.

The early years of the Philharmonic were full of problems and many disasters. A first-class honours Music graduate, Duffus had come to Hong Kong with a brief to solve these issues and set the orchestra on an international footing. With typical Scottish grit and determination, he overcame most problems, helping the Philharmonic become a true community orchestra with a growing international reputation.

Remaining in Hong Kong after his eight years with the Philharmonic, he describes more adventures presenting concerts and recitals around Asia with such artists as Pavarotti, Domingo, Carreras, Kiri Te Kanawa, Isaac Stern, Yo-Yo Ma and a host of others. He organised the spectacular Three Tenors concert in Beijing's Forbidden City in 2001 and Pavarotti's final concert before a paying public in 2005.

As managing director of Andrew Lloyd Webber's Asian companies, Duffus helped bring *CATS* and *Phantom of the Opera* to Hong Kong. He later established his own arts consultancy working with the Hong Kong Tourist Association and at the start of the West Kowloon Cultural District, both requiring much problem-solving. Most of the stories in this book have never before been published.

Contents

Preface . . . 7
Dramatis Personae . . . 9

1 Hong Kong on the Horizon . . . 14
2 Challenge #1: A Strange Music Director Appointment . . . 23
3 Challenge #2: Ling Tung's Dubious Qualifications . . . 32
4 Challenge #3: What Happened to Due Diligence? . . . 38
5 I Arrive in Hong Kong . . . 52
6 My Growing Love For Hong Kong . . . 64
7 Ling Tung Leads the Philharmonic into the Law Courts . . . 79
8 Things Finally Begin to Go My Way . . . 92
9 Discovering the Region and Being Discovered . . . 103
10 The Much-Disliked Ling Tung Finally Departs . . . 113
11 The Search For a New Music Director . . . 117
12 Jury Duty . . . 127
13 The New Music Director Unveiled . . . 130
14 Developing the Philharmonic . . . 134
15 New Audiences – Who? How? Where? . . . 141
16 Downs and Ups . . . 153
17 My Final Season: I Start Thinking About My Future . . . 171
18 My Final Season: China Tour, Glyndebourne, Lawsuit . . . 202
19 Disaster When Starting My Own Business . . . 219
20 Excursions into the Soviet Union . . . 222
21 Macao's International Music Festival . . . 236
22 Hong Kong Cultural Centre: Design Misadventures . . . 240
23 The Superstars: Pavarotti, Domingo and Carreras . . . 267
24 Musicals #1: My First Attempt to Present *CATS* . . . 278

25 Yet More of the Classical Superstars. .283
26 Musicals #2: The Desire for a New Adventure 293
27 Musicals #3: *CATS* and Broken Promises 304
28 Abject Failures at the Hong Kong Tourist Association 329
29 West Kowloon: A Great Idea Dramatically Watered Down . .356
30 Summary: How Much and Who Paid? 367

Afterword 377
Footnotes 385
Selected Bibliography 388
Acknowledgements 390

PREFACE

"Stop worrying about the potholes in the road and celebrate the journey."

I had never heard of the American physician, writer, educator and social activist, Professor Fitzhugh Mullan, until I started thinking about how I wished to start this book. It is not a history. Nor is it a diary. More it is a series of personal reminiscences of my time as an arts administrator in Hong Kong interwoven with thoughts about people, places and events over a period of close to four decades. Looking through a website of quotations, I came across this one which seemed to sum up my career rather nicely.

When I meet friends and family members, the constant refrain is always, "You have had an enviable career." I have never disputed this obvious fact, even in light of the whole series of potholes I had to navigate. As a student in the Music Faculty at the University of Aberdeen, I would have laughed if anyone had suggested I would go on to enjoy even a fraction of the opportunities which have fallen my way. I deliberately use the word "fallen" for as the reader will discover in the following pages, rarely have I ever gone out to secure any particular employment. My one ambition was that I end up working in the international music business. And that in itself was more than a little audacious because at the time – I was at University during the second half of the 1960s – I had precious little knowledge of what made up the "international music business"!

Over the ensuing half-century, less just a couple of years, my journey was to include broadcasting, opera company administration, the management of a symphony orchestra, regional directorships of the world's largest artists' agency and one of its most lauded entertainment companies. I had also founded and managed two companies which concentrated on the promotion of the arts and entertainment at the highest international level.

Although for most of that journey I was based in Asia, it was to see me travel quite literally all over the world. As I entered University, I had taken only two short haul flights. By the time I closed my second company in 2017 I had flown more than eight million kilometres, travelled on 32 round-the-world trips visiting well over 100 cities for business reasons, and at least as many again on the vacation trips I was able to make, both as short weekend hops during those round-the-world flights and in an effort to learn as much about our world as possible during scheduled vacation times. They also enabled me to attend some truly wonderful performances. Bach's B minor Mass in Leipzig's Thomaskirche with the grave of the great composer before us; a magnificent performance of Haydn's *Creation* on the exact day and time of the 200th anniversary of his death in the beautiful Haydnsaal in Eisenstadt where he worked for much of his life; operas too numerous to mention including *Der Rosenkavalier* in Dresden where Richard Strauss was Music Director; and a string of musicals in Broadway and London's West End.

With Asia as my base for nearly four decades, it is appropriate that I start these reminiscences with another quote, this time from the great Tang Dynasty philosopher Lao Tzu. "The journey of a thousand miles begins with a single step." For me that step took place at the dawn of 1979.

DRAMATIS PERSONAE

As a guide for the reader, the following is a list of commonly used abbreviations and key persons mentioned in the text specifically relating to the periods I was associated with their organisations. Titles are often abbreviated. Listing is in alphabetical order.

Acronyms

AFM	American Federation of Musicians
CCDC	City Contemporary Dance Company of Hong Kong
CPAA	China Performing Arts Agency, Beijing
CSD	Cultural Services Department of the Hong Kong Urban Council
GC	General Committee of the Hong Kong Philharmonic Orchestra
GIS	Hong Kong Government Information Services
HKAPA	Hong Kong Academy for Performing Arts
HKCC	Hong Kong Cultural Centre
HKPO	Hong Kong Philharmonic Orchestra
HKTA	Hong Kong Tourist Association
IEF	International Events Fund established by the HKTA in 1998
IMG	International Management Group, the worldwide athlete representation and sports management company founded by Mark H. McCormack
IMGA	IMG Artists, the arts and entertainment division of IMG
KGB	The Soviet Union's Committee for State Security, Foreign Intelligence and Domestic Security
LCSD	Leisure and Cultural Services Department of the Hong Kong Government

LEGCO The Hong Kong Legislative Council
RTHK Radio Television Hong Kong
RUG Andrew Lloyd Webber's Really Useful Group
SAR Special Administrative Region of the People's Republic of China
SCMP South China Morning Post, an English-language newspaper
TPC Theatre Projects Consultants, London
WKCDA West Kowloon Cultural District Authority

Hong Kong Philharmonic Orchestra (HKPO) under the auspices of the Hong Kong Philharmonic Society

Dr. Solomon Bard, Vice-Chairman, HKPO GC
John Boyden, recording producer
Selina Chow, independent event producer
Gerry Forsgate, Hon. Treasurer, HKPO GC and subsequently Chairman, Urban Council
Richard Gamlen, General Manager, HKPO 1976-78
David Gwilt, Member of the HKPO GC
Klaus Heymann, founder of HK Records, Marco Polo and Naxos CD record labels
Vennie Ho, Accountant, HKPO
Cynthia Hydes, Publicity Manager, HKPO
Kenneth Jean, Guest Conductor and co-Principal Guest Conductor, HKPO from 1984
John Koljonen, Principal Clarinet, HKPO
Philip Kwok, Chairman, HKPO GC from 1982
Lee Bo-luen, Orchestra Manager, HKPO
Lee Kin-cheung (known as K. C.), Marketing Assistant, HKPO and later project manager for many of the author's events
Maria Lui, Deputy General Manager, HKPO until 1981
John Mackenzie, Chairman, HKPO GC until 1982
Hans Günther Mommer, Principal Conductor, HKPO 1976-78
Peter Moss, Member, HKPO GC and Assistant Director, GIS

Carl Pini (known as Tony), Concertmaster, HKPO 1980/82
Sir Denys Roberts, HKPO Board Member, Chief Justice of Hong Kong
A de O. Sales (better known as Sonny Sales), Chairman, HKPO Board of Governors and Chairman, Urban Council
Mrs. Carmel Sandberg, Member and later Chairman, HKPO Ladies Committee
Kenneth Schermerhorn, Music Director, HKPO 1984-1989
Maxim Shostakovich, Guest Conductor and Principal Guest Conductor, HKPO 1983-86
So Hau-leung, General Manager, HKPO 1974-75
David Stone, Hong Kong Government Music Advisor
Basil Tschaikov, former Principal Clarinet and Chairman, London Philharmonia Orchestra
Ling Tung, Music Director, HKPO 1980-82
Margot Tung née Walk, wife of Ling Tung
Sun Man Tseng, Marketing Manager, HKPO
Su Villiers, Concerts Manager, HKPO
James Wong, PR Consultant to the HKPO 1978-79
Takako Nishizaki, violin soloist and wife of Klaus Heymann

Hong Kong Urban Council (but not listed under the HKPO)
Darwin Chen, Director Cultural Services 1980-1984
Helen Yu, Director Cultural Services from 1985
Choi Suk-kuen, Assistant Director Cultural Services
Lo King-man, Chairman, Urban Council Sub-Committee on the Arts

Hong Kong Cultural Centre
José Lei, Chief Government Architect
Sir Cameron Mackintosh, the world's most influential theatrical producer of the 1980s
Harold Marshall, Acoustic Design Consultant, Concert Hall HKCC
Alan Russell, Partner, Theatre Projects Consultants
John Wyckham, Technical Consultant, Grand Theatre HKCC

Hong Kong Tourist Association

Amy Chan, Executive Director

Johnny Chin, Executive, Sun Hung Kai Properties

Selina Chow, Legislative Councillor and Member of the IEF Committee

Patrick Condon, Australian Event Producer and Consultant

Douglas Gautier, Deputy Director

Dick Kaufman, PR Company Director and Member of the IEF Committee

Y. S. Lo, Chairman

Peter Wearing Smith, Entrepreneur and Motor Sport Enthusiast

Stanley Yip, Executive

Allan Zeman, Prominent Hong Kong businessman and Member of the IEF Committee

West Kowloon Cultural District

Michael Lynch, CEO West Kowloon Consultative Committee, 2011-2015

Graham Sheffield, CEO West Kowloon Consultative Committee, 2010

Andrew Lloyd Webber's Really Useful Group

Brian Barnes, General Manager, RUG Australia

Julie Brookes, Production Administrator, RUG Australia

Michael Chung, Event Promoter, Seoul

Garth Drabinsky, Live Entertainment Canada CEO

Patrick McKenna, CEO, RUG

John Robertson, co-Executive Director, Cameron Mackintosh Australia

David Tang, Hong Kong entrepreneur and Founder of Hong Kong's China Club

James Thane, Director of Cameron Mackintosh Australia and later RUG Australasia

Pavarotti, Domingo, Carreras and other major international artists

Herbert Breslin, Manager of Luciano Pavarotti
Harvey Goldsmith, Major International Pop Concert Promoter
Charles Hamlen, Founder of Hamlen/Landau Management which became IMG Artists
Don Harris, Head of Corporate Affairs, Philip Morris Asia
Kazuo Kondo, Head of IMG Japan
Edna Landau, Co-founder, Hamlen/Landau Management
Ian MacLaren, General Manager, Tibor Rudas' company
Cheryl MacLaren, Executive, Tibor Rudas' company
Mark H. McCormack, Chairman and CEO, International Management Group
Chris McDonald, CEO, Rolex Japan
John Webber, Executive in overall charge of IMG Artists worldwide
Tibor Rudas, Concert Promoter of Luciano Pavarotti for 20 years
Michael Storrs, Arts Management Executive, IMG Artists London

General

Victor Hochhauser, Artists' Agent and Concert Promoter
Lillian Hochhauser, Wife of Victor
Sir Ian Hunter, First Artistic Director of the Hong Kong Arts Festival and Chairman of Harold Holt Artists' Agency, London
Lee Lamont, CEO ICM Artists' Management, New York
Walter Legge, Founder of London's Philharmonia Orchestra
Sir Murray MacLehose, Governor of Hong Kong
Walter Nichols, Former American Diplomat and Founder of Azabu Artists, Tokyo
Wilfred Stiff, CEO, Ibbs & Tillett Artists' Agency, London
Walter Tautschnig, Director, Vienna Boys Choir

1

HONG KONG ON THE HORIZON

"John! I know you want to work overseas. Would you be interested in a job in Hong Kong?"

What a strange question, I thought. Surely everyone was aware I wanted to go west, not east, for I had set my goal on working in the United States. I knew virtually nothing about Hong Kong. Indeed, if someone had placed an outline map of Asia in front of me, I would have had difficulty identifying Hong Kong's location. Asked to place a pin on that map, I fear it might have been somewhere near Kagoshima in Japan.

No doubt this was in large part a result of geography classes at my school in Aberdeen, Scotland, during the 1960s having dealt with Asia in little more than one session. Perhaps also a result of travel to Asia by early 1979 being limited more or less to the richer classes in society or hippies off to visit exotic countries like India, Nepal and Thailand. Others taking the kangaroo route to Australia rarely stopped over in the two main Asian cities through which mostly British Airways and Qantas flew, Singapore and Bangkok. Mass tourism was still some years away.

I had been asked the question by David Richardson, then the General Administrator of the Scottish National Orchestra in Glasgow. When I queried why he thought of me, he said he had been asked to provide references for two applicants for the post of General Manager of the Hong Kong Philharmonic Orchestra. He believed my qualifications were at least as good. If interested, he would happily recommend me to the committee organising the interviews.

After earning a first-class honours degree in music at Aberdeen University, I had spent a short time as a trainee with the BBC in London before joining the still relatively young Scottish Opera in Glasgow as Personal Assistant to the General Administrator in 1971. Scottish Opera had been the brainchild of the conductor Alexander Gibson. Gibson had been the youngest ever Music Director at London's Sadlers Wells Opera (soon renamed English National Opera) before returning to his native Scotland as Music Director of the Scottish National Orchestra. With the orchestra having several free weeks in the early summer, Gibson was determined to use it by presenting opera, giving Scottish audiences the same quality of performances that could be seen in the two London opera houses. Its first season was a week of two operas in June 1962, Puccini's *Madama Butterfly* and Debussy's *Pelléas et Mélisande*. Within little more than a decade the number of operas and performing weeks had expanded dramatically and it was drawing accolades from both audiences and the national media. As a critic wrote in the *Financial Times* –

"At its best, Scottish Opera is unsurpassed by any other company in western Europe."

Given that Europe boasted three of the acknowledged top four companies in the world – La Scala in Milan, the Vienna State Opera and London's Royal Opera – that was praise indeed.

The 12-year period starting in 1967 were frequently called Scottish Opera's "golden years". It was a time when almost everything the company did was a success. For its tenth anniversary in 1971 it presented Richard Wagner's massive four-opera *Ring* cycle. Within two more years it was close to being a full-time ensemble presenting 130 full performances a year of a dozen different productions. And by 1975 it raised £3 million (more than £30 million in 2022 figures) to purchase and fully restore Glasgow's Theatre Royal as Scotland's first Opera House.

I had the joy of working for the company in three positions. Following three years as PA to the General Administrator, I jumped up the ladder to become Assistant General Administrator. Three years later, following a near breakdown in the Production and Technical Department due in large part to the major increase in the number of productions being presented each year, I was asked to take over as Technical Controller with a brief to introducing a raft of administrative reforms that would help introduce greater efficiency.

I was delighted to accept that position for I had long been fascinated by everything that went on stage behind the curtains. At the back of my mind, though, was an ever-increasing feeling that in order to progress further up that ladder and eventually run my own company I would need to move away from Britain. I was perfectly well aware there were gaps in my knowledge of the performing arts. At that time there were few major performing companies in the United Kingdom. If I was going to progress, almost certainly I would need to cut my teeth abroad where I could make my mistakes – as all arts managers do – far from the limelight and away from the large number of music and arts critics in the UK.

So I set myself two years to complete my task with Scottish Opera's Production and Technical Department. No matter that I loved working for the company, I felt eight years close to the start of my career with one company was enough. I needed pastures new. One of my closest friends and colleagues had moved to a well-paid job as General Manager of the Boston Opera. He suggested I fly to America and generally see what jobs might be available. Unlike today, when most arts-related jobs worldwide are well advertised in a host of publications and websites, in 1978 when I visited America I was quite literally flying blind. Only through word-of-mouth and with help from some of the artists' agents could one hope to have much clue which jobs were, or were likely to become, available.

I returned from America with only one possible job opportunity: running the tiny company in Omaha, Nebraska. Even today the company produces only 11 performances of three operas each year. That held absolutely no interest for me. It was after that trip that I was approached and asked the question about Hong Kong. Being 6,000 miles away and a part of the world about which I knew precisely nothing, my initial response to David had been, "Thanks, but no thanks." I was quickly to change my mind. Sitting at home that evening, I spent more time thinking about the suggestion. In an age without the internet, it was difficult to find out much about Hong Kong other than by a phone call to my former boss who was then Managing Director of Australian Opera. All Peter Hemmings could tell me was that he found Hong Kong a fascinating place. Of the orchestra, he knew nothing. He suspected the salary would be considerably higher than I was earning in Scotland, adding he felt it would be good for me to run my own arts organisation at that stage in my career.

The following morning, I called David to inform him I had rethought his suggestion. I would indeed be grateful if he would recommend me. Within days I was invited to travel to London the following week to attend an interview at the Hong Kong Government office in Grafton Street. In the meantime I had learned more about Hong Kong and the Philharmonic. A colleague of Sir Ian Hunter who had started up the Hong Kong Arts Festival a few years earlier knew little about the orchestra but reiterated Peter's comment that I would love being based in Hong Kong.

A musician from an orchestra which had visited the territory repeated that view. Although he had heard a concert given by the Philharmonic, all he would add was that I would find managing it a challenge. "Challenge" is often a code word. It implies there are problems – perhaps major – that would need to be overcome.

Not daunted, I flew to London on the morning of the interview and found my way off Bond Street to the location. After a short wait, I was ushered into a large room facing a group of three men. John Mackenzie was the Chairman of the Orchestra, a man I was soon to realise who knew precious little about music! David Stone had been a violinist in Yehudi Menuhin's Orchestra and an examiner for the Associated Board of the Royal Schools of Music which held its examinations in many parts of the world. Three years earlier he had found himself in Hong Kong. There he got to know a number of important people, including Sir David Akers-Jones, at that time the Secretary for the New Territories. With the territory's Governor, Sir Murray MacLehose, particularly interested in

Hong Kong establishing its own professional arts companies rather than exclusively, as in the past, importing performances from international ensembles, Stone had rather quickly been appointed the administration's Music Advisor, helping steer through a number of major changes to develop more musicians among Hong Kong youngsters. The third member of the panel was the Hong Kong Commissioner in London, Denis Bray. It seemed clear that Stone would be doing most of the questioning.

During the hour's interview, I felt extremely confident, even though my primary expertise till then had been in opera administration rather than specifically running an orchestra. I believed I answered the questions by giving the panel what its members wanted to hear. I was also able to amplify my answers by drawing on experience of, for example, Scottish Opera's youth programmes which were developing an interest in opera in many thousands of youngsters every year. I was soon to discover that expanding the Hong Kong Philharmonic's base was a key objective of its new General Manager. Another was developing the orchestra to international standards, a somewhat nebulous brief that even the panel members could not define.

After I had bid farewell to the panel, I walked down Grafton Street to Piccadilly and then right to the Tube station. I had arranged to spend the evening with old university friends I had not seen for some years. I would catch a flight back to Glasgow early the following morning. Yet as I walked, I started to experience a nagging worry. Having initially been extremely hesitant when first asked about my possible interest in the Philharmonic post, I had become far more than merely interested in the possibility of spending a few years in Hong Kong. I did in fact want the job. But during the interview almost everything seemed to have gone too well. Had I, I wondered, appeared over-confident, too sure of myself even with my lack of orchestral management experience? Had I overplayed my hand?

This concern burrowed into my mind to the point where, on meeting my friends, I was convinced I would not be offered the job. I kicked myself mentally but clearly I could not rewrite history. That evening we all met in a pub before going on for a simple dinner. With two free days ahead of me, I decided just to stay in London before taking the overnight sleeper train back to Glasgow.

I arrived back at Glasgow's Central Station around 7:00am. On entering my apartment I first left a brief message on my secretary's phone informing her I would not get to the office until the afternoon. Having slept very little on the train, I immediately had a shower and went to bed planning to sleep for at least four hours. Almost asleep, I was annoyed when the phone rang. Who would be calling me at around 8:00 in the morning? Since much of our lives in the opera company centred around attending evening rehearsals and performances, our office days started at 10:00am. Being late January, it was bitterly cold in the apartment and the phone was in the lobby. I decided the warmth of the bed and sleep were much more important. I did not bother to answer.

Fifteen minutes later, it rang again, this time waking me up. I just let it ring. After another 15 minutes, there was that ring again. Obviously I was not going to get much sleep until I found out who was calling. Shivering, I wrapped a dressing gown over my shoulders and answered. It turned out to be one of those surreal events which, had I not answered, could – perhaps even would – have changed the course of my career. On the line was David Stone.

"John, I am so glad we have found you. I have been trying to reach you for two days but had no idea where you were. We want to offer you the position of General Manager of the Hong Kong Philharmonic Orchestra and urgently need you to sign a contract. Can you fly back to London this morning to meet us in the early afternoon? Mr. Mackenzie has already signed the contract and all we need now is your signature."

Half asleep, I had difficulty taking this in. So I had the job! I was thrilled. But I still knew very little about the Philharmonic and the terms of a possible contract had not been outlined during the interview. Besides, I also knew little about a host of things regarding the orchestra, Hong Kong in general, including the cost of living and other key issues. I needed to play for time. I therefore apologised most sincerely before waffling on about having an important meeting in Glasgow that afternoon. However, I could fly to London early the following morning and be at the Grafton Street office around 10:30am. Thankfully Stone agreed we could meet again at that time.

There was now no chance of sleep that morning. So much had to be put in motion before I signed that contract. I really hoped Stone could arrange to fly me out to Hong Kong in the following day or two so that I could at least get the feel of the city and be briefed in more detail about the orchestra, its progress and what the Board's expectations were for its future. I also hoped that I could attend a rehearsal in order to assess its standard. When I brought this up at our meeting the following day, I was told there was no time for that. They needed my signature there and then. After I arrived in Hong Kong little more than a month later, I realised that even if an advance trip had been possible, it would not have changed my mind. I was to fall in love with Hong Kong almost as soon as I got off the flight.

I was also informed the salary and other conditions were non-negotiable. It was take-it-or-leave-it time. Given that the salary was double what I was then earning, I assumed it would enable me to live in a nice, centrally located apartment with at least a pleasant lifestyle. I was not then aware that Hong Kong had rapidly changed from being a sweatshop producing cheap goods for export and was in the process of becoming one of the world's major financial hubs. Nor was I aware that financing rented accommodation without a housing allowance would eat up a large part of that seemingly generous salary.

Even so, there was never even a remote chance that I would not sign. Thereafter I was informed Mackenzie expected me to arrive in Hong Kong on Saturday March 3 so that I could attend the closing concert of the Hong Kong Arts Festival being given by the Philharmonic on the following evening. This was an important event for the orchestra as HRH Prince Charles would be in the audience. He wanted me to spend a few days in London going through papers relating to the orchestra and the arts in Hong Kong in general prior to my departure. He also asked me to meet with the orchestra's newly appointed Music Director, a Chinese-American from a prominent Shanghai musical family, Ling Tung. I had never heard of Mr. Tung. On the other hand, there were a lot of American-based conductors whose names I did not know. Mackenzie seemed genuinely proud that he was to be in London conducting the renowned Philharmonia Orchestra for a second time, having conducted a concert with the same orchestra a year earlier and followed it with a recording of the Rachmaninov Second Symphony. In Scotland one reason for the extraordinary success of Scottish Opera had been the excellent working and personal relationship between the Artistic Director, by now Sir Alexander Gibson, and the General Administrator, Peter Hemmings. I genuinely hoped and expected I would be able to experience a similarly enjoyable and productive relationship with Ling Tung. Little did I realise that Tung had very different ideas.

Preparing to leave Glasgow in considerable haste for the few days in London prior to the flight to Hong Kong was difficult. The deadlines were really very tight. But I made it. On the afternoon of my final day before flying back to London, I popped into my previous home, Glasgow's Theatre Royal, where Sir Alex was conducting an opera with which he was particularly associated, Puccini's *La bohème*. The theatre was full apart from the upper two boxes. So I entered one and just lay down on the floor, letting Puccini's music and Sir Alex's marvellous interpretation flood over me. I knew I would miss opera, I would miss performances like this, I would miss working for a company which had come to feel like one enormous happy family. But I was prepared and ready for my new adventure. The contract I had signed was for two years, with the Philharmonic's Board having an option on a third. I reasoned that even if I found managing an orchestra was not right for me, being based in Hong Kong would at least give me a wonderful opportunity of getting to know some of the countries and cultures of Asia which I might never experience again.

Before the opera's end, I slipped out of the box, down the side stairs and through the pass door to the backstage area. I had already been given a farewell reception with the gift of a lovely Caithness Glass whisky decanter as a going-away present. So I merely waved and said goodbye once more to Bill, the stage door keeper. I took a taxi back to my apartment for one last night. I hoped I could sleep.

2

CHALLENGE #1: A STRANGE MUSIC DIRECTOR APPOINTMENT

I desperately wanted the London meeting with Ling Tung to go well. After all, we would effectively be partners in developing the Philharmonic at least over the following two years. I had planned to keep a very open mind for our meeting, but inevitably I wanted to learn more about him and his career, as well as to get his views on the Hong Kong orchestra.

Leafing through papers and documents at the Grafton Street office, I realised as a professional ensemble the Philharmonic had had a shaky first five years. Founded by amateur musicians in 1895 when its conductor was the local auctioneer, George Lammert, with encouragement and finance from the Hong Kong administration and the Urban Council (Hong Kong's equivalent to a city council in the UK), it had turned professional early in 1974. One of its key initial problems had been a lack of wind and brass players in Hong Kong. There were plenty of string players, many of whose families had been immigrants from the north where there was a long tradition of stringed instrument teaching. To enable the orchestra to become a full-time professional ensemble, wind and brass players had to be recruited in the main from elsewhere. It was no doubt fortunate that the conservatories and music schools in the United States were churning out considerably more musicians each year than there were jobs available for them. A good many therefore sought employment overseas. Thus these sections were filled mostly by young American musicians, a practice that was to continue for many years.

While this in itself must have seemed an ideal solution for both the musicians involved and the orchestra, it raised several difficult issues. First was accommodation. With a rapidly expanding population as a result of vast numbers arriving from the north over the previous decade, property developers could not keep up with demand. One result was the administration's decision to create several new towns in the New Territories virtually from scratch, in Tsuen Wan, Shatin and Tuen Mun. As an example, Shatin originally had a largely rural population of around 30,000. That grew to over 650,000 by the 2016 census.

In the mid-1970s, rentals in Hong Kong were starting to rise rapidly and leases were almost all for two years. A locally based violinist had probably already purchased an apartment for himself and his family and would be paying off a mortgage rather than paying rent. A trombonist from overseas on a two-year contract had no choice. He would have to find an affordable apartment and then come up with the estate agent's fee plus one month rental in advance and a two-month rental deposit. A way had to be found to provide funds additional to salaries if overseas musicians were to find playing in Hong Kong even remotely attractive.

Instead of simply being open about the problem, the answer had been to introduce a three-tier salary scale. Almost all overseas musicians were on the top tier, whereas many of the local Chinese musicians were at the bottom. Over time, this became a running sore. It reached a peak in the summer of 1978 when allegations started to surface in some of the many Chinese-language newspapers of racism in the orchestra. This was an issue that had somehow to be squashed but no-one on the orchestra's various committees seemed to know how to achieve it.

Secondly, the musicians arriving from overseas almost as soon as they graduated were generally relatively inexperienced in how to behave in a full-time professional orchestra. Members of orchestras must follow certain rules during rehearsals and performances in a professional and disciplined manner. Not all were doing so.

No doubt this was partly for the third reason. Professional musicians are unlike those in most other professions. They will almost certainly have been studying music and their instrument since early childhood. They then spend some years at a conservatoire or specialist music academy. By the time they join an orchestra, they know how to interpret Beethoven or Mozart or Brahms. It is second nature to them. Yet music is not a science. There is no one correct way to perform the work of any composer. And in an orchestra, no musicians can play exactly as they think a work should be performed. They must submit to the interpretation of the conductor, whether or not they agree with that interpretation and its subtleties.

The man on the podium must therefore be a first-class musician, have a thorough knowledge of the score, a complete understanding of each work and an overall vision and interpretation, added to which he must be able to explain and communicate that interpretation to the musicians in a relatively short time. In essence he is a teacher – the very meaning of the much-overused Italian word 'maestro'. If he lacks any of these qualities, life for musicians can eventually lose much of its satisfaction. And when between 60 and 100 musicians in a symphony orchestra lack faith in the conductor who spends many more weeks on the podium than any other – and in many cases holds the fate of their future in his hands – it should be time to part ways.

The Philharmonic had never enjoyed the quality of conductor that inspires musicians continuously to give of their best. In 1974 the conductor of the amateur orchestra, Lim Kek-tjiang, an Indonesian violinist who had turned to conducting, was asked to take on the artistic leadership of the newly professional Philharmonic. By all accounts, he was not especially suited to the job of moulding the disparate nationalities and qualities of the musicians. He left the post in 1976 and emigrated to Australia. In the meantime, the initial General Manager, So Hau-leung, had been sent to London for a course in arts administration at the City Polytechnic. Unfortunately for the orchestra, on his return he resigned from his position. The two top positions in a very young orchestra had suddenly become vacant and the Board had little idea how they should be replaced.

This is one problem that many young arts organisations face with some regularity. Boards and committees tend to be made up of the great and the good with very little representation from experienced practitioners of the art form. Soon after turning professional the Philharmonic underwent a major financial crisis. As a result, the governing structure of the orchestra was revised. In future it would virtually be controlled by civil servants and their appointees. An overall Board of Governors would remain as the ultimate decision maker, at least in name for it would only meet once each year. Under it would be the General Committee (GC). This body would be responsible for overseeing the daily operations of the senior staff and the implementation of policy. Under the new Articles of Association, six of its 12 members to include the Chairman would be appointed by the Urban Council, three by the Governor of Hong Kong and three by the independent Board of Governors. The Urban Council majority was understandable given that it was the Philharmonic's major paymaster. When I arrived in Hong Kong, there was only one full-time musician on the GC, David Gwilt who would eventually become Professor of Music at the Hong Kong Chinese University; and one who had had considerable experience as concertmaster and occasional conductor of the amateur orchestra, Dr. Solomon Bard.

As probably tended to happen in other far-flung outposts of the world, embassies, high commissions and consulates were no doubt consulted when posts like the Music Director of a young orchestra became vacant, since their cultural departments like the Alliance Française, the British Council and the Goethe-Institut would be better able quickly to discover conductors interested in spending some time in a city far away from the mainstream classical music circuit. Thus it was that the German conductor Hans Günther Mommer came to the attention of the Philharmonic.

Mommer had been an itinerant conductor. He spent some of the 1960s working in Iraq where he eventually became the Conductor of the Iraqi National Symphony Orchestra from January 1971 till July 1972. He then moved to South America where he worked with orchestras and youth orchestras. At the time the Philharmonic sought a Music Director to take over from Lim, he had moved again and was working for the Goethe-Institut which had assigned him to work in Thailand training the part-time amateur Pro Musica Orchestra (the predecessor of today's semi-professional Royal Bangkok Symphony Orchestra). He informed the Hong Kong Philharmonic he could be available to give up that position and work mostly full-time in Hong Kong. As I understand it, the Goethe-Institut subsidy would be available to help underwrite part of his salary in Hong Kong. So it was that Mommer was invited to become the orchestra's Principal Conductor.

A tall, heavy-set man, Mommer was not an ideal conductor for a professional orchestra made up of several nationalities. He lacked both the detailed experience for such a post and the patience essential to draw the best out of a young ensemble. Soon, in addition to Hong Kong Chinese and American players, there were in the Philharmonic's ranks musicians from the Philippines, South Korea, India and several other countries. Mommer knew his scores and brought a greater degree of professionalism to the orchestra, but that degree was relative. By now, the American musicians, especially those who had been in the orchestra for more than one season, were upset at Mommer's leadership. They also felt that some of the guest conductors engaged from time to time were below the standard the orchestra should have been employing. A small group therefore took it upon themselves and formed a faction within the ranks to assist in recommending conductors. One who had conducted the orchestra for a pair of concerts in early 1978 had been the Welsh conductor Alun Francis who was then Music Director of the professional Ulster Orchestra in Northern Ireland. His concerts had gone extremely well and he was immediately invited back to conduct the closing concert of the following year's Arts Festival in early March followed by a regular concert a week later. Another conductor recommended by this faction was the Chinese-American Ling Tung based in Philadelphia. Tung arrived in Hong Kong for his concerts in early December 1978.

It was at precisely this moment that the orchestra was facing not merely the racism allegations but two other major problems. In the space of little more than a few days, both Mommer and the General Manager, Richard Gamlen, had resigned with immediate effect. Following So Hau-leung's departure on his return from London, the orchestra had had little success replacing him. Two had been given the post but neither stayed long, one for just five days. The GC then approached Gamlen, the British horn player in the orchestra, to take over.

Mommer had placed himself in the unfortunate position where he had no alternative but to resign. He was becoming even more unpopular within the ranks of the orchestra, a result of his rather gruff manner and the increasing frustration he showed at rehearsals if he could not get what he wanted from the musicians. When one South Korean player particularly irked him, he had aggressively said to the young man –

"Why don't you go back to Korea and pick potatoes. That's all you're fit for."

The climax came in a speech he gave to one of Hong Kong's Rotary Clubs in early November. Since several of the news media always attended Rotary lunches, they were an ideal platform for communicating information to a large public. In what Mackenzie intended to be an upbeat assessment of the orchestra and its achievements, Mommer, by now virtually at the end of his tether trying to handle problems he simply could not solve, blurted out –

"Hong Kong has a $10 million fucking orchestra trying to exist on a $5 million budget. This cannot continue. Hong Kong does not deserve a professional orchestra."

The Urban Council with its inbuilt majority on the GC ultimately had to solve all these problems. Born in Guangzhou, the Chairman of the Council was a man of Portuguese descent, A. de O. Sales, better known as Sonny Sales. After being appointed to the Council in 1953, he rose through the ranks, making friends as well as enemies in the process until finally appointed Chairman in 1973. He was regarded by some as a sort of minor mafia boss who would look after his friends who had found themselves in trouble. One was the same John Mackenzie whom I had met in London. John had held a senior position in one of the major companies in Hong Kong. I believe it was Hutchison International. With a labyrinthine network of over 350 subsidiaries, it became substantially overstretched financially when the global stock market decline occurred in 1973/74, the worst since the Great Depression. With its stock price having fallen by close to 90%, in 1975 the company had to be rescued by the Hong Kong and Shanghai Banking Corporation (now HSBC). Following the rescue and the resignation of the chairman, there was a scandal which resulted in several top managers having to resign in some haste, Mackenzie being one. It was to give him back 'face' in the community that Sonny Sales made him Chairman of the Philharmonic's GC. Professionally, Mackenzie was then managing an electrical goods company.

Mackenzie had no interest in classical music, no clue how to run a professional symphony orchestra and even less idea how to solve the growing list of problems in the Philharmonic. To counter the racism comments, soon after they started to appear in the media he engaged a PR company run by two very public figures in the world of entertainment in the Chinese community, James Wong and Eunice Lam. He believed they would help overturn the negative views, particularly by placing positive articles in the Chinese media.

As regards a new Music Director, Mackenzie very quickly realised that fate had played right into his hands. Mulling over how to replace Mommer, he had a brief introductory meeting with Ling Tung after his arrival for his pair of early December concerts only weeks after Mommer's resignation. Immediately a bell rang in his mind. Here was a Chinese, albeit an American Chinese living in Philadelphia, who hailed from a very distinguished family of Shanghai musicians. He had read Tung's biography, knew he conducted two orchestras in the United States and that he had been 'invited' to conduct London's Philharmonia Orchestra, one of the most celebrated in Europe. After all, the Philharmonia had been directed by some of the world's finest conductors, including Wilhelm Furtwängler, Karl Boehm, Herbert von Karajan, Arturo Toscanini and more recently its then Music Director, Riccardo Muti.

No other conductor who worked with the Philharmonic had ever led an orchestra with such an exalted pedigree. Tung had to be a fine conductor, or so Mackenzie assumed.

After Tung handed him a copy of the LP of Rachmaninov's Second Symphony which he had recorded immediately following his concert with the Philharmonia earlier in the year, Mackenzie saw in front of him the answer to his biggest problem. If such an experienced Chinese conductor were to become Music Director of the Philharmonic, he could at a stroke halt the influence of the American musicians' mafia. At the same time, he saw how this could easily be engineered in the Chinese media to get rid of the racism allegations. It was a win-win situation. Or so he naively assumed! Win-win it certainly was not.

Did Mackenzie attend either of Tung's concerts that December? I do not know, but I suspect not. During my time as General Manager, as long as he was on the GC he attended only occasional important concerts, an Arts Festival concert or two, but never one of the regular concerts. As long as Tung could start the orchestra together and then have them stop together, that was enough for him. Towards the end of his week's engagement, John met again with Tung and his American wife, Margot, to ask if he might be interested in the Music Director position. As this narrative will later explain – and of which Mackenzie had no knowledge since he had not had anyone perform the due diligence absolutely vital prior to the appointment of a Music Director – the fact was Tung had to be interested if only because he had little work elsewhere, even in the United States. When the Tungs left Hong Kong for an engagement in Honolulu, Mackenzie went into overdrive. Within days he had majority agreement that Tung should be encouraged to return to Hong Kong as soon as his Honolulu concert was over to negotiate a contract as the Philharmonic's new Music Director. Days later, the Tungs arrived in Hong Kong to do just that, even though someone on the GC should have been aware that he had never in his life been the Music Director of any full-time professional symphony orchestra. Tung signed a two-year contract to lead and conduct the Hong Kong Philharmonic Orchestra for three periods totalling approximately 14 weeks each season. The GC also had an option for a one-year extension. Immediately Wong and Lam were contacted to get maximum mileage out of an announcement to be made as quickly as possible in the Chinese media.

No doubt Mackenzie and his wife Audrey had an enjoyable Christmas that year. He had solved two of his immediate problems. All he needed now was a General Manager and that could wait till January. Had he bothered to consult any of the American musicians who would be working with Tung, he might have felt slightly more uneasy that holiday period, for Ling Tung was not a popular choice. Not only had his recent concerts shown little to make him a serious candidate, word was filtering in from the United States not merely in respect of Ling Tung's ability, or lack thereof, as a conductor, but also at his way of manipulating what went on behind the scenes to his benefit. Fear was developing that his ideas on how to develop the Philharmonic into an international ensemble would be very different from those envisioned by Mackenzie, the GC and the Board of Governors.

Within months, the musicians were proved to be correct.

3

CHALLENGE #2: LING TUNG'S DUBIOUS QUALIFICATIONS

I had met many conductors in my previous employment. In general I found all easy to get on with. Perhaps I was rather naïve to assume my day in London with Tung would be the same. We met at the serviced apartment which he and Margot had rented prior to his second visit working with the Philharmonia. In mid-afternoon a limousine took us to the out-of-town Fairfield Hall in Croydon, a journey of about 45 minutes. Ling then prepared for his balance rehearsal with the orchestra before we would all have dinner prior to the concert.

This was odd. I had never before worked with any conductor who ate a full meal prior to a concert. So often in Hong Kong I was later to take conductors and soloists for dinner to one of the restaurants close to the City Hall Concert Hall. With concerts starting at 8:00 p.m. we would rarely start eating before 10:30 p.m. I simply could not work out how or why Tung would wish to conduct a concert on a full stomach of soup, steak and dessert.

That Sunday morning I turned up at their rented apartment in Pimlico at the appointed time of 10:30. Margot opened the door. A small, relatively young lady with long blonde hair and bright blue eyes, she welcomed me warmly and ushered me up the stairs to their apartment. A quick look around the living room gave me the impression this apartment, furnished as it was with mostly Ikea-like furniture, must have been inexpensive. In one chair was Tung, seemingly oblivious of my presence.

"John is here, Ling!", Margot remarked, whereupon Ling looked around and saw me.

He stretched out his hand without any recognition or smile on his face. He beckoned me to sit opposite him and asked Margot to bring coffee.

Of medium height and weight, it was obvious he dyed his balding hair, keeping one side of that hair longer than the other which he continually swept across his brow. His face was ever so slightly chubby. What felt odd was that face and his eyes rarely seemed to register any emotion. I had come prepared to make small talk and to find out more about him and his career before we got down to talking about our jobs in Hong Kong. I told him of some of the more amusing happenings in opera performances during my time with Scottish Opera both in Scotland and on overseas tours. It was as though he was not even listening. He was almost uncommunicative about his work in the US apart from saying that one of his jobs was as Music Director of the Grand Teton Music Festival. Now that is also rather odd, I thought. I had heard of the beauty of the Grand Teton National Park and that a music festival was held there every summer. But it was a part-time festival running for only four weeks using musicians taking vacations from full-time professional orchestras. I had been told by Mackenzie that Ling ran two full-time professional orchestras. Had he just assumed the Grand Teton orchestra had been full-time?

"You must come visit us one year. It's such a beautiful place," was as much as I could get from him.

When we got down to business, that is precisely how he seemed to view the discussion – only business. I had earlier been informed that most of the concerts during the upcoming 1979/80 season still had no conductors and soloists. In the previous few days I had visited many of the London artists' agencies and brought to our meeting a list of possible artists. I was not surprised that he also had a list mostly of conductors. He wanted to invite Thomas Michalak of the New Jersey Symphony, Kenneth Schermerhorn of the Milwaukee Symphony and Maurice Peress of the Kansas City Philharmonic. The first two were to appear in our first season, Peress in the second. I thought little of this at the time. It only dawned on me later that Tung's interest in these and other American conductors was not merely limited to finding good conductors to direct programmes in Hong Kong.

Tung then asked me what I thought about John Mackenzie. Not knowing much about his relationship with Mackenzie, I was circumspect and gave little away. I then said he had known Mackenzie for longer.

"How did you find him?" I asked.

"I only know that I do not trust him. And you must not trust him either. In fact, never trust anyone on that Board [by which he meant the GC]. They know nothing about running orchestras. You and I are the professionals and we will do things our way."

Had I really heard that? Why on earth would he say this to me at the start of our very first meeting? He and I were servants of the Philharmonic's Board and it was our job either to carry out their instructions or persuade them that an alternative course of action was a better one.

Yet again, he stated that the members knew nothing about running orchestras whereas he and I with our respective backgrounds were in a far better position to make decisions. I was now feeling quite difficult. I was perfectly happy lobbying and persuading the GC that what they might propose would not be in the best interests of the orchestra. But its members were responsible to the bodies which had appointed them and ultimately they controlled the purse strings. To suggest that Tung and I could move ahead on our own without the GC behind us was surely more than naive.

There will also have to be some changes to the playing personnel, he added. To this I could contribute nothing. In my ignorance, I assumed that the Hong Kong Philharmonic had a firm contract with the musicians which allowed for auditions, a probation period for new hirings to be followed a year or two later with tenure. This was how most full-time professional orchestras in Europe and the USA worked. I kicked myself that I had failed to ask any question about hiring procedures during my interview. As Tung continued on this theme, I realised I had made another mistake. I should also have asked to be provided with a copy of the orchestra's Articles of Association. By the time I finally did so after arriving in Hong Kong, I was in for a dreadful surprise.

He kept on the theme of the need to improve the orchestra and how only "we" could make the improvements. He suggested I should give a lot of autonomy to the Assistant General Manager, Maria Lui. He had met and liked her. She will be a great asset, he told me. We shall see, I told myself. Management is my responsibility and if I find her a "great asset" I was sure my life would be made easier. If not, I would be the one to take any required action.

Margot had prepared a light snack lunch. As we ate, Ling remained as uncommunicative as earlier. Now it was Margot's turn to do the talking and she echoed much of what Ling had been telling me, stressing that it was now up to Ling and me to develop the orchestra, not the GC. I started to wonder: who really makes the decisions here, Ling or Margot? She certainly seemed to have the stronger personality. Ling responded so little to my thoughts and suggestions that I had begun to think that if I were to punch him on the cheek, it would be rather like punching a marshmallow. I needed to find out a lot more about him.

I had my first opportunity of watching his rehearsal technique at the balance rehearsal that afternoon. He had had a rehearsal the previous day. The main symphony at the concert was the Berlioz *Symphonie fantastique*, not by any means an easy work. Working with London orchestral musicians, though, is hardly difficult for they are amongst the best sight-readers in the world. Less experienced conductors with less experienced musicians are often more interested in setting tempi and dynamics within a movement and then ensuring all the notes are right. Far more difficult is the issue of interpretation. London orchestras have played all the standard works in the repertoire dozens of times. They don't need or want to be told how to play notes. And with a less experienced conductor, their main objective is to play a work exactly as they played it before.

As a young conductor, my close friend and colleague at Scottish Opera, Sir Alexander Gibson, told me about his debut concert with the London

Symphony Orchestra. He had been given just one rehearsal prior to the concert. Halfway through, when rehearsing the first movement of the symphony, the concertmaster requested that he stop. He then said it was clear Alex knew the score extremely well; the musicians likewise. There was no need for further rehearsal. He suggested they all leave and just come back prior to the start of the concert.

Had Alex agreed, he would have lost the orchestra and probably not been invited back. Instead he informed the concertmaster that he entirely agreed that the orchestra could perform the symphony to a very high standard. But the musicians did not know his interpretation. He suggested they continue for another 20 minutes to go through some tricky passages and then finish the rehearsal. He had won that small battle and in doing so gained the respect of the musicians!

I found Ling's rehearsal technique rather strange. If he was not pleased with a certain phrase, he rarely spoke to the musicians. He would merely repeat it until it met with his approval. The musicians looked bored. To be fair, playing Croydon was far less interesting than at their more usual venue, London's Royal Festival Hall. At the concert the auditorium was less than half full.

In the limousine there and back, neither Ling nor Margot spoke much. As we approached a Tube station after the concert I thanked them for their hospitality and said I looked forward to seeing them on his first scheduled visit to Hong Kong at the beginning of May. Ling's final words were –

"Remember what we discussed. The future of the orchestra is in our hands and we must ensure the GC interfere as little as possible."

As I waited for my train to north London where I was staying with friends, I reflected on what had been a very strange day. It had been totally unexpected and I was left with many doubts. How could I work with this man who seemed to have little trust in me and little desire to know me more? He would be in Hong Kong for barely 14 weeks each year. I had to deal with Mackenzie and the GC on a daily basis. How could I do that with confidence when I really did not know what was on Tung's mind in terms of developing the orchestra? He had not even made any repertoire suggestions for the season starting in September. It was now late February when the schedules for most orchestras would be all but complete. We still had huge gaps. Did he look on me as a partner in terms of artistic planning, which is what I hoped and what I had seen work so well at Scottish Opera? I was anxious to commence a subscription season for ticket booking as selling each concert on a one-off basis was not only costly, it was extremely time-consuming. So as a means of attracting subscribers I had suggested we undertake a Beethoven cycle throughout the 1979/80 season. He liked the idea but made no suggestions as to which Beethoven symphonies and concertos he would like to include in his own programmes. We would need to have many long-distance phone conversations if we were to get everything ready for a public launch of the subscription season by early June.

As my train neared Muswell Hill, I became rather annoyed that I had been left in the dark on so many issues. In many ways it had been a wasted day. I began to feel that this had probably been a deliberate ploy on the part of Ling and Margot. If they had to put up with me as General Manager, they would do to me what they wanted us both to do with Mackenzie and the GC. Keep everything to ourselves – or rather for Tung to keep everything to himself and where possible away from me.

Nothing seemed to make much sense. Instead of as expected being excited by our forthcoming collaboration, I had a foreboding. In addition to finding out a great deal more about Tung, at the same time I would need to watch my back. I had the distinct impression he would prefer to see me well out of the picture. As time would reveal, I was to be proved right much earlier than I thought possible.

4

CHALLENGE #3: WHAT HAPPENED TO DUE DILIGENCE?

After we had both been in our respective positions for little more than a year, in April 1980 the GC took the decision to exercise the third-year option on Ling Tung's contract. It would now run to December 1981. For reasons which will be reviewed later, this upset a great many musicians in the orchestra. Resentment against Tung had grown considerably and quickly following his first concerts as Music Director in May 1979. So there was even more concern about what the GC might do when the time came whether to negotiate once again with Tung the possibility of yet another new contract in the spring of 1981 to start at the beginning of 1982. Before the GC had time to consider that issue, the musicians took matters into their own hands. A considerable majority of the players signed an open letter outlining his deficiencies. This was published on the front pages of several newspapers, including the English-language *South China Morning Post*, regarded as one of the most influential and widely read among the territory's movers and shakers.

Some members of the GC felt they had lost face as a result and that the musicians should be put in their place by giving Ling Tung a new contract. Now chaired by Philip Kwok who was to make an excellent chairman, so totally different from John Mackenzie, at the GC April 1981 meeting Tung was given time to express his views to the committee before a decision on any new contract was made. His lack of knowledge of how Hong Kong worked then became obvious. On entering the committee room, he went around the room handing each member a document with 67 legally-worded paragraphs. In essence, this stated that he had been humiliated and libelled by those musicians who had signed the open letter. Further, the GC had conspired in that libel by not immediately denouncing it. The only way of redressing the matter and restoring his reputation would be for the GC immediately to provide him with a new contract following the conclusion of his existing one. Failure to do so would mean he had no alternative but to resort to sue committee members.

Although I was asked to leave the room during the discussions, I returned later to learn the committee's decision. This was that the meeting would be adjourned for a week to enable Tung to back up his claim that a large number of musicians were actually on his side and had only been persuaded to sign the open letter under duress. He was asked to return with a delegation of the musicians who did support his demand for a new contract. Although I was not supposed to see that legal document, two members of the GC had left their copies on the table as they left the meeting. As usual, I cleared up all the papers. Thus I came to have and retain a copy.

A week later, Tung brought just one member of the orchestra to help back up his claim, the American timpanist Kristan Phillips. By now, members of the GC were universally angry that Tung had mentioned the law. This was not the way that matters in the arts were handled. Indeed, the very mention of the law had turned those few members of the GC who might have been disposed to consider a new contract totally against him. After he and Phillips left the meeting, the proposal that he not be offered a new contract was approved by all members. His controversial three-year period as Music Director had only months to run.

That it should have even have started was commented on by the distinguished British musician and administrator Basil Tschaikov in a report he was commissioned to prepare for the GC following Tung's departure and which is referred to in more detail later in this chapter. Of Tung's appointment, Tschaikov later wrote in his book *The Music Goes Round And Around* –

"Ling Tung seemed to have arrived with expectations far beyond what was possible and without the skill to make the best of what was available."[1]

At its next meeting I gave the GC a paper outlining how it should go about the process of finding a new Music Director. That process is in reality not difficult. First, a sub-committee should be formed to supervise a search process. Today, many orchestras will include one or more orchestra members on that committee. Time must be allowed to draw up a list of possible candidates. This will only be done after each likely candidate's background will have been thoroughly researched and checked. The eventual list should include conductors who have worked well with the orchestra at previous concerts as well as the names of two or three others whom the professional staff (including myself as General Manager and the concertmaster) consider could be ideal candidates. All the candidates under consideration should then be invited to conduct the orchestra. As noted earlier, there was amongst some members of the GC in my day a firm view that musicians should basically do as they were told. That may have worked in some parts of the corporate world but it definitely does not work in the world of orchestral music where that music is essentially created by the musicians themselves.

Mariss Jansons, one of the great conductors who died in 2019, once said this about the rehearsal process. He was referring to his then orchestra, the Concertgebouw in Amsterdam. In no way could the seven-year-old Hong Kong Philharmonic compare with one of the most distinguished orchestras in the world, but his comments apply to the musicians in all orchestras.

"They have an understanding of each composer like an actor understands his roles – they interpret, and shift into the appropriate character. It comes from a hunger to comprehend what is behind the notes. Notes are after all only signs, and if you only follow the signs they won't get you there . . .

"In rehearsals the players talk with you on a fascinating level about interpretation. So often rehearsals can be simply about organisation: you are expected to come in and say only, 'Here a little louder, here a little softer,' which is all very primitive. The Concertgebouw players expect something extra from you, an interesting interpretation, illuminating ideas, a fantasy. If you offer them that, they play with a passion as though for a new piece rather than a work they have played a million times before. This is what the players want – that higher level, when you forget about the notes and play the image, the idea."

Not all conductors employ the same tactics. In an interview in October 2022 prior to a concert with the Chicago Symphony Orchestra, the distinguished German conductor Christian Thielemann explained his technique –

"The first rehearsal is about making contact, but working on certain details so that they know: is he more of a rhythmical guy, or he wants us to play free, or he doesn't want too much vibrato, and so on. And then one sees how the chemistry works. I'm a big fan of chemistry and of not talking too much to an orchestra. It's better to show it with your hands. You have to show it your own way. And they have to know me and I have to know them. The first contact is always very interesting."[2]

As he specifically points out, "chemistry" between a conductor and his orchestra is so vitally important. That and there being no need to spend much time speaking at a first rehearsal. Thielemann lets the baton and his personality do most of the work. That was so different from Ling Tung who simply could not desist from his stop/start technique and his constant repetition of phrases even at the very first rehearsal. I was determined that that chemistry really worked as we sought a new Music Director. So, after each short-listed conductor's concerts, we let the musicians have their say about working with the conductor and express their feelings about the rehearsals and concerts. In particular, was that "chemistry" there with a conductor who enabled them not merely to play well but to lift their playing to a higher level? Above all, did they enjoy the experience?

At the end of the process, the views of all parties having been considered, one candidate will be at the top of the list. The General Manager must then commence negotiations with the conductor's agent in the hope that the terms and conditions of employment that the orchestra can offer will prove acceptable.

There was only one problem about my proposal. In essence, the entire procedure could last a good two years. As I was soon to learn, there were some on the GC who were still not sure of my own expertise and if I would be able to oversee the orchestra and all the planning, particularly the artistic planning, without outside help during that time. So as mentioned above, they commissioned a report from one of the United Kingdom's most respected musicians and administrators. In July 1981 Basil Tschaikov, known to all his friends as Nick, came to spend a week in Hong Kong meeting with me and my senior staff as well as the GC and the other stakeholders in the orchestra. During his long career, Nick had been Principal Clarinet in three of London's famous orchestras, ending with the Philharmonia Orchestra, at the same time being elected as chairman of that self-governing orchestra's board. For a time he had also been a Deputy Secretary General of the Musician's Union. When he came to Hong Kong, he was in charge of the National Centre for Orchestral Studies where graduates from the music schools and conservatories spent a year becoming familiar with the conditions of playing in a high-quality professional orchestra.

As Nick later wrote in his book –

"I soon found that John Duffus, their General Manager, was both charming and extremely capable but not strong enough to deal with the high-powered members of the Committee. They were all used to exercising authority, and wanted to make the decisions as to how the orchestra should be run. They were unwilling to let their manager do his job without interfering, believing their ability to be successful in their particular field of administration gave them the skills required to run an orchestra. This attitude has at times created similar problems for orchestras and opera houses elsewhere . . . I persuaded the Committee that for the next nine months they should give John Duffus the chance to do his job without interference (I was confident that he would)."[3]

When Nick's report was delivered, I was the one who was delighted. He stated firmly that I was the right man for the job, that my ideas for finding a new Music Director, auditioning new musicians and future development were ideal, and that I was fully qualified to take over artistic planning until the new Music Director was in place when we would work together on matters like selection of guest conductors and soloists and decisions on programming. One item he commented on was the absence of a musician's union in Hong Kong. He stated there was a need for the Philharmonic musicians to have their own committee to discuss issues relevant to their conditions of work. These could then be discussed with the General Manager and, if necessary, brought up with the GC. This would not be, as no doubt some GC members worried, a negative move. It would be a safety valve to ensure that problem issues did not fester and become deep-rooted discontent. Finally, he stated the GC had to place more faith in my judgement and let me do my job "without interference". After all the troubles during the Ling Tung era, I felt a huge sense of relief.

And so at the end of 1981 the turbulent Ling Tung years quickly came to an end. (There was to be a short postscript though and it was to appear towards the end of that year). That they should ever have begun was something I was determined to find out. The more I had come to know him, the less qualified I realised he actually was for the post of being in artistic charge of any full-time professional orchestra. For it had become clear that he never intended to follow through on Mackenzie's desire to develop the Hong Kong Philharmonic further as a full-time professional orchestra. He had other plans. A look back at his career – in other words, the due diligence that Mackenzie and his colleagues failed to undertake prior to their rushed appointment – would have made this very clear.

It was certainly true that parts of Tung's resume were impressive. A gifted violinist, he had been drafted into the US Army where he became a member of the Seventh Army Orchestra based in Stuttgart. Many excellent musicians were to find their way into the ranks of the orchestra and several conductors were to go on to major careers, conductors like

Henry Lewis and Kenneth Schermerhorn. In 1956 Tung was invited to take over as conductor in Stuttgart for two years. Ironically, Kenneth was to succeed Ling Tung at the Hong Kong Philharmonic in 1984 after the two-year search process.

On his return to Philadelphia, Tung joined the famous Philadelphia Orchestra where he played for six years under its distinguished Music Director, Eugene Ormandy. In 1964 he left to pursue what he believed to be his true calling, as a conductor. To this end he founded his first orchestra in the small city of Camden across the river from Philadelphia, the Camden Symphony. Camden may have seemed a somewhat innocuous name but it was well known amongst record lovers in the USA. It was the name of the budget label of the top recording company RCA Victor. Did Tung perhaps think that some might consider the Camden Symphony as a branch of RCA Victor?

When I was appointed to the Hong Kong post, I made enquiries with the many London artists' managers and concert agents about Ling Tung. Some were aware that he had conducted one concert with the Philharmonia the previous year; a handful that he had recorded the Rachmaninov Second Symphony. None knew of his career in the United States. This struck me as very strange. Many American musicians were coming to the UK to take part in concerts and recordings with British orchestras. More than a few British musicians were travelling in the other direction for concerts with a variety of the many hundreds of orchestras in the United States. Did no one know of his conducting activities in that country?

Mackenzie had proudly told me about Tung's two American orchestras. With no internet, and international phone calls still being very expensive, I wrote to two New York artists' agents whom I had come to know well and whose judgement I trusted. They informed me that Tung had only a very minor reputation in the USA. He had no full-time professional symphony orchestra. The two orchestras of which he was artistic director were freelance ensembles with each of which he conducted at most half a dozen concerts each year. One, as he had informed me, was at the Grand

Teton Music Festival in Jackson Hole in Wyoming. A small fledgling festival with no concert hall, in 1967 Tung had been invited to guest conduct its freelance orchestra. The concert was held in a tent. He and Margot loved the area – as all who visit it do – and quickly saw the potential to build the festival into a more important summer event. He was soon invited to become the festival's Music Director commencing in 1968. Margot became its business manager, effectively its CEO, but never using her married name. Instead she was known to the musicians who visited the festival each summer in those early years merely as Thea Walk. As Jay Humeston, one of the cellists in the Teton orchestra who was soon to become Principal Cello at the Hong Kong Philharmonic for many years, told me when I was in Jackson Hole, many times the musicians cursed "Ms. Walk" when weekly salary cheques were handed out just after banks had closed on Friday afternoons!

As the festival grew in stature, for a month each summer Tung would soon be conducting weekly concerts with an orchestra of excellent musicians, almost all of whom were full-time members of other professional US orchestras. This was possible for in those years it was not uncommon for musicians to have eight weeks' paid vacation in the summer. It so happened that Margot came from a wealthy Philadelphia family. Her mother Marguerite had been born in Amsterdam. She moved to America in 1939 where she married Maurice Walk. Through Maurice, the Walks were allegedly distantly related to the Pitcairn family which had founded the Pittsburgh Plate Glass Company (PPG) in 1883. In 2016 Forbes magazine estimated PPG to be worth US$31 billion and the Pitcairn family wealth as US$1.7 billion. Founder John Pitcairn moved to Philadelphia after his marriage and built the family estate there.

Both Maurice and Marguerite were to place some of their wealth into philanthropic foundations, two of which were devoted to projects related to the arts. Soon one was to provide much of the finance for the construction in Jackson Hole of an excellent, all-wood medium-sized 750-seat concert hall named the Walk Festival Hall. This opened in 1974.

The foundation also provided funds for a large endowment to help secure the future of the Grand Teton Festival for many decades to come.

In 1988 a major board controversy over an invitation to the New York Philharmonic to visit for a two-week residency at a cost greater than the festival's total annual budget resulted in Margot's immediate resignation. By this time the Tungs' marriage had fallen apart, leading to their divorce four years earlier. Tung remained as Music Director of the festival until 1996. Today the Grand Teton Music Festival continues under the direction of the superb conductor, Sir Donald Runnicles. Sir Donald became Music Director in 2005. In addition to a plethora of guest engagements with top international orchestras, he has been Generalmusikdirector of the Deutsche Oper Berlin since his appointment in 2009. This was recently renewed to 2027.

By enabling them also to bring their families, the musicians performing in Jackson Hole during the time of the Tungs may not have been paid more than a small fee each week but they had free accommodation, an opportunity for an outdoor family holiday, a relaxing schedule of only one major concert each week and, if they so wished, as much chamber music as they would like to perform along with other groups of excellent musicians from the orchestra. Not surprisingly, many of the country's finest professional orchestral musicians would eventually find themselves playing for the summer festival.

When I finally made it to the Grand Teton Festival in the summer of 1980, I was completely overwhelmed by the beauty of its setting and the quality of the one orchestral concert I was able to attend. As Ling proudly pointed out to me, there were seven concertmasters from major US orchestras in his violin sections, the Principal Horn was Bob Bonnevie, Principal Horn in the Seattle Symphony . . . and so the list went on. It was perfectly obvious this was not an orchestra which Ling had trained to achieve the quality I had heard. To suggest that it could in any way be a template for the Hong Kong Philharmonic made up of mostly young, relatively inexperienced musicians was not only patently false. It was just plain nonsense. And Mackenzie, in failing to do due diligence, had fallen for it.

As an aside, there is surely more than a touch of irony that in 2016 the Marguerite A. Walk Private Foundation and the Maurice Walk Fine Arts Foundation filed a 55-page lawsuit against the Grand Teton Music Festival regarding the use of donated money. The suit alleged that funds they had donated for specific purposes had been diverted for other uses. Acting on behalf of the foundations were Margot Walk/Tung and her sister Cynthia. As reported in the Jackson Hole News and Guide website:

"Margaretha 'Margot' Walk, whose family has helped fund the festival for half a century, has been in disagreement for about two years with the Music Festival about misuse of grant funds, she said Thursday by telephone."[4]

Finally, proof that it was primarily money from Margot's family which had helped fund Ling Tung's conducting activities in the more publicly impressive of his two part-time conducting posts.

Of Ling's other orchestra, there were some striking similarities to that in Jackson Hole. Although the city of Camden only had a population of around 70,000, it had no orchestra. As already noted, Ling assembled a group of freelance players and announced the formation of the Camden Symphony. Like Jackson Hole, it gave approximately six concerts but spread throughout the year. It always used freelance players, occasionally some who were old friends and still full-time members of the Philadelphia Orchestra if they had free time.

Fate has a habit of playing a role in many careers. So it did with Tung. An event that took place in 1964 on the other side of the Atlantic was to see a major change in Tung's fortunes. To understand why, it is necessary to go even further back in time to 1945 in the immediate post-war period in London. A British record producer and entrepreneur, Walter Legge who worked for the EMI record label, had decided London needed a world-class symphony orchestra to produce recordings of the highest international quality. He called it the Philharmonia Orchestra. The commercial introduction of the black vinyl long-playing record was on the horizon and larger 12-inch discs quickly became the world standard for commercial recordings until the introduction of the CD in the early 1980s.

Legge realised there were many conductors who had been active in Germany and Europe prior to the war whose activities were curtailed thereafter. In particular there were three conductors who had had Nazi connections – Wilhelm Furtwängler, Karl Boehm and Herbert von Karajan. All three and others had to serve two-year bans following the post-war denazification trials. Legge scoured the continent for such conductors, successfully persuading the authorities in London that the bans were only applicable for public concerts and not for private recordings. Thus a conductor like Karajan who had twice joined the Nazi party came to London to make over 150 recordings with the Philharmonia, many extremely fine, some superb.

Legge exercised a near tyrannical control over 'his' orchestra until the cost overruns became excessive. When his chairman, Sir Joseph Lockwood, cut the budget for classical recordings, the autocratic Legge decided to take an extraordinary step. He announced in a press release that he would be disbanding the orchestra. This took place in October 1964 following the completion of a recording of Mozart's *Magic Flute* conducted by Otto Klemperer. Klemperer had left Germany for America in the 1930s. Although he held a number of positions there, including the Music Directorship of the Los Angeles Philharmonic, he was never happy. After the war he returned to Europe to work with the Hungarian State Opera. Legge invited him to London to conduct the complete Beethoven symphonies. He was such a success that he became the Philharmonia's first and only Principal Conductor during the Legge years.

Klemperer plays a part in the Ling Tung story because of his dogged determination. When Legge disbanded the orchestra, he sold off all its assets, including its name.[5] To this day I do not understand how the name Philharmonia can be the subject of copyright, but in 1964 it clearly was. The musicians were understandably staggered when news of Legge's actions became known. They assumed they would all have to return to being poorly paid freelance musicians. They reckoned without Klemperer. He loved the orchestra. He knew that the London Symphony, London Philharmonic and the Royal Philharmonic orchestras were self-governing co-operatives. He persuaded the Philharmonia players to take the same route. The only problem was the name. How could they compete in the orchestral recording marketplace with a totally new name? But the word 'new' became their saviour. From henceforth the orchestra would call itself the New Philharmonia. Klemperer agreed to stay on as its Principal Conductor.

By the mid-1970s, all the difficulties arising from the bankruptcy proceedings had been settled. The orchestra and its board wanted to revert back to its original name. The board then instructed its General Manager of the time, Gavin Henderson, to find out who had purchased it and negotiate terms for its return.

Ling Tung now returns to the story. For whatever reason, it was he who had purchased the name Philharmonia and retitled his Camden Symphony, the Camden Philharmonia. What benefit this provided for either the orchestra or Tung is yet another unanswered question. But it was a flight to Philadelphia that took Henderson to the home of Ling and Margot Tung. We need to note here that even with his posts running the Grand Teton Music Festival and the Camden Symphony, Tung had undertaken very few other conducting engagements in the United States – or indeed anywhere else for over a decade. He did not even have an agent, an absolute essential for any conductor intent on a future in the profession. Had Mackenzie not been aware of this?

Agents are in the unique position of being in regular contact with orchestras around the country. It is part of their job to try and place their clients as guest conductors or even as Music Director for orchestras with a vacancy. As importantly, they are the first to be contacted when a scheduled conductor falls sick at the last minute. Most conductors will have their engagement diaries quite full up to two years in advance. With only two part-time orchestras where freelance musicians were invited to join them exclusively at his invitation and his conducting little more than a dozen programmes a year, Tung must have had a vast amount of free time on his hands over the years. Without an agent he had little or no chance of being engaged anywhere as a last-minute replacement. In New York alone there were many agents, large and small. Why did he not have one? Had he even tried to obtain one?

In the discussions with Gavin Henderson, Tung – or perhaps more probably Margot – obviously had one overriding objective. The New Philharmonia was one of the finest orchestras in the world. If they could engineer a deal whereby Ling could be invited to conduct the orchestra in a public concert in a major concert hall, it would not only look very impressive on his resume, it would almost certainly be a big boost to his career. I am sure this was exactly what Henderson wanted to hear. No financial transaction, merely a concert or two. After all, as he was without doubt only too well aware – but Tung perhaps not – almost all the London orchestras barring the BBC Symphony could be 'bought' by any conductor provided they paid all the orchestra's costs and fees. It was therefore quickly agreed that Tung would visit London early in 1978 for one concert in London's Royal Festival Hall. In early 1979 there would be a second concert in the out-of-town venue in Croydon, the concert that I attended.

Although Tung would not receive fees, there was a double benefit to the deal. Margot's money soon put up all the cash required to make a commercial recording in the days following the Festival Hall concert of whichever symphony was to be featured. For the orchestra, this was money in the bank. Commercial recordings paid orchestral musicians extremely well. For Tung it would prove an invaluable 'calling card', as good as proof to many of his status as a 'world-class' conductor.

The recording of Rachmaninov's Second Symphony which he handed out to John Mackenzie and others he met in Hong Kong received more than reasonable reviews from the professional critics. The public concert beforehand was less impressive. Basil Tschaikov had heard it and found Tung "competent enough but not inspiring."[6] That was more or less the impression I gained when I attended the Berlioz *Symphony fantastique* concert at the start of 1979, a performance lacking the essential excitement of that work.

I have gone into considerable detail to highlight the sort of background information John Mackenzie and the members of the Hong Kong Philharmonic GC should have unearthed before they very suddenly decided Ling Tung was the man to become the orchestra's new Music Director. If a conductor has only given invitations to the first-rate musicians he wants in his orchestras, how can he possibly work training up an ensemble of musicians on full-time contracts and develop that orchestra over a period of years? Once appointed, though, there were two other instances where Tung's lack of experience and Mackenzie's impulsiveness quickly made themselves felt. They were to result in lasting damage to the orchestra for many years ahead.

5

I ARRIVE IN HONG KONG

I now backtrack to my arrival in Hong Kong in March 1979. Inevitably I had to do the rounds of important people who played a role behind the scenes in the development of the Philharmonic. One was Barrie Wiggham, a career civil servant who worked in the Home Affairs Branch and who was in large measure responsible for supervising the administration's annual subsidy for the orchestra. He took me to lunch at the Eagle's Nest atop the Hilton Hotel and gave me so much detail I was unable to recall much of it after I left. Although not a member of the GC, he had a warm helpful personality. He and his wife, Mavis, were to become good and valued friends.

One of my most urgent tasks in my first weeks was to get the 1979/80 season into some kind of shape by filling in the many vacant slots for conductors and soloists, some as suggested by Tung. Before then, though, there was remarkably still one pair of concerts at the end of June in the present season that needed to be finalised. I noticed that the conductor was from Britain but I knew nothing about him. That in itself was strange as I knew of most British conductors. I therefore contacted two trusted agents to ask if they had heard of him. One had not. The other was more direct. Don't engage him, I was told. The man is an amateur and should not be near any professional orchestra. I had the first big problem on my hands as this conductor already had a contract.

I had arrived in Hong Kong only days earlier. It was a Saturday afternoon when the Air France 747 had landed at Kai Tak airport, arriving from the east through the Lei Yue Mun gap rather than the more usual approach over the Kowloon peninsula. The flight had been tiring as in those days there were no direct flights. British Airways did operate one daily 747 flight with a refuelling stop in Bahrain. All flights from other European destinations required either more stops or a plane change en route. The Philharmonic's Deputy General Manager, Maria Lui of whom the Tungs had spoken so highly, had ignored my request that I be put on the BA flight. Instead I received a telex asking me to call a London number for my flight details. This turned out to be Royal Jordanian Airlines. The routing she had booked had me flying to Amman where there would be a six-hour plane change for a flight to Bangkok. Then another three-hour plane change to Cathay Pacific for the final sector. There was absolutely no reason why I was not on the BA flight.

I was not prepared to take a flight with two long plane changes en route. I sent a telex back refusing to take it. The following day I was informed about the Air France flight. This would first see me fly to Paris, a relatively short change to a 747 to Hong Kong but thereafter en route stops in Dubai, Bombay and Bangkok. Then I discovered the final sector would be an hour longer than usual because Vietnam's airspace was totally closed due to its recent border war with China. Once again no reason was given why I could not be put on the BA flight. But I was happier with Air France than Royal Jordanian and I decided not to create more fuss.

The concert the following evening was conducted by the fine Welsh conductor Alun Francis. Having already conducted the orchestra in a pair of successful concerts almost a year earlier, the musicians had enjoyed working with him and hence he had been invited back for the Arts Festival concert and one featuring the Brahms Violin Concerto the following week. Having received my concert ticket from Maria, I was none too pleased at being given a seat near the front and far to the right of the auditorium. I had assumed that as the incoming General Manager I would be seated at least with a senior member of staff or even with Mackenzie and some of his colleagues on the GC. Instead I was left totally on my own.

I quickly realised that a very modest instruction I had given prior to my arrival had been totally disregarded. As with any new General

Manager, I knew the media would be keen for interviews. I had sent a telex from London that I would be very happy to do as many interviews as they wished, but only after I had been in the job for a week. I needed to hear and see the Philharmonic, learn more of its background from those who were involved and more about Hong Kong before I could give anything meaningful to the media. But waiting for me in a file of papers was a schedule showing a 'live' radio interview for the administration's radio station, Radio Television Hong Kong, at 8:30am on the Monday morning, and then an hour with the arts correspondent for the *South China Morning Post* on the Tuesday afternoon. These interviews were basically pointless. Sara Lupino Lane did the interview with the SCMP. The interview turned out much more interesting for me as Sara was a granddaughter of the famous British actor/manager Lupino Lane. I did my best to deflect all her questions about the Philharmonic. As she closed her notebook, she looked somewhat disapprovingly at me.

"I don't think I have ever done such an interview," she exclaimed, "where the interviewee has given me virtually nothing I can write about!"

I was actually quite pleased with myself!

I quickly put that to the back of my mind as I got down to business following the RTHK interview. What to do about this British conductor who should never have been contracted? I was then informed that this was done on the advice of the Programme Committee, a small group of members of the GC chaired by Dr. Solomon Bard. Solly, as everyone called him, was the loveliest man you could hope to meet. Born in Siberia, on the outbreak of the Russian Revolution his family had fled to Harbin in Manchuria, a cosmopolitan city that had become almost more Russian than Chinese. Even today there is an imposing decommissioned Russian cathedral in its centre and many streets are indicated in three languages – Chinese, English and Russian. It also boasted China's first music conservatory. Solly received his early education in Harbin and Shanghai before moving to Hong Kong to study medicine at Hong Kong University. Passionately fond of music and an accomplished violinist, for many years he was the concertmaster of the amateur Hong

Kong Philharmonic. When it turned professional, he became the Vice Chairman of the Board. Hugely respected and with so much musical experience, it was understandable that he be asked to chair the Programme Committee.

For me, this posed a major problem. Throughout my entire career I have been adamantly against the idea of programme committees. The board of any orchestra – indeed any performing organisation – has two primary duties: the appointment of an artistic leader (in the case of an orchestra, the Music Director) and a chief executive (General Manager/Director). If the board is satisfied with these appointees, they should be left to get on with their jobs in accordance with the board's objectives apart from occasional advice and assistance they may require from time to time. If they do not fulfil the credentials, they should not have been appointed or should be fired! Nothing in my fifty-year career has made me change my mind on this.

As an aside, in 1986 after I had left the Philharmonic to start my own company, the then Director of the Arts Festival, Keith Statham, had decided that instead of inviting overseas opera companies to take part in the Festival, each year he would create the Festival's own major production. For the opera in 1987 he decided on Wagner's *Flying Dutchman* to be directed by one of the world's foremost stage designers, Ralph Koltai, with Malcolm Donnelly and Phyllis Cannan in the lead roles, all of whom I knew well from my years at Scottish Opera. Keith did have a programme committee to which he had to report. With no final decision on mounting the Wagner opera and time becoming very short, he pressed for agreement to his plans. He later told me that one member who happened to have the title Chief Manager (Culture), Urban Services Department, said she would like to ask a question.

"Mr. Chairman, can the Director kindly inform the Committee who is this Flying Dutchman and what does he do?"

Since Keith told me this directly, I have no reason to believe it was not true. (Keith charitably assumed the lady had become confused for in the same festival there was a programme titled *The Flying Karamazov*

Brothers!) Assuming it was, it illustrated precisely why I have always been against the idea of programme committees, the more so one made up of people who really have little idea of the programmes they will be discussing!

Government officials later illustrated, shall I say, a lack of knowledge when communicating on arts subjects. One letter I received from the Inland Revenue Department had us all highly amused in the Philharmonic's office. In addition to symphony concerts, many of our musicians were given the opportunity to perform chamber concerts in the smaller City Hall Theatre. As with orchestra concerts, these would always be publicised with posters and flyers. One morning I received a form letter from the department. This listed a number of composers including Wolfgang Amadeus Mozart, Gabriel Fauré, Jacques Ibert and two or three more. It then continued –

"It has come to our attention that the above named took part in a concert in the City Hall Theatre on the above date. This department has not been informed of any visa requests permitting the above named to work and provide paid performances in Hong Kong. Will your organisation please provide at the earliest opportunity copies of the artists' contracts and details of the fees paid so that Hong Kong salaries tax can be levied?"

Clearly one alert civil servant had seen a poster and assumed long-dead composers were performers. What else could one do but laugh!

Back with the Philharmonic, how was I going to tell Solly that he had engaged a conductor who should be nowhere near a professional orchestra, and that I would propose to Mackenzie that the Programme Committee be disbanded? The Programme Committee would obviously be very dear to Solly's heart as it kept him in regular touch with the orchestra and its future plans. On the other hand, perhaps if I suggested we meet for a regular fortnightly lunch or even an early evening drink, I could make him feel at least as involved if not more so.

When we met to discuss this, I don't think he had any idea what I planned to talk about. Gently I steered the conversation around to engagements of conductors and soloists. Rather than start with the

British conductor problem, I highlighted another engagement that I felt should not have been made. To open the 1979/80 concert season, a Greek violinist named Spyros Tombras had been engaged. I knew nothing about him. On checking I learned that he was a member of the State Orchestra of Athens and played in various chamber ensembles. I could find no information about any international career outside Greece. I therefore made a decision on my own to maintain the engagement but to postpone his concert by a week so that he would be playing in an out-of-town concert. In his place, for the season opening concerts I engaged the wonderful cellist, Mischa Maisky.

Solly very much approved of this decision. I then tackled the British conductor problem. After going through his background and what I had heard from close friends in London, I asked point blank –

"Why did you engage him?"

I was certainly not prepared for the answer.

"His brochure looked so professional!"

I was flabbergasted! That a conductor who was to all intents and purposes an amateur should be facing an orchestra of professional musicians for four rehearsals and two performances on the basis that he had a nice-looking piece of PR was not merely foolish – it was almost laughable. As anyone in the management of the performing arts is aware, you can take a dreadful review of a conductor's last concert and with judicious cutting and editing make it sound as though he had done an amazingly fine job!

As delicately as I could, I explained that I was loath to go through with this engagement. To soften the blow, I told Solly that I would do my best to find another date for him in another season. He accepted this solution even though I suspect he realised it was not one I intended to follow through. But now I faced another problem. We had a pair of concerts at the end of the season and no conductor. I had so little time I estimated I had to find a replacement within at most two weeks.

I talked this over with my staff. They informed me that the musicians would by then be tired and ready for their holiday to start immediately after. This had been a long season for them and would have lasted for 16 months before it ended. When the orchestra had turned professional, the Board of Governors had decided to align it to the government's financial year starting on April 1 rather than wait a few months and begin professional operations at the start of the recognised international artistic year in September. By 1977 the musicians were still engaged on two-year contracts to end on March 31 1979. Towards the end of 1978 the GC finally made the sensible decision that the next contracts would start on September 1 each year. As a result all musicians were offered an extension to their existing contracts to cover the period from April 1. Within that extension was a clause informing musicians that they would be told on or before April 30 1979 if they were to be offered new contracts for the forthcoming 1979/80 season. Little did anyone involved with the orchestra's affairs realise that this seemingly innocuous decision would cause a firestorm that would take a full seven years before it could be put out.

In the meantime, another issue which had been nagging me was the composition of the Philharmonic's audience for its regular concerts. I estimated it was comprised of about 75% expatriates and only 25% local Chinese. This was something that had to be changed. How could an orchestra subsidised by public funds play to such an imbalance of the population, given that the Hong Kong population was well over 90% Chinese? In my mind, I decided that one of my goals had to be reversing that balance. Naturally I had no idea then how I could achieve it or, given the short term of my contract, if I would have anything like the years required. I felt, though, that these concert dates at the end of June could be a start. What if instead of a purely symphonic programme we changed it and made it into an evening of music from the movies? After all, Hong Kong was one of the movie capitals of the world and movies were one of the very few leisure activities enjoyed by most of the population. I would justify it by including in the programme a number of popular classical music items that had featured in Hollywood movies.

The office staff liked the idea. I assumed the musicians would as it would be a relatively easy end to the season for them. I assumed Ling Tung would not care as he would have had three weeks of symphonic programmes with the orchestra in May and be working in Grand Teton at the end of June.

As for conductor, we had one who had worked very well with the orchestra actually in Hong Kong at that very moment – Alun Francis. Over a drink one evening, I sounded him out about it. Might he be free and possibly interested? The answer was yes to both. Before the end of his week conducting the Brahms Concerto he informed me that he had confirmed the dates with his agent in London. All I needed was to negotiate a fee, decide on the programme and inform Tung.

Tung was never an easy man to get hold of. If he had only had an agent, communication by telex would have been simple. He himself did not have a telex machine and resisted my attempts to persuade him to get one. I was reluctant to spend too much time over the phone in view of the exorbitant cost of international calls. Most times, therefore, I would wait a few days until I had a list of items for discussion before I tried to call. On this occasion, I tried several times over several days and got no answer. Finally, Margot came on the line. Within moments Tung was on an extension.

I went through the other items, mostly relating to Board issues, programming and guest artists for the 1979/80 season. I then informed him about the June concert. At first, he gave the impression he had no interest. Then Margot suddenly interrupted.

"Why has Ling not been consulted on this before now? He is the Music Director and conductors and programming are his responsibility. Alun Francis has already conducted three different programmes in the space of a year and should not be invited back. We don't want conductors back on a regular basis."

"*We* don't want?" What did that mean? Given that Tung was only to be conducting in Hong Kong for less than one-third of each year, what would be his view if, like many orchestras, it was decided the

Philharmonic should engage a principal guest conductor who would certainly be working with the orchestra for between four and six weeks each season? But on and on she went to the point where I could hardly believe what I was hearing. With Francis having conducted two weeks of very successful concerts three months after Tung's appointment, there was absolutely no reason why one more pair of concerts just three months later could possibly be bad for the orchestra unless it was to cast a bad light on Tung's own conducting. Besides, these were pops concerts, not a regular symphonic programme.

During her rant, it gradually became clear that Tung had to be more than a shade insecure. Was he afraid of comparisons between himself and Francis? Eventually, Margot ran out of steam after I agreed to discuss the matter with the chairman. When I tackled him on the issue a few days later, John Mackenzie looked away from me for a moment. Surprisingly, and I felt shockingly, he then told me it would be best just to cancel the concerts outright. For what reason? Just because Tung did not want Francis back? I knew that getting dates in Hong Kong's main Concert Hall was not easy and now Mackenzie wanted us to waste a pair of them. I could have fought the decision and I could have won. The excuses from Tung were so flimsy and I had already come to a verbal agreement with Alun's manager over terms and conditions. On the other hand, it had become more than obvious to me, both from the discussions I had been having with Tung and from the hostility to his own appointment now being openly expressed by some within the ranks of the orchestra, there would be other more important battles I would have to win. Once again this one was just not worth fighting.

Mackenzie's decision that the concerts be cancelled was utterly bizarre. Was there something more here of which I was not fully aware? Did Margot know something I did not? Did Mackenzie know something? Since no-one was forthcoming about a lot of things related to the appointment of Ling Tung, I decided I needed to spend a Sunday alone in the office dredging through old files. There are, I believe, two character traits in my personality which have helped, and occasionally hindered, me in my career – I can be stubborn and I am inquisitive! Both had quickly come to the fore.

Perhaps rather innocently I had assumed that my Sunday might shed a little light on a rumour that had begun to spread that Tung had offered incentives to certain individuals to obtain the Hong Kong position in such haste. By this time some of the American musicians had spoken to their counterparts in the USA and learned about the Tungs' connection with the Walk family and their money. Could it be possible that money had changed hands to aid Tung being offered the Hong Kong position?

I started by considering this mere speculation. Yet Tung's appointment had happened just too quickly. I had begun to discover that the availability of Margot's family money had played a role in enabling him to finance his freelance orchestras in the USA. Given his near total lack of experience with any fully professional orchestra, I could not rule that speculation out completely as regards Hong Kong. Whether I would find anything damning in the files seemed highly unlikely, but perhaps there would be a nugget of information that would shed some light on what might have actually happened.

What I was not aware of until that Sunday was the role of Alun Francis in the saga. A highly experienced conductor, as noted earlier Alun had conducted the Philharmonic several months before Tung first appeared in December 1978, and had been invited back – a mark of his respect amongst the players and his popularity with the audience. What had I missed?

Then, as I turned a page in Alun's file, it all suddenly became clear. With Mommer's abrupt departure, there before me was evidence that Mackenzie had taken no time at all in deciding on a successor – and that successor was not Tung. Several telexes proved that Francis had been the only conductor Mackenzie wanted to succeed Mommer. Not only had he contacted Alun's manager in London, Audrey Frank, within days, sounded her out, received acknowledgement that Alun was interested, and made an offer regarding fee and expenses that was accepted; he had even gone as far as to courier an unsigned draft of a full Music Director contract to Audrey for her signature. All in extraordinary haste. Only a day or so later Tung had arrived in Hong Kong. Mackenzie's sudden change of heart seemed to affect him not one iota. It was another ten days before he bothered to contact Audrey again.

As soon as Tung had returned from Honolulu and put pen to paper, Mackenzie immediately sent the most rude telex to Audrey. He advised her that the Philharmonic had just appointed the "eminent Chinese-American conductor Ling Tung" to the post of Music Director. Tung would be in London in February to conduct the renowned Philharmonia Orchestra. Mackenzie would be –

". . . grateful if Alun could meet with Tung to brief him on the orchestra and to offer advice and suggestions based on his experience."

"Brief him on the orchestra?" "Offer advice and suggestions?" It was one of the most discourteous and insensitive requests I had ever read. Oddly, Audrey did not mention this to me when we were discussing Alun's terms and conditions for the June movie music concert. Thankfully there was clearly no long-term bad feeling as Alun had generously agreed to make himself available. Somewhat ominously, though, the Tungs had obviously been made aware of the earlier contract having been sent to Alun Francis. Finally, their desperation that he not return had become a great deal clearer.

What concerned me more than Mackenzie's seeming double-dealing was that someone had briefed Tung in considerable detail about the Francis saga and his aborted appointment. Did Mackenzie tell him, for only he had been a party to all the negotiations with both conductors? It then dawned on me that had he sent all those telexes to Audrey Frank by himself, he would surely have kept them in a confidential file in his own company's office. Yet here they were openly in the Philharmonic files for anyone to read. There had to be another person leaking such sensitive information.

No matter what had happened before my arrival, I had no choice regarding the June concert. I called Audrey and explained as best I could that the concert would not take place – without giving her the real reason.

While she could have made life quite difficult, given the short notice, she was wonderfully generous and understanding.

I, though, was now left with a number of major issues. A Chairman I neither respected nor now trusted. A Music Director who, the more I found out about him, the more I disliked and the less I felt could come anywhere close to fulfilling the Board's mission of developing the orchestra to international standard, and a Programme Committee that I now had to persuade the GC to disband. I had a lot of work in front of me.

But as the weeks passed I always had another nagging thought at the back of my mind: had I made a mistake? Should I have paid more attention when told I would find the orchestra in Hong Kong "a challenge"? With the Tungs' imminent arrival in early May just months after my arrival, I was to discover that things were about to go from bad to a great deal worse.

6

MY GROWING LOVE FOR HONG KONG

To say I fell in love with Hong Kong as soon as my Air France 747 touched down at Kai Tak on a gloriously sunny early-March Saturday afternoon is very much the truth. Perhaps initially it was a result of alcohol! During each of the first three sectors of the flight from Paris until it arrived in Bangkok, I'd had a small bottle of wine with the meals. For the final 3½ hour sector (the result of Vietnam's airspace being closed), I decided to celebrate my new life with a small bottle of champagne. The flight attendant apologised that they had run out of small bottles; she could only offer a half-bottle. Having been informed that I would be met on arrival by Maria Lui, I decided not to let that stop my mini-celebration. If I appeared in any way the worse for wear due to alcohol, I could put it down to weariness and jet lag for the flight was more than twice as long as any I had previously taken in my life.

Having had my passport stamped and collected my suitcases, I exited and walked down the ramp to the Greetings Area. I was slightly shocked. There was John Mackenzie and his wife, Audrey. I expect he realised I had probably had just a little too much to drink, but he did not remark on it. He drove me to Causeway Bay where the orchestra was putting me up for my first month in the Lee Gardens Hotel in Hysan Avenue, long since felled by the wreckers' ball and replaced by an upmarket shopping mall. The location was extremely convenient as the Philharmonic's administration office was little more than a five-minute walk down Percival Street to Harbour View Commercial Building at the corner with Gloucester Road. Across the road was the harbour and the Royal Hong Kong Yacht Club.

That evening I was on my own. As I wandered around Causeway Bay, I wondered how could anyone do justice in describing the little piece of Chinese territory named Hong Kong at the end of the 1970s? When I had first visited Manhattan only six months earlier, I thought there could be no more exciting place on the planet. I was wrong. The exoticism, the dynamism, the gorgeous views, the myriad of its more than 200 islands . . . I was to find so much so exciting in Hong Kong. In terms of topography, it was far more dramatic than New York with hills dotting much of the skyline as well as being situated on one of the world's great natural harbours.

The Philharmonic office took up the 20th floor of the building. On the Monday morning following the closing concert of the Arts Festival, Maria came to meet me and walk me to the office. She was extremely kind and pleasant. I had a large office at the front facing the harbour. Seated at my desk, I could barely keep my eyes off the view. If I leaned forward, this stretched from Victoria Peak right around Central, the soon-to-be-skyscraper-dotted Admiralty and Wanchai districts, across the harbour to Tsim Sha Tsui and, with a further stretch, to the runway at Kai Tak airport. Breath-taking was hardly an appropriate description. I began to wonder how I would be able to do any work!

My office had a glass partition so that I could see the staff in the large open space of the rest of the floor, and – importantly – they could see me. The layout appeared to have little logical organisation and I quickly decided I would rearrange everything to improve efficiency by creating a formal departmental structure. I had been well-briefed on the importance of *feng shui*. So, once I had decided how best to put the rearrangement into effect, I called the senior staff, all Chinese, into my office to outline my plans and the reasoning behind them. I stressed that nothing would be done until it had been approved in advance by a *feng shui* expert.

I looked over a sea of surprised faces. Is there a problem, I asked? You surely don't believe all that rubbish, was the reply! So much for my efforts to assimilate local customs!

Despite the skyscrapers and the veneer of extreme wealth, there were still parts of Hong Kong the government would have preferred visitors not to see. Accommodating the ever-increasing flood of immigrants from the north placed a huge burden on the territory's public services, especially housing and education. Squatter communities, now long since disappeared, still covered many of the hillsides, including at North Point within sight of the business district.

As I spent more time getting to know a little of Hong Kong, it was, I felt, a feeling of complete foreignness allied to an inevitable sense of the history of the place that made it so utterly unique. Surely it was no accident that John le Carré set part of the second of his George Smiley trilogy *The Honourable Schoolboy* in Hong Kong, for Hong Kong was also Control Central. Indeed, one of the characters in the novel is unashamedly based on the doyen of Hong Kong's foreign correspondents, the flamboyant and eccentric Richard Hughes, who had worked for the London *Times* in both Moscow and Asia. Hong Kong then was where every spy and China-watcher worth his salt came, the centre of a region still playing a major part in the Cold War, most of its gaze fixed across the hills to the north into the emerging giant that was China.

Although the Cultural Revolution had been over for almost five years, its effects were still unclear. What was happening in Beijing with the re-emergence of Deng Xiaoping was of keen interest to all the major powers, the more so since Beijing and Moscow had broken ties in the late 1950s and Washington and Beijing had cosied up to each other in 1971. A sea of satellite dishes dotted the hilltops along the eastern part of Hong Kong Island as spymasters did their best to discern and interpret the latest signals from Beijing.

As the weeks passed, several members of the GC remained virtually unknown to me. They had little interest in the Philharmonic and its new western manager. Others, though, were keen to get to know me and over the years were to be of considerable help. One was a fellow Scot, David Gwilt. Like David Stone, Gwilt had first visited Hong Kong as an examiner for the Associated Board of the Royal Schools of Music. He soon became a lecturer in music and subsequently professor at the Hong Kong Chinese University. With his background and a keen interest in composition, he was always interested in plans for the orchestra.

Another was Peter Moss. Peter had started working in Malaya during British rule there. An Anglo-Indian, he had been born in Allahabad. His initial education was in Calcutta before he moved to England just after World War Two aged 11. Never happy in England, he moved to Malaya in 1957 having made the 6,000-mile trip mostly by bus! There he worked as a journalist before his next move to Hong Kong in 1965. When we met, he had risen to the post of Deputy Director of Government Information Services (GIS), effectively the administration's spin doctors. Although he was not a frequent attender at concerts, he did have a genuine interest in music and in improving the image of the orchestra. He would rarely speak out at meetings, a mark I attributed to a degree of shyness. Yet he was a sociable and gregarious man, frequently inviting friends to his large government apartment in Conduit Road in Mid-Levels for a Malay dinner cooked by the Malaysian family he had brought with him to Hong Kong. These informal dinners would frequently mix people from different professions and careers. Peter had a knack for knowing who would get along with others.

In 1975, he and a friend had first rented and then purchased an old rather run-down house on the relatively unknown island of Ma Wan. A small island, it had an area of less than one square kilometre and its few inhabitants were mostly fishermen. Peter would sometimes stay there over weekends, always inviting friends out for a Sunday lunch. If I recall correctly there was only one morning ferry to the island. One Sunday, I took the little path from the pier to the house to be confronted by a spider's web spun between two trees with a huge spider lounging in its centre. I have never liked spiders and this one looked particularly nasty. Fortunately I found a way around the trees and did not have to confront it.

Peter always gave the impression, I am sure a correct one, that he never had many financial reserves. By the mid-1990s, though, his Ma Wan house was to make him a lot of money. On retiring from government service, he and his Malay family had moved to a house on the southern tip of Vancouver Island to be near his brother. Although the view was spectacular, Peter never settled in a country which he hardly knew and which was so far from the continent in which he had spent most of his life. After a fire had destroyed part of his land, he decided to sell up and leave.

Peter returned to Hong Kong where at least he still had the Ma Wan house. When a government employee, he had been on contract terms, meaning accommodation was provided only whilst employed and at the end of each contract he received a bonus in lieu of a pension. So he had no ongoing source of income. He was delighted when a publishing company gave him some work so that at least he could live. And then fate played its hand.

Hong Kong's new airport was being constructed on a flattened island to the north of Lantau. The infrastructure included a new airport railway and a motorway requiring the construction of several bridges. The government wanted part of Ma Wan to locate one of the massive pillars for the main bridge carrying both the airport train and the motorway. At the same time, with land in Hong Kong always at a premium for development, one property developer decided to purchase much of the rest of Ma Wan to construct high-rise apartments, a small number of townhouses and a small theme park. The villagers who lived on the island knew Peter well. They elected him to lead the negotiating team with the administration and the property developer. The deal he negotiated was that the head of each village household would be provided free with either one townhouse or two or three apartments. Having visited Peter in the 2000s after he had returned to live there, he told me he had received both a townhouse and an apartment. He immediately sold the apartment to obtain some capital and happily lived in the townhouse with, of course, his Malaysian family. Eventually he sold that as well for a handsome sum before spending his final years in his old hunting ground of Malaysia. He died aged 84 before I could visit him there.

Many remember Peter for the books he wrote about Hong Kong and its heritage. I remember him as a warm and humble friend who let me down only once during my time at the Philharmonic. Unfortunately it was near the start of my first contract and was to leave me with considerable public relations problems. It concerned two issues: the public announcement of our 1979/80 season which I wanted to signal as a new start for the orchestra, and that April 30 deadline for advising the musicians if they would be offered contracts for the upcoming season.

The Philharmonic gave concerts virtually every weekend. Some, the more important ones, were held in the territory's main concert hall, the City Hall Concert Hall. This 1,450-seat venue was part of a larger arts complex that included a 500-seat theatre and a 150-seat recital hall. All were located within the larger City Hall, the headquarters of the Urban Council. It was a perfect location, virtually at the centre of the north shore of Hong Kong Island with the Mandarin and Furama Hotels literally across the road and the Star Ferry pier only a two-minute walk away.

All concerts were marketed on a one-off basis. This was not uncommon in many parts of the world but it was very expensive. Each concert required a new design for the poster, flyers and newspaper advertisements. Interviews had to be set up for visiting conductors and soloists to gain extra publicity. Gradually some UK arts institutions were moving over to the American system of marketing concerts on a subscription basis. In return for members of the audience booking for a package of concerts over the course of a season, they would be given quite substantial discounts, often the same seats for each concert and various other benefits. For an orchestra this provided not just a considerable advance of cash for the seats sold by subscription, it ensured a guaranteed minimum audience for each concert without the need for a great deal of further publicity and marketing. Additionally, the renewal of subscriptions prior to each season was basically just one nicely designed flyer and a letter. The drop-out rate would usually be less than 15%.

I assumed subscription would appeal to all members of the GC. Not so to one who was particularly influential with the orchestra's main paymaster. Darwin Chen was the Director of the Cultural Services Department (CSD) for the Urban Council. In this position he was in charge of the civil servants who managed virtually all arts venues and, with the territory's lack of commercial impresarios, an ever-increasing department charged with filling the venues with arts events. When I raised the issue of subscription at my first GC meeting, he stated he would vote against it. During the discussion, I advised Mackenzie not to hold a vote. I would meet Darwin on a one-on-one basis prior to the next meeting, find out why he objected to the proposal and get him to change his mind.

My initial view of Darwin was that he wanted to run the arts in Hong Kong only his way and for a time we did not get on well. Over the years, though, I grew to have a much greater respect for him and especially, once I had realised the complexity of official regulations, his achievements. At our first meeting Darwin was very direct. He was perfectly aware that the orchestra's audience was mostly expatriates. He was concerned that subscription would merely reinforce this with the result that we would never increase the numbers of Chinese attending concerts. He was afraid the orchestra would become virtually an expat club.

I understood completely. I explained my belief that subscription was in effect one of the tools we could use to change the balance of the audience. Many of the orchestra's regular attenders were businesspeople or retired. They were never sure what they might be doing or even if they would be travelling outside Hong Kong three or four months later. A subscription programme committed an audience to attend six months and more in advance. I was sure there were more Chinese ready to commit to that schedule. To assuage Darwin's fears, I suggested that we place a cap on the number of subscribers for at least the first two years and then analyse the results. We eventually agreed on 55%.

The other key issue was financial. Ticket prices for Philharmonic concerts were extremely low with the highest being HK$20 – the equivalent at that time of around £2. Offering discounts on that price would reduce even further the orchestra's very low revenues from sales.

So I proposed that we increase the top price to HK$30 and the others by a similar percentage. Most who could afford HK$20 could easily afford HK$30. But subscription would sweeten the pill by offering 30% discounts. Effectively therefore prices remained almost the same, whereas many subscribers would assume they were getting a bargain!

Darwin withdrew his objections at the next GC meeting.

In discussion with Tung, I accepted that we would never be ready to finalise the entire first season in time to implement a full year subscription. We agreed that the first would be a half season, taking the orchestra from September until January. As noted above, James Wong and Eunice Lam were in charge of the orchestra's publicity. I was basically not pleased with what they were doing as most of it seemed geared to the upper echelons of society. I wanted the PR to be geared much more to the emerging Chinese middle class and below. I was convinced this was where our core audience would be found. After all, if the 12 members of the GC and the other 18-20 members of the full Board of Governors mostly being either senior government civil servants or successful businessmen in their own right rarely attended concerts, what was the point of gearing marketing campaigns to their business contemporaries and colleagues?

I wanted a subscription brochure that avoided all upper-class pretensions. For the first season James and Eunice were far from convinced about downgrading the design but I finally persuaded them. Discussions had been quite heated and we had to delay the date of the media announcement as they could not get the final brochure designed and printed in time. But it was only by a few days. And this is where I had my one major disagreement with Peter.

First, though, I had to address a concern that Ling and Margot continuously harped at during our phone conversations. He had told me in London that there were a few musicians in the orchestra who were poor and whom he would wish to replace. I felt this was hardly surprising. Many incoming Music Directors feel certain changes of personnel are required. Then again, most orchestras had set procedures to follow with regard to dismissing musicians on artistic grounds. I assumed the Philharmonic had the same. I was wrong. My third mistake when being interviewed in London was a failure to ask about the precise roles of the Music Director and the General Manager. As noted, I had assumed they would work together, very much as at Scottish Opera where Sir Alexander Gibson and Peter Hemmings had worked in almost complete harmony.

During one phone call, Ling or Margot had asked me to place on the next GC agenda an item for discussion which would confirm that Ling had total artistic control. I said this was not possible for in no way could the Music Director be given such total responsibility. Margot countered that I should read the Philharmonic Society Articles of Association. Had I done so? For whatever reason I had not. Then I suggest you do so quickly, said Margot, because you will note a certain clause which gives the Music Director absolute artistic control.

What? Total artistic control? I simply could not believe this. How can any arts organisation give its artistic director "absolute" control? In an orchestra, virtually all artistic decisions have financial consequences, and budgeting is always a CEO responsibility. There would also be political and other considerations to take into account.

"Ling signed a contract on the understanding he has total artistic control. It is important that everyone on the GC accept and reconfirm this. You will be at the next GC meeting and it is your responsibility to ensure a vote is passed."

I was simply not prepared to accept such dictatorial behaviour from the wife of the Music Director.

"I will read the Articles of Association as soon as this call is finished. But you must realise that total control does not mean 100%. If you plan to emasculate me as General Manager, then you will have to talk with Mackenzie and have him, as Chairman, inform me to place this item on the agenda and lead the discussion. I will have no part of it. You will then have to ask him if the orchestra has any requirement for a General Manager!"

Frankly, I should not have used such language but I was becoming very tired of Tung and his demands. There always seemed to be something behind his words. Having informed me about the conductors of American orchestras he would like to invite to come to Hong Kong, it did not take me long to discover that he expected this to be on a "you scratch my back, I'll scratch yours" basis. Kenneth Schermerhorn's manager later confirmed to me that Kenneth was very happy to come and conduct in Hong Kong. He would not, however, consider inviting Tung to conduct his orchestra in Milwaukee. In part this was because he was against the business of exchanges when it came to conducting professional orchestras. As importantly, he was leaving the Milwaukee orchestra that summer and no longer had a say on future guest conductor appointments!

I quickly discovered Tung was correct. The Articles of Association were worded exactly as Margot had stated. Article 73 concerned the appointment of a Chief Executive. It stated,

"The Board may contract retain or otherwise employ a Chief Executive who shall be responsible to the Board for the management and operation including but without limitation for financial matters *except in so far as artistic matters are concerned.*"

This was totally idiotic and unworkable, the more so with the orchestra being so relatively new. Obviously Tung then spoke to Mackenzie for I received a call informing me this item was to be placed on the agenda for the April GC meeting. As Tung wished, Mackenzie led the discussion. To be fair he did point out that he was only raising it because Tung had asked him to do so. David Gwilt and Dr. Bard were two members who disagreed. They said it was vital that the two senior employees jointly discuss and come to agreement on artistic issues. Only if there was failure to agree should the relevant matter be brought to the Committee. As far as the hiring and firing of musicians was concerned, this could not and should not be the exclusive preserve of the Music Director. The Articles had to be changed to reflect this.

At the meeting another matter was raised and agreed which had not been first discussed with me. Although the musicians were about to complete an extended two-year contract, Mackenzie proposed that contracts for the upcoming season should only be for one year. I was dumbfounded! How can you build an orchestra without providing your musicians with longer-term employment? It made no sense. Unfortunately I again detected the influence of Tung.

As the discussion continued, it was suddenly interrupted. One member made the point that it was impossible for the GC to alter the Articles. Only the Board of Governors could do this. It was not scheduled to meet until December. All the GC could do was ask Tung to inform the General Manager of changes he wished in membership of the orchestra so that the GC could be briefed prior to any changes being put into effect. But it had absolutely no authority even to enforce that.

Tung was therefore left with precisely what he had wanted all along: the absolute right to hire and fire as he alone wished. I was completely depressed. Soon after the meeting, Tung informed me of two contracts he wished issued as a priority. One was for a new tuba player. The other I cannot now recall. I had no leg to stand on. In view of the Articles and their reconfirmation by the GC, I had no choice. One worry concerned the two existing players in those positions. Should I tell them? Morally I felt I had to. On the other hand, if two of our existing overseas musicians were informed they would not have contracts following the end of the season, the news would spread like wildfire. I had no doubt, given the degree of control that had hitherto been exercised by the small group of American musicians within the orchestra, the rest of the season could be in considerable jeopardy. Worse, the bad press the orchestra had been receiving during the second half of 1978 would be revived. About to launch a new subscription season as a new start for the orchestra, this was the last thing I could let happen.

Perhaps it was because I had earlier realised the April 30 deadline was a major error that should have been altered several months before Tung's appointment and long before my job was even advertised. He had conducted only one programme in December. He would then not hear the orchestra until he returned for three pairs of concerts whose first rehearsal was after the start of May. How could any conductor make a reasonable decision on employment for the following season if he had

had only one opportunity of hearing all the musicians? The deadline should have been reset by the GC to May 31 prior to his appointment. It hadn't. And on April 30 the Tungs had still not arrived in Hong Kong. It was therefore left up to me to solve a problem that was entirely not of my making.

Rather than write individually to every musician, I decided to address them all at a short meeting following a rehearsal on the morning of April 30. The plain fact was that none had a right to any contract beyond the end of July as the existing contracts provided for no guaranteed renewal. But as I have previously stated, what is contractually legal is not always morally so, particularly for musicians who had been with the orchestra for more than just one contract. I needed to outline very clearly the reasons for the delay about announcing new contracts and to give everyone the opportunity to question me. Before going over to the rehearsal venue, I made a note of the various items I wished to highlight, the main one being that no musician would be offered a contract for the following season until June 1. I knew exactly what I intended to say. There had to be no doubt in anyone's minds about what I actually said – unless of course they had an ulterior reason for suggesting otherwise. Thankfully, that note I made prior to the meeting would assume a much greater importance a few years later.

In the brief discussion following the points I made, some suggested what I was proposing was not fair. But eventually all accepted they really had no choice in the matter. It was the Philharmonic Society which offered contracts. In the absence of tenure, contracts had a beginning and an end.

About two days later Ling and Margot arrived for his three weeks of concerts. I met them at Kai Tak and took them to their hotel. The following day he gave me a list of two or three more names and addresses of USA-based musicians he wanted to have contracted for the new season.

His three pairs of concerts that month went reasonably well. Usually there will be a special feeling around the first concerts by a new Music

Director. It should be a major event. Not so with Tung. They were just regular concerts. As usual, hardly anyone from the GC bothered to attend. One group, though, attended and were increasingly worried. The musicians had to be at each of Tung's five rehearsals and the three pairs of concerts. The spark some had hoped would be there was totally absent. Tung's rehearsal technique allowed for no interaction with musicians. What he wanted, he got – without discussion. The problem they found was that he did not know how to get what he wanted. As we have noted, his rehearsal method was merely repetition, a few words, more repetition, more words, more repetition . . . and so on. Of inspiration there was virtually none. As Basil Tschaikov was to write –

"The orchestra complained that the principal conductor [Tung] had far too many rehearsals during which he kept repeating the same passages over and over for no apparent purpose without improving the performance."[1]

During his first three weeks there was little I could do other than keep working on improving the administration of the office and desperately trying to get the first subscription season brochure finalised and printed. Some of the office practices I discovered were bizarre. One of my predecessors had insisted, for example, that a young lady in the accounts department spend part of each afternoon writing in a book the addressees of the letters being sent out that day and the amount of the postage stamp placed on each! I soon put an end to that.

The day before the Tungs left Hong Kong at the end of May, Ling presented me with two envelopes. Please give one to Mackenzie, he asked me. When I opened my envelope, I was shocked! Here were two lists. One contained names of members of the current orchestra to whom contracts should be offered for the following season; the second the names, addresses and orchestral positions of new musicians to be contracted for the same season. Whereas I had already issued contracts for four or five new musicians and had expected there might be one or two more, there in front of me was an orchestra list without 16 names. I was astounded. Tung planned to get rid of virtually 25% of the orchestra. I could not help wondering: why? Immediately I called Mackenzie and Bard. Both were horrified. Only now did I realise why Tung and Margot had been so desperate to have the clause in the Articles of Association re-ratified. They had manipulated the situation so precisely that nothing could be done. Besides, they were in the process of leaving Hong Kong and would not return till the autumn. I would again be left to sort out the mess.

Mackenzie accepted there was nothing he could do. To quote Shakespeare, he had virtually been hoist with his own petard! I am sure he realised he had been played by Tung – and lost. As had happened several times already with Tung, Mackenzie's own ignorance allied to his certainty that Tung had been the right man for the job had masked the need to tie him down to any specific course for improving the orchestra. Despite the Articles, if Tung's contract had in fact included clauses that changes in the orchestra personnel could only take place gradually and that his decisions would have to be made in consultation with the General Manager, I am as certain as I can be that he would still have accepted these as conditions of his contract. After years conducting only a few concerts with hand-picked musicians in freelance orchestras, he was desperate for his own orchestra!

What made me the most unhappy about this sordid mess was I believed some of the players on Tung's list were fine orchestral musicians. John Koljonen, the Principal Clarinet, was one and Tim Wilson, the Principal Flute, another. Dr. Bard and David Gwilt agreed. But I had no time to dwell on that. As instructed by the GC, I had absolutely no alternative. I issued letters to all the musicians. I expected to be inundated with phone calls from those not offered contracts. Surprisingly there was just an eerie silence. I was sure this was just the calm before an almighty storm.

It was at this point that Peter Moss re-entered my career. Three days following despatch of the letters, we had scheduled the major media conference to outline our plans for the new subscription programme. I wanted an upbeat conference. I planned to unveil to the media all the new ideas we'd be incorporating into the season and all the benefits that subscribers would gain.

I did not want it in a government office which would only reinforce in the public's mind how it was civil servants and political appointees who were still running the orchestra. I all but begged for it to be in a hotel. I was over-ruled. Peter insisted that it be held as all previous announcements had been held in the GIS Conference Room.

7

LING TUNG LEADS THE PHILHARMONIC INTO THE LAW COURTS

Prior to the media conference, Peter had suggested he and James Wong meet with me in his office at GIS to go over the main points. Neither had been made aware of the non-renewal of such a large number of musicians' contracts. They were shocked but relatively unconcerned. After all, nothing had yet appeared in the media. I made the point quite forcibly that it was bound to find its way into the media very soon and this would be the subject of yet more controversy for the Philharmonic. We should not wait for it to become public or we would always be on the back foot in countering the issue. I knew from my former public relations manager colleague and very good friend who had been the Marketing Director at Scottish Opera, Thomson Smillie, that a key part of any PR manager's job is always to keep bad news far away from the media. If that is not possible, then it is important always to take the initiative. I stressed I would take the initiative at the conference about to start by announcing a major change in personnel and make it into a positive element in the 'new' Philharmonic. That would at least get it out of the way quickly and hopefully take any PR sting out of it.

Yet again I was unprepared for what followed. I was absolutely certain Peter and James would agree with me. Not at all! Both were entirely against my idea. I was instructed to keep totally silent on the matter. If it did reach the media, the story would die within days. They both said they knew the Hong Kong media better than I. Again I objected. Again they told me they would not agree to my proposal. Nothing must be said about the non-renewal of contracts. For years afterwards, I was to kick myself for not having followed my own gut instinct.

As soon as we entered the conference room, it was obvious we were in for trouble. With the media representatives assembled in the front rows, there sitting on his own at the back was John Koljonen. Koljonen had not only been in the Philharmonic for several seasons, he was the leader of the group of mostly American musicians who had taken it upon themselves during the Mommer years to take a role in the way the orchestra was run. Being one of the musicians on Tung's list who would not be offered a new contract, he was certainly not there to talk about the new subscription season.

As best I could, I kept the conference upbeat, stressing the benefits of subscription in opening up the audience to more of the community, the Beethoven symphony and concerto cycle, and the quality of some of the guest conductors and soloists. Knowing what would follow, I paid little attention to the questions and answered them as best I could. As these seemed to be coming to an end, John Koljonen stood up.

"I wish to ask a question of the General Manager. The Music Director Mr. Ling Tung has just advised the orchestra that 16 of its members are being fired. Mr. Tung has disappeared back to his home in Philadelphia. Will Mr. Duffus please inform the media of the reasons for this massacre of the orchestra and why he and the GC allowed it to happen?"

It could not have been worse. How newsworthy was the launch of a subscription season when here was a far better story about a large group in the orchestra being "sacked" and mention of a "massacre" – even though both were false? The media smelled blood. As I had been perfectly well aware, from now on we were well and truly on the back foot. I could clearly see the headlines in the morning papers. However I and other members of the GC reacted, we could never be seen as anything but callous and cold-hearted. All I could point out as forcefully as possible was that Mr. Koljonen was incorrect with his information. No-one had been sacked. Mr. Tung had merely decided that some players were not up to the standard he had set for the Philharmonic and so 16 contracts would not be renewed. No one in the orchestra was guaranteed a contract.

I looked over to Peter Moss and James Wong. They knew the Hong Kong media. I wanted help. I got none. They were as angered as I that they had mishandled the proceedings and no doubt felt somewhat humiliated that I had been right and they had been wrong. James was a hugely respected figure in the Chinese community. Peter was a senior member of the civil service. They could, and I believe should, have backed up my comments, but they remained silent.

After the conference, we went back to Peter's office. There was so much I wanted to say, but what would be the point? The damage was now done. We had to move quickly into damage limitation mode for it was perfectly obvious this news would not be hidden on the inside pages. It was front-page material. Would James Wong do anything to temper the comments that would soon appear in the many Chinese newspapers? Would GIS have any influence on the three English newspapers? As we returned to the office, I asked Peter to call Mackenzie as the press would certainly be calling him for comments. Mackenzie would have to report the media reaction both to his fellow GC members as well as every member of the Board of Governors. Sonny Sales would be far from happy. The other main Board members included Sir Denys Roberts, the Chief Justice, several of Hong Kong's top businessmen including the two shipping magnates, C. Y. Tung and Y. K. Pao. Carmel Sandberg, the wife of the Chairman of the Hong Kong and Shanghai Banking Corporation and one of the territory's most prominent citizens, was co-chair of the Philharmonic's Ladies Committee. She would also have to be notified. The one member I wished to speak to myself was Dr. Bard.

As I knew, that so many contracts had not been renewed was headline news the following day. Koljonen's use of "sacked" and "massacre" had struck a powerful chord and were to remain in the media for weeks, no matter how much we denied it. The media wanted to discuss the matter with Tung. I had no hesitation in giving them his number in Philadelphia. For fairly obvious reasons, he was never available and so never quoted.

Worse was to come. Two days later in a banner headline across the front page of the *Hong Kong Standard* was an article which basically accused me of lying and that no potential subscriber should trust the information in the subscription brochure. It accused me of saying we had engaged a Korean pianist, Kyung-sook Lee, to perform one of the Beethoven concertos. Ms. Lee had never been asked to do so, the article stated. That was a blatant lie and both Ms. Lee and her husband were perfectly well aware of it.

Ms. Lee just happened to be the wife of John Koljonen. A fine pianist, she had been engaged as a soloist before by the orchestra. She was also perfectly well aware that in the business of professional music, there is a procedure which permits an orchestra or presenter to announce a soloist as long as the engagement has been what is termed "firmly pencilled". With contracts for so many artists to be finalised in the short time we had to prepare and launch the subscription season, it had not been possible to exchange formal contracts with each. Ms. Lee had been approached about the concert dates, agreed to both the concerto and the fee we had offered and had provided written acceptance of them. She had received but not by then signed the contract. To all intents and purposes the engagement had been finalised. While the *Hong Kong Standard* article could just be regarded as technically correct, I knew well that again I was on the back foot and the *Standard* editor would have no interest in printing our side of the story. All we got was a couple of paragraphs on an inside page the following day pointing out that I disagreed with Ms. Lee's account. Still, I determined that no matter how good Ms. Lee was, she would never perform again with the Philharmonic as long as I was in charge.

Another story printed by the *Standard* was relegated to the back page. It announced that Koljonen had been touch with the body in the United States which monitored the actions of orchestras outside the USA. It would now inform its members that the Hong Kong Philharmonic was on its list of banned orchestras and unable to contract American musicians. Koljonen effectively lied twice in that article. First he named an organisation that did not exist. I suspect he meant to say the American

Federation of Musicians (AFM) but got it totally wrong. Some weeks later I was in New York and made an appointment to meet the AFM executive in charge of monitoring overseas orchestras. I visited his Times Square office to explain exactly what had happened in Hong Kong. Our meeting was extremely cordial. He said he had not been advised of any problems with the Hong Kong Philharmonic (!) and stated that the AFM could not in fact ban any orchestra. All it could do was advise its members if it heard of problem issues which might affect American musicians and suggest they investigate further before signing contracts. But with no complaints against the Hong Kong Philharmonic, the AFM was perfectly happy for us to recruit new musicians from the USA. He expressed his thanks for my coming to visit him.

It was not many days following the stories in the *Standard* that I received official notification from the Small Claims Tribunal. It was a summons to attend on a certain date and time to hear a case that had been brought by the musicians whose contracts had not been renewed. Since lawyers were not permitted to attend, I went with our Finance Committee chairman, Peter Chan. No musicians turned up. Accordingly, the judge threw the case out.

I thought by then that we had perhaps turned the corner and could start working on steering public opinion back our way. I was wrong. The following month I was due to make a long trip overseas. I had earlier agreed with Mackenzie that as General Manager I would need to make a yearly visit to concert agents and promoters. This was largely to find out which conductors and soloists would be available to fill our annual concert seasons. That first year, we still had not completed the 1979/80 season and had almost no artists even lightly pencilled for 80/81 or 81/82. With our limited budget we simply could not pick and choose who we would like to work with the orchestra. We had to talk with agents to find out which artists would be elsewhere in the region in the hope we could persuade them to add an extra few days for an engagement in Hong Kong at a fee we could afford. Either that or find artists who would be happy to sign up to appear in Hong Kong in the hope they would find additional engagements thereafter. I estimated all this would normally take about two weeks. This year, though, with so many slots to fill and so many new agents to meet, I said I would need to allow three weeks. Additionally, Alliance Française had generously invited me to spend a few days in Paris to get to know the artists' agents and managements of the French performing companies. I would have to get myself there but once in the city they would organise everything, including a five-star hotel. So I would be away from Hong Kong for almost a month. I had reminded Mackenzie of his earlier agreement which he reconfirmed.

On the morning of the day I was due to leave for New York, an officer from the High Court came to my office and presented me with a summons. Fifteen of the 16 musicians had been provided with legal aid and were taking out an action in the High Court for breach of contract and deliberate misrepresentation. I had time only to call Mackenzie and then send the writ over to our honorary legal advisers. But it left me furious. The regulations for the award of legal aid were quite strict. A musician with even a reasonable instrument would almost certainly exceed the limit. How did this group of western musicians all get legal aid when many Hong Kong Chinese were routinely turned away? But my primary concern was that the courts could take years to settle the case and it would continue to be a thorn in our side as we tried to turn the orchestra's fortunes around.

I was relieved to get away from Hong Kong. All went well until half way through when I arrived in Paris after an overnight flight from New York. Alliance Française had not finalised my itinerary before I left. So Maria Lui agreed to coordinate with them and ensure I would be met at Charles de Gaulle airport and provided with a copy of the schedule. I was really looking forward to my four days for I had much enjoyed several earlier visits to Paris.

After clearing customs, I went to the arrivals area. I could see no-one with my name on a signboard. I waited for 30 minutes before checking at other exits. Nobody! After another 30 minutes, I knew something had gone wrong. I went to a telephone and found a number for the agency.

Getting anyone who knew who I was was difficult and took a good ten minutes.

"Oh, how is it you are here?" I was asked. "We had been told that you would have to reschedule your visit as you needed more time in New York."

What? I had never said such a thing to anyone in my office. Yet again, someone was out to make life difficult for me and I was becoming very angry about it. At least I was starting to have a very good idea who this was.

By the time I returned to Hong Kong, I had a long list of artists and conductors for Tung to consider as we worked on the next two years' planning in earnest. Given the legal situation, I was slightly apprehensive about returning and wondered how matters had progressed in my absence, despite my regular phone conversations with Maria. That apprehension was justified, although for a different reason. At the top of the pile of correspondence on my desk was a memo from Mackenzie. In it he asked why I had taken such a lengthy absence without getting GC approval. The time would be taken out of my annual leave entitlement, and he expected me to reimburse the Society for all costs!

I was incredulous! This was another piece of nonsense! The initial temptation was to phone Mackenzie and have this matter out with him there and then. I decided, though, that discretion would be more fruitful. Mackenzie knew full well that he had approved the trip. But it would certainly not be the first time – nor would it be the last – he had gone back on his word. After I finally got round to having a conversation with him, he suddenly remembered his earlier agreement! I doubted if he had taken it on himself to write the memo. Someone had prompted him to write. As with the aborted visit to Paris I needed quickly to find out who – and why. At times I felt it perfectly possible I was becoming somewhat paranoid about events affecting me at the orchestra, but I was being thrown into too many uncomfortable situations for them to be mere coincidence. Yet again, I was soon proved right.

Not much was happening on the legal front. In the meantime, Tung had brought in a group of mostly fine musicians to replace those whose contracts had not been renewed. It gradually emerged, though, that most of these musicians were on one-year terms of sabbatical leave from their full-time orchestras in the United States. The Principal Horn, for example, Bob Bonnevie, was perfectly happy for us to know that he was Principal Horn in the Seattle Symphony Orchestra. He was delighted to be working in Hong Kong but never had any intention of this being more than for one year. Most musicians in U.S. orchestras qualified for a sabbatical year after around eight years of continuous service. Something, though, was very wrong. Tung's responsibility as Music Director was to build an orchestra – not import one. If, as was to happen in most cases, these new musicians returned to the U.S. after just one year, Tung could no doubt fill the posts with yet more musicians also on sabbaticals, but there would have to come a time when the house of cards would start to collapse.

Almost all the new musicians, like Bonnevie, were known to Tung because they played in his freelance summer festival orchestra in the Grand Tetons. Tung himself became increasingly difficult for me to work with. It annoyed me intensely that at our London meeting he had laid such stress on not trusting the Board and the need for the two of us to present a united front. That "front" was rarely united. Whenever he was in Hong Kong, I always checked the draft agenda for GC meetings with him before the papers went to John Mackenzie for his approval. At least I was trying to present a united front. Yet, I started to lose count of the number of times when I would inform the GC that Mr. Tung and I were in favour of a particular course of action, only to have him whimper from the other end of the long table –

"But Mr. Chairman, I think the General Manager must have mistaken my views because I am very definitely not in favour of this course of action."

It was all lies. When he detected the wind blowing in a different direction, he would jettison previously agreed positions and go along with what he perceived to be the majority. So annoyed did this make me that I eventually purchased a simple recording device to place under my office telephone. Whether or not that was legal, I recorded all calls to and from Tung, as I was not going to permit my position to be undermined in such a fashion in future. Some weeks later, I went to discuss some issues with him at the Furama Hotel where he and Margot normally stayed in Hong Kong. I informed him I had told Mackenzie of his desire for something to be discussed at the next meeting.

It was Margot who spoke cloyingly, with her annoying habit of looking not into your eyes but about half a metre above them.

"Oh John, you must have that wrong. Don't you remember? Ling never requested you do that."

That did it! I pulled from my pocket a cassette tape.

"Ling," I told him, "because you consistently misrepresent what you say you have told me, I have been recording your phone calls for the last month. Yesterday, you told me very clearly the exact opposite of what Margot now claims you said. The evidence is here on this cassette. Shall we go to your room and play it so you can refresh your memory?"

The marshmallow analogy came back to me. He waffled, he slithered and dithered, before finally confirming that perhaps he was indeed mistaken. He was sorry. There was no need to play the tape. And that, for me, was just as well, for that tape was blank! It was one of a batch I had purchased earlier in the day and just happened to put in my jacket to load into the recorder as soon as I returned to the office. I never had that problem with him again!

Even before the cassette episode, it became clearer to me that my own position was in some jeopardy. On the opening night of the 1979/80 season in September with the superb cellist Mischa Maisky as soloist, I was standing at the back of the stalls when, just before the concert started, Kate McRae – a Scottish journalist who worked for *The Star* tabloid newspaper – rushed in. Seeing me, she stopped and came over. I'm really surprised you're leaving, she said. It's all over the newsroom. Why so soon after you've just arrived? I tried not to look surprised, assured her I had no intention of leaving and that it had to be some mistake. As she took her seat I wondered who would have started this particular rumour?

Two days later I was having a long lie-in on the Sunday morning. I received a call from the concertmaster, Jan van den Berg. Jan was something of an enigma. From South Africa, he was not the type of individual ideally suited to leading an orchestra made up of a group of musicians from almost a dozen countries. Nor was he a particularly outstanding player. Yet he loved Hong Kong and especially the life that Hong Kong offered an expatriate. That morning he was about to go out on someone's boat for a relaxing day at sea. But he first wanted to tell me that he had heard from several of the musicians over the previous two evenings that Ling Tung was "out to get me". He hoped I would be careful and look after myself.

I got out of bed. At the window I looked out at the glorious view over the channel to the west of Hong Kong and the islands of Lamma, Cheung Chau and Lantau. My small apartment was at the top of a skyscraper. No matter that I had begun to love this little flat and the island that was now my home, the constant problems with the orchestra and the personal attacks being directed at me had really started to wear me down. For the first time I became very depressed. I really did not know where to turn.

I decided to take a ferry over to nearby Lamma Island and crash on a beach for a few hours. That helped me focus on the issue. I returned knowing what I had to do. Having been out-voted in wanting to be pro-active at the June press conference, I now had no choice but to protect myself and put those attacking me on the defensive.

Before I had left London in March, my good friend the wonderful mezzo-soprano Ann Murray with whom I was staying had given me the name of a journalist friend in Hong Kong who wrote for *The Economist*. Paul Maidment and I had met several times for drinks. I arranged to see him again the following evening. I outlined the history of the various problems I faced, the situation I now found myself in and my concerns that whoever was trying to get me ousted might succeed.

Paul introduced me to a journalist who worked for the *South China Morning Post*. He was aware that the Philharmonic was filled with intrigue and that someone was not happy at the influence I was trying to exert. He promised to write a story angled around the rumour of my leaving and my denial. He told me not to worry! Sure enough, two mornings later on the right-hand side of the front page there was a half-column article headed: "Philharmonic Chief Denies Manager is Leaving." It outlined very succinctly the rumours and quoted John Mackenzie confirming they were simply untrue. Whether Mackenzie was in on the plot or not, I do not know. I suspect not. But his re-affirmation of my appointment and my two-year term was all I needed. It effectively killed off all further speculation regarding my immediate future.

Despite this, it was again clear some were determined to undermine my position whenever possible. It did not take much longer to realise that it was Tung and Margot. Their instrument? Maria Lui, my deputy. Margot saw Maria as totally pliable. Because of my background and my expertise in arts management, I was always going to be a threat to Tung if he wished to continue with his job, and both he and Margot were perfectly aware of this. I knew that I could not stay with the orchestra if he was to continue as Music Director. Our relationship had passed beyond that point. If I was going to stay, he would have to go. Just half a year into my contract, that was always thereafter close to the front of my mind.

Not all was as depressing, though. Sometimes there were amusing moments which helped relieve the tension. Soon after my arrival, the Ladies Committee whose members did sterling fundraising work for the Philharmonic invited me to dinner at one of their homes on the Peak. I asked my secretary Vivian what I should say in Cantonese after enjoying a very good meal. As I drove up to the Peak, I practised this phrase probably 50 times! The meal was indeed excellent. Before we all left, I turned to my hostess and uttered the phrase. Only I got the tone levels wrong. As a result, all the ladies laughed. Naturally they would not tell me what I had said and I was left wondering what howler that might have been. It was only in the office the next morning that one of the guys who worked in the PR department suggested I take more care with tone levels. What I had said was something like –

"I am a sex maniac!"

One of the great benefits of working in a city like Hong Kong is how easy it is to get out on the sea. Many friends and colleagues invited me to join them for a Sunday on their junks or larger corporate boats. Spending time chatting, drinking, eating and sunbathing was a lovely way to relax.

Another was visiting Macao. With jetfoils and hydrofoils to the gambling mecca departing every 15 minutes and taking little more than an hour, I regularly joined friends for evenings enjoying dinner at some of Macao's lovely simple restaurants. Early 1980s Macao was the total opposite of Hong Kong. Having been leased from China by the Portuguese since the mid-1550s and the residence for 19th-century China traders except for the few months each year when they could sail up the Pearl River and base themselves on Shamian Island in Guangzhou, for a first-time visitor Macao resembled a Mediterranean village lifted from that same century with its own very special sea-front charm. On arrival at Macao we would always take a taxi and go first for drinks on the terrace at the old-fashioned Bela Vista Hotel. Situated on a promontory looking over to Taipa Island, even though the hotel had seen better days it still retained a certain charm. Macao then was three separate islands linked by bridges. After leisurely cocktails we would take a taxi over to Taipa or Coloane for a splendid dinner at typical Macanese hostelries like Fernando's or Pinocchio's. Dinner was always remarkably inexpensive, made even more so by the excellent Portuguese wine on which there was no tax in Macao. If we had time before the return ferry, we would pop into the wedding cake-like Lisboa Hotel and spend 15 minutes playing roulette. These were perfectly lovely evenings, an ideal antidote to the difficulties earlier in the weeks.

A third benefit which has lasted for the remainder of my life was the relative ease in crossing the border to the rest of China. At the start of my second season I was surprised to receive an invitation to visit Guangzhou. As a result of China's gradual opening up to the west following the visit of President Nixon in 1971 and the establishment of full diplomatic relations at the start of 1979, a US consulate was opened in Guangzhou on the top floor of the Dongfang Hotel in August that year. The new Consul General, Dick Williams, knew the Hong Kong Philharmonic had some musicians from the USA and was keen to explore the possibility of their presenting occasional chamber recitals at the consulate.

In September 1980 I walked across the bridge at Lo Wu and made the slow train journey through agricultural country where farming was still undertaken in communes to the outskirts of Guangzhou. Driven through near-empty streets to the consulate, I was introduced to another of Dick's guests, the Director of Mission in Thailand, Burton Levin, alleged at that time to be the head of the CIA in Asia. Both diplomats were to go on to become the consuls general in Hong Kong.

Our business was quickly concluded as I agreed to facilitate the concerts Dick was keen to see in the consulate. The following morning, we all drove down to the river to see the area on Shamian Island that had been the location of the 13 'factories' (literally trading posts, derived from the Portuguese word 'feitoria') where western traders had their go-downs with living quarters above immortalised in the famous painting by George Chinnery. China had just started on the road to rapid modernisation. Walking along the waterfront, I was struck by the large mansions, presumably at one time the residences of the *cohong* merchants who were the essential intermediaries for foreign trade around the turn of the 19th century, many of whom became incredibly rich. Little could any of us have believed that, as with much of the rest of the country, Guangzhou would develop so quickly into a modern 21st-century metropolis. That short two-day visit became the first in a long discovery of the extraordinary history of one of the world's greatest countries with my thereafter making dozens of fascinating explorations to many of its provinces and cities.

8

THINGS FINALLY BEGIN TO GO MY WAY

For many members of the GC, as he entered his second year in 1980 Tung had become a huge disappointment. Far from endearing himself to the Hong Kong community, when in Hong Kong he and Margot largely kept themselves to themselves. The Music Director of any society's orchestra has to be a public figure and be seen as such. As General Manager, I was invited to a host of cocktail parties each month. I made it my business both to be seen and to talk about the orchestra at as many as I could reasonably attend. I cannot recall Tung attending even one civic function in his post as Music Director. He had certainly improved the quality of the playing, but that had come at the cost of building a permanent orchestra. Even some of those musicians he had recruited were unhappy with his rehearsal technique. One, another Grand Teton 'graduate', had been engaged to lead the Second Violin section. I assumed that Marcus Lehmann would have been one of his supporters. Far from it. Marcus quickly showed he did not like Tung at all. Prior to one concert, he even went into his dressing room and said he would shoot him! I assumed this was mere rumour, but it had been heard by several other musicians and quickly became known to many in the orchestra. Since no complaint was made to me, I could take no action.

Other conductors had much more success. In the first season, conductors like George Hurst, Sir Edward Downes and Kenneth Schermerhorn knew how to rehearse without the constant repetition used by Tung. Kenneth was particularly successful, having been engaged for the final three weeks of the season in June 1980. In addition to excellent concerts, he was fun to be with and liked by almost all the musicians. During his 12 years with the Milwaukee Symphony, Kenneth had steered it to become one of the finest of the second-tier orchestras in the United States. After a concert in New York's Carnegie Hall, the influential critic Andrew Porter wrote in the *New Yorker* magazine –

"A superb conductor. He is obviously a maestro of great versatility as his programme demonstrated. I should place him without further thought or qualification, amongst the finest conductors of any nationality now before the American public."

After a programme featuring the Shostakovich Symphony No. 10 with the New York Philharmonic Orchestra, Byron Belt wrote in the *New York Times*, "The most incredibly exciting performance of the Symphony I have ever heard."

On my annual visit to London in the summer of 1980, fortune smiled on me. In addition to meeting with the usual list of agents, a good friend had invited me to lunch with one of London's finest violinists, Carl Pini. Known to all as Tony, he was then the concertmaster of the Philharmonia Orchestra in addition to leading the London String Quartet. Tony brought with him two other members of the Philharmonia who also performed with the Quartet, the violinist Benjamin Cruft and the Principal Violist Ruşen Güneş. What they wished to discuss initially shocked me – but in the nicest possible way. They had learned a bit about the orchestra in Hong Kong from their encounters with Ling Tung. Tony was looking for a move away from London. His new young wife was keen to be closer to her family in New Zealand. Would the Hong Kong Philharmonic be interested in his becoming the concertmaster, with Ben joining the first violin section and Ruşen leading the violas?

This all seemed far too good to be true. Tung had decided that the orchestra required a more experienced concertmaster than Jan van den Berg. I had not the slightest doubt that everyone associated with the Philharmonic would be thrilled at the possibility of three such distinguished musicians from the Philharmonia coming to Hong Kong. Immediately their presence would give the orchestra a huge boost. Even better, the administration had agreed to the Jockey Club's offer to put up the cost of building an excellent Academy for Performing Arts (HKAPA) as their 100th anniversary gift to Hong Kong. Increasingly there was an understanding that the best musicians from the Philharmonic also teach Hong Kong's most promising instrumental students.

Back in Hong Kong it was accepted that to obtain the services of a celebrated musician of Pini's stature would require a substantial salary. With the government backing the proposal, funds were found which would include a mix of playing, conducting and teaching. By that stage, Ruşen had decided he preferred to stay in London. Ben, though, arrived in Hong Kong in time for the start of the season. Tony would not be free until the beginning of November which happened to coincide with the first of Tung's concerts that season. The second of his first pair of concerts in the City Hall Concert Hall could not have been more dramatic or better received. That weekend the soloist was the well-established Israeli pianist, Ilana Vered, performing the Mozart D minor Concerto K466. Her husband, a doctor, accompanied her. On the afternoon of the second concert, I received a phone call from the orchestra's concerts manager, Su Villiers. Ms. Vered was ill and her husband had confirmed she would not be able to perform. Finding a substitute soloist at only a few hours' warning was impossible. I feared we would have no choice but to cancel half the programme.

I called an urgent meeting with Ling Tung and Tony Pini. How should we handle this impossible situation? Immediately Tony came up with the answer. He had recently performed one of the Mozart Violin Concertos as soloist with the Philharmonia. If the Philharmonic's library had the orchestral parts, he would be happy to perform it at the concert, even without rehearsal. This was almost unbelievable! We had the parts and agreed to move the concerto to the second half of the programme. This would give Tung, Pini and the orchestra's principal players 15 minutes to talk through key matters like tempi and general interpretation before the concert restarted. When I went onstage at the start of the concert to announce the change of programme and how our new concertmaster would perform the violin concerto in place of the advertised piano concerto, there was loud applause. At the interval I went backstage to wish everyone the best of luck. Tony's debut was a triumph for him, for the orchestra, most of whom were sight-reading the concerto never having played it before, and I admit also for Tung who did extremely well to keep everything together.

Thanks to Pini, the following month he had persuaded the superb pianist Vladimir Ashkenazy to come to Hong Kong to perform the Brahms First Concerto with the Philharmonic and Tony conducting. Carl Pini was a total joy to work with. Nothing seemed to upset him and his experience alone was a massive boost to the orchestra. Only once did I have a problem to solve and it was no way his fault. One of Tung's conductor selections, the American one-time Music Director from the Kansas City Philharmonic, Maurice Peress, finally arrived in early 1981 for a week of concerts. Like Schermerhorn, though, Tung could not benefit from a conductor exchange because Peress had left the Kansas orchestra the year before!

For whatever reason, totally the fault of Peress, the atmosphere between Pini and Peress got off on a bad foot and never recovered. During coffee break intermissions it was usual for musicians to leave their instruments in their cases or on their seats. Returning from the canteen, Tony noticed that Peress had picked up his very valuable Carlo Bergonzi and was inspecting it closely. It was extremely unprofessional of Peress even to touch it without Tony's permission. He then made matters much worse. He said to Tony something along the line of –

"I hope this plays well because it looks quite old."

After Stradivarius and Guarnerius violins, Bergonzis are acknowledged as amongst the most valuable. Pini had purchased the instrument in 1960 for £4,500. He eventually sold it for US$500,000 in 1989. Peress' extraordinary statement and cavalier attitude rightly infuriated Pini. I was summoned and quickly agreed that Tony take the week off. I was certain that some other issue would arise if Tony was forced to work with a conductor he clearly disliked intensely.

Despite continuing disappointments with Tung, for almost the first time I had begun to believe the Hong Kong Philharmonic might be on a path that could eventually see it becoming as good as some of the region's finest orchestras in Japan.

The following summer, fortune was again to smile on me, and once again in the most unexpected way. Many conductors had already been booked for the upcoming 1981/82 season. We were still short of one, though, for an important concert during the February 1982 Arts Festival. With that Festival also including the Cleveland Orchestra with Lorin Maazel and the Zurich Tonhalle Orchestra with Ferdinand Leitner, we had to come up with a programme that would as far as possible match these two distinguished ensembles. That meant either a stellar conductor or outstanding soloist – or both. Tung was out of contract, thankfully. Given his unpopularity within the ranks of the orchestra, I had been surprised at the lack of discussion at the April GC meeting in 1980 when the option of his additional year had been discussed. There had been talk that his ability to 'hire and fire at will' be curbed, but that was about as far as it went. Some members of the GC reminded their colleagues that he was particularly unpopular and that the views of the musicians should be taken into account. Others stuck to their earlier line that the musicians should just do as they were told. If they did not want to work with Tung, they could leave and find other orchestra work elsewhere. Tung's one-year extension was granted with near unanimity. That extension was to be his last. Thereafter the contract was not renewed.

For the Arts Festival concert, no other conductors who had worked well with the orchestra were available. Filling that date was therefore at the top of my list. I arrived in London on a hot June morning. After dropping my case with the friends with whom I was spending these few days, I went back in to central London for an early afternoon meeting at the home of Victor and Lillian Hochhauser, legendary agents and concert managers who for years had promoted the best Soviet Union artists in the UK. That had changed in 1974 when they had helped the famed cellist Mstislav Rostropovich and his wife, the Bolshoi Opera's Prima Donna

Galina Vishnevskaya, defect to the west. Doors to the Soviet Union were then closed.

I especially liked Lillian. She was a warm-hearted lady with a lovely smile and a genuine desire to help when needed. A year or so later, she was rather shocked that I had never enjoyed afternoon tea at the legendary Ritz Hotel in Piccadilly.

"My dear, this is something you must do at least once. Are you free tomorrow?"

Thus I entered one of London's great hotels for afternoon tea with Lillian. I was only glad that she was paying and not me!

I was later to meet Victor on several occasions when he came through Hong Kong after visits to other parts of China to finalise deals to tour performing companies to the United Kingdom. During one visit at the end of the 1980s, I had the USSR State Symphony Orchestra giving three performances in the City Hall Concert Hall. The Orchestra's Music Director was the famed Russian conductor Yevgeny Svetlanov, a friend of Victor's. I remember particularly Svetlanov's conducting of the final movement of Rachmaninov's First Symphony at the first concert. After a few bars it starts on a fanfare-like March theme. Svetlanov gave the down beat and then kept his hands rigidly at his side for nearly 40 seconds letting the orchestra just play. It was very impressive.

Unfortunately Victor arrived in Hong Kong on the day of the third concert when the assistant conductor was on the podium. We could not find Svetlanov and so Victor said we should instead just go to the Mandarin Grill and have a nice dinner. Once our entrées arrived, the Filipino waiter made a great show of removing the tureens to show our dishes. Unfortunately Victor's plate was empty! We just laughed.

Victor was such fun to be with as he was always full of anecdotes. For some years when he was still persona grata with the Soviet Union he had toured the Red Army Choir around the UK. Of course, he told me, hardly any had been in the army! On one tour, a member of the choir had unfortunately died and his coffin had to be sent back to Moscow. When it came to the last day of the tour, one of the KGB officers who always toured with Soviet ensembles came to his office.

"Mr. Hochhauser. You have a contract to fly 60 members of our group to and from Moscow. Isn't that correct?"

"Indeed, it is," replied Victor.

"Well, as you know we will only be 59 returning to Moscow. Can you therefore give me in cash the amount you have saved as a result of our unfortunate member not being with us on the return?"

On several occasions I suggested that Victor had to find time to write his autobiography. I am sure it would have been both fascinating and hilarious. Sadly, I believe he never did.

Back in that summer of 1981 I went through with Lillian the list of dates for which I needed conductors and soloists, starting off with the February Arts Festival concert. Without batting the proverbial eyelid, she slowly broke into a big smile, held it for a moment and then said –

"I know exactly who you want and I am certain it is beyond anything you will have dreamt of."

I was aware that the conductor son and pianist grandson of the great Soviet composer Dmitri Shostakovich, Maxim and Dmitri, had defected from the Soviet Union on a visit to Germany less than two months earlier. Unknown to me, Lillian was helping establish Maxim in the west. She took a file from her desk drawer, opened it and the smile returned.

"Both are available for your Arts Festival date. Why don't you consider inviting Maxim to conduct and Dmitri to perform the First Piano Concerto? You could also end with one of the Shostakovich symphonies. In effect, you will be the first orchestra outside the Soviet Union to have three generations of Shostakovich on the same stage." She laughed!

I thought it a marvellous idea. It would not only inspire the musicians, it would bring untold benefits in term of PR. It will be remembered that David Stone was the government's Music Advisor and had been on the panel for my interview in London. Only recently did I read in his biography on Wikipedia the claim that "he [Stone] was instrumental in Maxim Shostakovich's first conducting engagement after his defection to the west (Hong Kong Philharmonic 1981)." Frankly, that is absolutely untrue! It was a deal done exclusively between Lillian and me. In any case, the concert was in 1982, not 1981.

In a rather sad way this was typical of Stone's overreaching himself in one way or another. I have no doubt he was a very fine violinist and he certainly achieved a lot of good for music education in Hong Kong. This was especially true when he oversaw much of the planning for the HKAPA. But in an official paper regarding the future of the Hong Kong Philharmonic that I read during my days working out of the Hong Kong Government office in London, I noted he had proposed himself as being more or less the ideal Music Director. I thought no more of that until one Arts Festival concert in the early 1980s when he conducted a work by Handel with the Hong Kong Youth Orchestra and Choir. This was a difficult work requiring in addition to the orchestra and chorus a small group of continuo players. Sitting in a box with Barrie Wiggham, I was shocked when it became all too obvious that the three groups were gradually coming apart. David just did not have the talent as a conductor to pull them back together. It got so bad he had no alternative but to stop, turn to the audience and say –

"We'll start again. It happens to the best of orchestras!"

It hardly ever happens to any orchestras! I have no idea who he thought might believe that, but it was deeply embarrassing, mostly for the youngsters he was trying to lead and their families in the audience.

The Shostakovich concert was a huge success for the Philharmonic. Although Maxim was hardly the finest conductor I had ever seen, he was ideal for that programme and, I felt, a lot more. He brought spontaneity and flair to the podium, two qualities sadly lacking in Ling Tung. If we could just persuade him to return for a few weeks a year in the role of Principal Guest Conductor, we could benefit immensely from his continued presence. I, though, was not yet in a position to offer this. I did however contact Lillian to tell her how successful the concert had been, while at the same time sowing in her mind the possibility of an offer for a titled position in the not-too-distant future. We did not have to wait long. By September Maxim had agreed to become the Philharmonic's Principal Guest Conductor for a period of three years.

With Tung no longer associated with the Philharmonic and the GC in possession of the report submitted in the summer by Basil Tschaikov, Philip Kwok the new chairman invited me to lunch. He told me he fully agreed with the comments about me in the report and would back me to the hilt in how I wished to manage the orchestra. He said there was only one thing he asked of me. If ever a situation arose where the orchestra would be appearing negatively in the media, he wanted to know beforehand. His door would always be open to me. Equally, he wanted me to know that it would be open to members of the orchestra. But he would always inform me of the subject of any such discussions with musicians. I could not have asked for more.

One couple whom I had met at my first concert in 1979 were Klaus Heymann and his wife, the excellent violinist Takako Nishizaki. They kindly invited me to dinner to talk over orchestral matters as both had once been involved with the Philharmonic. At their New Territories home, I became aware that Klaus had come to Hong Kong in 1967 to work as a journalist. He soon started up a mail order business largely for many of the American troops who visited Hong Kong on rest-and-recreation breaks during their tours of duty in Vietnam and who wanted the latest cameras and hi-fi equipment sent back to their families. As the war ended, he remained in the business of hi-fi equipment, adding to it the licensing of a number of record labels and organising occasional concerts with artists contracted to those labels. Having been invited to join the Philharmonic's GC when it turned professional, he had recently married one of Japan's finest violinists. In 1964 Takako had been runner-up to arguably the finest violinist of the day, Itzhak Perlman, in the prestigious Leventritt Competition. Contracted to a major American music agency, she found the constant touring around the USA tiring and not artistically fulfilling. She decided to return to Japan where she met and later married Klaus.

With Klaus based in Hong Kong, he proposed that Takako also be contracted as one of the soloists. Neither found their roles satisfactory. As Klaus told me, he felt the GC had no interest in his ideas, while Takako found the first Music Director very difficult to work with. Both left with more than a degree of bad feeling. Three years later, learning of the Philharmonic's intention to record a popular Chinese work for orchestra and violin soloist titled *The Butterfly Lovers Concerto* for the Philips record label, Klaus took another major decision. He would start his own label and record the same concerto with Takako performing with a Japanese orchestra. The Philharmonic's version sold a few thousand copies. Thanks to his expertise in business and much greater knowledge of the recording market, Takako's version soared to eventual sales of hundreds of thousands.

Klaus' dislike of those in charge of the Philharmonic did not prevent him from later arranging with me to commence a recording relationship with the orchestra. By then he had started up Hong Kong Records and then Marco Polo Records before launching Naxos as the world's first budget CD label in the mid-1980s. I was at first delighted at our association for half a dozen recordings for all three labels. Making new digital recordings of initially popular repertoire but using excellent but less well-known orchestras, conductors and soloists, Klaus kept his fee structure low and never paid royalties. Soon Naxos was outselling all the more established record labels with its CDs costing around one third of those issued by the major labels. At the same time, Klaus expanded the repertoire to include much more from a less popular repertoire and also rarely recorded contemporary music.

One story told to me by the late Anthony Camden illustrates his approach to recordings. An excellent oboe player who had been Principal Oboe with the London Symphony Orchestra for 14 years, Tony had also been the self-governing orchestra's chairman, a post he held for a dozen years. In 1993, Tony came to Hong Kong as Dean of the School of Music at the HKAPA. Although he had made several recordings as a soloist in London, he was particularly keen to record a CD of oboe concertos by the baroque composer Tomaso Albinoni. He approached Klaus as Naxos had no recording of the works in its increasingly extensive catalogue. Klaus was not initially very keen. He did not believe it would sell well. So Tony made a proposal that he would assemble and pay for a group of London's finest musicians and an excellent recording venue. In return, Klaus could pay him a royalty rather than up-front fees. Klaus was hesitant in view of his no royalty policy. On the other hand, this would expand his repertoire at little extra cost. He therefore agreed.

After the CD had been on the market for some time, Tony said he'd like to record another set of Albinoni concertos. He would be happy for the same royalty arrangement. Klaus paused and looked through reams of paper on his desk. No, he said. He had checked the latest sales figures and seen that the first Albinoni CD had sold in the region of 185,000 copies – far higher than the 50,000 average for Naxos CDs. He would be happy to make another recording, but only on the up-front fee basis, the same as all Naxos' other recordings!

During our first dinner, Klaus and Takako gave me snapshot profiles of many involved with the orchestra. None was complimentary. Klaus believed the governance of the orchestra was overly political with few on its committees having any real interest in classical music and even less in developing an orchestra. They wished me well, but suggested I would be in for a considerable amount of trouble. As things turned out, that was initially very much an understatement!

9

DISCOVERING THE REGION AND BEING DISCOVERED

With my initial contract only for two years, as I was determined to learn more about the region, its peoples and cultures, I realised I would be taking all my annual vacations in neighbouring countries. Although I only had three weeks of paid vacation, Hong Kong had a very generous 17 days of annual public holidays as it observed both Chinese holidays and many of those observed in the UK. I could therefore split my vacations into several smaller ones.

For my first, I opted for a week in Penang followed by a few days in Bangkok. Knowing little about Penang beforehand, I decided to stay in the then rather dilapidated Eastern and Oriental Hotel by the sea. My large room opened on to the garden by the rocky waterfront where I would take my breakfast in the morning sun. Unfortunately, I also shared the room with a colony of ants, albeit a trail of ants leading from a corner of the ceiling, down the wall before disappearing somewhere under the floor. The only part of the hotel that had been renovated was the bar. With plush colours and soft sofas it was a pleasant watering hole to enjoy a drink in the evening. It also had a galaxy of old pictures and framed fading newspaper articles on the walls. One was an advertisement clipped from a copy of *The Times* in London dating from the 1930s. "The E & O Hotel: The Finest Hotel East of Suez," it boasted.

I thoroughly enjoyed wandering through the small capital city of Georgetown. This was to lead to one of my funniest encounters. I loved the sights, smells and sounds of the Malay quarter, the very different experiences in the Chinese quarter and the yet greater differences in the

Indian quarter. Somewhat tired from my afternoon walk in the high heat and humidity, I found a bar named the 'Hong Kong' bar. Where better to refresh myself with some cold beer? Around 40 minutes and two beers later, I decided it was time to get back to the hotel for dinner. As I left the bar, a middle-aged Indian man approached me.

"Hello," he exclaimed. "Where are you going?"

"Back to my hotel," I replied.

Getting close to my ear, he asked in an almost conspiratorial whisper –

"Wanta a girl?"

"No! No!" I replied. "I have to go back to my hotel for dinner."

He would not give up. Another whisper –

"Wanta a boy?"

As I declined, I walked rather quickly away. Goodness, I thought. I have certainly arrived in Asia!

I found Penang fascinating but without much to do to occupy a week. Someone in the hotel had told me about the island of Langkawi to the north. She added it was very undeveloped and only had two hotels in those days. But she suggested it was worth a two-day visit. So, the following day I was on the ferry to the mainland, then a bus up the coast and another small ferry over to Langkawi. I had taken as reading material Anthony Burgess' series of novels *The Malayan Trilogy* and thoroughly enjoyed his amusing tales as I experienced some of the countryside he described.

Langkawi had a rather simple country club which was an ideal base for exploring the small island. I remember little of it now apart from a lovely mosque that seemed to be situated in the sea. I came upon it when the tide was out and the only way to get close was to wade through the thick wet mud. Looking now at a map of the very developed island, I think it must have been the Masjid Bukit Malut, but am far from sure.

My only other memory of Langkawi is of a short flight back to Penang. I had assumed I would have to retrace my steps by ferries and bus but the hotel receptionist told me there was a daily flight in the afternoons.

It took little more than 15 minutes. So, I booked a ticket and found my way to what was merely a small airstrip cut from the jungle. The 'terminal' was a small Nissen hut manned by a young man who can have been no more than 16. After taking my ticket, he asked if I would like a drink. Being thirsty, I told him I would indeed like one. He then went out by a side door, clambered up a palm tree and cut down a coconut which he opened and presented to me. Once again I realised I was well and truly in Asia! When the incoming aircraft arrived, it was tiny with a small box-like fuselage and seated around 12 passengers.

For a first-time visitor with no prior experience of Asia, Bangkok with its magnificent temples and palaces and its crowded streets buzzing with activity well into the evenings was jaw-droppingly amazing. Even in the intense heat of April I spent much of my time wandering around just taking in all the sights and smells from the many dozens of hawker food stalls.

Soon after my return to Hong Kong, the GC exercised its option on the third year of my contract. So my vacations took me further afield. In November 1980 I flew to Nepal for a stunning six days. After exploring the many sights in Kathmandu, I hired a taxi for a day to spend time in the wonderful old Kathmandu Valley cities of Bhaktapur and Patan. I had read about the erotic carvings on some of the temples. For a boy brought up in the small Scottish city of Aberdeen, perhaps I should have averted my eyes. But I marvelled at the culture which had created them. I then took the short flight to Pokhara for the main purpose of the trip: to see the Annapurna range as dawn broke. On the mid-afternoon flight I was disappointed because the mountains were covered in thick cloud all the way. Landing in Pokhara it was also cloudy. Pokhara then was little more than a poor village with a pot-holed main street dotted with guest houses. My taxi from the airport had a large crack on the windshield and its driver seemed no more than 15 years old. We passed a lake which was having construction work done. I felt so sorry for the men and women hauling baskets of rocks up an incline, the baskets held by thick cloth bands stretched over their foreheads. At the guesthouse, the friendly landlady explained how to see dawn break over the Annapurna range on the other side of the valley, I had to get up at 4:30 in the morning. She would leave a thermos flask of tea, some sandwiches and a torch for me to take as I walked for almost an hour from the guesthouse till I reached a small track leading up to the left. It was then a long trek gradually up a gentle hill to a viewing point at Sarangot.

Before dawn, it was pitch black. All I could make out were some faint clouds in the sky. There can have been no more than half a dozen of us that morning, all with cameras at the ready. Eventually the sky slowly lightened. I then realised that what I had assumed were clouds were in fact mountain tops. Before reaching the horizon, the sun hit the tops of the mountains. As the light slowly moved down the huge peaks, the snow changed colour from deep pink through various shades of orange until it was bright white and we could see the sun emerge from the edge of the universe on our right. That morning was miraculous, an intense visual experience that seemed almost religious made even more impressive by the absolute silence apart from the flapping of the wings of a few birds. I returned to Pokhara 26 years later to refresh that experience in my mind. My 1980 photos had all turned slightly pink and I hoped to recreate them in digital splendour. It was a mistake. Pokhara had become a thriving city of close to 500,000 inhabitants bustling with tourists, many hotels located in the extensive new district around the lake. The trail up to Sarangot had become a paved road and merely a 10-minute drive. Once there, I was in the company of more than 100 others, mostly young Japanese and Koreans, all jostling for the best camera positions. Unfortunately, there had been a cyclone in the Bay of Bengal and cloud trails extended as far as the valley. I was slightly disappointed that my photos lacked the crystal clarity of 1980, but no one can be disappointed for long when so close in front of you is that extraordinary mountain range with 30 peaks of over 6,000 metres in height of which 13 are over 7,000 metres. The main Annapurna peak is over 8,000 metres, the tenth highest mountain in the world.

In April the following year, I planned three weeks split between Bali and Tokyo. After three nights at the luxury Oberoi Hotel I had decided to move up to a small hotel just outside the artists' village at Ubud. The Tjampuhan hotel across the bridge as you leave the village could hardly be called a hotel even then. It was essentially one large open building which served as the dining room and a series of huts on a hillside leading down to a stream. The huts had gauze rather than glass for windows and the showers were more than basic – buckets with holes in the bottom attached to a rope slung over a beam. After filling the bucket with water, the hope was you could raise it high enough to get some water over you before it all drained out of the bucket. None had electricity and so we were given paraffin lamps when retiring for the night.

Yet I so enjoyed that little hotel. The staff were all so genuinely friendly towards the guests. Every morning a lovely breakfast would be left outside my door. On the hillside was a small Hollywood-style pool. The Tjampuhan had been home to the German artist Walter Spies who lived in Bali in the 1930s and started a Balinese cooperative to encourage young Balinese to take up painting. Although he was gay, the American heiress Barbara Hutton fell in love with him. He obviously liked her and agreed to her demand that she would only visit him in Bali if he built a Hollywood-style pool for her. Although Spies complied with her request and his white pool was very much a feature of the hillside, she never did visit.

I loved Bali and its people so much I called my secretary and asked her to cancel Tokyo. I spent the entire three weeks there, totally immersing myself in the island's distinctive culture. I was to return twice a year for five years. I eventually returned 20 years later. As I had found in Nepal, though, the advent of mass tourism had by then all but spoiled the island for me. The simplicity of the artists' town of Ubud had been almost destroyed by becoming a tourist magnet.

I finally made it to Tokyo following auditions in the USA that summer of 1981. With Tung on the way out, the GC had finally agreed to my proposal that, in addition to Hong Kong, there be open auditions in three centres – London, New York and Los Angeles, to which Chicago with its nearby excellent music faculty at Northwestern University would eventually be added.

Instantly I loved Tokyo. I began to visit about six times each year until I found myself working there for two years from 1990. I continue to return regularly for it remains one of my favourite cities. It was during one of my early visits that I met Walter Nichols (of whom much more later). He in turn introduced me to Tadashi Yokoyama. Yokoyama held a senior position in the Japan Foundation. I was seeking any information I could about subsidies for engaging Japanese artists or financial assistance if a way could be found of inviting the Philharmonic to give concerts in Japan. It was at that meeting that Walter informed me about the Osaka International Music Festival, then Asia's most prestigious music festival. This chance meeting was quite amazingly to lead to our giving two concerts at the Festival in April 1983.

It took me some time after moving to Hong Kong to realise that there were no other westerners working in the business of music management in the whole of Asia. The most active music centre was Japan where there were many concert halls and many more in the planning or construction phase. Whereas Berlin had six professional symphony orchestras and London five, Tokyo alone had 12. Tokyo also had an opera company and many fine concert and recital halls. Consequently there was a large number of concert managements. I felt it very important that I start to get to know them and they get to know both me and the Hong Kong Philharmonic which was still virtually unknown in Asia outside Hong Kong.

I also found myself visiting Seoul on many occasions. Although not nearly as active in the presentation of western classical music, it had two major orchestras in the KBS Symphony Orchestra (KBS is the South Korean equivalent of Britain's national broadcaster, the BBC) and the Seoul Philharmonic established by the Seoul city government. Initially I found it slightly bewildering that much musical activity in Korea was underwritten by the some of the major newspapers, notably the influential

Dong-A Ilbo. In Japan the Yomiuri Nippon Orchestra had been founded in 1962 by a media consortium including the *Yomiuri Shimbun* newspaper. But I knew of no others. On each visit to Seoul, as in Tokyo, I would find out which artists and conductors they were planning to bring to Korea and if any could also visit Hong Kong.

Visiting Seoul presented particular difficulties because martial law was still in existence. Indeed, South Korea was not to become democratic until 1992. As a result, there was a curfew between midnight and 6:00am. If found on the streets after midnight, there was always the danger you could be shot. If out for a dinner engagement, getting a taxi back to my hotel was far from easy. At around 10:00pm everyone who was out wanted to get home, leading to a rush for taxis. I discovered the only way to get to my hotel was to stand by the roadside holding a fistful of Won, hoping that a taxi would stop for me. If one did, it would usually have one or two other passengers. If I was going where the taxi driver was going, he would take me. If not, I'd have to wait for the next one.

I had thought my first overseas visit in the region would be to Taiwan. Early in 1979 one of my first visitors was a concert promoter and agent from Taipei, Hsu Po-yuen. Along with Lucretia Kasilag, the Director of the Cultural Centre of the Philippines, the previous year they had founded the Federation for Asian Cultural Promotion (FACP) of which Po-yuen was the Secretary General. The FACP was a loose-knit body of promoters, artists' managers, venue managers and others involved in the presentation of the arts in the Asian region. Po-yuen invited me to attend the annual conference to be held later that year in Taipei. With members from most regional countries, this seemed an ideal way for me to get to know them and for them to get to know me. When I applied for leave to make the trip, though, the request was denied. It was a regulation that no Hong Kong civil servants could visit the island of Taiwan. Although I was not a civil servant, most of my masters were and so my request was denied.

I rather put the FACP out of my mind until 1984 when the annual meeting was in Tokyo. Apart from being a talking shop, FACP did very little throughout each year. It also had no Articles of Association and, worse, no money. I therefore suggested that a sub-committee be formed to draft a set of Articles and report back at the following year's conference scheduled for Seoul. This was accepted. I was rather surprised when I was elected chairman of the sub-committee. I suspect this was only because I travelled in the region a great deal and could therefore easily meet committee members individually. At the Seoul conference, the new Articles were adopted and I was voted on to the Board of Governors.

The next conference in December 1986 was once again back in Taipei. No longer with the Philharmonic, I was free of restrictions and delighted to attend, although once again I was in a territory with martial law in force. Until I got there, though, I was not aware that a small palace revolution was under way within the FACP. The Japanese always formed the largest delegation. This year they were determined to force a change of office bearers. With increasing arts activity in China, they felt a secretary general from Taipei was a hindrance to membership from other Chinese cities where the arts were starting to flourish. When it came to the election of office bearers, just before the nominations were to be submitted for the top positions, the two Japanese board members informed me the Japanese delegation wished to nominate me as secretary general. I was somewhat dumbfounded, as well as embarrassed. If the current secretary general was effectively booted out on his home turf, a great deal of face would be lost. But by this time I knew and liked my Japanese colleagues. I therefore consented. When the votes were counted, I was the new secretary general, a post I was to hold for five years.

Even during my tenure, FACP never was able to achieve much. But it did give me a great deal of 'face'. I was regarded now as a major regional promoter. Little did I then realise that this could become the root of yet another set of problems for me!

Internationally I was to become far better known – again through a quirk of fate. A UK publishing company had decided to launch a new trade magazine aimed at the growing number of managers working in the arts around the world. As editor of *International Arts Manager* it selected

Graeme Kay with whom I had worked at Scottish Opera. Graeme called me one day to tell me about the magazine and his desire to have the first issue feature an arts manager working in an 'exotic' part of the world. Would I be interested? Naturally I was, and so it was my photograph that adorned Volume 1 No. 1. Taken on the Peak, there is actually little of Hong Kong to be seen in the photograph. But for years afterwards I would often be regaled at conferences with comments like, "I know we have met but I just cannot recall where!" In most cases we had never met. It was only my cover photo in their memories that made them assume we must have done!

Back in Hong Kong much was happening in the arts. The CSD had started up and financed a Chinese orchestra, a repertory theatre and a dance company. The privately founded and run Hong Kong Ballet soon was added to the list of performing companies in receipt of official government subsidy. Perhaps the most successful of all the performing companies was the City Contemporary Dance Company (CCDC). Founded privately in 1979 by Willie Tsao who was passionately interested not only in contemporary dance and with a burning desire to spread that interest to the people of Hong Kong, Tsao's company was very quickly taking part in the 1980 Arts Festival production of Stravinsky's *The Soldier's Tale*.

Willie himself was later to take his passion to Beijing and Guangzhou, in both cities establishing professional dance companies. With his commitment to the entire population of Hong Kong and a donation of HK$500,000 from his family, Willie avoided the main up-market centres of the territory and instead based his company in an old school building in the depths of Kowloon very close to the famous Wong Tai Sin Temple. In addition to more and more regular performances, the company ran evening and weekend dance classes at the school. Within a decade it had started to become one of Hong Kong's most travelled cultural ambassadors with invitations to give performances by more than 270 organisations worldwide.

I had watched the development of the company with increasing interest. It was therefore with great pleasure that I accepted an invitation to join its executive committee in 1985. I am not sure how much I was able to contribute until the issue of applying for regular government funding came up. With my experience of various branches of government and civil servants, I worked closely with the chairman, Kennic Lui, in drafting the application. I was then absolutely delighted when it was approved and the government started regular annual funding of CCDC.

10

THE MUCH-DISLIKED LING TUNG FINALLY DEPARTS

As noted earlier, in April 1981 the GC finally decided not to offer Tung a new contract. His term as Music Director would come to an end in December. His attempts to oust me were not over, though. That summer, with Tung out of the picture in terms of recruiting new musicians, we now had formal auditions in several major music centres. Joining me on the first of what was a very enjoyable if quick round-the-world trip were Carl Pini and David Gwilt. My job was basically administrative, making sure the local organiser I had hired in each location had all the paperwork ready for each candidate and copies of all the music required for sight-reading for each instrument. Unobtrusively, I had a secondary role. The GC and I were concerned that some of the musicians hired by Tung did not fit well into the orchestra. They lacked the discipline required for working in a young full-time professional orchestra. I would therefore do my best to assess the character of all those attending the auditions. Far from an easy task, given that each audition only took between 10 and 15 minutes. It was probably also unethical from the point of view of the musicians' unions in each country!

I don't think I had realised that auditioning was such an exhausting process for Tony and David. When they had to listen to up to 20 or more horn players each day all playing the same pre-arranged excerpts from, for example, the important solo parts in the first movements of the Brahms First and Second Piano Concertos. I wondered after they had heard the last player in the afternoon how they could recall the playing of the first player in the morning. Each evening, therefore, it was almost essential that we go out and enjoy dinner with a lot of jokes as a release mechanism. This was especially enjoyable in Los Angeles where Tony took us to a delightful seafood restaurant he knew at nearby Marina del Rey.

Even with the GC having finally decided not to renew Tung's contract, he (or again, was it Margot?) was not finished trying to get rid of me. That summer after the auditions and my visits to concert agents in London and New York, I have already mentioned my decision to stop in Tokyo on my way back to Hong Kong. Even though the fees paid in Japan were higher than we could afford, it would be very useful to find out which conductors and soloists they might be bringing so that I could try and negotiate for one or more before or after their Japanese concerts. At the very least this would reduce our airfare costs.

I stayed in the large Keio Plaza hotel as it was close to Shinjuku station with easy rail and subway access to much of the city. With my first full day being a Saturday, I decided to start exploring this city I was to come to love almost as much as I was loving Hong Kong. I decided to find the main opera and concert venue, the Bunka Kaikan in Ueno. I always like looking at the design of concert posters as I am usually able to pick up ideas I can use later for my own concerts. About to leave, I noticed one for a visit being made later in the year by the opera company from La Scala. One of the operas in the season would be Verdi's *Simon Boccanegra* conducted by Claudio Abbado with whom I had worked at the Edinburgh Festival on a much-praised production of *Carmen* in 1977 and 78. I decided I had to get a ticket, no matter that tickets were much more expensive than I had been used to in London and elsewhere. Once back in Hong Kong I booked a package tour around the date.

The Giorgio Strehler production of *Boccanegra* designed by my old friend Ezio Frigerio with Mirella Freni, Nicolai Ghiaurov, Piero Cappuccilli and Veriano Luchetti was a truly wonderful evening. I was so pleased I had taken this short holiday. Back at my hotel, though, there was an urgent message for me to call the office. Early the next morning I was horrified to learn that someone had sent unsigned, undated letters in plain envelopes to the Hong Kong Governor, the Philharmonic Board of Governors, the members of the GC and a host of other important people in Hong Kong. This basically alleged fraud on the part of someone in the orchestra's management. It was to do with return air tickets issued to overseas members of the orchestra being purchased overseas prior to the start of their contracts. Once the musicians arrived in Hong Kong, the Philharmonic staff kept the return portions in a safe. The letter alleged that these unused return portions had then been submitted for refunds and the proceeds pocketed.

This was utter nonsense. To say I was livid would be a total understatement. After the utter joy of the previous evening, I now had another problem to solve in Hong Kong. I spoke to our accountant and asked her to go through the accounts for the previous two years as I knew this letter was a blatant lie. I then called Philip Kwok. He had just returned from a short overseas trip and had not seen the letter. Not having seen it myself, I could only describe it in general terms. I told him it was an outrageous untruth and I sought his permission to call in the auditors as well as the police. He agreed.

By the time I was back in the office the following day, it had been proved that no air tickets had been refunded. Discussing the matter with the police, I was asked who might have a grudge against the orchestra. I could think of about three people, Tung and two former musicians. Was there any clue in the letter, they then asked? One thing had bothered me as soon as I had read it. The letter included the word "bilked". I had never heard of it before. I soon realised that it is a word rarely used in the United Kingdom but quite commonly in the United States, meaning essentially to obtain by deceit or to defraud.

It was only then I recalled a discussion I had had with Margot Tung two years earlier. It had been common for the orchestra to purchase just one-way tickets for overseas musicians for their outward journey to Hong Kong. She had suggested it would be much cheaper in the long run if we purchased return one-year tickets and kept in a safe the return portion for use at the end of a season. In discussion at the time with our accountant, this seemed a very sensible suggestion. Not only were return tickets less expensive than two one-way tickets, if purchased in the United States for the US musicians, they would also be less expensive than purchasing the same tickets in Hong Kong. Margot had a friend who was a travel agent in Philadelphia. She organised these tickets for us.

So that was it! No one else in the Philharmonic was aware of this arrangement other than Vennie Ho the accountant, the honorary treasurer and I. It became perfectly clear, given the amount of specialist detail in the letter, that one of the Tungs had to have written it. But it had been posted in Hong Kong. The Tungs had not been in Hong Kong for several months. I then became certain that Maria Lui must have sent Margot the list of names and addresses who thereafter returned to her the sealed envelopes with the letters ready for posting. Reflecting on it later, it was such a simple and utterly stupid attempt to spread a lie when disproving it was so easy. No doubt it had been sent primarily as an embarrassment to me.

I was delighted I would never again have to have any dealings with either of the Tungs. They had created so much havoc in such a relatively short space of time. I also had had enough of being undermined within the office and gave Maria Lui the opportunity of resigning before being fired. Still wending its way through the courts was the lawsuit resulting from Ling's non-renewal of the 16 contracts in the summer of 1979. By this time, the number of plaintiffs had been reduced to six. Although that would not come to a resolution until July 1986, from that day in October 1981 forwards I felt we were finally able to get down to the serious business of really developing the orchestra into a fine fully professional full-time ensemble.

11

THE SEARCH FOR A NEW MUSIC DIRECTOR

I have always believed that fate has played a considerable part in my career – that and being in the right place at the right time. After the decision had been taken not to renew Tung's contract, we set about the search for a new Music Director. In view of his depth of experience, his reviews of major concerts in New York and the fact that he had worked so well with the Philharmonic, Kenneth Schermerhorn obviously had to be high on the list. But as I was now in almost total charge of selecting conductors and soloists, I wanted to invite a number of younger conductors whom I believed would work well with the orchestra. These included Gerard Schwarz, then Music Director of the Los Angeles Chamber Orchestra and the Mostly Mozart Orchestra in New York, and the young Korean Myung-whun Chung. Myung-whun had come to world attention when at the age of 21 he had won second prize at the 1971 International Tchaikovsky Piano Competition in Moscow. But his real interest was in conducting. Accepting that he needed to spend some time working with a lesser-known orchestra in order to learn the repertoire and gain much needed experience, he had accepted the post of Chief Conductor of the orchestra in Saarbrücken in Germany. Despite his relative lack of experience, I brought him to Hong Kong for two periods of two weeks each, during one of which the orchestra performed its first Mahler Symphony, the Fourth.

Everyone enjoyed those weeks and not surprisingly he was high on our list of potential new Music Directors. Unfortunately he informed me he would not wish to be considered. If we were based in Seoul, then he would certainly take the position. Understandably perhaps, he had decided that future concerts in Asia should concentrate on orchestras in his home country.

There was one occasion during our search when there was a strange and rather unique occurrence. While annoying at the time, I did not realise it would result in another change in my career.

I received a handwritten letter from an agent in London I had never met nor even heard of. Charlotte Nicholls ran a small company with very few artists. One was the world's most celebrated double bass soloist, Gary Karr. She explained that Karr visited Japan regularly and she hoped the Philharmonic would be interested in offering a concert around the time of one of those tours. Engaging a double bass soloist was never something I had considered, partly because I knew none and partly because I was aware that the repertoire for double bass and orchestra was extremely limited. However, it seemed an interesting idea and I wrote back to Ms. Nicholls to say we might indeed be interested. She then suggested I contact Gary's manager in Japan, the same Walter Nichols who was to enable our visit to the Osaka Music Festival, as he would be co-ordinating Karr's Asian tour schedules.[1]

Walter was to become an extremely useful contact as I shall explain later. In the meantime, we worked out dates for Gary to visit us towards the end of the 1982/83 season. I then made a major error! For political reasons, I was asked to make concert dates available for a young Hong Kong-born conductor who had a freelance ensemble in New York and who should at least be considered for the Music Director position. Given that he had never had his own full-time professional orchestra, he fell outside our guidelines for Music Director candidates. But the political pressure increased. By then unfortunately we had no out-of-town dates available. I therefore paired him with the hugely experienced Gary Karr. In this book I shall merely refer to the conductor as David.

The problem which reared its head was the nature of the repertoire. I am sure David assumed he would be asked to conduct one of the warhorses of the repertoire like a Tchaikovsky, Brahms or Rachmaninov

Symphony. But there is no double bass repertoire that fits any of these composers. Instead, Gary performed two much shorter works: a Dragonetti concerto to end the first half and some Paganini Variations in the second. Domenico Dragonetti had been a virtuoso bass player and composed the concerto at the end of the 18th century. In a typically florid style, it requires an elastic tempo often dictated by the soloist. Gary's performance required close liaison with the conductor to keep orchestra and soloist together. Unfortunately, David was used to more regular sustained tempi when conducting and found it extremely difficult to keep up. Finally, in frustration, he did something no conductor should do. At the final rehearsal in the City Hall Concert Hall, he stopped the orchestra and asked Gary to pay a little more attention to the score's tempo markings!

It was an astonishing comment. When told of it, I was reminded of a story told to me by the great virtuoso pianist Earl Wild who came twice to perform with us. As a 16-year-old, Earl had been engaged as resident pianist of the Pittsburgh Symphony. At one concert, the composer Sergei Rachmaninov was a guest soloist for a performance of his Second Piano Concerto. The conductor was Fritz Reiner, an especially dictatorial conductor who became known as a hirer and firer of musicians, even though he later made the Chicago Symphony into a very fine orchestra. On a particularly cold day early in 1930, Rachmaninov arrived for the rehearsal and sat at the piano, his fur coat draped over his shoulders. Wild remembers –

"A minute or two into the first movement, Reiner stopped the orchestra by tapping his baton on the stand. He leaned over the piano and said to Rachmaninov. 'Don't you think we could take this a little faster?' Rachmaninov was *not* pleased. He rose, rather slowly, looked Reiner squarely in the eye, and replied in his low, resonant voice, 'I wrote this piece!' He then walked, equally slowly, off the stage."

He refused to return until Reiner was fired from conducting the concerto. The orchestra's assistant conductor took over.[2]

David's remark had illustrated not only a failure in conducting technique but how not to speak to a celebrated soloist, particularly in front of the entire orchestra. Gary could have walked out as Rachmaninov had done in Pittsburgh, but he was too professional for that. Besides, he realised he was working with a very inexperienced conductor.

As is usual with concertos, the Dragonetti has a cadenza just before the end of the first movement. Cadenzas are rarely rehearsed – merely topped and tailed. In other words, after the orchestra ends on a dominant chord, the soloist may play the first bar or two of the cadenza, then stop and end with the final trill which is the signal that the orchestra is about to re-enter. With the Dragonetti being such a short work, it was not expected that at the concerts the cadenza would last much more than a few phrases. Gary, though, decided he would play a little game. As he came to a trill in the cadenza, David raised his baton ready to bring the orchestra in when it ended. Instead, Gary then continued with the cadenza before there was a second trill. Again expecting its conclusion, David raised his baton. Once again Gary was not finished. And so on it went for almost three minutes before it finally came to an end. At least in front of the orchestra, David had looked more than foolish.

At lunch with Gary the following day when the concert was to be repeated, I apologised sincerely for having paired him with such a young and inexperienced conductor. Lovely man as he is, he just said something like "these things happen". But, he added, wait till he hears what I plan to do tonight. It will not be three minutes. The cadenza will be six minutes! I then did something no general manager should do, but it was too tempting. I told him that David and the orchestra were anticipating three minutes. Why not make it ten seconds? I added that he must make sure the principals in the orchestra knew what would happen so that they would be ready to come in even though David not. Gary loved the idea. And that is what happened. At the start of the cadenza, David put his baton down on his music stand and stood back with his arms folded. Before he knew it and with arms still folded, the orchestra came back in and the movement finished. It was no doubt a major embarrassment for him, but perhaps he had learned an invaluable lesson for a conductor.

As usual with Gary, when he took his first encore he always brought the Principal Double Bass from the orchestra to perform with him – a wonderful gesture. Asked the secret of his success as a bass player, Gary had no hesitation in saying it was due to his spending time being taught by the distinguished American mezzo-soprano, Jenny Tourel. Thereafter he was to regard the bass as his voice.

One of the joys of working in the business of music is that I have become friendly with musicians based in many parts of the world. Gary and his pianist and partner, Harmon Lewis, have been two of the loveliest friends anyone could hope to know. Gary had made his debut whilst a student in one of the televised educational concerts with Leonard Bernstein and the New York Philharmonic Orchestra. For that concert, Bernstein had asked what he would like to play. He mentioned a concerto by, I believe, Paganini. Bernstein thought that particular piece had not been orchestrated. Gary assured him it had and he would bring the score and parts with him to the rehearsal. In fact, it had not previously been orchestrated. Gary spent the entire night writing orchestral parts.

The television concert was a huge success. The following morning, more than a little hung over, his phone rang. When he answered, a Russian voice congratulated him on the success of the concert. She claimed to be the widow of the famed conductor of the Boston Symphony and celebrated double bass soloist, Serge Koussevitzky. Thinking this had to be one of his contemporaries pulling his leg, he made some sort of less than polite remark. But it was indeed Olga Koussevitzky. She said she was sure that Gary was her husband's successor and would like to donate to him his bass, a hugely valuable instrument then assumed to have been made by the Italian Amati brothers, Antonio and Giralomo, in early 1611. The son of Girolamo Amati, Nicolo, became a teacher of the even more celebrated Antonio Stradivari.

The instrument came to be known as the Karr-Koussevitzky bass. Gary travelled the world with 'Koussy' and generously lent it to aspiring bass players. In mid-2015, though, the instrument was examined by an expert who determined that the wood could not have come from early 17th-century Italy. It was more likely to have been made in France around 1800. After his retirement, Gary donated the instrument to the International Society of Bassists.

On one visit to New York soon after my tenure at the Philharmonic I had the pleasure of spending a day with Gary and Harmon in their Connecticut home. More recently after they had emigrated to Canada, I have twice been a guest in their beautiful home on Vancouver Island. When I started Pacific Images on leaving the Philharmonic I was determined to present them in recital. In addition to the more regular classical repertoire, one item on the programme was *The Last Prima Donna in Las Vegas* for soprano, bass and piano. In this Gary played the bass and sang/spoke the rather outrageous words of the soprano. Much later in December 2005 I was at their final public recital in Yokohama when the work was performed again, this time with Gary having learned all the dialogue in Japanese.

Japan was very close to both their hearts and they had been performing there for decades. On one occasion Gary recorded the Dvořák Cello Concerto on the bass with the Osaka Symphony Orchestra. In Tokyo in 1980 they were honoured to receive an invitation to perform at a special intimate afternoon recital for the Imperial family. Following the small recital and knowing that the Empress was an accomplished pianist, Gary asked if she would do him the honour of performing with him. He had learned some famous Japanese melodies and the Empress was clearly delighted. This was to be the beginning of a long, happy friendship that was followed by several private visits to the Imperial Palace when Gary would perform accompanied by the Empress.

In March 2011, the dreadful earthquake and tsunami hit north-eastern Japan. Gary and Harmon watched the events unfold on television and spoke with many of their friends in Japan. Eventually they decided they would like to make one more tour, this time at their expense and to play for some of the displaced families. How to organise? They did not want their agent involved as this would require commissions. They wrote to their contact at the Palace to ask his advice. He wrote back thanking them for their generous and kind gesture and to advise that all the arrangements would be made on their behalf.

And so the following year they found themselves back in Tokyo for final preparations for concerts up in Sendai in the north. As Harmon was later to write –

"The evening after we arrived, we were invited to the Palace. We were greeted by the royal couple, sat and talked, and were surprised when a light supper appeared."

After Gary and Harmon had played through the programme they would be taking up to the earthquake region in Sendai, Gary again invited the Empress to perform a well-known Japanese song with him. Then as time came for them to leave, Harmon continues –

"The royal couple graciously walked us to the door. We bowed, saying our polite goodbyes. Then Gary and I were much taken aback when the Empress hugged each of us, and kissed us on both cheeks. Most unexpected and I imagine very unusual! She said, 'Tonight I will sleep very, very well. Thank you for a most wonderful evening.'"

Sadly Harmon died after a long illness in January 2023. I miss him greatly.

Other friends I made died many years ago and their names, once known throughout much of Asia, are now all but forgotten. From my earliest days as General Manager, one of the most trying aspects of the job was parrying requests from the cultural departments of consulates like the Goethe-Institut, the British Council and Alliance Française to engage their nationals who either wanted to perform in Hong Kong, or were allegedly passing through and "wouldn't it be a good idea . . . the more so since their fares are already paid?"

The assistance from such organisations was only rarely useful if they were able to help bring out an artist we wished to engage. But well over 95% of the time, we'd have no interest in the artists being proposed and it required a variety of diplomatic niceties to keep saying "No" in a polite fashion.

Other artists were more entrepreneurial. They would arrange their own tours, put considerable time and effort into making them happen and then try to add in a date with the Hong Kong Philharmonic. A year before I moved to Hong Kong, the orchestra had engaged one such couple, indeed a married couple who spent most of their working lives at the Metropolitan Opera. Joann Grillo was a mezzo-soprano and her husband, Richard Kness, a tenor. They were what was generally known as "covers", artists on salary at the Met to understudy principal roles. If a major artist fell ill at short notice, it was often difficult for the Met to fly a replacement from Europe. So the cover would go on. And from time to time, the Met would sweeten the pill for covers by giving them an occasional performance.

To be fair to Joann and Richard, they did sing quite a number of comprimario parts and occasionally solo roles. Joann had sung more than 250 performances over some 20 years, no mean achievement by any means. Her Carmen had been particularly singled out for praise.

After their appearance in Hong Kong, Joann and Richard were very keen to return and were to write to me regularly. Ling Tung did not like the idea, and other orchestras in Asia were mostly of a similar view. Joann, though, was very determined. She had spied an opportunity. Not much took place musically in Southeast Asia over the summer months. She therefore formed a company, *Ambassadors of Opera and Concert Worldwide*, and assembled a group of fellow Met singers each year along with a Met repetiteur to play piano. With this group she organised evenings of operatic excerpts, often sprinkled with some operetta and Broadway. Joann always had a knack of selecting some extremely good singers to join her tours. In one of the early years, there was Aprile Millo, then singing a number of major roles in top opera houses. On another, I renewed my acquaintance with Klara Barlow who had been a member of the Bavarian State Opera when engaged by my old company Scottish

Opera and sang a wonderful Isolde, a role she also sang extremely well in Munich and at the Metropolitan Opera.

On a few occasions, Joann's ensemble would be engaged to be principals in a local opera production. More often, though, Joann would have to make arrangements with local hotels to present her concerts in a dinner concert format in their ballrooms.

This concept was not unusual in Asia for theatre. The popular British comic actor, Derek Nimmo, had been packaging and touring West End plays (invariably with small casts) around the Hilton Hotel circuit for years. The largely expatriate audiences loved it, and the hotels generated good profits from food and beverage sales. It only took one or two managers to see the link between plays and opera, and take a punt. So, for several years Joann, Richard and their ensemble toured Asia, latterly adding some hotels in the Gulf states. It was not a hugely profitable venture, but it provided an opportunity to travel and, importantly, to actually perform.

Despite my not being able to engage them, through my own love of opera and experience with Scottish Opera, I found I enjoyed their company and looked forward to annual dinners with them full of the latest opera news and gossip. One year I happened to be in Seoul during their visit there. They were to be giving a concert in the Convention Hall next to the Hilton. The evening before their concert, the Convention Hall was hosting a concert with the popular singer Julio Iglesias. Joann and Richard invited me to join them as their guest at the Hilton general manager's table.

Mid-way through the concert, Julio Iglesias announced to the audience that he was going to do something very special – he would teach one member of the audience how to sing! To the accompaniment of a drum roll and a spotlight searching the tables, Iglesias made great play of pretending to choose one person, then moving on to another, then another, before finally the spotlight beam narrowed to the general manager's table – and Richard. Richard was the last person who needed to be taught how to sing. His cries of "No! No!" were taken to be false modesty, whereupon two assistants pulled him from his chair and led him to the stage.

Iglesias then proceeded to instruct Richard about the technique of voice production. With just the hint of a gleam in his eye, Richard played along. He was asked to copy Iglesias and sing a short phrase. Richard croaked it out. Iglesias corrected him, advising him to relax the throat muscles and breathe from his diaphragm, not the top of his lungs. Richard tried again, this time showing noticeable improvement.

"You see," said the star. "It works! Now we will sing a duet and you will realise how easy it is!"

That was a big mistake! As Iglesias launched into a popular song, Richard hesitatingly followed suit. But not for long. After a few phrases, he gradually thrust out his chest, opened his lungs and sang as he would at the Met. Iglesias looked at first confused, then dumbstruck – and finally angry. Walking offstage to the cheers of the crowd, Richard told me afterwards that Iglesias turned to him and asked in a none-too-pleasant voice: "Who the fuck are you?"

In many ways I was sorry that I could not do anything professionally for Joann and Richard. They were very much larger-than-life. Joann died tragically in 1999 at the early age of 59. I never saw Richard thereafter. Only later did I learn he had died aged 70 in 2005. I was sad, for their friendship had been genuine and one I had never expected.

12

JURY DUTY

Amidst all the dramas, disasters, joy and fulfilment, one event stood out, one that put all else into perspective. In the middle of my term as General Manager, I was called for jury duty. I had no idea what to expect, but what I found in the courtroom was almost surreal. Here in this territory where well over 90% spoke Cantonese, I felt as though I was in a courtroom lifted out of middle England. The judge was a British expatriate, my fellow jurors were mostly British and the proceedings with the legal teams in white wigs and black robes were held in English. It all felt alien in Hong Kong for the defendants, two teenagers still not having reached their 20s, were Chinese, dependent on a translator close to them in the dock. All the spectators in the public benches were Chinese, many being members of the two defendants' extended families.

The case involved the death of another young Cantonese in a snooker hall brawl. The deceased had been in a fight with the two defendants for reasons I cannot now recall. He was beaten with snooker cues and succumbed to his injuries. We had to decide if they played a part in the brawl. If they had, what was the degree of their guilt? Had one or both struck the fatal blow or merely been caught up in the action? Had it been deliberate or merely accidental?

After the judge gave us our instructions, the case started. At the morning break, the clerk of the court asked our preference for lunch in the jury room. I had not thought about meals but assumed they would be sent in from one of the nearby Hilton Hotel restaurants. Now the proceedings descended into a sort of farce. We were handed menus. McDonald's hamburger, McDonald's fillet of fish, McDonald's cheeseburger and so on with a choice of water or Coca-Cola. This was the daily fare over the ten days of the case. It was almost as though the court wanted us to reach a decision as quickly as possible before our stomachs gave up.

The need for translation inevitably slowed down the proceedings, sometimes to a crawl. I had not realised that Hong Kong courts did not use stenographers. Everything depended on the judge's notes. During our jury deliberations, we had on several occasions to request that certain evidence be repeated. That meant a return to the court room, entry of the judge who would look through his extensive paperwork and come up with the appropriate response. I could not help wonder how detailed it would be possible to make notes of questions and answers unless any judge was fluent in shorthand. I believe none was.

Throughout the trial the young men in the dock were clearly nervous. They answered questions quietly if not always truthfully – at least in our collective judgement. As the trial progressed it was obvious they had not only taken part in the attack on the victim, one had certainly struck the fatal blow. In our deliberations we could not decide which one that would have been. But we had been informed that in law this was relatively immaterial. An attacker aiding and abetting effectively a murderer is equally guilty of murder. Although there were some small areas of doubt, I believe it took us little more than a day to find both guilty. In a time-worn choreographed scene, an attendant then placed a black cap over the judge's wig and he pronounced sentence. The now guilty teenagers would be taken to a place where they would be detained at Her Majesty's pleasure (What a ridiculous statement! What pleasure would they find there or Her Majesty enjoy?) until they were taken to a place of execution where they would be hanged by the neck until they were dead.

I had heard this said in endless films and television programmes. Absolutely nothing prepared me for hearing it in person. I quickly found myself short of breath and starting to sweat. How could these men's lives be snuffed out before they had had any reasonable chance to live them? As these thoughts flashed through my mind, a loud wailing commenced from the public benches. It grew louder and seemed never-ending. Sentence pronounced, the judge thanked us for doing our duty, we all rose as he returned to his chambers and the guilty were dragged downstairs to their eventual death. Only we were all well aware that Hong Kong had abolished the death sentence some years earlier. All death sentences were automatically commuted to life in prison. I could not help wonder. If they were not to die, why would those two boys and their families be put through the appalling agony of hearing that the local government would execute them? It was a totally absurd piece of theatre. I felt utterly sick.

Making my way out of the Supreme Court building, the afternoon sun was welcoming. I knew, though, that work was impossible. I would be totally unable to concentrate as what I had just witnessed remained at the front of my mind. I drove home to my apartment and sat on the balcony. The beauty of the view of the islands to the west of Hong Kong and of the many cargo and other vessels sailing through the Lamma Channel did little to make me feel better. Reviewing all that had happened during the previous ten days, I knew one thing for certain. I could never again be on a jury in a murder trial. No matter how serious the crime, no matter how damning the evidence, I simply could not go through that experience of hearing another human being condemned to death knowing that I had cast a vote for that action. As I basked in the gradually setting sun, not even the knowledge that the sentence would be commuted helped. I was filled with an emptiness I had almost never felt before.

13

THE NEW MUSIC DIRECTOR UNVEILED

Even before we had really started the Music Director search, I was pleased we had been able to make several positive changes in the management of the Philharmonic. The subscription scheme which had got off to such a bad start with its media conference hijacked by one of the musicians whose contracts had not been renewed had resulted in more and more subscribers with each half season. We had enlarged it to give subscribers several options rather than committing to every concert, and we had increased subscriber numbers every season. One reason for this were the incentives we gave to existing subscribers to renew each year. For example, when I learned that the Berlin Philharmonic Orchestra and its legendary conductor Herbert von Karajan were to be giving concerts in Japan, I persuaded the Japanese promoter to sell us two very good tickets at a discount. Cathay Pacific then donated a three-day Discovery Tour to Tokyo at the time of the concerts. We were therefore able to offer this in a lucky draw for renewals. By the time I left the orchestra in mid-1986 I believe we were up to around 55% of all tickets sold by subscription for the main City Hall concerts. The vast majority were purchased by Chinese.

Within months of arriving in Hong Kong I made two appointments vital for any symphony orchestra. The young lady who had been the concerts manager for about a year was not really up to the job and so was reassigned. The concerts manager is basically responsible for liaising with artists and agents after contracts have been issued, then on rehearsal scheduling and generally looking after guest conductors and soloists once they arrived in Hong Kong. A knowledge of the classical music repertoire is almost essential, as is personality. I was extremely fortunate that there was an expat wife in Hong Kong, Su Villiers, whose husband worked in GIS. Su had worked in the UK with one of the main London orchestras and was to prove a godsend for many years. She really looked after our artists. I had informed all the orchestra's staff who worked with visiting conductors and musicians that it was vital they be given an enjoyable and professional environment. That way they would spread the word to their agents and others that Hong Kong, still an orchestra that was relatively unknown, was one where making music was very enjoyable and where they were extremely well looked after.

PR had always been a major issue for the orchestra. I felt it essential that we have someone on staff able to deal with the main English media as one outlet, the *South China Morning Post*, was read by most of the movers and shakers in Hong Kong. That person obviously had to have writing skills and generally know many journalists working in Hong Kong for both local and overseas media. Soon after my arrival I had been interviewed by Cynthia Hydes, then working on a radio programme with RTHK. After asking around, I believed that Cynthia would be a good appointment. She was keen and quickly on the staff.

These two appointments were to get me in some hot water. At one GC meeting, Dr. Denny Huang criticised me for not having advertised the positions and then held open interviews. An Urban Councillor, Dr. Huang was well known to be a regular critic of the way Hong Kong was being run, frequently criticising administration policies, putting forward a pro-Beijing view and even describing the Urban Council as "backward". In this case, I fully accepted his criticisms of my actions as valid and so informed the meeting. All positions in a publicly subsidised body should be open and I so stated. But I added that the time factor and the Philharmonic's very particular and very urgent problems made it impossible to go through an open interview process that could take many weeks. I agreed I would deal differently with future positions.

I was especially pleased that I had finally been able to persuade the GC that the three-tier system of salaries for musicians had to be changed. As in all orchestras, Principal and sub-Principal players who are effectively soloists would continue to receive higher salaries, but for the most part all others would be on the same rate. With Philip Kwok's help, the Chairman and CEO of Hong Kong Land, Trevor Bedford, helped in launching a fund to purchase apartments which could be used for accommodation for overseas musicians. By the time I left, only a few had been purchased, but it was an important start.

Thanks to increasing government and Urban Council support, we were in a position to start raising both salaries and the number of musicians in the orchestra. Naturally the musicians would have preferred more and by late 1983 with the success of major concerts in the 12,000-seat Coliseum we were finally able to add a small "pops" bonus to basic salaries.

By the end of the season in the summer of 1983, it had become very obvious that the one conductor whom the orchestra admired, who was available and extremely interested in becoming the next Music Director was Kenneth Schermerhorn. Quite unlike his predecessor, Ken exuded charisma. Tall, slim and elegant with wavy white hair, he entered the stage rather like a cross between two of the finest conductors of the day, his mentor Leonard Bernstein and Herbert von Karajan, although considerably taller than both. As a conductor and Music Director he was hugely experienced, he knew the musicians well, had just made a major success of the recent tour to Singapore, Bangkok and Osaka, knew me extremely well, knew several members of the GC and he loved Hong Kong. Although by this stage he had assumed the Music Directorship of the Nashville Symphony in the United States, in discussions I commenced with his manager in New York, Bob Gardiner, it became clear that dovetailing the two orchestras' schedules would not be difficult. If there was a problem it concerned fee. Bob was holding out for a reasonably high weekly fee covering a pair of concerts plus the administration expected of all Music Directors. This was considerably more than the Philharmonic had been paying to Ling Tung and I knew some members of the GC would voice objections. When the matter was raised, I pointed out that

Ken would achieve greater standards with the orchestra in just one year than Tung had failed to achieve in three.

By then I had deliberately inflated Bob's requested fee by 50% as I knew this would be out of the question. Sure enough, I was instructed to discuss it in detail with a senior civil servant not directly involved with the Philharmonic. He informed me we must not agree to it. I said confidently that I was sure I could negotiate it down by between 10% and 15%. This would still be too high, I was told. Perhaps I should press hard for a reduction of 30%. In other words, this was precisely what Bob and I had provisionally agreed! Ken quickly signed a contract for three years.

In November Ken made a special trip to Hong Kong for the formal media announcement. Beforehand it was important that the musicians be informed. Prior to a regular rehearsal, I entered the rehearsal hall with Philip Kwok and requested a few moments from the conductor for an announcement.

"Ladies and gentlemen," said Philip, "it gives me great pleasure to introduce to you – once again – your new Music Director, Maestro Kenneth Schermerhorn."

When Kenneth then entered there was near universal applause and smiles all round. It was a very popular appointment. At the media conference later that day, it was announced that his three-year contract would commence in September 1984. I could not have been more pleased.

14

DEVELOPING THE PHILHARMONIC

One of the tasks requested of Ling Tung was that he draw up in consultation with me a five-year plan for the orchestra. Never having developed any professional full-time orchestra, Tung asked me to draft the paper. Apart from greater funding to allow the orchestra to increase the pitifully low salaries and the number of musicians, issues with which I was in total agreement, Ling had little to add. There were several things we desperately needed including some specialist instruments and our own rehearsal venue, but I knew these would not be possible in anything like the short to medium term. In completing the plan I did include the vital importance of two other activities for any young aspiring professional orchestra – making recordings and overseas touring. The former becomes a mark of quality, calling cards that give those both in and out of the business an indication of an orchestra's quality. The latter is vital to any orchestra. It improves morale, it is exciting to find out how audiences in other countries react to your performances and it breaks up the routine of always presenting concerts in the same venues. It also brings considerable prestige back at home base. Touring, though, tends to take considerable time to set up. This would become a priority.

Walter Nichols in Tokyo, the agent whom Lottie Nicholls had suggested I meet in connection with the engagement of Gary Karr, became a very important figure in my career as well as the orchestra's development. As we were finalising Gary's dates, I arranged to meet him in Tokyo on one of my many visits. I had slowly begun to get to know this fascinating city but finding Walter's office was a problem. So we met at one of the most famous intersections, Roppongi Crossing, under the pink and white striped awning of the famous Café Almond. At the appointed time I met this tall, late-60s American and we walked down the hill to the Sweden Centre where his company Azabu Artists had its office.

A chain smoker, Walter had been born to American parents who were missionaries in Japan. Apart from the war years, he had spent all his life in the country. He had even been a member of MacArthur's staff following the conclusion of the Second World War. Eventually he joined the American Embassy where he was given the responsibility of handling cultural affairs. Coinciding with the start of the country's economic boom, the 1970s were a period of major growth for the country in general and for classical music in particular. Being fully bilingual, Walter was often contacted by the Japanese concert agents to ask for advice on matters like contracts. He also had the opportunity of meeting many artists and ensembles who toured Japan, some with official embassy backing.

When it became time for him to retire, Walter had decided to stay on in Japan for some years before moving back to the United States. He had married a younger Japanese and they had a small son, Aki. He and his wife had agreed that Aki would receive his primary education in Japan, moving to an American school when he entered his teens. His wife had little faith in the Japanese secondary school system!

Bombarded by artists whom he had met and who were unable to obtain representation from the established Japanese concert agents, to fill his days Walter decided to set up Azabu Artists. And it was in his small smoke-filled one-room office that we had our first discussion. Gary Karr was one of only a small roster of artists he worked with.

With his vast knowledge of Japan and the Japanese, Walter understandably knew everyone in the concert business. I had only recently started visiting Japan regularly for meetings with a few of the main Japanese agencies. Walter introduced me to more.

It was, as readers will recall, Walter who made it possible for the Philharmonic to perform at the prestigious Osaka International Music Festival. Naturally Walter knew Mrs. Michi Murayama who was the President of the Festival. Within weeks, I had received an invitation for the Philharmonic for the two concerts in the Spring of 1983. We would be in the most august of company, for also appearing that year were the National Symphony Orchestra from Washington D.C. with Mstislav Rostropovich conducting, and the Vienna Philharmonic with Lorin Maazel. It would be the biggest possible boost to the orchestra's morale, even though neither Walter nor Mrs. Murayama had by then heard our orchestra!

I felt it important that we precede the Osaka concerts with others in the region. The Philharmonic was not used to touring and it was important the musicians get used to performing the programmes in other cities. Fortunately I was able to line up two concerts each in Singapore and Bangkok. I was equally fortunate to engage the legendary Polish violinist, Ida Haendel, to perform the Brahms Concerto, long considered one of her signature works. A child prodigy when younger, Ms. Haendel was to be fondly remembered by all, both for a stunning account of the concerto as for her range of wide-brimmed hats. I knew she had already written her autobiography with the uninspiring title *Woman With a Violin*. Over lunch in Singapore, she told me so much had happened in her life since publication that she had thought about writing a follow-up, but her publisher hated the title and it never got written. She had wanted to name it *One Night Stands*!

We had only one slight hiccup before the tour started. In one of the early discussions we were to have over several years, Walter had told me there was little communication between artists' agents, concert promoters and venue managements in Japan. Being a foreigner, everyone gladly told him of their plans knowing he would not reveal them to others. Sometimes, he would be asked to translate artists' contracts. He was aware, though, that it not infrequently happened that, say, the Festival Hall in Osaka would be booked by one management for an afternoon concert by a prominent visiting American orchestra and by a second management for an evening concert by an equally prominent American orchestra!

I found evidence of this when I flew to Osaka with Kenneth Schermerhorn, whom we had invited to conduct the tour concerts, for a press conference announcing our participation about ten days beforehand. Just before we entered the room where the media was assembled, I saw a programme of the full festival. Flipping through its pages, I was particularly interested in the programmes being presented by the two other orchestras. I was then horrified to see that both our orchestra and the National Symphony were scheduled to perform Tchaikovsky's Fifth Symphony. This was ridiculous! I had no doubts we would perform the symphony well, but as Ken agreed, we were not yet anywhere near the quality of the Washington Orchestra. It was Ken who suggested that we could easily change to the Fourth Symphony instead. After a quick word with Walter and Mrs. Murayama's representative, this was agreed and the programme change announced. Yet I could not help wondering: why had no one in the festival told us in advance and suggested months earlier that one orchestra change the symphony? Typically, no one had wanted to lose face.

Inevitably orchestral tours have their own set of problems. We had made the ticketing arrangements directly with Cathay Pacific, with which we enjoyed a very close association. This included the freight required for the instruments and equipment. Leaving Hong Kong for Singapore on a Sunday morning, I spent most of the day before in the office. I decided to treble-check our bookings by calling the airline. No problems. All the bookings were in order. I then checked with the freight department. Panic! The representative I spoke to claimed there was no booking for crates of large orchestral instruments flying to Singapore. Thankfully I had a good friend who worked for the airline and just managed to catch him at home. All was well. For some reason our instruments were under a different booking number.

At the airport the next morning, panic number two. A Canadian brass player in the orchestra had recently renewed his passport. He brought the expired one. I got him to hand over his apartment key and there was just enough time to get one of the administration staff there and back with the valid one.

The tour as a whole was more successful than I think we had ever dared hope. The musicians certainly enjoyed it. Through their enthusiastic applause in all three cities, audiences had very much also enjoyed the concerts, and the concert organisers had all been fulsome in their praise. I believe it was on this tour that the Hong Kong Philharmonic finally turned the corner in terms of community acceptance and its relations with the general public in Hong Kong. We had taken some Hong Kong journalists with us and the reviews back home gave readers an insight into the quality of the performances and the rapturous receptions we received. Even the respected region-wide magazine, the *Far Eastern Economic Review*, was unstinting in its praise, commenting that the Philharmonic was –

"a musical unit which can hold its own anywhere in the world."

The tour to Singapore, Bangkok and Osaka had not been our first. During the early summer in my first year, I had received a call from an old friend, Paul Findlay, then the Assistant General Director at London's Royal Opera House. He was organising a tour for the Sadler's Wells Royal Ballet in Asia during the autumn of the following year. Might we be available to accompany the ballet for part of the tour to Kuala Lumpur, Penang, Bangkok and Hong Kong? I jumped at the chance. It was a perfect opportunity to take many in the orchestra overseas with a repertoire that would not be overly taxing. There was a catch though.

Paul needed an additional £50,000 before he could firm up the tour. Did I know anyone in Hong Kong whom he could approach? I had absolutely no idea but I did know someone who might. Immediately I called Caroline Newbigging, a member of our Ladies Committee whose husband, David, was the chairman of one of the territory's oldest trading companies, Jardine Matheson & Co. She said we should speak with John Thresh, then chairman of Barclays in Hong Kong who loved ballet. She and I attended only one meeting. Within days Barclays had agreed to put up the £50,000.

The tour achieved all the goals we set ourselves. The only real problem arose in Penang where the air conditioning in the theatre broke down just as we were starting a final warm-up rehearsal and could not be repaired. The venue had just two large fans. I insisted one had to be in the orchestra pit. In that intense tropical heat and humidity, it was horribly uncomfortable for everyone, but especially the poor dancers. When one did a long pirouette, seeming sheets of water poured off her. As we neared the end, I got our stage manager and librarian to join me buying beer and soft drinks for the orchestra as I knew they would be utterly exhausted and extremely thirsty.

The following morning as we boarded the flight to Bangkok, I had been informed the aircraft would be a THAI 737. My concern was what to do with the smaller instruments as I knew there would not be enough room in the overhead lockers. A member of the ground staff came to the check-in desk and told me there was no problem. Three seats on the right side of the first row were not occupied. We could put some of the instruments on them and she would arrange with the purser to have two extra-long seat belts to make sure they stayed in place. I had never come across anything like this before, but these were our instructions. And so a dozen or so violins and small woodwind instruments, all in their cases, were piled up and then belted in place. All seemed to be fine until the captain came out of the cockpit. He nearly had a fit. This has to go, he said.

"It will not be safe *when* I crash."

Thankfully everyone soon realised his piloting skills were considerably better than his command of the English language!

I kicked myself that I had not asked Paul for a commission for the orchestra's funds in return for getting him that £50,000; even more so when John Thresh came up with an extra £250,000 to enable the ballet to undertake another, longer Asian tour two years later. This time they would be using another orchestra. I was later informed that Imelda Marcos, wife of the Philippines dictator President Ferdinand Marcos, had said she would welcome the company to Manila but only on condition that the ballet company's president came with the dancers. This was Britain's Princess Margaret, the sister of the late Queen Elizabeth II!

After one performance Mrs. Marcos had invited the entire company for dinner. Only dinner for the dancers was not what they expected. While Marcos, Princess Margaret and the VIP guests including David Rockefeller dined, the dancers were told they were expected to dance. They were then ushered to a different room for the separate and very simple supper that had been laid out for them. The dancers were far from happy.

15

NEW AUDIENCES – WHO? HOW? WHERE?

For anyone with a background in arts management in the west, there is an assumption that marketing concerts means appealing to a section of the community which has at least some interest in or basic knowledge of classical music. Most of the expats in Hong Kong who attended concerts seemed to assume, quite wrongly, that classical music concerts would have little appeal to the Chinese community. Marketing had almost always been geared to that small expat group.

During the time they were employed to assist the Philharmonic with marketing, James Wong and Eunice Lam also seemed to believe that. One tool they employed was paying the *South China Morning Post* for a regular Wednesday column in the centre of a page that described what the Philharmonic would be performing the following weekend. Only it was written by an academic who seemed to think that describing the themes and movements of a symphony would actually sell tickets! It was a total waste of money.

Not that marketing an orchestra and its concerts is easy. It isn't, as orchestras all over the world are well aware! When I occasionally had to interview young professionals for marketing assistant posts, I always asked what sections of society did they anticipate would make up a concert audience. The first word inevitably uttered was "Students"! That's great, I'd say. Many may well be interested in classical concerts but I doubt if many will have much money and so will only purchase the cheaper seats. Who is likely to purchase the many more expensive seats that we have to sell in order to meet our budget targets? This would always be followed by a lengthy pause. Most had no clue. Businessmen was a popular answer. Teachers was another. The fact was that none had bothered to undertake any research, none as far as I can recall had even attended a concert and none had any reasonably sensible ideas!

To be fair, I had come to Hong Kong having worked for an opera company which had increased its total audience from around 7,000 in its first year of operation to more than 150,000 about 15 years later when I left. Even I, though, would have had difficulty in answering my own question when it came to Hong Kong for I, too, had not done my own basic research.

Very stupidly, it took me well over a year to realise that the vast majority of the Hong Kong Chinese community probably hadn't the faintest idea what a western symphony orchestra was! Yes, they would be aware of its general sound through watching some movies or listening on the radio. But of what it comprised in terms of musicians and instruments, and what the concert experience was like, most had no clue. As soon as this dawned on me, I realised our entire marketing strategy was based on sand. There is no point trying to convince such a public of the merits of a Beethoven concerto or a Tchaikovsky symphony. We had to scrap all our preconceptions and get right back to basics.

We did that initially by trying to convey one simple message – symphonic music is fun. Come to a concert and you will be surprised at how much enjoyment you gain from it. For our third year of subscription concerts, I even stole an idea I had seen at one of the orchestras in the United States. Instead of drawings of composers, beautiful photos of mountains or lakes or other images which implied "high class", we used the photograph which I specially commissioned of an ice-cream cone with several different coloured scoops. The sales pitch was the simple message *Experience the Unexpected*. Until then I had not realised that taking photos of ice cream rarely worked. Under lights it starts to melt before the camera is ready. The photographer used coloured mashed potato instead!

From having worked almost exclusively on formal concerts and with occasional chamber groups going to schools, we also decided we had to divide the orchestra's work into a series of different types of concert. It took a few years and the opening of two stadia – one, the 12,000-seat Hong Kong Coliseum (a more intimate space than the capacity might suggest), and the other, the 3,300-seat Queen Elizabeth Stadium in Morrison Hill – before we could eventually get close to our goal.

We saw the need to programme several different types of concert. At the top of the pyramid would be the subscription concerts, the core of the orchestra's music making with a varied classical repertoire and interesting conductors and soloists. One step down would be the non-subscription concerts in concert halls where more popular classical programmes would be presented at slightly lower ticket prices to attract those with just a modest interest in music. The third tier would be what we termed more aggressively popular classics or pop music with a classical theme in a non-traditional venue. The Queen Elizabeth Stadium fitted the bill, even though it required amplification for the orchestra. Our concerts in that venue included a Tchaikovsky night and a programme of Mozart music from the popular movie *Amadeus*. This we presented with the inclusion of actors wandering through the audience playing the roles of Mozart and Salieri and quoting parts of the Peter Shaffer play which led up to the relevant musical excerpts. The actors spoke in Cantonese, with brief English summaries flashed up on the scoreboards.

The fourth tier of concerts took place in the Coliseum. I was initially very reluctant to use it for Philharmonic concerts. The space seemed far too large, the acoustic was dead and I seriously doubted that we could find a new audience to go anywhere near to filling it. Despite my concern I came under intense pressure from the CSD to find a way of developing a much larger audience for pop concerts than we would normally achieve in the far smaller City Hall Concert Hall.

I owe the concept of the Philharmonic becoming involved in popular music concerts to Selina Chow. With a career in television and more recently as a member of Legco, she had started up her own entertainment company. In 1982 she persuaded us to perform in a short series of concerts in the Queen Elizabeth Stadium with the very popular singer and architect Michael Kwan. This presented problems aplenty but the concerts were a major success. She could easily have booked a group of freelance musicians, but with friends as members of the Ladies Committee, she took a plunge by asking the Philharmonic to take part. My only request was the orchestra have a section when it could play on its own. So it performed John Williams' *Star Wars* Suite to great audience approval. With the Hong Kong Coliseum about to open in 1983, Selina arranged a test concert there with six local Cantopop singers including Michael Kwan, Liza Wang and Danny Chan. That success was to lead to the Coliseum becoming the major venue for all manner of popular concerts.

To test whether we could successfully market a concert to a much larger, new, younger audience, I decided to revisit the idea which I had been forced to abort in my first summer when the GC's chairman John Mackenzie cancelled planned movie music concerts. Almost everyone in Hong Kong went to movies. For most it was their major form of leisure time entertainment apart from television. So in the autumn of 1983 we took a gamble and scheduled three concerts in the Coliseum of a programme featuring movie music. I engaged the Japanese conductor, Yoshikazu Fukumura, who had had success with such programming in his home country. He also knew where to obtain good orchestral arrangements. These would be important because nothing annoys an orchestral musician more than having to play boring arrangements. Best of all, Fukumura had a friend who was an excellent Japanese sound technician. He came to devise a complete sound system that required up to 40 microphones along with quality amplifiers and speakers to deliver the best possible sound.

I also felt that in such a large space, we would need some simple lighting and perhaps the occasional dramatic effect. I had hoped we would be able to rent clips from the movies scheduled in the programme but this proved both difficult and too expensive. So we kept everything simple. Prior to the start of the theme from *Bridge on the River Kwai*, for example, we blacked out the auditorium before having two tightly focussed spotlights beaming across the audience as might have been the case in a prison camp. At the very least, this created an expectation for what was about to be played.

I had great fun working out the detail of these concerts with my administration team and Fukumura. We had decided ticket prices would be slashed to less than half what we charged for our standard classical concerts. As they went on sale, we also increased our regular concert marketing budget by almost four-fold. During the ticket sales period, we were all amazed at how quickly they sold. By the time of the first of these three concerts, all 35,000 seats had been sold. I was completely dumbfounded. Never had I believed we could attract so many to a Philharmonic concert series. When sales indicated we would be close to a sell-out, we decided we had to find some way of getting the names and contact details of as many of the audience as possible to feed into a new database. We then ensured that every member of the audience had a lucky draw card which they could submit and win quite handsome prizes. Those who attended clearly loved this totally new entertainment experience. The attendance comprised mostly a much younger audience, many of whom would never have considered going near a regular symphony orchestra concert. The value of the 8,000 names we obtained to start our database quickly became evident when sales for future programmes in the arena all sold extremely well.

By this time the general manager of the main artists' agency handling Hong Kong pop singers, Capital Artists, was none other than So Hau-leung who had been the Philharmonic's first general manager back in 1974 (and was to return as CEO for a year in 2009). Hau-leung was keen for some of his younger artists to work at a Coliseum concert with the Philharmonic. So we arranged one with three of his singers: Lui Fong, Anita Mui and Leslie Cheung. Remarkably, we did not quite sell out the Coliseum. Had we only waited just an extra few months, we could probably have marketed ten concerts rather than three, for Anita and Leslie were on a fast track to becoming legends in the field of entertainment, and not merely in Hong Kong but also in much of Asia and many other parts of the world with large Chinese communities. We were fortunate to have Leslie also as a guest artist in another programme which we titled *Romance at Christmas*. Talking with him for a few minutes before he went on stage, I was struck by how completely natural he was and how easy to talk to. That two such superstars should have died so young – Anita was 40 and Leslie 46 – was tragic.

The 35,000 attendance at the first movie music concert in the autumn of 1983 had not proved a flash in the pan. By 1985 we were presenting four such popular programmes each season, each with at least three performances. Attendance never fell below 25,000. The programmes we devised for these large-scale concerts included a Valentine's Day *Love* concert. We also had a special Beatles concert with the little-known two-piano concerto featuring John Rutter's arrangement of the band's music in a piano concerto format, and a popular Broadway excerpts concert featuring dancers from Willie Tsao's excellent CCDC.

Naturally several of our programmes featured Chinese music. At one which included Takako Nishizaki performing the *Butterfly Lovers Concerto* followed after the interval by the *Yellow River* Piano Concerto, both preceded by some specially orchestrated theme tunes from television soap operas, we achieved our record attendance of about 52,000 with two additional performances having to be added. For another, we commissioned a new oboe concerto from Chen Gang who had been a co-composer of the *Butterfly Lovers*. This was given its premiere in the Coliseum in October 1985 by our excellent Principal Oboe, Peter Cooper. Nor did we only engage Chinese conductors for these Chinese music programmes. Kenneth Schermerhorn was delighted to conduct several.

I absolutely loved planning and putting these concerts together. I had always wanted the orchestra to play before much larger audiences but it was rarely possible. In December 1979 we had been asked by the Jockey Club to inaugurate the infield Penfold Park at the then relatively new Shatin Racetrack. I invited the distinguished American acoustics specialist Chris Jaffe to design a simple stage to be placed just beyond the race track and a detailed (and expensive) sound system that would relay the true sound of the orchestra to the full length of the stands. Around 10,000 turned up to hear the concert which also featured the popular Hong Kong singer Roman Tam.

Although performing to such large audiences was obviously satisfying for the orchestra to a certain extent, conditions in such a massive acoustically unsuitable space like the Coliseum with the requirement for extensive amplification was always a trial. We did not construct an acoustic shell, partly on account of expense but partly also because this would have meant losing almost 3,000 saleable seats behind and at the side of the orchestra. To make life easier, the sound technicians fed the orchestral sound back to the stage area roughly half a second later. This enabled all the sections to hear each other and at least give them the impression of some reverberation. With the profits generated from these concerts, it was not difficult to persuade the GC that the musicians should be provided with the bonus for each Coliseum concert series.

This type of programming had two massive benefits. On the one hand, our total annual audience numbers soared, much to the delight of our paymasters – the administration and the Urban Council. Total audiences each year which had been under 25,000 when I arrived in March 1979 were now over 200,000. We could at last justifiably make the case that we were a real community orchestra, playing for the benefit of the whole community, not just one for a small group made up mostly of expats.

The second benefit is that we noticed through a professional audience survey carried out in early 1986 there was a definite trickle-down effect. Invert the pyramid of four types of concert and some of that initial pops audience had become subscribers. By that year, the number was 93 – not an especially large number but certainly far from insignificant.

Having expressed my concern about having to report to a programme committee and finally managed to get it disbanded, there are some committees which form an essential part of most orchestras' existence.

One I came to rely on was the Ladies Committee. Comprising the wives of top businessmen and government leaders, they virtually kept the orchestra's activities 'alive' as a subject of conversation amongst their friends and colleagues. They also worked hard on a major fundraising event each year. One year they invited several prominent (and rich) young socialites to take part in a quiz on one of the TV stations. On another, they persuaded Stanley Ho, the gambling king of Macao, to bring to Hong Kong many gambling tables and his croupiers to set up an especially elegant casino on the ground floor of the recently opened Landmark mall in Central. All these events raised valuable funds. One was even what should have been the most amusing and entertaining evening in many a year.

The much-loved actor and comedian, Danny Kaye, was passionate about classical music. He loved orchestras. He loved conducting orchestras, even though he could not read a note of music. Even better, through his conducting, he loved raising much-needed funds for orchestras. One of the Ladies Committee had a direct connection to one of Kaye's friends. Would there be any possibility, she asked, of Danny Kaye coming to conduct the Philharmonic? What she and many others knew was that Danny Kaye adored Chinese cuisine and was an excellent chef – so much so that when he toured for fundraising concerts he insisted that there be a Chinese kitchen in his suite. He also loved Hong Kong.

Soon, in January 1983, his manager of more than 30 years, Herb Bonis, was in Hong Kong to discuss the idea in more detail. A concert would indeed be possible, he said, and we were given some dates in April which worked for the orchestra. The deal itself was pretty straightforward. Danny Kaye would conduct for no fee. He was to receive first class travel expenses, the best suite at the Peninsula Hotel with a Chinese kitchen installed, and all local expenses. A key condition, though, was that the orchestra had to raise a minimum of US$100,000 net of all costs for its musicians' pension fund.

One last condition was vital. Since Danny Kaye only conducted one programme and so the same jokes and visual gags were always repeated, everyone involved, including the orchestra members, would have to sign a binding confidentiality agreement not to reveal them to third parties. We agreed to all the terms and the ladies who were chairing the special Danny Kaye concert set to work to organise the fundraising and social side of the evening.

Unfortunately, only a few weeks later, Danny Kaye had to go into hospital for what turned out to be major heart bypass surgery. A concert in 1983 was therefore no longer possible. Whilst obviously a disappointment, everyone agreed to reschedule the concert to April 1984. By early March that year, the ladies had several major sponsors on board, the hotel and flight arrangements had been made, and every ticket in the 1,450-seat Concert Hall had been sold.

But that rescheduled concert was also not to happen. Danny Kaye fell sick again, this time with a very heavy cold which turned into a form of pneumonia. I was certain nothing major could be organised at such short notice until one of the committee, I believe Judy Green, asked if I thought Tim Rice would be a draw with an evening entitled *Tim Rice and Friends*. He had given this show in Australia but nowhere else. As two of the great West End stars, Elaine Paige and Colm Wilkinson, would be with him along with a musical director, I thought it would be perfect. Within days we knew we had the artists for the planned Danny Kaye date, airline tickets and hotel suites were donated, notices went out about the change of artists and programme – and I do not recall any ticket holders asking for refunds.

It was a superbly witty, entertaining, hilarious evening punctuated with some wonderful singing. We absolutely could not have expected anything nearly as successful as a replacement for the great Danny Kaye. The audience was thrilled, giving the artists and the orchestra a long standing ovation at the end. Sir Run Run Shaw, Hong Kong's legendary movie mogul, came up to me at the end and said he had not enjoyed an evening as much for a long time.

As a 'thank you' to Judy for getting Tim involved and helping pull everything together, I invited her to dinner. I took her over to the village of Stanley on the south side of Hong Kong Island where there was a lovely little French restaurant open to the sea breeze. During dinner, I was reminded what a different world I lived in from many other Hong Kong residents. After we had ordered and I expressed my profound gratitude, we somehow started discussing personal finances. Judy mentioned something about how difficult some people were finding living in Hong Kong with only half a million dollars in their account. I looked at her and said I had nothing like such a sum. She looked bemused.

"Do you mean to say the manager of our symphony orchestra doesn't have $500,000 saved up?"

I replied that I didn't even have $50,000 in my account.

"How can you possibly live without US$50,000 in the bank?"

"But Judy, I am talking about Hong Kong dollars, not US dollars!" (The total in my account was then worth less than US$6,500).

She just could not believe it! And when I gave her an indication of what managers of performing arts organisations were paid, she almost choked!

But I understood her point. In the circles in which she and her colleagues moved, US$500,000 was virtually nothing. I rather hoped that for their fundraising project the following year, they might raise some money to help boost staff salaries!

The sad postscript to our Danny Kaye concert was that he was never to come to conduct in Hong Kong. He died early in 1987, of hepatitis and internal bleeding caused as a result of the transfusion of contaminated blood during his cardiac surgery four years earlier. Fortunately for the world, though, a 1981 concert he gave with the New York Philharmonic is available for viewing on YouTube. Although the humour is obviously somewhat dated, much of it remains hilariously funny.[1]

For our regular subscription programmes, as a result of my annual visits to concert agents and artists' managers in addition to word of mouth from artists who had come to work in Hong Kong, the Philharmonic was becoming increasingly well-known. More and more internationally celebrated conductors and soloists were becoming interested in performing with us. My old friend and colleague, Sir Alexander Gibson, came for two pairs of concerts. A winner of the Sibelius Medal, his performance of the First Symphony was particularly fine. The distinguished Czech pianist Rudolf Firkušný gave a glowing account of the Brahms First Piano Concerto. When Gidon Kremer performed the Brahms Violin Concerto, the audience was startled to hear the first movement cadenza by Shnittke rather than the more usual one by Joachim for whom the work was composed. Teresa Berganza with whom I had worked at the Edinburgh Festival *Carmen* in 1977 and 78 graced our stage twice during my tenure. In one of our non-subscription concerts, the orchestra gave an impressive performance of Berlioz's mighty *Grande Messe des Morts* conducted by Sir David Willcocks with the Bach Choirs from the UK and Hong Kong and many additional instrumentalists.

Another British conductor, Sir Charles Groves, came for a pair of City Hall concerts. As always, either I or one of the staff would meet the artist at Kai Tak. On this occasion, our PR manager Cynthia Hydes was desperate to meet Sir Charles. Kai Tak airport had always had a shambolic arrivals area, and Cynthia had a little trouble picking out Sir Charles with his beard. After welcoming him to Hong Kong, she asked him to walk a small distance to the waiting limousine. On the way, she expressed surprise that Sir Charles' wife, Hilary, had not joined him as expected.

"Lady Hilary? Who is Lady Hilary?"

"Your wife," said Cynthia.

But I am not married, said her bemused guest.

"Are you not Sir Charles Groves?"

Cynthia had picked up the wrong bearded man!

During one half season, we concentrated more on 20th-century music and featured composers like Pendercki, Lutoslawski and Berio. I had also invited the Scottish composer Thea Musgrave to fly from her California home to conduct her Horn Concerto. For this I engaged the celebrated horn player Barry Tuckwell for whom the work had been written. Thea's concerto is a splendid work. It calls for the four horns from the orchestra to be positioned at different parts of the auditorium and for the soloist to wander around the stage. The audience loved it. Indeed, I was delighted if somewhat surprised that for an audience not especially accustomed to classical music, programming contemporary music seemed to have little effect on attendances.

In a later season I had also engaged two artists at the very top of their professions. Heinz Holliger was regarded as the finest virtuoso oboist in the world in the early 1980s and Yo-Yo Ma was fast rising to equal Rostropovich as the finest cellist. Certainly he was in huge demand. Both were engaged for our Philharmonic subscription series. Sadly neither was to appear.

16

DOWNS AND UPS

With Hong Kong being relatively isolated from more major musical centres, cancellations by soloists or conductors for one reason or another were always a problem we could never anticipate. We had already had the scare with Ilana Vered's illness in late 1980. Thankfully that was extremely unusual. Very occasionally the problem might not arise from an outright cancellation but an artist who is released from a signed contract. Such was the case on the first occasion we were to have worked with Yo-Yo Ma. Over several visits to New York, I had gained the confidence of his manager, Lee Lamont. She had finally agreed that he would come to perform the Elgar Concerto with us. When I much later received a request that we release him to enable him to take up an offer of a concert tour with a major international European orchestra, there was never any question of trying to hold him to the contract. Having been offered alternative dates in a future season, of course I readily agreed.

With Ma being one of the most sought-after artists on the concert circuit, this was obviously a major disappointment. The withdrawal, though, was at some months' notice. The young Canadian cellist, Ofrah Harnoy, was fortunately still available and so I contracted her to take over the dates.

A week before the Elgar concerts we were to have the pair of concerts with Heinz Holliger. Our regular concerts were on Friday and Saturday evenings, so these would normally necessitate the arrival of the soloist no later than the Wednesday evening in time for a preliminary rehearsal the following day. When I arrived at the office on Tuesday morning, there was a telex from his agent cancelling the engagement on the grounds of

Mr. Holliger's ill health. If finding a pianist or a violinist can be relatively simple, top international oboe soloists are a far rarer breed. I really did not know how to start. But I knew who would. Late that afternoon, as soon as the London offices were open, I called June Megennis, a friend for more than a decade from her days as artistic administrator at the London Symphony Orchestra. June was then managing the Chamber Orchestra of Europe and in as good a position as anyone to know who might be the most ideal replacement should they be available at such short notice.

The name Maurice Bourgue meant nothing to me, but June recommended him most highly. June found out that he happened to be free and, as she later informed me, was mad enough to get a flight from Paris the following day to arrive in Hong Kong on the morning of the rehearsal. He proved a joy to work with, as fine a musician and player as Holliger in my view. We'd now had our one major cancellation and one withdrawal for the season. The rest of the season would sail by – or so I thought!

The following week, our concerts with Harnoy playing the Elgar Concerto happened to be on Wednesday and Thursday. I first had meetings to attend in Seoul and so flew to Korea on the Monday afternoon, arriving in my hotel around 9:00pm local time. At the reception desk there was a message waiting for me marked "Urgent". It was from Lee Bo-luen, our Orchestra Manager. Opening the envelope I saw that just a couple of hours earlier Ofrah Harnoy had cancelled, also on the grounds of ill health! I sat down on the bed as certain as I could be that replacements were out of the question. There were exactly 48 hours before the first concert was due to start. Flights from Australia departed Sydney in the morning, and with it being well past midnight there, it was too late to find a cellist. Similarly, it was around midday in Europe, making it all but impossible to get someone on to Hong Kong flights, most of which in those days all tended to depart around late afternoon. North America seemed even more out of the question. That only left Japan.

Although it was very late in Tokyo, I called Walter Nichols at home. Was he aware of any Japanese cellist who might be able to fly to Hong

Kong first thing the next morning? During what became an increasingly negative discussion, he suddenly paused and exclaimed "Tsutsumi"! I had heard of a Japanese cellist of that name and had a vague recollection that he worked in the USA.

"He does," said Walter who not surprisingly knew the entire Tsutsumi family. Walter seemed to know everyone! A noted soloist and teacher, Tsuyoshi Tsutsumi was then based in Chicago. But, added Walter, he might just fancy the challenge – if he is free. While Walter called him, I tried to work out how to get him to Hong Kong in time. Fortunately, having to fly in so many soloists, conductors and musicians from many parts of the word, I always had the two thick volumes of the ABC airline timetables on my desk. I was aware there was an overnight Singapore Airlines flight departing San Francisco around midnight that arrived in Hong Kong via Honolulu around 6:00am. By this time it was 8:00am in Chicago. If he was willing to drop everything, Tsutsumi would be able to reach San Francisco and connect with that Singapore Airlines flight. The one benefit of this madness was that he could go straight from the airport to the final morning rehearsal, stay on Chicago time, sleep in the afternoon, perform the concerto at what would for him be the early morning, repeat the routine the following day and then fly back on Friday.

It was a crazy schedule that most artists would not even consider. Would he accept? Was he even available? Within half an hour, Walter had called back to say he was free and would play the concerts – if he could get to Hong Kong on time. I then outlined the travel schedule. Again I waited while Walter spoke to Tsutsumi. By around midnight, it was all agreed, including the fee. I would worry about the PR in the morning. I went to bed wondering how you express your gratitude to someone prepared to fly halfway around the world at the shortest of notice quite literally to save a pair of concerts.

Illness once an artist had arrived in Hong Kong never resulted in cancellations, only in the 1980 concert necessitating a change of concerto with Carl Pini taking over from Ilana Vered. More distressing is when an artist is clearly ill but keeps it quiet until becoming obvious in performance. I was delighted to have engaged the celebrated Cuban-born American Jorge Bolet, rightly acknowledged as one of the world's finest pianists with a long list of distinguished recordings. One of Bolet's teachers had been a pupil of the composer/pianist Franz Liszt. I was therefore thrilled when we engaged him to play one of the Liszt Concertos during my final season. Thankfully Kenneth Jean was conducting the concerts. Although born in New York to Cantonese parents, Ken had been educated in Hong Kong. He was then the Resident Conductor of the Detroit Symphony Orchestra working under successive Music Directors Antal Dorati and Gunther Herbig. He was later to move to the Chicago Symphony Orchestra as Associate Conductor under Sir Georg Solti. In 1984 we asked him to join the Philharmonic as a Principal Guest Conductor along with Maxim Shostakovich, a post Ken filled for ten years.

Ken was an excellent conductor who was always totally at home with the music. In this case, he also showed how well he could keep an orchestra together when a soloist loses the place. Unknown to us all, Bolet was ill. He would later undergo a brain operation and eventually and very sadly die of AIDS-related complications. His performance started with the sort of excitement we expected to continue. Suddenly he skipped a few bars. Later he would both skip bars and return to phrases he had played moments earlier. Ken was magnificent. Piano and orchestra could easily have come totally adrift but the musicians were aware that something was seriously wrong with Bolet and were on the ball when Ken shouted bar numbers to keep all more or less together.

Writing in early 2023, it must be hard for those not then at least in their early teens to understand that we lived in a pervading atmosphere of fear and often desperation that had descended at the start of the 1980s with the discovery of HIV and AIDS. Believed to originate in monkeys in the Congo in the 1920s, the virus had lain largely dormant until being discovered among small groups of gay men in New York and Los Angeles in 1981. It was soon to spread and affect many in most of the world through infected blood transfusions and unprotected sexual encounters. That there was no magic bullet to cure those infected led to a time that for many bordered on terror. If you discovered you had the virus in your system, it was a death sentence. The devastation wreaked in the world of entertainment and the arts wiped out almost a generation of talented and committed individuals. One of the greatest ballet dancers of any generation, Rudolph Nureyev; choreographer Alvin Ailey who had founded the Alvin Ailey American Dance Theater which visited Hong Kong twice in the 2000s; the wonderfully talented Broadway director Michael Bennett who had devised the musical *A Chorus Line*; Larry Kert who had played the lead role in the original Broadway production of *West Side Story*; fashion designer Halston; tennis legend Arthur Ashe; pop icon Freddie Mercury – all were just some of the best-known names to die from AIDS. By the end of the decade, drugs had begun to appear that would inhibit infection. AZT had to be used in combination with other drugs and had considerable side effects. It also came with a price tag. One year's treatment cost $17,000 in 2022 dollars.[1] It was not until the mid-1990s that a new class of far more effective antiretrovirals finally resulted in those infected being able to live basically normal lives. By then roughly 50,000 had died worldwide. According to the World Health Organisation, that number mushroomed to nearly 40 million by 2021.[2]

By far the worst occasion when a different illness manifested itself for the Philharmonic was in June 1985. For me it was especially unfortunate because it was largely my own fault. This was especially true as we had increased the number of concerts to three and they all but ruined the last month of Kenneth Schermerhorn's first season as Music Director.

When appointed to the post, Ken had been very keen to have a major choral or operatic work in the final month of each of his seasons. For 1985 we had programmed the popular Beethoven Ninth Symphony preceded by excerpts from Beethoven's only opera *Fidelio*. Finding a dramatic tenor became the easiest part of the jigsaw to fill. In Hong Kong for a few days was the former coloratura soprano Jenifer Eddy. Australian-born, much of her career had been in the United Kingdom before returning to Australia to open up an artists' management agency. Over lunch, she told me that one of her artists had been an old colleague from her days at Sadlers Wells Opera in London. When Sadlers Wells (or English National Opera as it was renamed) presented Wagner's *Ring* cycle, the company's tenor Alberto Remedios had been universally singled out for praise in the role of Siegfried. It so happened that Alberto had married an Australian and so visited regularly. There he signed on to Jenny's agency and I was told he would be free for the Beethoven evenings.

Finding a mezzo-soprano and bass baritone locally for the Symphony was easy. Michael Rippon was a very distinguished British bass-baritone who had decided to give up his active performing career to come to Hong Kong as Head of Voice at the Academy for Performing Arts. When he first came to see me to talk about the possibility of moving to Hong Kong, I expressed surprise at his being prepared to give up his career in opera, oratorio and recordings in the west.

"I can no longer handle the stress," he told me. "I am almost paralysed by nerves before I go on stage."

I had known of other singers who suffered from major anxiety and stage fright. For Michael it was to prove a perfect move as he was also able to pick up a number of freelance engagements in Hong Kong and was ideal for our Beethoven concerts. All we needed to complete the jigsaw was a dramatic soprano. The previous summer I was discussing this with several agents in London when one, Wilfred Stiff at the Ibbs & Tillett agency, suggested Linda Esther Gray. I had known Linda quite well. She had made an astonishing debut at Scottish Opera seven years earlier when she had been summoned to the Theatre Royal in Glasgow at just a few hours' notice to take over between Acts the role of Eva from an ailing Elizabeth Harwood in David Pountney's splendid production of *Die Meistersinger*.

Linda was a massive success in the role. Thereafter, with her big, natural full-throated voice, her career took off. Contracts were agreed with La Scala, with the Met in New York, San Francisco Opera and other major houses for several of the heavier roles, including Brünnhilde. For a while, all went well. An Isolde for Welsh National Opera was a triumph as were debuts as Sieglinde in Dallas and concerts at the Hollywood Bowl. An added benefit for us was that she knew Alberto extremely well and they had sung together on a number of occasions.

For reasons which remain uncertain even today, although some have pointed to the style of tuition of her teacher, the famed Dame Eva Turner, Linda's voice left her remarkably quickly. Appearances in several major productions were cancelled to the point where, as the news filtered out, she was asked to withdraw voluntarily from most of the other engagements in her diary. To those in the opera world, by the summer of 1984 when I met with Wilfred her short stellar career was all but dead.

Ibbs & Tillett was the oldest established London agency, then in the midst of its own long decline. Its managing director, Wilfred, had taken over from the formidable Emmie Tillett, often called "the Duchess of Wigmore Street", a reference to the location of her old-fashioned offices. Wilfred was an agent very much of the old school, quite unlike those who headed the smaller, more boutique agencies which had started springing up in the mid-1960s. Ibbs & Tillett still managed the careers of such illustrious artists as mezzo-soprano Dame Janet Baker, but the days when the agency had controlled much of musical life in Britain were long gone.

While I knew Wilfred, I do not remember having previously engaged any of his artists. Why I happened to speak to him about the Beethoven concerts is now a mystery to me. Speak to him I did, though, and he immediately recommended Linda. Returning as I had to Britain every year, I was well aware of Linda's vocal difficulties and was not remotely enthusiastic. Linda, I was assured, was much, much better, the voice had returned and she was now picking up quite a number of engagements. He cited in particular a Mahler symphony she would be performing a month before our Beethovens at the Brighton Festival. I still did not feel that this would be sufficient justification for engaging an artist who would have to start a concert with the extremely taxing "Abscheulicher" Act II aria from *Fidelio*, but I could not rule it out.

It soon became apparent that finding a soprano for that repertoire on our dates was extremely problematic. I spoke to Ken several times and he said he just could not come up with any additional thoughts. As we were running out of time and an engagement became more pressing, I returned to Wilfred's suggestion. If Linda was indeed on the road to recovery, perhaps a few items from *Fidelio* and the Ninth Symphony away from all the western media scrutiny might indeed work – both for her and for the Philharmonic. So with Ken's agreement I issued her contract.

As that 1984/85 season progressed, I gave little thought to the June concerts. When I did get round to it, the more I thought about it, the more concerned I became that I had made a big mistake in engaging Linda. I talked again to Wilfred in London. You are being silly, I was told. She is in extremely good voice and she will sing wonderfully. Yet, in a discussion soon after with Jenifer Eddy about Alberto, she came up with an idea I kicked myself for not thinking about first. Why not have someone fly to Hong Kong to stand by and cover the concerts? If Linda sings well, the cover will have a nice week's holiday and a small fee. If not, then you have a replacement at your fingertips. She even suggested that another of her artists and one who had worked before with Alberto on the English National Opera *Ring* cycle in the 1970s, Rita Hunter, then based in Australia, was available and would probably agree to come to Hong Kong if we paid for an extra air ticket for her young daughter.

I felt utterly stupid that I had not considered Ms. Hunter in the first place. But I did not know that she had emigrated to Australia. I could also not understand why Jenny had not mentioned her as a possibility when we were discussing Alberto's participation. She would have been perfect! Still, the idea of having an artist like Rita on standby was hugely appealing. I asked Jenny to pencil her in whilst I spoke to Ken about it.

It was during my conversation with Ken, who generally agreed with everything I suggested, that I decided I would have to inform Wilfred. If Linda's voice was still in a fragile state and she discovered on arrival in Hong Kong that Rita was sitting in on rehearsals, it might shatter her confidence. She had to be made aware of it. And so I called Wilfred again. This time he was even more adamant than before. Engaging Ms Hunter would be a pointless waste of the orchestra's money. Linda was perfectly fine and would sail through the concerts. I thought long and hard about this. Finally, I made the wrong decision. I took the word of the agent rather than what my brain was telling me. I did not engage Ms Hunter.

I did arrange for Linda to arrive a day earlier than usual to give her more time to get over the long flight. We also accommodated her in the luxurious Mandarin Hotel, just a short walk from the Concert Hall. Although not required for the preliminary rehearsal three days prior to the concert, she asked if she could attend. Afterwards, Ken called me to ask what all the fuss had been about. Linda's voice, he said, is in superb shape. The difficult runs and arpeggios of the "Abscheulicher" had presented absolutely no problems. He was really looking forward to the concert.

It was the same when Alberto joined at the next rehearsal and at the general rehearsal in the Concert Hall. It was as though Linda's vocal problems had been laid to rest. They hadn't!

Prior to the first concert Su, our concerts manager, told me that Linda had arrived at the hall a couple of hours early and had been practising parts of the "Abscheulicher" at least 200 times! At the start of the concert I was sitting with friends through Ken's rendition of the *Leonore No. 3* Overture and awaited the entrance of Linda and Alberto. The "Abscheulicher" aria came first. It started tentatively, then began to blossom before catastrophically collapsing towards the end. Linda just seemed to go to pieces. I could only imagine how awful she must have been feeling. I felt dreadful for her, for Ken, for the orchestra and the audience, as well as for my own stupid, stupid lapse of judgement.

Alberto's aria was magnificent. In the duet Linda did not improve. In the second half Symphony, she cracked again as she approached the high notes. I was in agony, my mind racing, desperately trying to work out how we could find a new soprano to salvage the other two concerts on the following evenings. It was perfectly clear that Linda would be in no state to sing.

At the end of the concert, I went straight to Ken's dressing room, full of apologies. As usual he generously said he shared the blame. I told him my first priority would be to call Walter Nichols in Tokyo. Everywhere else was impossible due to flight timings. Even if we could not find a Leonore, we should at least be able to get a soprano from Japan where Beethoven 9s were performed a dime a dozen in the run-up to Christmas.

In those days before mobile phones and faxes, I raced over to the Mandarin where they kindly let me make my calls. Walter said he would try for a soprano early in the morning, an exercise which proved futile. He did wake a couple of sopranos he knew. Neither possessed a valid passport!

As this was going on, I finally found time to go up to Linda's room. I knocked. No answer.

"It's John," I said, asking her to let me in. Soon the door opened revealing a heavily tear-stained face.

"Have you come to send me home?" she asked plaintively.

"No," I said, "I have come to take you downstairs to get something to eat, because I am sure you have eaten nothing all day!"

Soon we were in the hotel's coffee shop. As we ate, there was no blame. It was far too late for that. I tried merely to make her comfortable and at the same time to get her own views on what had been happening to her voice, the more so as she had sounded so magnificent in the early rehearsals. Apparently it was the same as had been happening in her career for at least two years. The voice was there one day; gone the next. She had not really wanted to come to Hong Kong but had done so because she had known me from our Scottish Opera days and Wilfred had strongly pressed her into coming. (What?) At one point I asked what she thought about our killing the *Fidelio* excerpts – we could slot in another short orchestral work to fill up some of the time – and instead concentrate only on the Symphony. No, she said. She had no confidence that would work. She would just let us down again.

Despite the difficulty I now faced, I felt so much sympathy for Linda. I had no idea if her problem was principally with the voice or the brain, or a combination of the two. And she did not know either! An addiction to alcohol or a damaging substance can be treated. Many artists and actors had enjoyed success following such treatment. With a voice that continuously breaks down, however, there is no clinic or regime that can guarantee a cure. In Linda's case, the more I talked to her, the more I felt it had to be psychological. She did not agree.

Linda returned home to London the following evening. By a stroke of luck, Catherine Lau, the wife of our assistant conductor, was a soprano and singing in the Beethoven Chorus. She knew the soprano part of the Symphony. She possessed a light, accurate voice and filled in admirably for the work in the second and third concerts.

More than 20 years after those concerts and my departure from the orchestra a year later, Linda published her autobiography, *A Life Behind Curtains*. She writes of two engagements that summer. Of Hong Kong she says only this –

"Surprisingly I go off to Hong Kong . . . to fulfil a concert engagement . . . Alberto Remedios is the tenor and is very kind to me during our stay there, but I am terrified."

She then adds –

"That I tried to fulfil these engagements is a mystery to me, and it was misguided of me to waste people's time in such a way because it was obvious to me by then that I was a mere shadow of my former self. It may, however, surprise you to know that even at this point people would not accept that I could no longer sing and were still trying to get their pound of flesh . . . it was the end of my career."[3]

I had at no time insisted that Linda fulfil her obligation. While I certainly signed the contract for the concerts, if anyone had been seeking their pound of flesh in insisting she could indeed sing, it was her manager Wilfred Stiff. On reading her book, though, I felt more than a slight sense of disappointment. She had mentioned Alberto but not the kindness and understanding we had all shown her in Hong Kong. In such a horrible circumstance, no doubt the bad sticks in the memory more than the good.

On a more positive note, in addition to concerts, I had always believed that recordings were vital to a young developing orchestra. They exposed the orchestra to a wider public, not just in Hong Kong but with the right distributor also in some overseas markets. Here Klaus Heymann was a great asset. He was keen to start up a series of concerts for his two labels, HK Records and Marco Polo. He wanted us to start with Chinese repertoire to get a better idea of the orchestra's marketing appeal. He was not prepared to offer us a fee. Instead we would receive a royalty on each copy sold, an incentive for us to assist where possible with the marketing.

For the first recording of popular Chinese classics, Klaus had these short works re-orchestrated in Japan. As a recording venue he booked the new concert hall in Tsuen Wan. With the compact disc just having been introduced to the international market, he wanted the best digital audio possible for an eventual transfer to CD and so an experienced Japanese production team was also engaged. Long before the concert with Jorge Bolet, Kenneth Jean was beginning to work regularly with the Philharmonic and was engaged to direct these first recording sessions.

Colourful Clouds would sell many tens of thousands of copies. So successful was it that Klaus decided to record a second volume in 1984, this time titled *Under The Silver Moon* also with Kenneth Jean. In between, he had engaged the conductor of the Utah Symphony, Varujan Kojian whose brother Miran was to join as us concertmaster after Carl Pini left us, for a recording of popular Hong Kong TV and movie themes titled *Everlasting Love*. With the Philharmonic now becoming used to recording conditions, only one problem had arisen – and it was external. At the front of Tsuen Wan Town Hall was the local bus station. While the sound of buses passing on the road by the hall might not have been noticed on ordinary LPs, the extra frequency range of digital sound picked up their low rumble. This proved an annoying distraction, but with the recordings being of short works the producer would either work around it or just restart another 'take'.

One of the benefits to the Philharmonic of the association with Kenneth Jean was his ability to speak fluent Cantonese. This was to become extremely useful in some of the education concerts which the orchestra undertook. Under Mommer, the orchestra's education programme had involved just splitting the orchestra into two groups during weeks with no formal public concerts and sending the musicians out to schools for short performances in their assembly halls. Kenneth felt these were basically a waste of time and the format had to be changed. School was the children's primary environment. They felt comfortable and at home there. If they were going to become the building blocks of future audiences, it was essential that we take them out of their comfort zone so they could get used to a more alien concert hall environment and understand what attending a real concert was like.

That apart, the goal of these concerts was very simple: to impart a feeling of enjoyment and fun, exactly the message we were slowly getting across to our subscription audiences. We realised that 1,450 children from various schools in the concert hall would soon be a recipe for a degree of chaos. If the teachers had handed them the simple programme notes we had sent in advance, inevitably some would make them into paper darts which would fly around the hall. There would also be a lot of chatter. So these concerts, mostly devised by Kenneth, would commence with the houselights being dimmed, the stage lighting being increased and the entrance of Kenneth. As he bowed from the podium, the children applauded. Kenneth then turned around and started conducting. The only problem was there were no musicians on stage.

At once, Ken had got all the children to focus on the stage. Inevitably a murmur would arise. "What is he doing?" "Isn't this supposed to have music?" Hearing this noise, Kenneth would tap his music stand, wave as though to stop the imaginary orchestra, turn to the audience and speak directly to them in Cantonese.

"Why are you talking? Were you not told this is a serious concert and you are supposed to be absolutely silent?"

Although these concerts were aimed at younger children, inevitably someone would get up and say –

"But sir, where are the musicians?"

"Oh," Kenneth would respond. "I was told you were coming to see ME! So you want musicians. What kind of musicians do you want on the stage?"

Again inevitably, someone would say, perhaps, "violins". Over the next few minutes, all the sections of the orchestra would come on stage, mostly prompted by the children. As a result, within that short space of time, Kenneth had not only introduced the various orchestral sections, he had the total attention of 1,450 children. With this being the first orchestral performance most of these younger children had ever experienced, Ken fully accepted that attention spans would be short. His objective in drawing up the one-hour programmes was that no work being performed would be more than about five minutes. After 45 minutes, he would turn to the children and say –

"Right! For those of you who have hated every minute of your time this morning, I dare you not to enjoy what we will play next."

He would then launch into John Williams' very popular suite from the *Star Wars* movies. The end result was we had a concert hall full of children who had been dragged along to a concert hall certain they would be bored who left having had, as hoped, an exciting and fun time. Thanks to Kenneth we had sowed seeds. So successful were these concerts we desperately wanted to expand our educational programmes in two ways. Firstly, to follow up with those who had come to the original concerts with others that were slightly more 'meaty'. Then to devise and implement a series of programmes for older children. Sadly all this proved impossible. Most of the concert halls were very heavily used and dates for short concerts difficult to book. Secondly the concerts were substantially more expensive to present than sending musicians out to schools. We just could not find the extra finance.

On the recording front, on the basis of the earlier Chinese music recordings it was clear to Klaus that the Philharmonic was ready to move into the much larger classical repertoire. Understandably he did not want standard repertoire recordings as the record stores were filled with the works by Beethoven, Mozart, Schumann, Mendelssohn and other popular composers. And so we made recordings of orchestral works by Glazunov, two CDs of rarities by Richard Strauss, the Villa Lobos Choros Nos. 8 and 9 and another of works by César Cui.

Only once did Klaus call me about my views on making a CD of a more popular composer. He had been checking through the record catalogues and noticed there was no digital version of the Brahms *Hungarian Dances*. Also, he could find no evidence of one being recorded. Would we be interested? It took just a second to say yes. And so the orchestra was soon with Kenneth Jean again recording these popular works. It was not long before there were copies of the resultant CD on my desk. We were all delighted. And then I thought no more about it.

Soon an extremely unfortunate incident occurred at the same hall where we were making the recordings. We had started a series of concerts in the two new towns of Shatin and Tsuen Wan. Each year we had agreed to give Klaus's wife, the excellent violinist Takako Nishizaki, a solo concerto, in the City Hall Concert Hall in alternate years and in one of the out-of-town halls in the others. For this particular concert, she wanted to perform the Mozart Sinfonia Concertante for Violin and Viola. I was very pleased at the choice because it so happened we had an equally fine Principal Viola, Mark Braunstein. It is a mark of his quality that when he left Hong Kong he was appointed Assistant Principal Viola of the esteemed Cleveland Orchestra.

I cannot now remember why the Japanese conductor Yoshikazu Fukumura was engaged for this concert. I believe the original conductor had cancelled and we required a replacement. What I do know is that Takako had had a say in the appointment because I would never have asked her to work with a conductor without her agreement. So I engaged Fukumura who knew the orchestra, lived close by in Japan and had recently started working with the orchestra, even though mostly as a conductor of our pops concerts.

All seemed to be going well until the afternoon prior to the concert. As the Mozart was being rehearsed, something happened. Klaus was soon on the phone to me to say that there was a problem with Fukumura.

"He just cannot conduct this work and Takako cannot work with him."

I thought at first it had to be some sort of joke, although Klaus rarely joked! When I quickly realised he was being serious, I told him that if she did not perform as advertised, she would ruin our concert. It was too late to arrange a replacement soloist. I asked him nicely if he would kindly talk with Takako to point this out and request that she change her mind. About ten minutes later, Klaus was again on the phone. Takako had considered my request but could still not agree to perform in the concert.

I simply could not allow the concert to be imperilled because of some issue between the conductor and soloist. I had to do something. So I was quite adamant with Klaus that Takako had left me with no alternative. If Takako broke her contract and refused to perform, I would have no alternative but to sue her. I would also make sure that while I was General Manager of the Philharmonic she would not perform again as a soloist. I realised only too well this was being heavy-handed, but I believed I had been left with no option. Klaus became angry. I could not do this, he said. I'm sorry, Klaus, I replied. I can do it and if you force my hand, I will do it. As I put the phone down, my hand was shaking.

I was, of course, bluffing. Suing a soloist like Takako who had a very high profile in Hong Kong would be madness. Denying future engagements was a more plausible threat, but again one which could cause me more problems than Takako in the future. I had no choice but to wait. After another ten minutes, Klaus confirmed that Takako would perform – under duress. And perform she did, extremely well. During the applause, though, she would not come on to the stage to take a bow with Mark Braunstein. I can understand that being annoyed at Fukumura she would not wish to take a bow with him. But it is customary at all concerto performances for the soloist/s to take one bow together. That she did not even do this was to a large extent an insult to Braunstein.

Over that weekend I knew there would be repercussions. Klaus was a very strong-willed man and he would not forget what I am sure he regarded as my 'slight' as far as his wife was concerned. He soon made his anger known. On the Monday morning I received a call from his secretary. Mr Heymann wanted me to know that the recording sessions which were scheduled to take place in a few weeks' time were now cancelled. Although we had no further sessions scheduled thereafter, I was certain Klaus would not consider working again with the Philharmonic until he had got over his anger. I suspected this would be more than just one year.

Soon after our version of the Brahms had been issued, it turned out that Klaus's spies had fed him incorrect information. Just as we were recording the Brahms, another conductor was recording the same works. Unfortunately for us, it was one of the world's finest conductors, Claudio Abbado, with one of the world's finest orchestras, the Vienna Philharmonic. With only two CD versions in the record stores, it was highly unlikely that record buyers would opt for the Hong Kong Philharmonic version.

The next problem occurred some months later during my last season. One of our Double Bass players, Charles Martin, popped into my office and laid a Naxos CD on my desk. It was a recording of the Brahms *Hungarian Dances* with a Hungarian orchestra and a Hungarian conductor. Neither was known to me. What's so special about this, I asked Charlie? Well, he said, it has absolutely nothing to do with Hungary. It's our recording but billed as a different orchestra and conductor!

I found this all quite hard to believe. We had a contract with Klaus. Offhand I could not remember all the fine print about marketing and labelling. If Charlie was correct I felt that Klaus should have told me about it in advance, rather than my hearing it from one of my musicians. I called him. It turned into one of those occasions when I almost wished I hadn't. He had not had a new recording made, he explained. It was indeed our Philharmonic recording. But it was, he told me, perfectly legal. If I was not happy with his explanation, he referred me to a certain clause in the contract. Besides, he added –

"You know as well as I do from the statements I send you that the sales of your recording are desperate. No record buyer wants a Hong Kong version of the Brahms when it is in competition with the Vienna Philharmonic. Far better I withdraw it and re-release as having been recorded by Hungarian forces. You will not get the credit but at least you will still get the royalties." There was nothing I could do.

17

MY FINAL SEASON: I START THINKING ABOUT MY FUTURE

Now that our relationship with Klaus and his record companies had soured, I still wanted the Philharmonic to make more recordings. To discuss how to go about this, I called an old friend, John Boyden. John had been the Managing Director of the London Symphony Orchestra but before then was the CEO of EMI's budget *Classics for Pleasure* record label. In 1974 he had produced an excellent LP of excerpts from my old company Scottish Opera's *Der Rosenkavalier*. Perhaps ironically John had also produced Ling Tung's 1978 recording of the Rachmaninov Second Symphony with the Philharmonia. By 1985 John was a consultant for the Pickwick label in the UK. He told me it was looking to expand its repertoire. What would we like to record? I had spoken with Ken Schermerhorn. He had discovered a young American coloratura soprano with an extremely high range, rather appropriately named Beverly Hoch ("hoch" meaning "high" in German!). She could hit a high A flat three above middle C. Very few sopranos can get within a few semitones of that note! Ken was very keen that we engage her as a soloist for concerts. Immediately thereafter we could record an album of coloratura arias. Both could include the virtuosic *Air with Variations* by the 19th-century Austrian composer Heinrich Proch, one of the few works with that horribly high A flat.

John said that he could be available to produce our recordings in the HKAPA and fly out to Hong Kong with a top recording engineer, Tony Faulkner. Since he would prefer to come for a week rather than just three days, we agreed to make a second recording. Ken was keen that this be

Tchaikovsky's Sixth Symphony (the *Pathétique*) which the orchestra was performing the week before Beverly's concerts. Pickwick was happy with this.

Beverly's concerts and recording went remarkably well. Hearing any soprano sing such a high note bang in the middle is a spine-tingling moment. Beverly had become a big fan of Kenneth. As she stated in an interview for Ken's biography about working on the recording –

"Maestro Schermerhorn was extravagant, elegant, mercurial, creative, passionate, unpredictable, and extremely witty. His rehearsal style was quick-paced and efficient . . . he always listened closely and let the orchestra play, and allowed the music to breathe and be elastic and fresh, edgy, exciting, and heartfelt."[1]

It was a thoroughly deserved tribute.

The Tchaikovsky posed problems, though. John called me just before the last session to tell me that while most of the recording was extremely fine, he was afraid he might not be able to release it. There are some exposed viola passages in the first movement which our section, the weakest of our string sections, just could not get 100% right. John had talked with Ken and they would spend much of the final session trying to improve things. He just wanted to alert me that if there was no improvement, a commercial release might not be possible.

He was right. John and Tony left Hong Kong in the hope that they might be able to edit their way out of the problem. In London a few weeks later, I listened to the final edit. Much of the performance was indeed exciting. But those viola passages were just too weak. Unfortunately I cannot do any more with it, said John. I thought for a moment. I then looked at him.

"John," I said. "You have often told me how you can work miracles in editing, even making lousy conductors seem like very good ones. What if I were to find some extra cash? Could you find a venue with a similar acoustic, hire some good freelance viola players in London, re-record those short passages and splice it all together?"

John looked back at me with his usual wry smile.

"John Duffus! I never thought I would hear you prostituting yourself like that!"

I had actually been quite serious, but knew the chances of realising an acceptable match was near impossible. John agreed. There were limits to the tricks he could get up to and still produce an artistically acceptable CD. So our *Pathétique* never got released. Later I was to regret we never thought of licensing just the other three movements, one or more of which could have been used in some of the many compilation CDs which would be filling the marketplace some years later! On the other hand, as I left my post at the Philharmonic at the end of July, perhaps that is indeed what happened.

After the problems with Klaus Heymann, I rarely spoke to him for eight years. There was really no need. I had left the orchestra in the summer of 1986 and embarked on new adventures. Returning to Hong Kong in the early 1990s after a visit to Scotland to spend time with my mother who had suffered a debilitating stroke, however, I bumped into Klaus in the Cathay Pacific lounge at London's Gatwick airport. In such a small space it would have been churlish to have avoided even a brief 'Hello'. I knew that his Naxos label had just received the *Label of the Year* award from the annual record industry conference in Cannes, and so I went up to offer my congratulations. The ice was broken. Thereafter, we met for lunch on occasion. I remain in awe of his monumental achievements with Naxos. Our problems notwithstanding, I also remain extremely grateful for all the help he gave me especially at the start of my Philharmonic career.

Following the departure of Ling Tung and Basil Tschaikov's very positive comments about me as General Manager in the report he subsequently submitted in the summer of 1983, the GC gave me a much longer contract that took me to the end of the 1985/86 season. It had also accepted Tschaikov's proposal that I be given a much greater say in programme and artistic planning. Working alongside such an accomplished and experienced Music Director as Kenneth Schermerhorn was a joy. By late 1984, though, I had come to the decision that I should seriously consider leaving the Philharmonic after the end of that contract.

During what would in total become seven-and-a-half fruitful, exciting, tough, challenging, yet ultimately extremely rewarding years I had especially enjoyed building a completely new audience for the orchestra, getting the number of full-time musicians increased from 67 to 84, the budget increased by some 400%, watching the orchestra become much better known worldwide and even more of having the opportunity of building an excellent administration team almost from scratch.

During this time I was frequently asked about arts management and what makes a good manager. In the early 1980s there were few academic institutions worldwide offering courses in arts management. We all basically had to learn on the job by observing our peers and making our own mistakes. But my view had not changed since I started working for Scottish Opera in 1971. The basic essentials are twofold. One is to create the conditions whereby all the artists – and by artists I mean all personnel involved in a presentation, be they soloists, orchestral musicians, opera singers, stage managers, electricians, technicians, wardrobe and wigs staff, etc. – can give of their best. For we all know that artists not giving of their best are not only letting themselves down, they let down everyone in the team and the audiences who have paid to attend the performance. Secondly, whether the company which they head is subsidised by the public purse or from private donations, it is important to ensure that the funds are spent wisely and efficiently. It can turn out to be a difficult balancing act.

For an orchestra CEO, this can often involve awkward decisions. Several times I received important messages from our Orchestra Manager that a conductor wanted more rehearsal time, meaning they needed approval to go into overtime. Apart from the fact that overtime payments are very costly, it was important for me to know why the request had been made. As importantly, I had to assess whether the scheduled rehearsal time up to that point had been used properly. Had the conductor cut some rehearsals short? If granted overtime, would he make good use of it? Indeed, was it essential to the success of the concert? In most cases the answer was always 'no' and I would have to rush to the rehearsal to speak personally with the conductor to explain my reasons.

But during my last contract I was starting to fear that spending more years developing the young orchestra would all but wear me out mentally. I was no longer as enthusiastic about solving the problems that arose week-in, week-out, and coming up with more new initiatives that would be needed to develop it further. Even more draining was the constant grind of dealing with officialdom and civil servants. Thankfully the Hong Kong Philharmonic of mid-1986 was vastly different from – and far superior to – the one I had inherited in early 1979. I was happy with what I had achieved. But I knew it would soon be time to go, time for another challenge.

For some of my final two years I was thinking of opening a small concert and artists agency following my time with the orchestra. The seed for this had been sown by Walter Nichols, whom readers will recall had already helped me in so many ways. Walter was such a wonderful source of knowledge about the music business in Japan that I always looked forward to lunching with him on my increasingly frequent visits to Tokyo. Not long after the Osaka Music Festival concerts, on yet another visit to Tokyo, Walter told me about the promise to his wife that their son Aki would be educated in the United States. With 1986 or 87 being the likely year of their departure, he would therefore start to wind down the agency. Walter was well aware of my growing love for Japan. Towards the end of one of our lunches, he suggested that since I was planning to leave the Hong Kong Philharmonic, maybe I should consider taking over his little company. He did not want any fee, for it was making hardly any profit. But it definitely had potential with the growing number of artists wanting to give concerts in the country. At first it seemed the most natural career progression for me, and perhaps a way for Walter to keep in touch with his business – albeit from afar. Initially I was hugely excited. A new challenge. A new country. A new direction for my career. On my return to Hong Kong, the more I thought about Walter's suggestion the more excited I became.

Yet despite it being what I really wanted to do, I was soon to realise it would make no sense even if I could obtain the relevant work papers and learn the language. For the time being, the doors to the Japanese agents had always been open to me principally because I was a foreigner and they had learned to trust me. As Walter had pointed out, they were perfectly happy for me to be aware of their future plans, but they would never reveal them to any of their competitors. So those open doors might well slam shut were I to take over the running of Azabu Artists, the more so as expansion was essential if it were to become profitable. However polite and welcoming Japan appears to the casual visitor, even as I write it remains essentially an insular society where the interests of the group will always take precedence over those of any individual. It would take many years before I could be accepted as part of the group.

Sadly, therefore, Japan was not going to be an option. Hong Kong, on the other hand, had no concert agency specialising in the classical market. Not only were most concerts arranged and promoted by the CSD of the Urban Council, there was no co-ordinating body, for example, for the booking of soloists for the emerging orchestras around the region. With each booking soloists and conductors separately, an artist would fly all the way to Hong Kong for a pair of concerts, and then fly all the way home again. The same would be true elsewhere. I felt sure there could be greater co-operation so that at least some worked for two or even three regional orchestras on one tour, thereby reducing travel costs for everyone.

As plans developed in my mind, I decided also that a new Hong Kong company's main objectives would be twofold: the mounting of an annual subscription series of recitals by the world's great artists, and starting up regular touring of Broadway musicals, one of my earlier passions.

During my last year with the orchestra I received some advice about the difficulty of opening an artists' agency. A dear friend, Jennifer Hodgson, had arranged a small dinner party for Sir Ian Hunter. Ian, chairman of the London-based artists' agency Harold Holt Ltd., had had a distinguished career, which included being Artistic Director of the Edinburgh Festival as well as starting up and directing a number of overseas arts festivals,

Photographed on the Peak for the front cover of the first issue of International Arts Manager in 1987

Above: Hong Kong Island in 2005 – the City Hall Concert Hall is located in what had been the Urban Council Chambers, now merely a tiny building in front of the HSBC headquarters left of the green Star Ferry

Below: A news photo of Hans Günther Mommer leading the Pro Musica Ensemble in Bangkok prior to his appointment as Principal Conductor of the Hong Kong Philharmonic in 1977

Top: Ling Tung, the controversial Music Director of the Hong Kong Philharmonic for three years from 1979

Middle: The recording of Rachmaninov's Second Symphony with London's Philharmonia Orchestra which so impressed the Hong Kong Philharmonic's chairman John Mackenzie

Bottom: The promenade at the exterior of the Grand Teton Summer Festival Concert Hall where Ling Tung was Music Director from 1968. The Hall was named after its principal donors, the parents of Ling Tung's wife

Kenneth Schermerhorn first conducted the Hong Kong Philharmonic for three weeks in the summer of 1979 and returned several times including to conduct the very successful 1983 tour to Singapore, Bangkok and the Osaka Music Festival before being appointed Music Director from September 1984

Above: Maxim Shostakovich, Principal Guest Conductor of the Philharmonic from 1982-1985, with Mrs. Carmel Sandberg, the Hon. Michael Sandberg, chairman of HSBC, Cynthia Hydes and me

Below: at a reception with Lady Pamela Youde, wife of the British Governor of Hong Kong, Barrie Wiggham and Mrs. Caroline Newbigging, wife of the then chairman of Jardine Matheson & Co.

Above: The cover of the Philharmonic's first digital recording of popular Chinese classics, Colourful Clouds
Below: The final recording made by the Philharmonic during my time as General Manager – the soprano Beverly Hoch singing coloratura arias for the UK's Pickwick label after Naxos CEO Klaus Heymann suspended the Philharmonic's recording contract

Above: The Hong Kong Philharmonic recording made at the request of Klaus Heymann. When it was discovered that another version had also been recorded by the Vienna Philharmonic Orchestra conducted by Claudio Abbado, the Philharmonic's version was withdrawn and re-released as having been recorded by a Hungarian orchestra and conductor.

Below: The recording made of works featured during the Contemporary Chinese Composers' week following the February 1986 tour to three cities in China

Page 2

South China Morning Post

MONDAY, AUGUST 5, 1985

Playing in tune with our needs

The Hongkong Philharmonic is an institution in which we can all take pride. It has added lustre to our international reputation. Along with such events as the Festival of the Arts and the Asian Arts Festival, the Phil and other artistic groups have given the lie to the old claim that Hongkong cares only about money.

The orchestra has shown that local people can read musical scores as well as balance sheets and are concerned about culture as well as cash. But the Philharmonic remains in the red. Last year the deficit was $2 million and is expected to be double that this year.

One reason given for this increase is the cost of holding concerts in the New Territories. But we must be prepared to bear this. The Phil is taking music to the people and the people live increasingly in the new communities beyond Lion Rock.

Making music popular is what the Phil is all about. The general manager, Mr John Duffus, and the music director, Kenneth Schermmerhorn, are both in their own way remarkable men who have done a great job in making the Philharmonic truly a living part of our community.

Mr Duffus says the Phil will continue to play its merry tunes in the new towns.

Quality never comes cheaply. If Hongkong wants a world-class orchestra the community must be prepared to pay for it.

Above: On the Great Wall during the Philharmonic's 1986 tour and the August 1985 SCMP editorial praising the Philharmonic's accomplishments
Below: left, the great solo bass Gary Karr on a visit to his beloved Japan. Right, the cover of the autobiography of the superb virtuoso pianist Earl Wild whom the author brought three times to Hong Kong

The series of pops concerts we presented annually at the Hong Kong Coliseum did not only feature western music. This from 1985 was exclusively of Chinese music and featured popular Hong Kong-based soloists Takako Nishizaki, Wong On Yuen and Gloria Ku with the Philharmonic's Principal Oboe, Peter Cooper

My last concert of popular music from the Coliseum Series – music by the Beatles including the special two-piano concerto of the group's songs written by composer John Rutter for the piano duo Peter Rostal and Paul Schaefer who came to Hong Kong especially for the performances. When Rostal approached Paul McCartney about creating a concerto, McCartney was immediately enthusiastic. Since its composition in 1977 it has been recorded and performed all over the world.

Above: the December 1984 Coliseum concert arranged with Capital Artists featuring three of its most popular artists: Leslie Cheung, Anita Mui and Lui Fong. Within months Leslie and Anita would go on to become true Hong Kong superstars. Sadly both were to die tragically young.

Left: a still from a 1981 movie showing Danny Chan – who had sung in the Philharmonic's first-ever popular concert – and Leslie Cheung

Three vital members of the Hong Kong Philharmonic administration team during my term as General Manager. Above left: with Vennie Ho at the Philharmonic's opening concert of Bangkok Week in October 2023. Above right: Lee Bo-luen in a photo taken during my visit to Toronto in the mid-1990s. Below left: a more recent photo of Sun Man Tseng who has become one of Hong Kong's most experienced arts administrators and educators. Below right: K. C. Lee who started with the Philharmonic during my last years and then worked closely with me on many projects over the following 20 years.

Two iconic cultural venues. Above: Sydney's Opera House, designed by Danish architect Jørn Utzon and home to the Sydney Symphony Orchestra and Australian Opera. Below: Frank Gehry's titanium-clad Disney Concert Hall, home of the Los Angeles Philharmonic Orchestra

Above: the bare exterior of the Hong Kong Cultural Centre in Tsim Sha Tsui designed by the chief government architect José Lei who was enamoured with the functional Nordic modernism of Finnish architect Alvar Alto

Below: the warm interior of the Cultural Centre Concert Hall following its two renovations which included extending the stage forward to allow for a larger orchestra and a more effective acoustic canopy over the stage

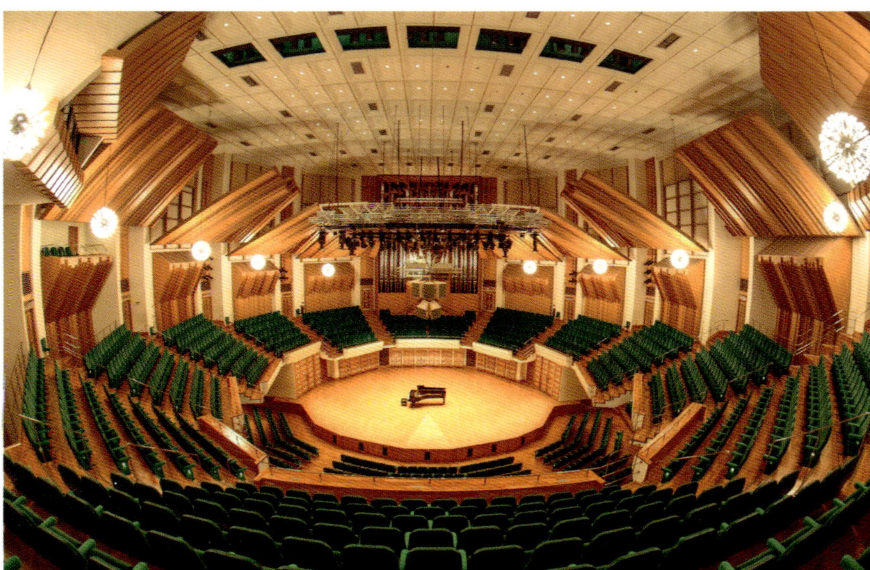

Two photographs show the difference in the interior layouts of the Christchurch Town Hall, the model José Lei took for his design for the Hong Kong Cultural Centre Concert Hall. Although at first glance both may look similar, Christchurch has greater depth and width thereby permitting more audience seating – 2,500 against just under 2,000. Although the Christchurch stage may seem smaller, it is virtually identical in size to the Hong Kong stage on the facing page. The stalls area is much larger as is the back balcony seating. The main feature is that the Christchurch hall is more circular, and with greater width and height, the sound is better balanced and has greater space to reverberate. Perhaps the most startling feature is the wooden louvres above the audience which are much larger and therefore much more effective than those in Hong Kong.

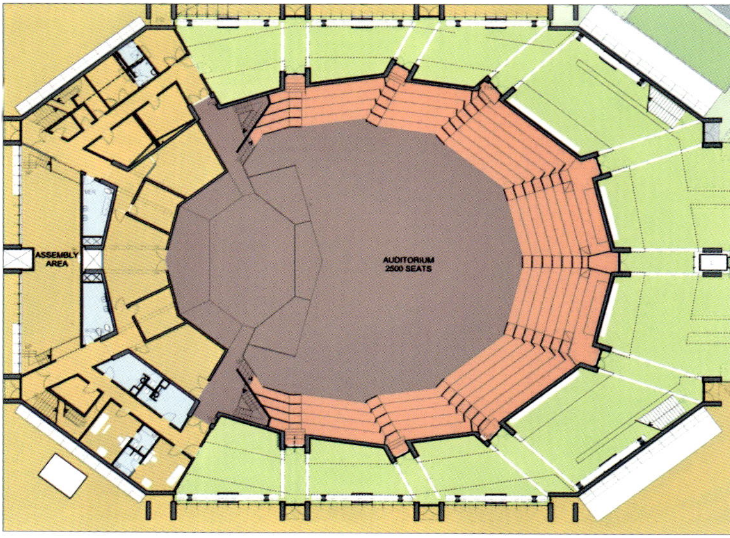

Although this rough comparison of the layouts for Christchurch (above) and Hong Kong (below) is not to scale, it illustrates several major differences. The back five of the balcony tiers in Hong Kong stretch out over the back of the stalls. Christchurch is more circular with a much larger open stalls area making it much more acoustically ideal. The most obvious difference is the significant narrowing of the almost egg-shaped footprint in Hong Kong resulting in a very small backstage area compared to the far more spacious area available in Christchurch.

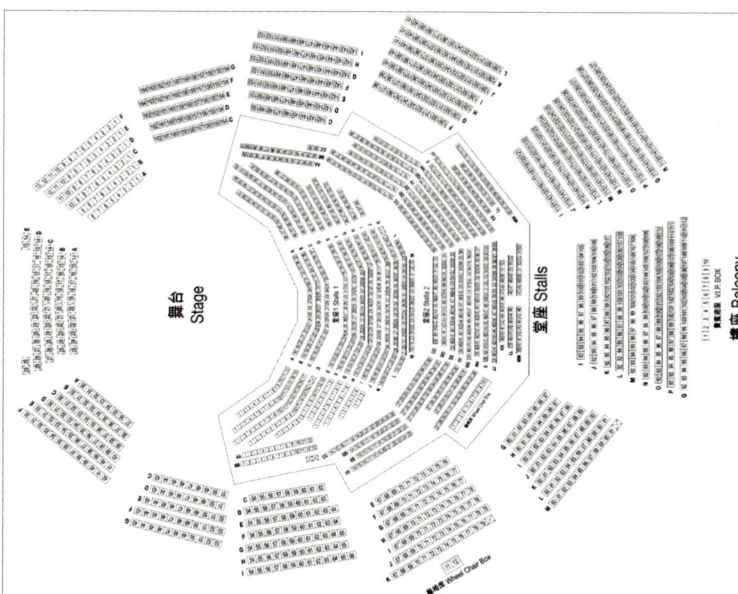

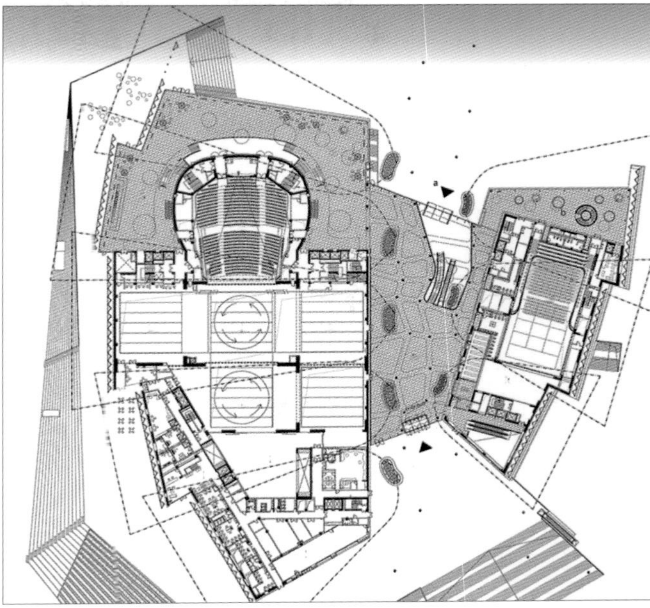

Ground plan drawings of the new opera theatres in Wuxi (above) and Harbin (below) illustrating auditoria in front of inverted T-shaped stages, the type of backstage area lacking in the Hong Kong Cultural Centre Theatre

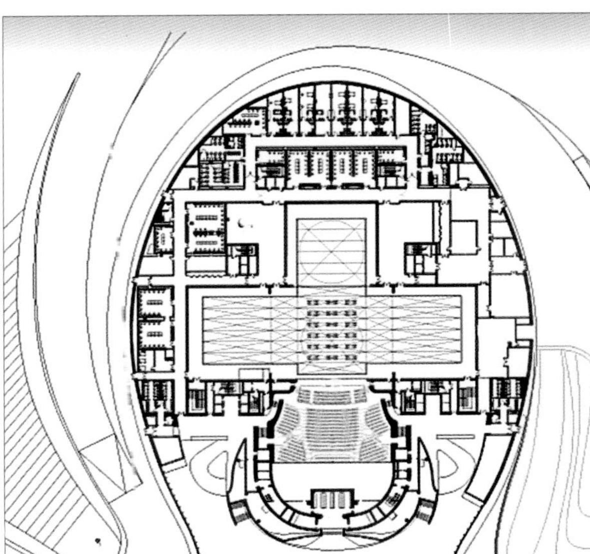

Luciano Pavarotti signing autographs at the Philip Morris sponsors' dinner following his first concert in Hong Kong in February 1990. Alastair Blount, the marketing manager of Cathay Pacific, is behind Pavarotti's right shoulder and I am behind his left.

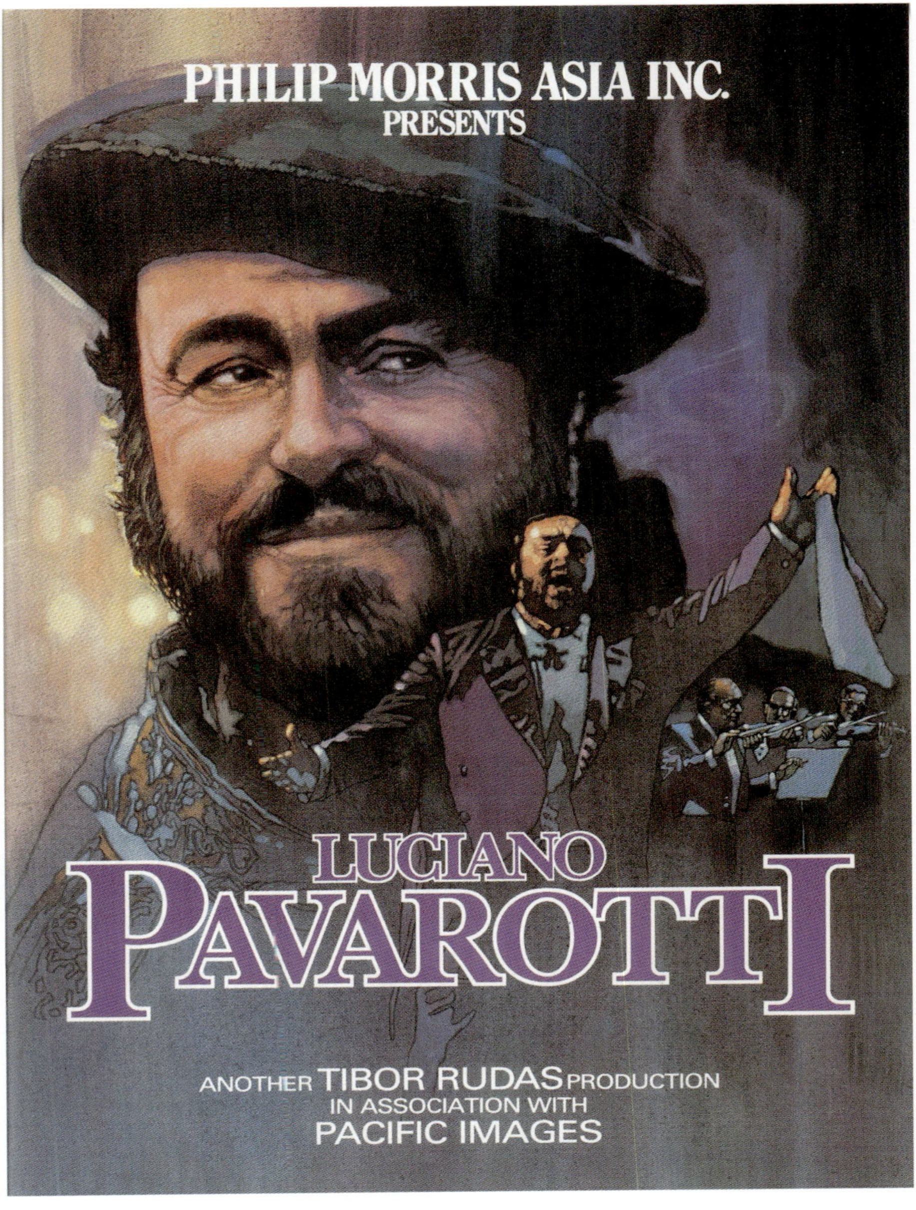

The programme cover for Pavarotti's first Hong Kong concert. It had originally been scheduled for December 9, 1989 in the Hong Kong Coliseum. After Pavarotti was invited by the Italian president to participate in the draw for the 1990 World Cup in Italy, the date was changed to December 5. Subsequently it would be changed again to February 11, 1990 and the concert moved from the Coliseum to a hall in the much smaller Exhibition Centre in Wanchai.

Above: In conversation with Tibor Rudas, the exclusive concert promoter for Luciano Pavarotti, at the Grand Hyatt Hotel prior to the media conference for the tenor's second concert in Hong Kong in June 2001

Below: Enjoying a day off at sea prior to the debut recital of José Carreras in Hong Kong in 1991. Joining me were Lorenzo Bavaj, José's pianist, Jutta Jäger (later Mrs. Carreras), and José Carreras.

Above: Dining with Dame Kiri Te Kanawa at the time of her Hong Kong debut recital in August 1987

Below: The stunning setting of Beijing's Forbidden City for the special Olympics Day Three Tenors concert in June 2001

Above: With violinists Isaac Stern and Young Uk Kim, cellist Yo-Yo Ma and pianist Emanuel Ax after their three chamber concerts at the Hong Kong Cultural Centre Opening Festival in November 1989

Below: Ted Chapin, president of the Rodgers and Hammerstein Organisation, and Mary Rodgers, daughter of composer Richard Rodgers, in Shanghai for the opening performance of The Sound of Music tour

Above: with Andrew Lloyd Webber when CATS was being presented in Hong Kong in 1994

Below: The 20,000-seat open-air Taichung arena on December 14, 2005 with Luciano Pavarotti rehearsing the last concert he was ever to sing before a paying public before his death from pancreatic cancer in 2007

A variety of backstage passes enabling me to gain access to the stage and back stage areas of concerts with which I was involved as promoter or presenter

including Hong Kong. I knew Ian, but not well, and so Jenny, knowing of my plans, seated me next to him.

Ian did not beat about the bush. Hong Kong would be a very difficult centre for an agency, he suggested, if only because the agencies that already existed in the bigger markets of Japan and Korea precluded any work in those countries. He doubted if there would be enough engagements coming out of Southeast Asia to make an artists' agency profitable.

"If I were doing it," he advised, "I'd sign up every artist I could and get exclusivity for this part of the continent. Your business would only be profitable on volume."

Before I had time to outline my other plans, he rather quickly ended the discussion, but offered to take me for lunch when I was next in London to discuss it further. Prior to the London visit, I sent Ian a telex to remind him of our conversation. He replied with a date and time for a meeting in his office after which we'd go somewhere for lunch. After the pleasantries, Ian said he was not really feeling well that day. There had been a bad accident overnight. I expressed the hope that no one had been badly injured.

"I'm afraid so. My wife's parrot died!"

As I was wondering what on earth one says to console the bereaved on the death of a parrot, Ian asked if I was hungry, quickly adding that he was not. Before I could even answer, he suggested that we just skip lunch and have a drink instead. What could I say, other than that would be nice? Anticipating a large vodka tonic, Ian got up and walked over to a drawer, opened it and pulled out a half-full bottle of what had once been sparkling mineral water.

"Perrier all right for you? Good!"

And that glass of flat Perrier was virtually the most productive part of a highly unsatisfactory meeting.

18

MY FINAL SEASON: CHINA TOUR, GLYNDEBOURNE, LAWSUIT

The peak of my time at the Hong Kong Philharmonic came mid-way through that last season. Once the British and Chinese negotiators had reached agreement on Hong Kong's future after 1997, Philip Kwok and I spoke about the desirability of the orchestra performing in some of China's main cities. We believed this would make a strong statement about our presence and our quality, in addition to doing something to help the morale of Chinese orchestras. These were only just emerging from the Cultural Revolution when most had to rehearse in filthy conditions akin, I was told by Li Delun, the distinguished conductor of Beijing's Central Philharmonic, to a pigsty. Mao's wife and a leader of the Revolution had insisted that orchestras were only able to perform a handful of Chinese revolutionary works. Western music was banned.

Philip asked me to fly to Beijing to try and set up a tour. Rather as Gosconcert was the official Soviet agency acting on behalf of the Ministry of Culture for Soviet artists and tours outside the Soviet Union, a part of the Chinese Culture Ministry had been let loose from its parent partly to arrange for similar commercial cultural exchange projects. Our meetings at the China Performing Arts Agency (CPAA) were extremely cordial and the idea of a tour was welcomed. It was hoped we could visit in February of 1986 when the new Beijing Concert Hall would be open. We would therefore be the first non-Beijing orchestra to perform there.

The orchestra's marketing manager, Sun Man Tseng, accompanied me on advance trips since he spoke Mandarin well. After one visit, we had to get up very early for the one daily flight back to Hong Kong. This Air

China flight departed – or was scheduled to depart – around 8:00am. After we had checked in and arrived at the gate we saw we would be on a 747. We sat and waited – and waited – and waited! We watched as engineers and technicians brought a ladder and started working on an engine of the aircraft, sometimes frighteningly looking as though they were merely hammering to get some part in place. By 10:15am we finally boarded – and then stayed on the ground. Within less than an hour we were told we would have to disembark again. Our flight was soon cancelled.

This posed a problem as we were now totally stuck in the airport for our visas had been cancelled on check-in. There was a tiny snack bar in the circular departure area. It quickly ran out of food. The real problem was that we had no idea when we might get a flight back to Hong Kong. Would we have to overnight in that uncomfortable departure area? By early afternoon we were informed that another Air China 747 would be arriving in the late afternoon from San Francisco via Shanghai. It would take us to Hong Kong. After that plane had landed and the passengers disembarked, we did not have to wait as long as I thought might be necessary before we boarded. On the flight down to Hong Kong in the early evening, I asked one of the flight attendants if this was her first flight of the day. I was astonished when she told me that she and the rest of the crew had flown in from San Francisco, including the pilots. Her shift would not be finished until the 747 arrived back in Beijing after the turnaround in Hong Kong. I was shocked. Flying time of at least 20 hours with an hour's preparation time prior to San Francisco departure and at least four hours for stops on the ground. I prayed that the cockpit had a double crew.

Naturally, like all visiting artists, CPAA made it clear we would have to pay for the privilege of their organising our tour and this took up most of our negotiating time. It was not long, though, before we had settled on a six-concert tour – two concerts each in Shanghai, nearby Hangzhou and concluding in Beijing. Kenneth Schermerhorn would conduct and we selected two soloists, the young Chinese pianist Li Jian and American violinist Stephanie Chase. To aid our negotiations, Sun Man and I organised a small lunch in our hotel for the head of the CPAA, Li Delun, and Professor Wu Zuqiang, the charming and highly respected Dean of the Central Conservatory of Music in Beijing.

In Shanghai we gave performances in the Concert Hall, a converted theatre that had become a cinema before a further transformation back to a concert hall in 1959. After the first performance we headed back to the old Jin Jiang Hotel in the French quarter for a banquet hosted by the local cultural officials. Earlier that day some of us had gone to hear the Shanghai Symphony Orchestra rehearse. The orchestra had been established as far back as 1879 when it was essentially just a small band of about 22 musicians (16 years before the amateur Sino British Orchestra, the predecessor of the Philharmonic, started in Hong Kong). By 1922, an Italian, Mario Paci, had assumed the post of Music Director and started expanding it into a formal orchestra named the Shanghai Municipal Council Symphony Orchestra. Paci was adamant that the local Chinese who had hitherto been banned both from its indoor concerts and outdoor summer park concerts be permitted entrance. Within a few years he was no doubt pleased that Chinese were to make up almost 25% of his audiences. The name was shortened to the Shanghai Symphony Orchestra in 1956, the name by which it is known today.

From Shanghai we boarded a train for the 180km journey to Hangzhou. Lee Bo-luen had done an advance trip to check all the concert venues and so we knew that its theatre was not only a barn of a place, it would be extremely cold in February. We had therefore insisted in the contract that the heating be turned on in the hall the day before our first concert and the days of the concerts themselves, a concession for which we had to pay a large amount for the coal – in advance. This heating had not been switched on and the coal money had simply disappeared. When Bo-luen confronted the hall management he was informed they had decided to open the theatre for two days to show movies. The presence of audiences would heat up the hall! It did not. The temperature got so low that Bo-luen had to have the orchestra take a vote on whether they would – and could – play in such conditions. All the musicians realised the importance of the concerts and voted to perform. Once again they played extremely well.

Although I had many months earlier announced my departure from my post as General Manager at the end of the season, I was still working with Ken on planning for the following two seasons. We were both very keen to try and get the orchestra to undertake a tour to the USA. To that end I arranged for a good friend in New York, the publicist Audrey Michaels, to join us on the tour and bring with her three representatives of the American media. While Audrey had been with us since our departure from Hong Kong, Shirley Fleming, the editor of Musical America, Fred Winship of the Christian Science Monitor and Byron Belt from the extensive Newhouse Group of newspapers all joined us in Hangzhou.

Here in Hangzhou we were accommodated in the luxurious new Shangri La Hotel situated by one of the lakes for which Hangzhou is famous. Many of us were in lovely villas on the hillside. After the first concert we had the customary banquet and speeches with sightseeing on the schedule for the following morning. As we concluded dinner after the second concert we were all anxious to get to bed for we had to catch a flight to Beijing late in the afternoon – from Shanghai. Since there were so few trains, we had been booked on one departing shortly after 7:00am. Yet another short sightseeing trip in Shanghai had been arranged for the orchestra to cover the time between arrival of the train and the Beijing flight departure.

Leaving dinner at close to 11:30pm, the tour organiser from CPAA said he needed to speak to me. I told him I was tired and suggested we talk on the train in the morning. No, we needed to talk now. So I asked Sun Man to join me to act as translator.

From the moment we started negotiations for this tour, I had insisted that we be allowed to choose our hotels. After all, we were paying CPAA for them! China had few western-standard hotels even in those relatively recent days and I was determined that the musicians would not have to stay in one-star establishments. Our deciding on the hotels was not possible, I had always been told. We could approve the hotels from a list provided by CPAA, but as was usual they would organise the rooms and make the payments.

So far, Shanghai and Hangzhou had worked out well thanks to Bo-luen having approved them on his advance trip. In Beijing, we had agreed to be accommodated in a new hotel in the Qianmen district very close to the new Concert Hall. On a visit the previous November, Sun Man and I had been shown some of the existing rooms which were barely acceptable, but we were advised we would be in a new wing to be finished the following month. Reluctantly we agreed, but we insisted that the conductor and soloists along with Su Villiers, our concerts manager, and the media accompanying the tour had to be in a western hotel. The Great Wall Sheraton Hotel which had opened barely two years earlier and was one of the first western-style hotels to open in the city was perfect for that group, even though it was located miles away.

Looking embarrassed, Sun Man and I were told CPAA had been let down by the Qianmen Hotel. They had double-booked all our rooms. Double-booking such a large number of rooms seemed such a lame excuse as to be quite implausible. But we were not to worry. CPAA had been working ceaselessly on our behalf and had found us new and acceptable accommodation. We had to tease it out of him but it soon became clear that we would be in not one but three different hotels – and one would not have phones in the rooms. To say we were furious would be putting it mildly!

Changing hotels to ones we had not inspected and approved was a breach of our agreement. Besides, it was perfectly clear that CPAA must have been aware of the situation many days earlier. Indeed, I just assumed that the new wing had not been completed in time. No doubt expecting an argument, his CPAA's colleagues had probably told him to wait till almost the last possible minute before telling us.

I had a quiet word with Sun Man. I realised we were going to have a sleepless night wondering how to break this to the musicians, so I decided the CPAA representative should also have a sleepless night wondering how he would convey what I was going to say to his bosses.

I told him that CPAA had broken the contract. As a result, there was now no contract. So I gave him a choice. Either CPAA find us one hotel in which all rooms had telephones and private baths or showers, preferably of better quality than the one which had allegedly double-booked its rooms. If he informed us by noon the following day that this had been done, we would continue on to Beijing and perform our two concerts there. Or CPAA could decide to do nothing. In that case, I would cancel the Beijing concerts, and arrange with our travel agency to get the entire orchestra on to flights to Hong Kong late the following afternoon. In that event, I reminded him, when the Minister of Culture and officials from the government's Hong Kong and Macao Affairs Office gave a banquet for the Hong Kong Philharmonic in the Grand Ballroom of the Beijing Hotel the day after our expected arrival, we would not be there. It would be up to CPAA to explain why.

It was of course bluff. We were all very anxious to show audiences and officials in the capital city how much the Hong Kong Philharmonic had developed. Besides, with my chairman already in Beijing and a clutch of international media with us, there would have been a humongous diplomatic row. But I counted on such a junior functionary in the organisation not realising this.

As soon as I got to my suite, I called my four senior staff to a meeting. Su could do little as she would be looking after the group staying in the Great Wall Sheraton. The two who could help me most were Sun Man and Lee Bo-luen. Bo-luen had been a very effective orchestra manager for four years and had got us out of several sticky situations in the past.

After briefing everyone on the discussion with the CPAA representative, I added my view that there was in fact nothing we could do. It was the middle of the night and we were in the middle of a provincial city in China with no direct-dial phones. I saw no possibility of our contacting hotels and coming to any sort of deal before we had to leave for the early morning train. Besides, we had already paid CPAA for the hotel in

Beijing. I had no approval to exceed the agreed tour budget other than a small contingency which might cover a handful of rooms at most. We were over a barrel. How were we to explain all this to the orchestra?

It was Bo-luen who made me rethink. He was as angry as I.

"I've heard this has happened before with orchestras visiting China. They pay a lot for hotels but agreements are not adhered to. We have to find a different solution."

We all agreed we had to try, and slowly we mapped out a plan. We thought of all the hotels in Beijing which might be up to an acceptable standard. There were not many but we intended to call each of them. We did have a certain leverage as Chinese New Year had taken place only two weeks earlier. As this is the major annual holiday, many businesses would just be reopening and there was a chance that one or more hotels might still have up to 50 available rooms. We each took down the names of the few hotels we would call. How we would pay for rooms, I had no idea. I would cross that bridge later if I had to.

I got nowhere with the first hotel I tried. My second was a new Holiday Inn slightly out of the city en route to the airport. By an amazing co-incidence, the night manager had been seconded from the Holiday Inn in Hong Kong and spoke excellent English. Very quickly he grasped the situation and confirmed he had 50 rooms. But he could only hold these without further authorisation until 10:00am. The maximum discount he could offer was 10%.

I said I would call him back. After talking to the rest of my colleagues, we agreed we had to make this work. And then I remembered that See-foon Koppen was a member of our Ladies Committee. Her husband, Rudi, was a well-known figure in Hong Kong and just happened to be the regional head for Holiday Inn Hotels. Even though I had no phone numbers for them, I had to find a way of getting in touch with one soon after 9:00am at the latest.

That settled, we agreed that the others would accompany the rest of the party on the train to Shanghai while I stayed behind in Hangzhou to try and finalise a deal for the hotel. If I could get the rate lowered significantly, there was a possibility that it would not be much more than the amount we had already paid CPAA. They could therefore pay direct to the Holiday Inn.

Before he left for the train, I informed the CPAA official of our new plans. For our part, I made it seem essentially a take-it-or-leave-it situation. I asked for assistance from the local cultural officials. Once I had spoken with Hong Kong and finalised the hotel, I would somehow need to get to Shanghai to meet up with the others, or fly directly from Hangzhou to Beijing if there was a flight. Sheepishly he told me I would be provided with all the assistance I needed. Later I laughed. The moment the buses departed for the train station I was quite literally on my own.

By a near-miracle I did manage to get through to Mrs. Koppen and thankfully her husband was in Hong Kong. He immediately agreed to a 25% discount and promised his staff would take over liaison with their Beijing hotel. I was massively relieved. With help from the Shangri La's business centre I discovered there was no train to get me back to Shanghai in time to catch the flight to Beijing. But there was an early afternoon flight to Shanghai. So I arrived at Shanghai's Hongqiao airport about 30 minutes before the buses bringing the orchestra. My staff could see from my smiles that what had seemed an insurmountable problem had been solved.

One solved and another about to hit. Having checked in for the flight to Beijing, we were informed it had just been cancelled. Expecting a near riot from an orchestra whose members had had little sleep the previous night, luck now was on our side. Whereas we had managed the 1983 tour to Singapore, Bangkok and Osaka on our own, for China I had engaged a tour manager from American Express Travel. He more than earned his fee when he discovered that within less than an hour of our scheduled departure, another 747 flight would be leaving for Beijing even though it was not on any airline schedules. Then he managed to get seats for all our party. We therefore arrived in Beijing only an hour late.

With the hotel problem more or less solved, all I had to do was contact my chairman as soon as I got to Beijing to brief him on events and request approval for an additional budget in the event CPAA played hardball over the hotel payments. Philip could not have been more understanding. He would sort it out, he said with a smile. And that, I suggest, is what chairmen are for – if only in part!

The following day was free for the orchestra and we had arranged with CPAA that everyone visit the Great Wall followed by the Ming Tombs. On the Great Wall, despite the fact that it was freezing, we arranged a photograph of Ken conducting some brass players. I was delighted that this made it into many of the world's newspapers. Before visiting the Tombs, we all assembled in a local restaurant for lunch. With a spare seat beside me, I used it for my knapsack and sheepskin coat. I never gave a thought to the waitresses arriving at the tables with three dishes in their hands and a couple more balanced on their arms. I wished I had, for when the young lady came to place the dishes on our table, one slipped off her arm and right on to my coat. I could tell immediately that this was going to leave a very greasy stain on the sheepskin – and so it did. Back at the hotel I used paper, dishcloths and an iron to try and get the grease off. Even in Hong Kong that proved difficult.

The banquet in the huge Beijing Hotel ballroom that evening went without a hitch. We had earlier asked Li Delun what he would like as a small gift and he answered without any hesitation: some scores and orchestral parts. Much of his library had been destroyed during the Cultural Revolution and so we had been delighted to have Philip make a presentation on stage. One of the works was a Sibelius symphony, especially appropriate as Ken had been awarded the Sibelius Medal for his championing of the composer.

On the day of the second Beijing concert, there was a slight scare when Su was unable to locate Fred Winship in the Great Wall Sheraton Hotel. Calling from outside the hotel, she slowly asked the operator to be put through to Mr. Winship's room. The operator spoke little English and so struggled to inform her there was no Mr. Winship staying in the hotel. More slowly, Su asked her to look again for a Mr. Win-Ship. Again no luck. So next she spelled it. Still no luck. She was put through to the reception desk.

"Ah yes, now I have his room number. I'll put you through to Mr. Wee Shit." Fred made it to the concert – but thereafter he was stuck with the name!

The Beijing concerts were a huge success. Once the orchestra had left for the Holiday Inn Hotel after the final tour concert, Cynthia Hydes, Su and I decided drinks were in order. So we went with the media to the China Great Wall Hotel where the three of us parked ourselves in the coffee shop for a late dinner and several drinks. With the release of all the tension leading up to this tour and on the tour itself, we burst into a fit of laughing that saw at least one of us collapsed on the floor! All the orchestra had loved the tour. On our Cathay Pacific flight back home, some of the string section got out their instruments and serenaded all the passengers.

Thanks to Audrey, her friends had provided a great deal of very positive coverage in the American media. Ken particularly was singled out for praise, further justification for our having selected him as the orchestra's Music Director.

There was only one real disappointment on that China tour. Audrey had arranged a major media conference for Ken, Philip and me to explain more about the Hong Kong Philharmonic and how pleased we were at showing the way to greater cultural exchange between Hong Kong and other Chinese cities. With little happening in China, Audrey called me the previous morning to inform me that virtually all the Beijing-based foreign correspondents would be attending. Sadly international politics was to intervene. News was just reaching Beijing that People Power in the Philippines was about to oust the hated dictator Ferdinand Marcos. Not surprisingly, by the following morning every foreign correspondent had departed Beijing bound for Manila. Our media conference had to be cancelled.

The Hong Kong media, though, was fulsome in its praise. Although I still had another five months of my contract before I left the orchestra,

I felt this was well and truly the high point and did not care too much about what happened thereafter. I had proved that I could take a young faction-ridden orchestra with poor direction at board level and a Music Director who should never have been appointed and help develop it into an ensemble that could play extraordinarily well. I was massively proud of the administration team. And I had proved to myself that I was capable of handling almost all the crises that can beset the CEO of any orchestra.

As I was about to enter my last season a few months earlier, there had been an editorial in the *South China Morning Post* which particularly pleased me for it illustrated the complete turnaround in the orchestra's profile in Hong Kong in recent years. It started by stating that the Philharmonic was an institution of which the community could take pride. Towards the end, it wrote –

"Making music popular is what the Phil is all about. The general manager, Mr. John Duffus, and the music director, Kenneth Schermerhorn, are both in their own way remarkable men who have done a great job in making the Philharmonic truly a living part of our community."

Had our season ended there, I would without doubt have retired on a very high note. I was perfectly well aware, though, that one leftover from the Tung years still required resolution. The court case brought by many of those musicians not offered new contracts in the summer of 1979 had been proceeding at a glacial pace. By this stage, the original 16 musicians had been whittled down to just six and a final court date had been set for June. The case itself had also undergone some changes. After a couple of years, the initial judge had thrown out the part of the lawsuit which alleged breach of contract. There could obviously be no breach if no one had actually been promised any contract! That left the issue of misrepresentation which directly affected me as it related to the points I had made verbally when I met with the orchestra after the rehearsal on April 30. Within a year or so of the original writ, the judge informed the plaintiffs that there were deficiencies in the writ as submitted. I thought it was then extraordinary that he gave the plaintiffs more time to submit an amended writ. Before the case finally reached the High Court, though, we had another problem on our hands.

Soon after our China tour and still elated over that tour's success, the orchestra had yet another success. A composer himself, Ken had been very keen to get together composers from greater China to spend a week merely rehearsing new works with the composers present. So it was that several young composers from all over China met and worked together. It was an extraordinarily productive week, particularly the insight it gave us into the work then being done in other parts of the country. Some was very experimental and remarkably interesting. Very fortunately, Klaus Heymann recorded the works for his Marco Polo label.

But then we had to get down to what we knew would be a more complex three weeks of rehearsals and performances. For the opening of the HKAPA the Philharmonic was playing for two of Glyndebourne Festival Opera's finest recent productions in the excellent Lyric Theatre – Mozart's *Don Giovanni* and Benjamin Britten's *A Midsummer Night's Dream*. This was going to be a taxing time for the orchestra as it had performed little opera and was not used to playing in an orchestra pit when virtually unable to hear the singers.

The late Richard Bradshaw conducted very stylish performances of *Don Giovanni*. *A Midsummer Night's Dream* was a different kettle of fish. Britten's music was very new in Hong Kong and proved much more difficult for the smaller chamber-sized orchestra. Jane Glover was clearly worried that rehearsals were progressing too slowly and made that concern known to the APA management. This found its way to my desk and to Philip Kwok's, but as I told him, there was little I could do. I could not make the orchestra members try harder for a work that was very different from the usual concert repertoire. In the end, all worked well although it became clear that the APA authorities had made a very big mistake by opening the week with the Britten rather than the Mozart. Being such a major occasion, several hundred VIPs had accepted invitations to attend. The majority, especially those with minimal interest in classical music, probably expected Mendelssohn's very tuneful Incidental Music to *A*

Midsummer Night's Dream. They were shocked when they realised after hearing just the opening string glissandi of the Britten opera that they were in for a very different type of evening. Had I been asked to schedule that week I would absolutely have insisted it open with *Don Giovanni*. But I was not even consulted. The result? Roughly half the invited guests disappeared after the interval. Someone had made a major error!

As the season continued towards its end, I spent more time with our lawyers preparing for the court case. I could not believe that an event which had taken place in my first few months with the Philharmonic would not reach its conclusion until my very last month. I am certain there are some who thought it would just gradually disappear without ever going to court. After the initial PR disasters, many were clearly embarrassed about it. At the Board of Governors meeting in December 1979 the Board Chairman Sonny Sales had decided it would not even be an item on the agenda. Mid-way through the meeting, one member had referred to difficulties with the Music Director. At that point the Chief Justice Sir Denys Roberts spoke up, saying he was aware of the court case involving the musicians whose contracts the Music Director had decided not to renew and he would like a briefing for the Board. Sonny Sales as Chairman would have none of it.

"Sir Denys. Is this matter related to the agenda item we are discussing?"

"No, Mr Chairman. But I do think the Board should be more informed about it."

"There will be plenty of time, Sir Denys, when we reach the final item on the agenda, 'Any Other Business.'"

But Sales was determined there would be no discussion. When the meeting came to 'Any Other Business', he said quickly –

"Is there any other business?" and then without even a pause, "Good. No other business. I declare the meeting closed."

He then turned to Sir Denys.

"Now, Sir Denys, I understand you wish to discuss an issue regarding contracts."

The Chief Justice therefore had no opportunity to discuss the background to the case with its being recorded in the minutes. Since it was a legal matter and I suspect there might have been the possibility of a conflict of interest regarding the position of Sir Denys, I outlined the situation as briefly and diplomatically as I could. And that was it! Sales had effectively silenced the Chief Justice.

We knew that the Legal Aid Department had engaged a Queen's Counsel, a top lawyer from London, to lead the prosecution team. QCs received very high daily fees and were accommodated in only the best hotels. How it was that musicians with assets were still able to have access to taxpayers' money in this way was not my concern. I was just delighted that the Philharmonic's honorary legal advisers had engaged a barrister who had worked in Los Angeles and had some experience in suits involving musicians and entertainers. Cameron Maxwell Lewis showed great flair in the courtroom. During his cross-examination of one witness, the Filipino timpanist, he used a trick I had seen before in a movie.

The discussion centred on this musician's location within the orchestra at the time when I stood on the podium and made my comments. As he asked more questions, Maxwell Lewis gradually lowered the volume of his voice. Soon, he was asked by the witness to repeat a question. Maxwell Lewis did so. Following the answer, he asked two more questions before the witness claimed he just could not hear the questions.

Maxwell Lewis than asked about the approximate distance between himself and the plaintiff. He said he was not sure. Maxwell Lewis suggested it was little more than a metre. He then stated, given that a timpanist is usually located near the back and to the side of an orchestra, at the rehearsal in question he was probably considerably over six metres away in a much more reverberant hall. On the witness stand he was therefore much closer and in a much quieter ambience than he had been back at the rehearsal in 1979.

"Would you say that is correct?"

"Yes, I think so."

The trap had been set.

"Turning to this morning in this court and your inability to hear my questions, can you please inform the court how it is that you are having difficulty hearing me when you say you clearly heard Mr. Duffus on the morning of April 30? Yet you have admitted to the court that on that date you were seated much further away from where he was speaking than you are from me today?"

That must surely have sown doubt in the mind of the judge about the plaintiff's ability to hear exactly what I had said. Even so, when it came to the verdict delivered some two weeks later, the judge found only one of the plaintiffs had a plausible claim. He awarded this same timpanist the sum of 2,000 Philippine pesos, a sum he alleged he had lost as a result of having purchased land for his family following April 30 which he then had to sell at a loss. I could not believe it, but that was the verdict. The case brought by all other plaintiffs was thrown out.

The judge also stated that a lot of questionable evidence had been provided by witnesses. The only one who in his opinion answered the questions put to him truthfully was the General Manager, Mr. Duffus. After two days on the witness stand, that pleased me. Yet I could not help wonder at the humongous amount of public money which had been thrown at this case by both sides when over the previous seven years 16 plaintiffs had been reduced to six and only one had been found to have a case acceptable in law. Two thousand pesos was no doubt important for the timpanist but it amounted to no more than US$70. Could there not have been a vastly simpler way of resolving the issue? Would all the musicians initially involved have been far better served and gained more had they merely bothered to turn up at the Small Claims Tribunal back in 1979? Questions that cannot be answered.

In the days before my contract ended, I knew there was no chance of any farewell gift from the GC. That was merely an issue of lack of precedent and certainly not a mark of displeasure on the part of the members. Philip Kwok did arrange a small private lunch at his office for me along with some of his friends with whom I had also become friendly since he became chairman of the GC. I got even more pleasure from the lunch and gifts given to me by the administration staff. I had given many of them their jobs over the years and they had more than repaid my confidence by becoming a very effective team. One, though, had been part of the administration when the orchestra became professional in 1974. Vennie Ho had become our Assistant General Manager in charge of accounts. As I write, after a long absence with family in Canada and another position in Hong Kong, she returned to work with the Philharmonic where she is now in the post of Executive Director immediately under the Chief Executive. If anyone deserves a splendid farewell gift when she finally retires, it is Vennie.

My last formal association with the Philharmonic was negotiating the extension of Kenneth Schermerhorn's contract as Music Director. This took him up to the summer of 1989. His five years had seen major developments in the orchestra but he was finding the commute from Nashville increasingly difficult. He wanted to spend more time there developing the Nashville Symphony. I was sad not to be able to see him regularly, although I did once get to Nashville for the opening concert of their season with the pianist Van Cliburn playing a work I had never heard before, the MacDowell Second Piano Concerto. I found this first major American Piano Concerto premiered in 1889 a delightful work with strong hints of Brahms. I felt it should be part of the standard repertoire but remains rarely performed.

At other times Ken and I spoke frequently on the phone during my annual visits to the USA. He was particularly thrilled that funds had been raised for a new concert hall in Nashville to be called the Schermerhorn Music Centre. This was to be opened in September 2006 and he insisted I come as one of the guests of honour. Sadly I did not make it. Ken, always a keen tennis player, had fallen ill after a game while on vacation in Florida. He died only two months later in April 2005 of non-Hodgkin lymphoma aged 75.

Several musicians who were in the Philharmonic during my tenure went on to play in some of the world's finest orchestras. I have already mentioned Mark Braunstein who moved to the Cleveland Orchestra. David Washburn, a superb trumpet player, is a member of the Los Angeles Chamber Orchestra as I write. Peter Cooper, our Principal Oboe, spent some seasons with the San Francisco Symphony Orchestra. Dan Silver, the Principal Clarinet, has taken part in several concerts in New York's Carnegie Hall under the batons of Lorin Maazel and David Zinman. He has also worked with Leonard Bernstein, Mstislav Rostropovich, Seiji Ozawa and others. Peter and Dan were among the few who took the trouble to learn some Cantonese. One was a bit of a magician and loved doing small tricks on the MTR subway for any children who might be in the carriage. More than any they sought every effort to integrate themselves into the Hong Kong community. I could not have been more delighted that both had been among the first to join the orchestra following the agreement to hold open auditions.

19

DISASTER WHEN STARTING MY OWN BUSINESS

Having flagged my departure for almost two years, I had little emotion as I walked out of the Philharmonic office for the last time. In the interim, I had found both a business partner and my first client. Philippe Delhaise had been the General Manager of the Belgian Bank. In 1986 it had celebrated an anniversary and engaged the Philharmonic for a special celebration concert with Maxim Shostakovich conducting. During the preparations, I had got to know Philippe well. When I had told him of my plan to start up Pacific Images, a new arts management company, he expressed an interest in investing in it. He had a love for music and musicians. He made it clear that he would essentially be a passive investor but could occasionally help us with financial and other matters. One was that he was starting up a travel business for his wife with an office in Central District's D'Aguilar Street. There was more space than she required and so he would be delighted if I wished to locate my office there at no cost. I did. I came to realise that Philippe's main reason for becoming involved was the desire to meet and mix with the artists I brought to Hong Kong. He came to many post-concert dinners, being especially delighted when we had a recital by arguably the world's finest flautist Jean-Pierre Rampal and I asked him to chair the dinner.

My client was none other than Kenneth Schermerhorn. His initial Philharmonic contract was coming up for renewal and he preferred that I handle the negotiations rather than his manager in New York. This was a lifeline for my young company as the commission on the contract was more than substantial. Unfortunately, though, through my own stupidity and lack of forethought, I ended up throwing much of our initial investment away in a venture which was massively overambitious.

Setting up concerts for the first year of operation was not easy given all the work I was doing with the Philharmonic at the same time. So when I received an offer from the agent for an ensemble based in San Francisco about possible concerts that first December, I was extremely interested. *The Brass Band* was a small group of virtuoso players from California. When they all had free time from their other posts they had been touring with a show which illustrated their virtuosity on their instruments and their love of humour. Keith Statham had booked them for the 1986 Arts Festival in February. They had been such a success that they quickly sold out four concerts in the 500-seat City Hall Theatre.

Given that in my view it was more than certain that others would have tried to get tickets and been unable to do so, I assumed there was a potential audience of well over 2,000 if I were to book the band. Instead of playing safe, I decided to book three nights in the 1,070-seat Lyric Theatre in the APA in December 1986. It was a huge mistake. I had forgotten one golden rule: that a success in one venue in one festival will not automatically translate to similar demand in a larger venue outwith a festival setting, the more so in the same year. In Hong Kong, many festival patrons booked for several events. The opera, ballet, concert and recital offerings might well have been the major draw, but adding a concert by *The Brass Band* either might just seem like a fun addition or, more importantly, help them obtain a larger subscription package discount.

I had my designer Peter Wong come up with an excellent eye-catching poster and flyer. We got media coverage and I took out two expensive newspaper advertisements. I assumed that as soon as tickets went on sale, we would quickly get rid of at least 500, if not 1,000, expecting those who had enjoyed the Arts Festival concerts to jump at the chance of hearing *The Brass Band* again. Even when the report of the first few days' sales arrived showing well under 500 seats sold, I was not so worried. A week later when we had still not reached 500 seats, I was quickly reduced to a state of panic. Two weeks later we were under 1,000 seats. I remember wondering how was I going to face Philip to inform him that this event was almost certain to lose us a large chunk of our investment.

Had I just kept the engagement to two concerts in the City Hall Theatre, the company would have made a nice profit. By failing to realise there were many reasons why 2,000 seats sold in February would not easily translate to 3,000 seats only ten months later, I had as-it-were bet the shop – and lost. The performances went well and ticket sales did improve. But it was a harsh lesson. Unfortunately it was one that I failed to learn.

Capturing the top end of the classical music recital market was always one of my primary goals. That was a good deal easier. By 1987 we had a six-recital series lined up with artists of the calibre of James Galway, Henryk Szeryng, the Labeque Sisters and Julian Bream. Sadly Szeryng, with whom I had worked in Scotland and never an easy artist to work with, died some months before the advertised recital. Thanks to Keith Statham who had left the Arts Festival soon after I left the Philharmonic to start up his own PR company, I obtained substantial sponsorship from Cartier. Thus the annual Cartier Master Musician Series was born. It went on to become a major success over several years.

20

EXCURSIONS INTO THE SOVIET UNION

When I left the Philharmonic and started Pacific Images, in Hong Kong there was one very obvious gap at the top end of the classical market – artists from the Soviet Union. It was well known that the British administrators of Hong Kong would do nothing to incur the displeasure of the government in Beijing. The Sino-Soviet split during the Cold War meant that no Soviet artists had appeared in Hong Kong for more than 25 years. With Gorbachev's rise to power in the mid-1980s and his policies of *glasnost* and *perestroika*, however, there seemed at last an opportunity to prize open that door. Not only would this enhance my own reputation and that of my new company in Hong Kong, it might enable me to engage artists at fees which were still below those of their western counterparts. Lee Lamont, the president of ICM Artists, who had very good Soviet contacts, had suggested I just go to Moscow and start direct discussions with Gosconcert, the Soviet artists agency, rather than deal through an intermediary. She kindly paved the way with some correspondence informing Gosconcert that a meeting with me could be mutually beneficial.

My initial problem had been obtaining a visa since there was no Soviet issuing office in Hong Kong. Not to worry, said Lee. I was to be in New York for a few days prior to Moscow. She said she would arrange one as long as I could spare a day from a New York trip to fly to and from the Russian Embassy in Washington. That I did. Once I had arrived in London I got on the daily British Airways flight to Moscow. On a frigid February morning in 1987 I expected to be met at Moscow's international airport by an interpreter and taken to the Ukraine Hotel, one of the six wedding cake-style Stalin-era buildings dotted around the capital with a *babushka* on every floor holding the room keys. I had been warned in advance that Moscow hotels rarely had bath plugs and had brought a small selection hoping one would fit. I had also been advised that every room would be bugged. Whatever I said on the telephone would be overheard by someone, somewhere. I don't think I even ended up using it.

Seated in the third row of the aircraft, I was one of the first to reach Immigration. The officer scowled at me, looked me over, checked my height from the lines marked on the glass between us and then growled something. I had no idea what he said and asked him if would kindly repeat it. Virtually shouting he said "hotel voucher". I had not been given a hotel voucher, merely notification of the hotel. That was not good enough. So I was asked to wait at the side while the rest of the nearly full aircraft was processed. I was sure the interpreter could be found and sort out the problem, but no one was prepared to bother looking for mine.

Having waited more than 40 minutes, I was therefore the last passenger to finally be passed through Immigration. I have no idea who the officer had called but the mention of Gosconcert might have carried some weight. With all other passengers long before having collected their bags, mine was the last on the carousel. I passed through Customs and looked for someone holding a placard with my name. Nobody! This is ridiculous, I thought. But then I realised I was in the Soviet Union and would just have to wait. After 15 minutes, I decided to get a taxi to the hotel. I exchanged some sterling into roubles at the criminally high official rate and went outside into minus 20 degree celsius. At least there were only six in the taxi queue. I assumed I should have one in less than five minutes. Wrong! Within 20 minutes only three had arrived. By this time, despite a sheepskin coat, I was starting to freeze. I returned to the terminal where at least I could warm up.

I had never been to Russia before and still had no idea what to do. Although only late afternoon, the airport was all but empty. So I went up to the short queue at the information desk hoping one of the assistants there would help. As I was waiting, a girl who can have been no more than 17 approached me.

"Are you Mr. Duffus?" she asked.

This was my interpreter! She had been at the airport waiting for my arrival. When I did not appear, she assumed I was not on the flight and taken the car and driver back to Gosconcert to report my non-arrival. Phone calls were made and she was told to return. Rarely have I been so pleased to see someone looking for me. She was hugely apologetic. It turned out she knew quite a bit about music as there were several well-known instrumentalists and singers living in her family's apartment block. She delivered me to the Ukraine Hotel, made sure all was in order regarding my room and gave me her home phone number in case I had problems.

The following day prior to my meeting, she gave me a short sightseeing tour which included Red Square. As I stood there in the light snow with the Kremlin Wall on my right and the GUM department store on my left, I stared ahead at the multi-coloured domes of St. Basil's Cathedral. I was totally overawed by the square's size and overwhelmed by a sense of history. Then we went to the large Novodevichy Cemetery to see the graves of Shostakovich, Prokofiev and Chekov and the most impressive grave of Russian bass Fyodor Chaliapin. I was fascinated.

In the afternoon, I had my meeting with two officials, a man named Kiseleov and his colleague Elena Tikomirova. After formal introductions and an outline of my plans, they expressed a desire to work together. I stressed that in view of the political situation relating to Beijing it was my hope to start in a small way with perhaps one recital and to work from there to more ambitious projects. I wanted them to feel confident that I could not only organise recitals and importantly obtain visas (an issue I had earlier been informed in Hong Kong that could take as long as six months), I would also provide the most professional conditions.

We agreed on a visit by the pianist Dmitri Alexeev. I could have engaged him just by going through his London management, but I wanted this personal relationship in Moscow. With everything agreed in principle, I could enjoy the remaining 20 hours of my visit. That evening my guide took me to the famed Tchaikovsky Concert Hall to hear a recital of Russian songs by the excellent bass-baritone Yevgeny Nesterenko. With the temperature outside back to minus 20 degrees, I had worn mountaineering underwear to keep out the cold. Sitting in the box on the right side of the auditorium near the stage, I became so hot I was sweating. At the interval I had to rush to the men's washroom to take it off.

After more sightseeing the next morning, we returned to the hotel for a late lunch prior to my flight back to London. Lunch was a buffet in the hotel's dining room. By the time we arrived there was virtually no food left. Probably there had not been that much available when lunch started! I was determined, though, that I could not leave Moscow without some caviar with vodka as I had noticed caviar listed on a small à la carte menu. The caviar duly arrived, but without the vodka. When I asked my interpreter to have the waiter bring the vodka, he simply growled something in Russian. She translated. Vodka was forbidden before 4:00pm. "Gorbachev's orders!"

Almost a year later, Alexeev arrived to perform my recital followed by a Beethoven concerto with the Philharmonic. It was front-page news. Tickets had sold out within days. I even had the concierges from top hotels begging for tickets for their guests. The visit was a massive success. I then had to decide how to follow this.

When considering possible options, I received a request in early 1988 to attend a meeting in the office of the Director of Cultural Services of the Urban Council in Hong Kong, Helen Yu. Helen had succeeded Darwin Chen who had been transferred to head another government department. Also present were the Assistant Director, Choi Suk-kuen. Helen said she needed my assistance on what she claimed would be a delicate mission. It concerned the opening of the new Hong Kong Cultural Centre (HKCC) in November 1989, now less than 20 months away. So far they had failed to engage a major international ballet company. They knew I had opened a dialogue with Gosconcert. Would I be prepared to act as their agent in getting Moscow's Bolshoi Ballet to come for the festival?

I paused and took a deep breath. I had engaged just one Soviet artist. I had promised Gosconcert I wanted to proceed slowly. I had not envisioned a Soviet orchestra or one of their top international companies visiting Hong Kong in the first years. The political situation was just too delicate. I pointed this out, adding that my major concern with a company of well over 120 dancers, technicians and administrative staff was their visas. She was surely aware that on all major Soviet tours there would be two or more officers of the KGB masquerading in some guise. This would be especially true when visiting a territory like Hong Kong where the KGB would have a very special interest in finding out what might be going on in Beijing. Before I would consider any discussion with Gosconcert I wanted formal written confirmation that all members of the company would receive Hong Kong visas should the company be free to come. Without such a guarantee I simply could not consider moving forward.

Confidentially, I was told, the matter had already been discussed at the highest level of the local government and word had been received that visas would indeed be issued. I was sceptical. I wanted it in writing. Helen suggested we meet after she had spoken again with the government's Security Branch. At the next meeting I was once more assured there would be no problem with the visas, provided all names and other details were submitted at least six months in advance. My requested confirmation letter had not been prepared. I was informed this was because it was too sensitive a matter to put in writing. So confident were Yu and Choi that I informed them I would start to make preparations for what would be my second visit to Moscow in 16 months. I sent a telex to Gosconcert asking for a meeting in June to discuss a number of possible future projects. Subsequently I decided to dangle the carrot of the HKCC's opening festival as this would have worldwide significance. I hinted that perhaps we could move faster than anticipated and should discuss a visit by a major Soviet company.

With such high-level assurances, I was not especially worried about the lack of paperwork from Hong Kong's Security Branch. I should have been. The evening before my Moscow trip, I was at a cocktail party at the residence of the Australian Consul, Penny Wensley. As I took my leave to return home and start packing, Helen entered. Why are you leaving so soon, she enquired? As you know, Helen, I said, I am departing for Moscow tomorrow to do your business.

There was a pause that was slightly too long.

"Oh, you are off to Moscow," she repeated. "Before you leave, can you come and have a quick word with me?"

The following morning I sat in her office as with increasing unease she informed me that the Urban Council could not proceed with the invitation to the Bolshoi Ballet. I had difficulty restraining myself. Apparently, having been assured more than once and in no uncertain terms that Security Branch would approve visas, that assurance had now been withdrawn – or that is what I was told. I went over the history of our discussions. I reminded them that I had put my own reputation on the line with Gosconcert at her specific request and with her specific assurances. Now my money was also on the line as travelling to Moscow was not inexpensive. But I knew when it came to civil service officialdom, I could argue for days but still not win. I stormed out of the office saying I would be sending them an invoice for my travel costs and my time.

I went to Moscow, spun some yarn about the reason for my visit and talked about other artists for the following two years. On my return, I remained furious. I arranged a meeting with Gerry Forsgate. Gerry had been one of my main supporters as the Finance Committee Chairman on the Philharmonic's GC and had by my return taken over as Chairman of the Urban Council, as Hong Kong's de facto mayor. In his office, I went through the entire Bolshoi saga. He knew of the background and confirmed the proposal had been vetoed by the Security Branch, but he had forgotten I was directly involved. He agreed I was certainly due financial compensation. He suggested I arrange a meeting with the chairman of the relevant sub-committee of the Council. I knew Lo King-man well and respected him. He invited me for lunch. Again I went through the facts. He also agreed that I should receive financial compensation. He proposed I send a short one-page memo with copies of my expenses for him to present to his committee. Some six weeks later I received the response. The letter informed me that the sub-committee had considered my request and decided there was no case for compensation, this despite two of the most senior members of the Council having confirmed I should receive at least reimbursement of actual costs! Then, in a second major slap in the face, it added –

"We look forward to working with you again in the future."

I was never again to work with that department. Not long after, there was the usual turn of the merry-go-round in senior levels of the civil service including the CSD. Some years later it happened that I knew quite well one of the civil servants who had been moved into a senior position in that department. At an appropriate moment, I told him the history of this Bolshoi episode and how angry I still felt about it. While he was clearly in no position to do anything, he promised to review the files. When we next spoke, he informed me confidentially that one memo seemed to be missing from the file. He would not have been aware of this had not reference been made to it in another piece of correspondence. I was well aware that civil servants looked after their own skins and the missing memo no doubt had to do with the promise made to me about Security Branch approving the initial approach and my expenditure as CSD's agent. I had been screwed. I just had to accept it.

News of my first visit to Moscow in 1987 had also filtered through the region with considerable interest. Until then, major Soviet artists and performing companies had only appeared in Japan. Soon, though, I received another important request. On one of my regular visits to Seoul, a promoter who worked for the largest circulation newspaper, the *Dong-A Ilbo*, invited me to lunch. At the appointed hour, I was ushered into a large black limousine and driven out of the city in a convoy of three limousines to an exclusive club in the hills above Seoul. There I was extremely surprised to be introduced to Dr. Kim Sang-man, the

Chairman Emeritus of the Dong-A Ilbo Group, who was to be my host at lunch.

Dr. Kim was a committed anglophile. His company had presented performances by the Royal Opera in Seoul in 1979 and 1986, as a result of which he had been presented with an honorary knighthood, the first from South Korea to receive the award. Like many Korean newspapers, the *Dong-A Ilbo* had a large arts promotions department which presented many classical music performances each year. He explained they had tried to bring Leningrad's famed Kirov Ballet to Seoul for the Arts Festival just prior to the Olympics in the summer of 1988 but without success. He asked if I might act as their agent in facilitating performances for 1989. He was sure this ought to be possible since Soviet athletes had taken part in the Olympics that year. I went through the history of my relations with Gosconcert and my desire to move relatively slowly. But as this was a personal invitation and did not involve Hong Kong, I felt confident enough initially to bypass Gosconcert and at least start talks directly with the Director of the Kirov, Oleg Vinogradov.

Off I went to Leningrad after spending Christmas in Scotland. On a miserably cold December day at the end of 1988 with the roads covered in grey slush, I made my way by underground to the famed Mariinsky Theatre where I was ushered into the stalls to watch the end of a rehearsal. Once again it was the history of the theatre that made the experience so special. This had been home to the Imperial Ballet, the most famous ballet company in the world at the end of the 19th century. This was the company from which the impresario Serge Diaghilev had recruited the dancers for his summer visits to Paris with his *Les Ballets Russes*. Until then, ballet outside Russia had mainly been an art form to show off the ballerina. Diaghilev changed all that by bringing many superb male dancers, including arguably the most famous the world has ever seen, before or since – Vaslav Nijinsky. Others included Serge Lifar and Leonid Massine. Among the ballerinas were Anna Pavlova (after whom the Pavlova dessert of meringue, fruit and lashings of fresh cream is named) and Lydia Lopokova who in 1925 married the celebrated British economist Lord John Maynard Keynes. In addition to the dancing and choreography, Diaghilev broke the mould by commissioning many original works from composers including Stravinsky, Debussy, Prokofiev and de Falla, from designers many new to ballet like Léon Bakst, Henri Matisse and Pablo Picasso, and costume designers like Coco Chanel.

In more recent times it was from the Kirov Ballet that the dancers Rudolf Nureyev, Mikhail Baryshnikov, Natalya Makarova and Alexander Godunov defected to the West while on tours outside the Soviet Union in the 1960s and 70s.

As my mind was wandering in the past, Vinogradov arrived and was introduced to me. We went to his office to discuss details. Yes, he said. Performances in South Korea would indeed be of great interest and could perhaps be tied in with the company's next visit to Japan where contracts had always been handled by the Japan Arts Agency. But Japan Arts had no rights for Korea and he saw no reason why I could not be the agent for that territory.

Once back in Hong Kong, I informed Dr. Kim's office. They were extremely pleased and I was thrilled. It was not to last, however. The following day I received a strongly worded fax from a company in Australia run by the promoter Michael Edgley. I was well aware that Edgley held the rights for major Soviet artists in Australia. The fax pointed out that these rights extended to the whole of Australasia apart from Japan. I was shocked. Surely Vinogradov must have been perfectly well aware of the company's contractual position regarding Asia, especially South Korea? Another Soviet project had collapsed.

Although without the Bolshoi Ballet, for the HKCC's opening festival I still had three chamber concerts with Isaac Stern, Young-uk Kim, Nobuko Imai, Yo-Yo Ma and Emanuel Ax which Lee Lamont had asked me to contract and look after. As I explain in the next chapter in dealing with the origins and events surrounding the construction of the HKCC, the chief government architect in charge of the design, José Lei, had decided to model the Concert Hall within the Cultural Centre on that in Christchurch, New Zealand. This posed a very specific problem.

Christchurch is a large space with a near perfect elongated circular shape. Acoustically it is a splendid space for classical concerts and recitals. José Lei, though, had designed the HKCC from the outside in rather than the much more usual inside out. The footprint for the Concert Hall tapered at one end, resulting in the Concert Hall being much smaller than Christchurch and effectively looking like an oval with a kink. This had a major and serious effect on the acoustics.

Like Christchurch, the HKCC had large wooden louvres at the top of the walls which could be lowered and raised to assist the acoustic depending on the type of event taking place. For chamber concerts, these were supposed to be lowered, thereby creating a more intimate space. When Isaac Stern and his colleagues came on stage to test the acoustics, he took an instant dislike to the louvres being in the down position. After playing a few notes on his Guarnerius, he called for the technician and demanded they be fully opened. After some awkward moments with the acoustic consultant, they were opened and remained that way for the three concerts.

I gave a small lunch for Stern and his fellow musicians on the day of the final concert. I was surprised to discover that none, apart from Stern, had been up to Victoria Peak on Hong Kong Island. I therefore decided I would organise a short trip for the others following the sponsors' dinner after that evening's concert. Outside the Regent Hotel, I waited in a stretch limousine. I had with me some glasses and a couple of bottles of champagne so we could see Hong Kong's glittering diamond-like skyline in style. Returning after half an hour taking in the superb view, I asked the driver if he could stay on an extra few minutes as I had not eaten and was desperate to find even a McDonald's. I had only worked once before with Yo-Yo Ma, not only one of the greatest cellists of the century but also one of the nicest and kindest musicians on the international concert circuit. On hearing my request, Yo-Yo insisted that I come back to the hotel and we'd go to the coffee shop. Now well past midnight it was closed, and so he invited me to his suite where he'd order room service. I protested that it was too late as he had an early departure for his return to Boston the following morning. He would not take no for an answer. Room service, though, was going to take around 40 minutes. That finally persuaded him it was not such a good idea. But as I was leaving, he thrust into my arms all the fruit, chocolates and other goodies the hotel and well-wishers had sent to him.

His generosity of spirit was evident more than 20 years later when I arranged for him to perform in Bangkok with his marvellous *Silk Road Ensemble*. Everything had to be organised virtually at the last minute because I had been able to take advantage of a gap that had suddenly opened in the ensemble's schedule. On those days I was supposed to be joining all my extended family in Scotland to celebrate my sister's 70th birthday. So I agreed with Mary Pat Buerkle, Yo-Yo's long-time manager, that I would make sure the hotel arrangements were perfect, meet everyone at the airport, and attend the rehearsal and the evening concert. But I would leave for London very early the following morning, some hours before Yo-Yo and the ensemble left for Singapore. As soon as I had welcomed everyone at Bangkok's international airport, I told Yo-Yo the reason why I would not be able to see them all depart two days later. It was, as I expected, not the slightest problem.

If I had had concerns about how the Bangkok audience would react to the very different repertoire for the ensemble when some might have come expecting the Dvořák Cello Concerto, I need not have worried. The cheering at the end was extraordinary! After chatting with some of the musicians backstage, I went to Yo-Yo's dressing room to thank him and remind him of my absence the following morning. John, he said, I must ask you to do something for me. When you get to Scotland and you see your sister, will you please wish her the happiest of birthdays from me! I was hugely touched that he had even remembered the reason for my early departure. We embraced as they departed for dinner and I to finalise my packing.

Most artists I engaged had their fees remitted directly to their managements. Two years after the opening of the Cultural Centre, following solo recitals I had arranged in Taipei and Hong Kong, Yo-Yo had wanted his two fees paid in cash. Just as I handed over the envelope in his suite there was a knock on the door. I prepared to leave but he asked me to stay. He'd value my opinion on what he was about to buy. In came a middle-aged man in a rather threadbare jacket who took from his pocket a small black pouch. Inside were several large diamonds. Which do you think is best, asked Yo-Yo? I had absolutely no clue about jewellery and merely asked what it would be for. It was for his wife's birthday as he planned to have one made into a ring! That he would even consider asking for my view was remarkable.

Almost the only other artist to request cash payment was another cellist, the marvellous Russian Mstislav Rostropovich. A wonderfully outsize personality, he had given a magnificent recital the previous evening with his regular pianist Lambert Orkis. After obtaining a substantial amount of cash from the bank, I was not surprised when he asked for it to be counted in front of him. I made a rather silly comment suggesting he not spend it all in one shop, to which he replied "It's already spent!" He added he would appreciate a small van in addition to the limousine to the airport that evening.

As eight large suitcases were bundled into the van, I wondered what on earth he had bought. It turned out he spent almost the entire fee on a new wardrobe of made-to-measure suits and shirts. Checking the bags at the airport, I watched as the weight counter cleared 150kgs and ended up at just over 170kgs. How is he going to pay for that, I wondered? With a conspiratorial smile, he then took from his inside pocket a clear plastic folder. Inside was what looked like a somewhat moth-eaten letter which he handed over to the Air France check-in assistant. This had been written 16 years earlier by the then president of Air France, the gist being that Maestro Rostropovich was a valued traveller and requesting all Air France staff to offer him every assistance. A supervisor was summoned, phone calls made and eventually the excess baggage was waived through without payment!

When the assistant then asked him for the US$20 departure tax, he searched his pockets before turning to me.

"My dear John, I seem to have no money. May I borrow this from you and I promise I will return it?"

I handed the assistant the tax, Slava's boarding pass was issued and I walked him to the entrance to the Immigration area. Turning to me he said –

"You have been most kind. I have enjoyed my visit so, so much. Thank you! Thank you!"

Whereupon he gave me the three-cheek Russian kiss. Unfortunately he had not shaved that day and it felt like especially rough sandpaper scraping over my skin. I waved him goodbye. I knew I would never see that $20. And I didn't! But what a privilege to work with such an artist!

In 1988 there was another fee issue we had to deal with, this time regarding a change in the hiring charges for venues run by the Urban and Regional Councils. Until then, the Urban Council and the CSD had a policy of subsidising rentals of venues intended for culture and arts events. This was in the expectation of keeping ticket prices lower than might otherwise be the case and thereby encouraging greater numbers of the public to attend. To the extent that it kept ticket prices lower, it succeeded. Whether it actually encouraged those who did not plan to attend a concert or other type of performance to change their minds is much harder to say. The one venue where a stiff 20% rental charge was levied was the Hong Kong Coliseum but that usually housed commercial pop events. When the Philharmonic hired it, though, we again benefitted from a subsidised rate.

Having moved into the private commercial sector and started bringing many of the top international artists to Hong Kong, the subsidy was clearly enabling lower ticket prices. Now that a decision had been made that the hire charge for all major venues be raised to 20%, our business strategy was very adversely affected. I wrote a letter with my objections as did Klaus Heymann. They had zero effect.

The decision had been made without any discussion with me and others who occasionally presented concerts. It would not be reversed. I believed the massive increase was more than just a commercial decision.

The Cultural Services civil servants, who basically sat behind their desks waiting for agents to contact them about the possibility of their presenting an artist who would be on tour in the region, were annoyed that I was bringing in many more top international artists on a regular basis because I actually took the trouble to visit agents and managers around the world. In effect I was to a certain extent stealing what they believed should be their thunder!

With my small company, it was obvious I had to become even more efficient at controlling costs. It also left me basically with two options: reduce the international quality of artists I would present in future, something I was not prepared to consider given that my intention in forming Pacific Images had been deliberately to capture the top end of the recital market. The alternative was to branch out into larger, more expensive projects in the hope of generating higher returns. As we shall see, this was to result in my ending up in a sea of red ink and having to sell my small company in early 1990.

The general effect of the rental increase was substantial and inevitably resulted in a considerable rise in ticket prices. When Dame Kiri Te Kanawa returned to Hong Kong for a second recital in 1989 following her hugely successful debut recital two years earlier, top ticket prices had to rise by 60% even though total costs excluding venue rental had risen by no more than 10%. Along with a good friend with whom I had worked in the past, the Swiss concert promoter Manfred Gerber, I had agreed to engage a French orchestra for two concerts the following year. With the new charges for the Concert Hall, I had no option but to abandon that tour just weeks before the contract should have been signed. I would certainly have made a significant loss had the concerts gone ahead.

21

MACAO'S INTERNATIONAL MUSIC FESTIVAL

Outside Hong Kong I had a more leisurely assignment. In 1986 Macao had taken the first steps towards changing its international image. Known to most of the world as a somewhat sleazy gambling mecca, with most of the gaming halls owned by Hong Kong's Stanley Ho, the Tourism Department decided to start up a Macao Music Festival. As its Artistic Director it selected the Lisbon-based pianist and concert organiser, Adriano Jordão. Adriano was an immensely likeable character and in many respects ideal as a festival director. From his activities in Europe he knew a great many musicians. His presence in Macao would unquestionably help persuade some to take part.

The reason I was approached was to lend my experience to the festival in a number of ways. First, Macao had no reasonable venues for performances of classical music. Many had to be held in a hall at the University where the air conditioning was much too loud. Larger concerts were held in the Macao Forum, a sports stadium with absolutely no ambience. In those early years, concerts rarely sold well with the result that many tickets had to be given away, often to schools whose pupils would have preferred almost anything to attending a recital of classical music. The one event which was always full was of a mass or other semi-religious work performed in Macao's Cathedral.

In the first of my three years working as consultant to the festival, seeking out new venues was of paramount importance. Back in the 1980s there was a permanent burlesque show called *The Crazy Horse Revue* held at the Dom Pedro V Theatre. Historically this was an important building.

Not only was it one of the first theatres to be built in Asia, it was the location for the very first performance in Asia of Puccini's opera *Madama Butterfly*. On one of my many visits to Macao, all liberally laced with excellent meals and plenty of fine Portuguese wine, we went to check on the theatre. It had obviously not seen any renovation for decades and the auditorium gave the impression of a seedy, run-down space that would need a great deal of work to make it suitable for classical music recitals and chamber concerts. But it certainly oozed potential – and Macao had the money. It would soon close down before finally being fully renovated and reopened in 1993.

There was, though, one superb location which I felt would be perfect for smaller-scale recitals. Close to the centre of the city is the Lou Lim Ioc Garden. Constructed by a local merchant at the start of the 19th century and based on the glorious formal Chinese gardens in Suzhou, it had been handed over to the local government which used it merely as a park. What made it special was a Chinese pavilion set right in its centre. One of its rooms would be large enough to accommodate an audience of about 200. Not that it was in any fit state on my first visit, as it was not used apart from occasional small art exhibitions. Like the theatre, it was in desperate need of refurbishment. Yet the garden was a gem and I felt there had to be some way to incorporate the garden as an integral part of the pavilion. It was I believe the editor of the main Macao newspaper who suggested that a section of one wall could be knocked down and replaced with floor-to-ceiling glass. With a small platform as a stage in front of it, audiences would not only see the performers, they would also see the magnificent flood-lit garden behind.

This was precisely what happened. In 1989 and 1990 there were several remarkable recitals given by such outstanding singers as Teresa Berganza and Christa Ludwig. These were made even more special when the audience could mingle with the artists on the terrace surrounding the pavilion after the recitals. Both these artists were among the finest whose recitals would immediately sell out at the world's most outstanding festivals. To have the opportunity of hearing them in such an intimate surrounding was quite extraordinary.

I remember enjoying a glass of wine with Christa Ludwig and mentioning I was delighted she had included in her programme some songs by the much-lauded composer/conductor Leonard Bernstein who had died less than two weeks earlier. She had been a great friend of Bernstein. She told me that about 10 days prior to his death, he had sent her a fax. This informed her that the prognosis for his illness was bad. As long as he could sign his name he wanted to tell her what a joy it had been to have known her and to have made so much wonderful music together. He sent her all his love and all his good wishes for her future career. I found that very touching.

All the artists stayed at the Mandarin Oriental hotel. I remember going to the pool one sunny morning and seeing Madame Berganza. I had in fact worked with her several times before. I had been the technical director when as already mentioned she made her debut in the role of Carmen at the 1977 Edinburgh Festival. I had also invited her twice as a guest soloist during my time with the Philharmonic. So we knew each other well and she quickly invited me to sit on the lounger next to her. We spent a lovely hour chatting about many friends and old times.

There was nothing we could do about a venue for larger concerts until Macao opened its Cultural Centre about ten years later. In the meantime the University and the Forum just had to make do. For 1990 Adriano had assembled a stellar group of artists. In addition to the pianist Dame Moura Lympany, there was a galaxy of singers including Berganza and Ludwig, the gorgeous soprano Ileana Cotrubas, the tenors Alfredo Kraus and Peter Schreier, and the young Italian bass baritone Ferruccio Furlanetto.

One reason Adriano was able to attract such major artists was not merely that they were his friends. He paid well. As part of their contracts, all concerts were to be televised by the relatively new Macao television station. And not just in Macao. Having persuaded his masters that they could better achieve their objective if the concerts were made available around the world, each artist's contract allowed for worldwide television rights. This was extraordinary. Occasional worldwide rights were not unusual for special events. What Adriano envisaged was not having each concert or recital offered worldwide. Instead, a one-hour programme compilation would be assembled and this would be offered to worldwide networks. So if Teresa Berganza took part in three events and the sum total of her contribution to the one-hour compilation was just ten minutes, she would still receive three large worldwide television fees.

This was one specific area where the committee wanted my input. Was this reasonable? Naturally I said 'No!' Lesser fees could relatively simply be negotiated even if Adriano and the TV station were still uncertain about the parts of the programme to be included in the compilation. It would certainly have been possible to have inserted a clause in the artists' contracts stating that if any part of any performance was included in an international television programme, then a specific additional fee based on time on screen would be added. I more than earned my consultancy fees with that advice alone!

22

HONG KONG CULTURAL CENTRE: DESIGN MISADVENTURES

In the weeks after I arrived in Hong Kong in 1979 one of my early visitors had been Alan Russell, then running an office in Hong Kong for the London company Theatre Projects Consultants (TPC). Alan was in charge of the design team for the new Hong Kong Cultural Centre on the Kowloon waterfront. As the Philharmonic would be the most regular occupant of its Concert Hall, he was anxious that he go through the plans with me to ensure they met with my approval. There was a degree of urgency in obtaining all approvals because the schedule at that time was the full HKCC should open by 1983. Coming under the overall brief of the Chief Government Architect, TPC had been asked to present final designs for approval within months of our meeting.

The HKCC was intended as a symbol of Hong Kong's rapid development in the performing arts. Comprising a state-of-the-art Concert Hall with 2,100 seats, a 1,750-seat Grand Theatre for opera and other large-scale lyric performances, and a smaller 500-seat experimental theatre capable of many different configurations (known in the business as a "black box"), it would not just complement the ageing and smaller facilities in the City Hall Complex on the other side of the harbour. It would create entirely new spaces for audiences and performers alike with views from Kowloon of one of the most magnificent harbours in the world. It would put Hong Kong firmly on the international arts map.

At least that was the plan. Following its long-delayed Opening Festival in November 1989, the Grand Theatre within the complex soon became the most in-demand performing venue in the territory. To that extent, the HKCC can be deemed a success.

If only everything had been that simple!

Like most public buildings for the performing arts in Hong Kong, the cost of the HKCC was borne by the local administration. Similarly, organisation and management of the new complex would be entrusted to the rapidly mushrooming CSD of the Urban Council, absorbed after 1999 into the larger Leisure and Cultural Services Department (LCSD) of the SAR government. As a result, its senior officers should have been closely involved at every stage in the planning.

The project was first conceived many years earlier at the start of the 1970s. Multiple delays then ensued. Only two things were initially certain: that the Centre would be located on the site of the old Kowloon-Canton Railway terminus at the tip of the Kowloon peninsula, and that its exterior design would be entrusted to the government's Chief Architect, José Lei.

Mr. Lei's department was already designing the cultural venues for the town halls in the new towns of Tsuen Wan, Shatin and Tuen Mun. These, though, were relatively simple, basically updated versions of the City Hall Concert Hall on the opposite waterfront. What is not known is if those in charge of the relevant government departments realised that Mr. Lei and his colleagues had virtually no experience of the enormous complexities involved in designing major international and much more highly specialised performing spaces.

Of paramount importance in all concert halls and all opera house/lyric theatres is their acoustics. In just the previous couple of decades a great deal had been learned internationally about new performing spaces and how their acoustics work. Before then it was often more a matter of trial and error based around a few obvious principles. By the final quarter of the 20th century, acoustics had become a science in its own right.

There are very specific reasons why the 'sound' in certain performance venues is superior to that in others. Three primary issues need to be considered – the volume of air in the performance space within which sound waves can first blend and then reverberate, the layout of the audience seating which to a large extent dictates exactly how that sound will reverberate, and the type of materials used in construction which assist in reverberation and in determining the quality of the overall sound. Taken together, in large part they dictate how successful or otherwise the space will become for both performers and audiences.

Given the vital importance of the interior acoustics, by the late 1970s most architects accepted that acoustic specialists must be brought in to the design process at the earliest possible stage. After all, audiences come to hear a symphony orchestra, a solo recital, or to watch an opera or other theatrical performance. Performing spaces should be developed from the inside out. The exterior architecture is of much less importance to those attending and performing inside.

Albeit many years too late, the then Music Director of the Hong Kong Philharmonic, the distinguished international conductor Edo de Waart, made this clear in a paper to the Home Affairs Department in relation to the West Kowloon Cultural District in 2009. He wrote –

"Concert hall acoustics are profoundly determined by the shape of the room. It is for this fundamental reason that the acoustic needs of the hall must be understood before any external design concept can be commenced. This inside-out approach is crucial to the success of concert hall design and requires a very close relationship between the acoustician and the architect before the first pencil is lifted."[1]

Despite this, for whatever reason almost impossible today to comprehend, Lei decided first to design the HKCC exterior. The Kowloon site in Tsim Sha Tsui had a very considerable plot area that certainly permitted a reasonably large degree of flexibility for design. Lengthy discussions with acoustics and theatre consultants could – and should – have been undertaken long before any exterior shape was finalised. They were not.

Unfortunately, Lei was enamoured with the functional Nordic modernism of Finnish architect, Alvar Aalto, who had designed Helsinki's somewhat severe Finlandia Concert Hall. Aalto was an unfortunate model. After that Concert Hall opened in the early 1970s, its function was immediately a major problem. As one journal commented, it had "acoustics that horrified performers and audiences alike."[2] Major and expensive changes including to the elevation of the stage and the lowering of the ceiling height had later to be undertaken to make it barely acceptable for symphonic concerts.

Perhaps nowhere is the difficulty of accommodating performing spaces within fixed exterior architecture better illustrated than in Sydney. Opened in 1973, Jørn Utzon's Sydney Opera House is a stunning marvel of design and engineering, one of the world's most iconic buildings. As celebrated architect Frank Gehry stated when awarding architecture's highest honour, the Pritzker Prize, to Utzon in 2003 –

"Utzon made a building well ahead of its time, far ahead of the available technology . . . a building that changed the image of an entire country."[3]

Today the Sydney Opera House remains by far the country's largest tourist destination, attracting almost 11 million visitors annually. Many consider the Opera House itself a work of art built for the performance of works of art.

But inside is a very different story. Within those imposing shell structures, both the Concert Hall and the Opera Theatre continued until very recently to present a myriad of huge difficulties. It is known that Utzon's rough concept designs had paid little attention to the interior spaces, as he never expected he would win the international design competition which had attracted 233 entrants. In fairness, though, many of these problems were to result from extensive political interference in the years immediately prior to its opening long after Utzon had been fired from the project, issues that need not be examined here. The only relevant point concerns the largest space. Originally intended as the Opera Theatre, quite late in the construction this was changed to become the Concert Hall. Some of the political powers-that-be feared there would not be a sufficiently large audience for regular opera performances to justify nearly 2,500 seats. Thus the much smaller theatre intended for drama became the Opera House. Never having been designed for opera, it was hopelessly inadequate with little wing space at each side of the stage and an orchestra pit incapable of handling other than medium scale forces.

Across from the now smaller Opera Theatre, creating a Concert Hall from the much larger space resulted in many major design issues. First was the fly tower for scenery which allegedly had cost around A$500,000 and which was now not necessary. It was jettisoned. Then the problems arising from making it into a concert venue necessitated major acoustic adjustments. Although several series of changes were made over the coming decades, until recently the acoustic in the Concert Hall remained a near disaster.

Writing in 2007, the long-time critic of the *Sydney Morning Herald*, John Shand, described a space with "low frequencies which turn to sludge, high frequencies ping around, and the presence of drums makes jazz sound like the *1812 Overture*." Five years later, music critic Bernard Zuel described "awful sound . . . woefully thin and scattered."[4] Only the most recent two-year closure for renovations, costing a whopping A$150 million and unveiled in August 2022, seems finally to have resulted in much applauded improvements. While audiences have marvelled at the very positive changes in the sound within the Hall, it is the musicians in the Sydney Symphony Orchestra who have been perhaps most impressed. Andrew Haveron, Concertmaster of the Sydney Symphony, described the new acoustic as "a miracle."[5]

The recent renovation is only the latest of many. In 2017 a major transformation of the Joan Sutherland Opera Theatre was completed after a seven-month closure. In all, renovations over a decade have cost a whopping A$300 million. If this illustrates anything it is that spending time on what is vital at the outset will always save vast sums later in the life of an arts building. That necessitates the engagement of acknowledged experts in their various fields.

In choosing José Lei as the architect rather than putting the HKCC project out for an international design competition or even for discussions with a small shortlist of possible architects, Hong Kong was stuck with that very severe, fixed exterior structure imposed by Lei. The two main spaces required height – in the Concert Hall primarily for acoustics and in the Grand Theatre to hide the rectangular cube above the stage housing the fly tower. Lei solved this with curved roof shapes slanting upwards and outwards towards the edge of each end of the structure. He then slanted the overall design into a gentle V-shaped structure.

There was a strong rumour at the time that the overall shape of the HKCC was meant to be viewed from the air – the outstretched wings of a large bird floating over the Kowloon peninsula. That dictated the angle at which the two large elements of the Centre were to be seen by passengers flying into the old Kai Tak airport from the west. Were that allegation to have any element of truth, within just nine years it became all but redundant when Kai Tak airport was closed and the new airport to the north of Lantau opened. Few would thereafter see that 'bird' shape.

The physical constraints presented by this V-shape resulted in many complex problems. To solve them, the government engaged TPC. Since construction had been given top priority, TPC opened its office in Hong Kong and Alan Russell arrived from London in 1978 with a brief to create interiors with world-class symphonic and lyric/operatic facilities.

Russell confirmed to me in correspondence in late 2017 that Lei had informed him at the outset the exterior footprint of the 'bird' shape was sacrosanct, despite the obvious problems it posed for the interiors. One in particular was lack of space at the stage end of the Grand Theatre. Russell wanted much more width for the stage. By the 1970s it was becoming common for the full stage area in a new lyric theatre to have large computer-controlled side and back stages – three near-identical areas as luxuriously spacious as the main stage itself. The result is an inverted "T" shape with the audience sitting in front of the centre at the top of the "T". This shape permits three complete scenes to be prebuilt in advance of curtain-up with one area remaining empty. To change scenery, at the press of a switch the entire stage picture that had just been seen by the audience moves into the empty space and the next act slides in to take its place. That whole process can take little more than a few minutes.

Lei's design footprint did not have anything like this width or depth for the Grand Theatre stage. In this respect the exterior is very similar to the restricted width offered within the individual shells in what became the Opera Theatre in Sydney. Citing Sydney's major liabilities for opera, acclaimed opera director Sir David McVicar has bemoaned that they result from "a very limiting blueprint" (by which he means footprint.)[6] That same criticism can rightly be made of the HKCC venues.

Naturally, when opera and large-scale spectaculars are not being performed, the result is a considerable amount of unused space. But the cost savings resulting from the inverted "T" layout on manpower, technical and performance time can become very considerable over the years. With adequate sound-proofing, each area can when required be used for rehearsals. Some opera theatres get by with just two additional stages, but within the HKCC footprint there was still not sufficient space for even one.

Nevertheless, Russell and his team set about their task hoping that Lei could be persuaded to make some modifications to the exterior design. They were not successful. Lei would not budge! TPC's internal design for the Grand Theatre was basically a traditional opera house horseshoe shape, thereby making it ideal not only for opera but also for smaller-scale lyric performances and drama. In a unique twist, the tier blocks for audience seating closest to the stage could be opened out in order to create a larger proscenium opening, thereby making the space more suitable for larger opera productions and the blockbuster Broadway musicals that would start coming to Hong Kong in the 1990s.

TPC's Concert Hall envisaged a basic rectangular shoe-box design, the same shape that is to be found in the world's concert halls with traditionally the finest acoustics – the Grosses Musikvereinsaal of the Vienna Philharmonic, the Concertgebouw in Amsterdam and Boston's Symphony Hall being amongst the most notable.

By the 1970s architects and acoustics specialists were certainly experimenting with different auditorium shapes. Herbert von Karajan, one of the finest conductors of his time, wanted a more intimate audience experience for the new Concert Hall being built for his Berlin Philharmonic Orchestra. That hall which opened in 1963 places more of the audience at the sides and back of the stage in a design that has come to be known as the 'vineyard' shape. Extremely rare is a circular or oval shape, if only because controlling sound waves and creating an even reverberation is far more complex. Virtually any variation to the traditional rectangular shape requires far greater time for acoustic design modelling prior to any other design work being considered.

It is worth noting that as the HKCC was in the process of planning and design, in other parts of Asia many superb and ultimately far superior arts facilities had either been opened or were in the process of design and construction, both by the public and private sectors. Symphony Hall in Osaka, said to be the favourite concert hall of von Karajan, Tokyo's Suntory Hall, Seoul's excellent Arts Centre Concert Hall and Taipei's National Theatre and Concert Hall had all opened by 1987. In the 1990s Kuala Lumpur's 900-seat Petronas Concert Hall with superb acoustics designed by Kirkegaard Associates, Shanghai's French-designed Grand Theatre, the Takemitsu Hall in Tokyo Opera City and a host of others all opened. Of the Takemitsu Hall, famed cellist Yo-Yo Ma is on record as saying –

"This hall simply has some of the best acoustics in which I have ever had the privilege to play."[7]

I have attended concerts in all of these halls, including more than two dozen in Taipei's shoebox-shaped Concert Hall. Its seating capacity of 2,077 is virtually identical to the original design capacity of the HKCC Concert Hall. The feeling of size and the acoustics could not be more different. Whereas Hong Kong's has a cramped feel and an overly dry and patchy acoustic, especially in the stalls, Taipei's has a glorious resonance throughout, as ideal for solo recitals as for full symphonic concerts. I particularly recall one concert with the Staatskapelle Dresden under the late Giuseppe Sinopoli consisting of excerpts from Wagner's *Ring* cycle. Not even at the opera house Wagner himself designed at Bayreuth have I heard such rich and wondrous sound. A much more recent all-Bach recital in 2017 by the acclaimed pianist Sir Andras Schiff attracted a full house of relatively young Chinese who were so enrapt you could have heard the proverbial pin drop. When Jaap van Zweden conducted the New York Philharmonic in that hall in a programme of Brahms and Stravinsky early in 2018, he must have wondered when Hong Kong would finally have a similarly excellent Concert Hall worthy of the Hong Kong Philharmonic of which he was then Music Director.

Here, though, I must pause to glance back not merely at the long history relating to a Cultural Centre in Kowloon but a more general history of the arts in Hong Kong, and in particular venues for music and the arts. In the 1950s and 1960s two businessmen with a love of the arts, Harry O'Dell and to a lesser extent Harry Weinrebe, had brought some performers including violinists Isaac Stern and Alfredo Campoli, pianist Louis Kentner and the excellent Academy of St. Martin's in the Fields chamber orchestra with conductor Neville Marriner from London. O'Dell in particular relished his role as Hong Kong's first classical impresario. Venues for classical music were a problem, though, as none was more than barely acceptable.

In 1956 the Los Angeles Philharmonic Orchestra had to present concerts in an open-air basketball stadium in Mongkok. When the Vienna Philharmonic, then the world's finest orchestra, performed three years later its conductor, von Karajan, refused to give performances in an outdoor venue. Alterations were made to the old Lee Theatre at the top of Causeway Bay's Percival Street to provide a barely acceptable concert venue.

By that time, planning was being finalised for Hong Kong to have a purpose-built Concert Hall with 1,450 seats and small 500-seat theatre as part of a new City Hall complex on the Central waterfront. But these would not be ready until early 1962.

With no government department then involved in the provision of arts and culture in Hong Kong, it was decided that responsibility be taken on by a new CSD within the Urban Services Department of the Urban Council. This no doubt came as some relief to the councillors and their staff whose other responsibilities up to this time had included the far less glamorous functions of city cleansing and hawker control.

But it posed a problem. Hardly anyone in Hong Kong had any experience of running any cultural facilities, let alone helping design them. Many were later to comment that the City Hall Concert Hall auditorium is remarkably like a scaled-down version of London's Royal Festival Hall with the seats themselves being an exact replica.

Once the design was finalized, another branch of CSD had to find product to put in the new facilities. This proved less problematic than at first thought. Concert agents around the world had been taking note of the rapidly growing interest in classical music in Japan. Some of the artists travelling to Japan would soon be offered to the CSD. Other agencies, as well as diplomats responsible for the arts in Hong Kong's consulates, also began offering artists. Along with local amateur companies and the regular official functions it hosted, it was not long before the City Hall Concert Hall had become a magnet for a variety of international visiting artists and ensembles. Few were of top international standard but only because the seating capacity of the Concert Hall prevented the CSD from offering the level of fees such artists demanded. Not unnaturally, though, the CSD was rapidly growing in size to cope with the demand.

The arrival of Sir Murray MacLehose as Governor in 1972 was to play the next vital role in the development of the arts in Hong Kong. MacLehose was no stranger to China, having worked variously in Fujian, Hankow and Beijing. He had developed a major interest in Chinese culture and spoke Mandarin fluently. It was perhaps an indication of the enthusiasm for the arts in general shown by Sir Murray and Lady MacLehose that, even though I was a total newcomer to Hong Kong, as the incoming General Manager of the Philharmonic I was invited to a small private dinner party in Flagstaff House during the week of my arrival (the official Government House was then closed for the installation of air conditioning). MacLehose believed strongly that simply importing artists and ensembles was only a small element in instilling a real interest in arts and culture among the general population. Just as Japan, South Korea and the Philippines had their own professional orchestras and other performing companies, so Hong Kong should develop similar performing software in addition to constructing venues.

British Airways was then the only carrier permitted to fly direct services between London and Hong Kong. Linking with the London impresario and former director of the Edinburgh Festival, Sir Ian Hunter, it had a small department dedicated to developing arts festivals in various parts of the world. The idea was far less philanthropic than financial. BA knew only too well there were times each year when its passenger loads to certain destinations took a dive. A festival would not only fill seats with the large numbers required by orchestras and ballet companies. It could generate some additional passenger traffic with arts lovers. On top, there might be subsidies for helping put a host city/territory on the international arts map.

Although traffic to Hong Kong had always suffered a downturn around the period of Chinese New Year, the territory had not been considered a viable centre for an arts festival due to its distance from the UK. Then fate stepped in. During 1972, while finalising plans for a festival in the Caribbean, the host country pulled out. BA was left with a festival and nowhere to locate it. Charles Hardy, a logistics manager with BA, came up with the idea of Hong Kong.

So it was that in early 1973, the Hong Kong International Arts Festival, run by professional arts managers in London and not local civil servants, was born. The much respected and admired local businessman Sir Kenneth Fung Ping-fan agreed to chair a high-powered local committee to swing public opinion round to the festival. The entire event was a major success and planning started to make it an annual event. Inevitably virtually all the early performers were imported from overseas. As Hong Kong developed its own professional performing companies in ensuing years, each would eventually be incorporated into the annual festival programmes.

Again with MacLehose's encouragement, the amateur Hong Kong Philharmonic Orchestra turned professional at the start of 1974. As with many orchestras with limited resources and, to be frank, a lack of experienced professional direction despite the enthusiasm of those involved, as we have seen it took some years before its teething problems were brought under control. With more professional arts companies being funded as the years passed, the need for a second arts facility on Kowloon was revisited.

When TPC was engaged for the HKCC project, it worked hard to squeeze in all the requirements of the brief for top international facilities. But the government's priorities suddenly had to be rescheduled when Hong Kong entered a period of recession in the early 1980s. Somewhere in the administration it was decided that TPC was no longer required. One reason given at the time was that the TPC plans had gone much too far over budget – due it must be said to the need for the late and hugely costly addition of an underground car park. A termination payment was negotiated. Allegedly this amounted to £1 million.

By the time planning got back on track, much of the budget for consultants had been spent on the TPC termination fee. Then the most irrational decision was made. Instead of going back to TPC, José Lei decided to start on the interior designs from scratch. Despite his lack of knowledge of international opera houses and concert halls, he decided to produce, out of a hat, design drawings and models that would fill the brief, fit into the exterior shape he was determined to have and come in within the budget.

Yet another allegation that has not been disproved is that Lei then looked at books illustrating concert halls around the world. From these he selected as template for the HKCC Concert Hall the very unique design of the town hall in Christchurch. Certainly, when you look at the footprints, architectural drawings and photographs of their interiors, the similarity between the two halls is more than striking. Each is basically an unusual circular/oval shape with audience seating in front, at the sides and behind the stage.

Selecting Christchurch as the model led to very specific problems, though. Acoustics is not merely a question of the physics of sound and how sound waves will behave within a given space. A knowledge of the differing acoustical properties of the various instruments of the orchestra and the art of music is as important as the engineering of the space in which the music is to be produced. As noted, extensive acoustic modelling is essential well in advance – especially to ensure an ideal balance and reverberation time.

The acoustic requirement for a symphony orchestra varies considerably. In general a reverberation time of between 1.8 and 2 seconds is felt to be ideal, although some like Tokyo's Suntory Hall go up to 2.1 seconds. The relatively new Elbphilharmonie in Hamburg with its stunning exterior has a reverberation time of 2.3 seconds.

Of equal importance is ensuring an even balance both of the multitude of sound waves and of the volume of the sound throughout the entirety of the space. There is little point having wonderful acoustics and excellent balance in part of a concert hall if both are inferior in others. At the same time, the stage itself must offer an excellent balance for the orchestral musicians since it is vital that all the different groups of instruments be first able to hear and then blend with each other.

A lyric theatre suitable for opera generally requires less reverberation time than that for a classical symphony orchestra concert hall. It is partly for this reason that the original opera theatres were built with a large stalls area and tiers of boxes rising high around it. That horseshoe shape provides plenty of air within which the sounds from the stage and orchestra pit (nowadays sometimes involving more than 200 artists and musicians) can blend and reverberate. Most experts agree that ideally an opera theatre needs a reverberation time of around 1.5 seconds.

As discussed earlier, the result is obvious. Designing from the outside in too often leads to excessive compromise – and not a few times to disaster. Lei's key problem now was that he had already decided on his austere exterior bird shape. Inside there was virtually no option. The Concert Hall and the Grand Theatre had to be squeezed in to the spaces within the bird's wings. Those spaces were simply not large enough to fulfil the brief. Many of the resultant problems continue to this day.

The space allocated for an oval-shaped Concert Hall loosely modelled on Christchurch was much too small. The plot ratios are quite different. Hong Kong has neither the same width nor the same length. Christchurch has a large auditorium with 2,500 comfortable seats. A quick look at the footprints of the two halls makes the difference abundantly clear. The Christchurch auditorium is a more circular shape. It then opens up to a very large stage and backstage area. Because the HKCC Concert Hall footprint is shorter and narrows dramatically from front to back, the auditorium and the backstage area had to be progressively squeezed, resulting in side balcony sections and a backstage area that are much smaller.

Inevitably this had a major effect on the acoustics of Hong Kong because the sound waves behaved very differently from Christchurch. Apart from a greater volume of air, the Christchurch acoustics can be altered through the positioning of a double set of massive louvres almost completely circling the auditorium. These start immediately above the top row of the audience and extend most of the way to the ceiling. Visiting artists of the calibre of Leonard Bernstein, Dame Kiri Te Kanawa and Sir Bryn Terfel lavished praise on those acoustics.

Had the HKCC Concert Hall capacity been downsized to provide for, say, 1,500 seats, that oval might have been more successful. But the CSD was determined to provide a flagship Concert Hall with more than 2,000 seats. Just as the exterior footprint was sacrosanct, so were the interior requirements. It was a classic example of the unstoppable force meeting immovable object. The latter won.

This all resulted in a smaller volume of air within the hall with less space for reverberation. Worse, the louvres which are such a vital feature of Christchurch had to be placed much higher up the side walls with space only for one set, not two. Since these are also much smaller, their effect is also reduced. To ram in as many seats as possible, the back of the stalls area had to be extended well up underneath the first-tier overhang, creating yet more acoustical quirks for those sitting there.

Worse for patrons, the physical seats selected for the hall may have been comfortable in the stalls where there is a wider distance between rows, but resulted in zero leg room in the upper tiers. Sitting upstairs for any length of time was hugely uncomfortable. The seats have since been modified but the increased legroom remains infinitesimal.

Lei's team had also failed to estimate the amount of space on the stage required for each musician. Consequently the stage proved too small to accommodate large orchestras, particularly when bigger percussion sections were required. The only way to comfortably fit 80 or more musicians and their instruments on that stage was to build temporary extensions to the front, thereby reducing the number of seats in the stalls and again playing havoc with the acoustics. That temporary ad hoc solution has since become permanent with the Concert Hall seating reduced to just over 1,950.

By far the biggest problem was the fact that the hall's acoustics were very different depending on where you sit. The sound is neither even nor balanced throughout the auditorium. I once sat close to the extreme right of the front stalls for a concert by the Asian Youth Orchestra. During the piano concerto, I could actually hear the action of the piano keys!

The louvres, such a key feature of Christchurch, were found to be all but useless. We have already seen what happened when the distinguished violinist Isaac Stern entered the stage with his colleagues to check the balance for their chamber music concerts. The louvres had been in the down position, supposedly ideal for chamber music. Stern disagreed. He ordered the louvres raised. And that is how they played their three chamber concerts.

For years the hall's acoustics continued to present problems for audience and musicians alike. With so much criticism the government had little choice but to turn to yet another set of consultants, Ove Arup & Partners. With the stage by now permanently extended and audience seating reduced, in 2011 after two years of studies Arup designed a new over-stage reflector canopy. This greatly assisted the balance for the orchestra on the stage and to a certain degree in the rest of the auditorium. But the overarching problem of the hall's variable acoustics has never been solved. These have been variously described as poor, patchy, unbalanced – to as bad as appalling.

The Grand Theatre also suffered from the lack of consultants' inputs at design stage. With 1,750 seats, it looks larger. Indeed, some have remarked that it is like a typical post-war Rank Organisation cinema in the UK. At least the seats are more comfortable and the acoustics more acceptable for opera performances.

Far less acceptable is that there is no intimacy. In the auditorium the first tier starts almost at the back of the stalls and the second tier starts almost at the back of the first tier. There is little overhang. Consequently there is a huge distance between the front of the stage and the back row of the top tier. Indeed, that distance is greater than even that at London's Royal Opera House. Yet the Royal Opera is a traditional horseshoe shape and has 500 more seats than the HKCC Grand Theatre!

At least in designing the Concert Hall, a call had gone out relatively early in the process for assistance from Professor Harold Marshall who had headed the acoustics design team for Christchurch. But with Hong Kong's fixed exterior shape imposing so many restrictions compared to Christchurch and the insistence that there be at 2,100 seats in a space too small to accommodate them without having an adverse effect on the overall acoustic, it soon became clear there was little Marshall's team could achieve.

For the Grand Theatre, technical consultants were obviously near the bottom of someone's list. Eventually a theatre consultant was finally engaged, but this time at an extremely late stage. During 1989 John Wyckham was commuting from London as a primary technical consultant for the Opera House within the Seoul Arts Centre due to open three years after the HKCC. As John told me on one visit to Hong Kong, he had been belatedly asked to stop over on his trips to Seoul to try to solve some of the many technical issues that kept on arising with the Theatre. What particularly annoyed John was not simply that many could have been avoided if he had been brought in at an earlier planning stage. The administration would also not pay any portion of his air tickets! He could therefore only be in Hong Kong to work on practical problem-solving as dictated by his Seoul commitments. One example of a key issue he would certainly have solved became clear almost as soon as the Grand Theatre opened.

The theatre's expensive power flying system for scenery had been donated by Jardines. Neither the specifications nor from whom it was purchased is known to this writer. What is certain is that it did not work as a well-thought-out flying system should work. Despite TPC having been removed from the project years earlier, that same company was finally approached in 2000 to replace it in its entirety. With work only able to take place when the stage was not in use, replacement was not completed until 2005. That proved an extremely costly solution to a problem that would not even have arisen had a specialist consultant like Wyckham or an expert from TPC been engaged in the theatre's early planning stages.

Backstage in the theatre there is hardly any wing space on stage right (the left side as viewed from the audience) and elsewhere insufficient space for changing scenery and scenery storage for complex productions. Now that major lyric theatres have also opened in Shanghai, Guangzhou, Beijing, Harbin, Dalian, Wuxi, Tianjin and other Chinese cities, each with vastly larger and much more impressive backstage facilities, the possibility of Hong Kong being part of a circuit for big-scale productions touring to China's major cities is stymied simply because the Grand Theatre cannot offer anywhere near similar facilities.

The narrowing of the footprint of the Concert Hall as it nears the stage end has already been discussed. Yet even an issue as simple as dressing rooms was to cause yet more major headaches. Since concerts normally involve only one conductor and one soloist, the Concert Hall was designed with just two dressing rooms at stage level. Each is nicely equipped with mirrors, cupboards and showers. The key problem is they are absolutely tiny. With the oval tapering off at that end, they could not be anything but tiny!

The HKCC opened with great fanfare in November 1989 with a pair of concerts given by the Hong Kong Philharmonic and the distinguished American diva, Jessye Norman. I was delighted when asked by Ms. Norman's New York manager, Harold Shaw, to look after her during her visit to Hong Kong.

She loved her suite at the Regent Hotel. With the Berlin Wall coming down, the first thing she did was send a fax to her dear friend, the distinguished conductor Kurt Masur, who had been in constant communication with the East German government to help avoid bloodshed as that government collapsed.

Indeed, all went well until she saw that dressing room at stage level. She was utterly horrified. She immediately said she would not use it. It would be impossible! "This is worse than a cupboard," she announced. Accustomed in other opera theatres to far larger spaces, she said no singer could possibly prepare for a performance in such a space. Singers must spend considerable time vocalising prior to a performance. This requires spending time singing both *piano* and *forte*. To do so in a tiny room the reverberation could negatively affect eardrums. Worse, she wanted windows so that she could inhale unairconditioned air. Singers especially hate air conditioning because it quickly dries the vocal cords which must always remain moist. When I had worked with Dame Kiri Te Kanawa in the height of summer two years earlier, she had even insisted on the air conditioning being switched off in her suite at the Mandarin Hotel, despite the build-up of heat.

Hence Ms. Norman insisted on a larger room. The only possibility was to accommodate her in a room on the first floor. But this was open to the audience. Screens were quickly found, but they were not large enough to prevent some members of the public seeing her head as she moved between that room and the stage. It was intensely embarrassing for the Concert Hall staff as much as for one of the world's most celebrated artistes.

If audiences are largely unaware of some of the difficulties I describe above, they cannot fail to notice the lack of windows in the entire audience circulation areas. This surely had to be some form of design madness. How any architect anywhere could even consider designing a building situated on one of the world's great natural harbours without allowing artists, audiences, or even just casual visitors the opportunity of seeing that view over to Hong Kong Island remains as mysterious as why no one in government appears to have put up any serious resistance to José Lei's severe exterior design. Sixteen years after its opening, Lei was still defending his windowless structure and dismissing the constant criticisms from so many quarters. To this writer his comments illustrate an almost total lack of understanding of the purpose of an iconic cultural building. He wrote –

"The Hong Kong Cultural Centre is environmental [sic] friendly. Any use of glass means you allow sunshine and heat to enter, which translates into huge cost for air conditioning and electricity . . . I was instructed to build a cultural centre rather than something for people to enjoy the harbour. People go to the toilet and have a drink rather than looking at the harbour during intermission of a concert."[8]

Lei's comments about what audiences do at intermission are amazingly depressing, providing proof he had little clue about audience behaviour and the purpose of performing arts complexes. The performance is only part of the totality of the audience 'experience'. He is correct in implying that many concert halls do not have impressive views. But in a much larger number, including most of the more recent arts facilities, if there are views architects always make it a point to enable those views to be seen. Looking outward is a perfect accompaniment to always looking inward during performances.

Lei also totally failed to understand that a beautifully designed iconic building can be a huge boost to tourism and in attracting a new public to the arts. Examples abound. The Sydney Opera House attracts nearly 11 million visitors annually. Frank Gehry's glorious Guggenheim Museum in Bilbao has led to what is called "the Bilbao effect". Gehry's iconic titanium-clad building housing part of the Guggenheim's vast collection completely altered that city's economy. In 1995, two years before its opening, Bilbao hosted 25,000 tourists. In 2019 that number had increased to over one million. The museum hosted 531,000 visitors in 2021, it is one of Spain's leading tourist attractions, it has transformed the tourism economy of a traditionally depressed city and witnessed the location of many new businesses.

More recently, in its first year the stunningly located glass-clad Elbphilharmonie Concert Hall in Hamburg not only doubled the number of subscriptions for classical concerts; the total number of visitors was an astonishing four million. The building now attracts 17,000 a day, most just to see around the building's interior and its views.[9] That the tip of the Kowloon peninsula has merely a characterless, solid lump with zero exterior attraction for residents and tourists is endlessly depressing. Indeed, one question really needs to be asked: has the existence of the HKCC as a structure resulted in any new visitors to Hong Kong whatsoever over the last 33 years? I consider it unlikely in the extreme.

For yet another of the key criticisms of the HKCC, it is important once again to revisit that exterior shape. Squeezing the two main performing venues into the bird's wings resulted in a huge amount of wasted space between them. The lobby atrium area in the HKCC is massive. It has been described variously as utterly soulless, looking more akin to the world's largest public toilet, a vast expanse decorated by small pink tiles and containing nothing but four staircases. Given his comments above, I wonder if Mr. Lei ever considered the wasted cost of the electricity required to air-condition that massive space night and day!

Unlike most performing arts buildings being planned and built worldwide around that time, its food and beverage outlets remain archaic. It operates a queue and ticketing system that is amongst the most user-unfriendly anywhere around the world that I have ever experienced in my long career. I still remember my first visit to the Bavarian State Opera in Munich in 1975. At the intermission, it was so utterly simple to purchase a glass of *sekt* even with a full house. I also had time to follow that with a small bowl of fresh warm raspberries with ice cream.

Instead of one huge atrium hole, each floor above could have had that space covered to provide several levels accommodating comfortable bars, coffee shops, restaurants and other audience facilities, thus avoiding the need for everyone to descend to ground level, purchase coupons and, rather like pupils at school lunches, join long queues for one red or one white cheap wine in a plastic cup. That the latter practice continues is an ongoing and damning criticism both of the CSD and now the LCSD who have been managing the venue for almost three-and-a-half decades.

But where were the civil servants when the HKCC was in its design stage? How many had visited major arts facilities overseas to see how interior cafes, bars, other refreshment areas and even restaurants are part and parcel of the concert- and theatre-going experience? Properly run, these can generate very significant ongoing commissions for the management of the cultural facilities. But then, José Lei had determined his structure would have no windows. It is hard to estimate how much revenue has been lost resulting from the lack of nicely designed interior food and beverage outlets, even on days when there are no performances. Uninterrupted views over the harbour to Hong Kong Island would be priceless in drawing patrons and visitors to such facilities.

The foyer area is a disaster for another key reason. One huge foyer catering to two major venues is far from ideal. Arguably the most successful theatrical producer in the world as I write is Sir Cameron Mackintosh, with *CATS, Les Misérables* and *Phantom of the Opera* amongst his major credits. He has always believed it is vital to start creating the atmosphere for any production as soon as an audience walks through the main entrance. He told me he much prefers small foyers with low ceilings and some degree of crush. He believes this anticipatory buzz before an audience actually enters the auditorium greatly aids his work as the producer and equally the audience for what they are about to experience. This completely echoes comments made to me by the late Michael Hampe in

1975 when he was the Artistic Director of the Cologne Opera with its massive foyers in the post-war Opera House.

In essence, as soon as one arrives in a concert, theatrical or other performance venue, the space you enter should immediately take you away from everyday life and into something that is obviously special. There has to be a feeling of expectation. The HKCC has none!

I have to add in fairness that whatever the many criticisms and no matter the building's defects, there is no doubt that the HKCC has made a contribution to the development of Hong Kong's arts and culture. Who could have believed in 1989 that the Hong Kong Philharmonic would become a truly world class orchestra under Music Director Jaap van Zweden, despite the many faults in the Concert Hall? Who would have believed that all three venues within the HKCC would have attracted such a variety of productions and concerts – and sold so many tickets since it opened?

When rendering criticism, however, I just happen to believe it was an act of supreme folly not merely to fail to look at the other far superior performing spaces being built in the region at the same time, but also to look back at the errors which the administration made when the City Hall performing arts complex was going through an eerily identical planning process.

In this context, it is instructive to review the deliberations of the Legislative Council. At its meeting on February 20, 1952, the Hon. Kenneth Barrett, Chairman of the Urban Council, made the following statement –

"It is our earnest wish, Sir, that the new City Hall shall be a building which is more than just architecturally sound. It must dignify and embellish its magnificent setting of harbour and hills."

Waxing lyrical in his speech, he then went on to defend government architects in general.

"In short, Sir, it must be the building of Hong Kong's twin cities, to be spoken of as the great buildings of the past were, and some of them still are, spoken of – the Parthenon at Athens, the Pharos at Alexandria,

King Solomon's Temple at Jerusalem, the Temple of Heaven at Peking, the Hanging Gardens of Babylon, the Pyramids. All these, Sir, so far as I can trace, were designed by government architects."[10]

What an extraordinary statement! That Legco meeting agreed not to put the project out for tender. Instead design would be undertaken by the government's Architectural Office of the Public Works Department under the control of the Chief Architect. The vote was 16 in favour and one against.

I cannot believe that anyone, even at its opening in 1962, can possibly accept that the City Hall structure "dignifies and embellishes" its harbourfront setting. It doesn't! It looks like a small office building, pure and simple, for few notice the building close to the ground which houses the arts facilities. Further, in absolutely no way does it merit any comparison whatever with the iconic buildings quoted by Mr. Barrett. He had totally failed to draw attention to the glaringly obvious fact that whereas one government architect might be a genius, the next few hundred are more than likely to be average at best.

Some of the faults in the City Hall Concert Hall can be put down to inexperience. Others are inexcusable. That there was no air conditioning backstage at stage level would have been regarded as near-idiotic by any experienced orchestra manager or even player. Instruments in an orchestra need to be tuned. This is not just a case of all playing together the 'A' sounded by the oboe once everyone is seated on stage. Once an instrument moves from a non-air-conditioned space with a summer temperature around 30 degrees Celsius to a stage where it is closer to 20 degrees, the instrument requires more than a few minutes' time to adjust. When I attended my first Philharmonic concert in early March 1979, I was surprised and more than slightly upset to hear so many members of the orchestra come and play their instruments on stage many minutes prior to the silence as the concertmaster made his entrance. Only later did I learn about the air conditioning problem.

Very sadly, it is perfectly obvious that no member of the administration in the 1970s took the trouble to look back at that history. Had they done so, surely there would have been much greater opposition to awarding the design of the HKCC to a chief government architect with no expertise in the design of performing venues of the highest international standard?

I trust that those who made the decision to award the design to José Lei and who are still alive now accept that the design process for the HKCC was a hugely wasted opportunity. Had they been less narrow-minded, Hong Kong might conceivably have been given a stunning, eye-catching iconic structure at the tip of the Kowloon peninsula, its performing spaces far more suited to the excellence of those now gracing its stages and a tourist mecca attracting many millions over the years. Instead, the city has a monstrous, pink-tiled, windowless albatross. The lessons arising from the design process of the City Hall complex were never heeded.

Earlier I mentioned a performance I had attended of excerpts from Wagner's mighty *Ring* cycle in the glorious acoustics of Taipei's National Concert Hall. Given the HKCC's many failings, in summing up the HKCC saga I end with a quotation from one reviewer who attended the Hong Kong Philharmonic's epic performances of *Götterdämmerung* in 2018. This appeared on the Interlude website –

"Much as *Götterdämmerung* marks the HK Phil fully coming of age, the Hong Kong Cultural Centre is in its desperate dotage. It simply cannot decently accommodate an extended performance such as *Götterdämmerung*. The uncomfortable seats, irregular acoustics, and horrid public areas are bad enough. A six-hour Wagner evening points a spotlight on the shocking food and beverage outlets, consisting of a small Starbucks and an even smaller cash-only bar serving cheap drinks in plastic cups and industrial sandwiches filled with what certainly must also be plastic . . .

"If only it were the twilight for the Hong Kong Cultural Centre, and this city would finally get a performance venue worthy of its global status and of its world-class orchestra."[10]

* * *

As a postscript, I have been enormously impressed not only by the performances but also by the sound quality of the Naxos 'live' recordings of the Philharmonic's *Ring* cycle. I wrote to Klaus Heymann who still ran the label to congratulate him on their success. I particularly offered congratulations to the sound engineers as I had absolutely no idea how they made such a poor acoustic in the Concert Hall sound so amazingly good. He wrote back, "Neither do I!"

Those concert performances of *Götterdämmerung* took place at the Cultural Centre as a prelude to the celebrations for the 30th anniversary of its opening in November the following year. As an aside, the plan had always been for the Hong Kong Philharmonic to open the Concert Hall with a full symphonic concert. During my final season with the orchestra in early 1986, I had received a letter from the CSD confirming this honour. It stressed the installation of the large pipe organ and expressed the hope that we would select a work for orchestra that would heavily feature the organ.

There is really only one standard repertoire symphonic work that fits that bill: Saint-Saëns Symphony No. 3 with its prominent organ part in the final movement. But I felt we really needed to feature a work that could involve more organ, greater forces as well as a large choir. I was thinking about the monumental *Te Deum* by Hector Berlioz. In six movements lasting approximately 50 minutes it has a major part for the organ in each movement that is almost as prominent as the considerably expanded orchestra. It also requires massive choral forces including a large boys' choir. The final movement *Judex Crederis* is guaranteed to bring the house down! The other benefit is that it requires only one tenor soloist for just one of the movements. There would be no requirement for several fees for several artists – just one. I believed no other work better fitted the bill for the second half of the programme. After agreement from Kenneth Schermerhorn, I wrote to make the suggestion to the Committee.

Amazingly, I received a response advising that in the committee members' opinion the Berlioz did not feature enough of the organ. What? Not enough? This was so utterly ridiculous I could hardly believe I was reading it! I even suspected not one member of the Committee had actually heard this work. So I wrote back informing members that Ken and I had wracked our brains and could not come up with another suggestion barring a very lightweight Handel organ concerto with a cut-down orchestra. I threw the question back to the Committee. Which work would it recommend that we consider?

The response was laughable. It suggested Beethoven's Symphony No. 9. Beethoven's Choral Symphony certainly has the benefit of a large choir but it does require four soloists for the last movement. Extraordinarily, though, it has no part for organ! I felt as though we were all part of a sketch in the *Monty Python's Flying Circus* television series! Surely the committee members, the supposedly great and the good who controlled much of what took place in the arts in Hong Kong, could not be serious!

Before the symphonic programme for the opening concert of the HKCC could be finalised, the Committee learned that the diva Jessye Norman would be free following a Japan tour to sing at the pair of opening concerts. Although she had been booked by the CSD, I received a last-minute call from her manager, Harold Shaw, asking if I would drop everything and look after her. A problem had occurred in Japan when the conductor who was also scheduled to conduct the Hong Kong concerts had turned up for a concert of 20th-century music not knowing some of the detail of the scores. Woldemar Nelsson was then fired from all remaining concerts on her tour. For Hong Kong, Claudio Abbado's assistant at the Vienna State Opera, Ion Marin, had been engaged at just days' notice. Harold was concerned that he had never worked with Jessye. Should any further problems materialise, he said he believed I would be better able to sort them out than the staff at CSD who would have so many other programmes and artists to look after.

As mentioned earlier, I was absolutely delighted. I flew to Tokyo and accompanied her on the flight back to Hong Kong. At the concerts she sang arias by Mozart and the famous *Seguidilla* and *Habanera* from Bizet's opera *Carmen* which she had recently recorded with Seiji Ozawa conducting. Having taken her to the rehearsal, I marvelled once again at that glorious voice. Additionally I soon learned that she was a master of the quick repartee and had a wonderful sense of fun.

With about ten minutes remaining of the final rehearsal, someone remembered that one of her big fans would be in the audience that evening, Britain's Prince Charles. The British national anthem would have to be played and Ion Marin had never conducted it. So the Hong Kong Philharmonic's librarian raced to find and distribute the parts. With only seconds left, Marin raised his baton and the familiar strains of *God Save the Queen* were played.

It was not generally known outside Britain that the full 14 bars of the anthem should only be played when the Queen as head of state, or someone officially representing the Queen, is present. For other members of the royal family, just the first six bars are played. So Marin stopped the anthem without launching into the final eight bars. Jessye Norman was sitting in the stalls while I was on the stage.

Immediately she asked, "Why not the full anthem?"

Marin admitted he had no idea. I therefore volunteered the information that it was because "the Queen herself would not be present." With a chuckle, her large and deep voice boomed from the darkened stalls –

"What do you mean the Queen will not be present? *I* am the Queen!"

23

THE SUPERSTARS: PAVAROTTI, DOMINGO AND CARRERAS

During the 15-year period between 1990 and 2005 I was very fortunate to spend much of my time working on concerts with the three great tenors of the age, Luciano Pavarotti, Plácido Domingo and José Carreras. These started with Pavarotti's first concert in Hong Kong in 1990 followed by others in Shanghai, Beijing, Taipei, Taichung, Seoul, Manila, Singapore and again in Hong Kong in 2001; Domingo's concerts in Singapore in 1990 and Hong Kong in 1992; and several regional tours with Carreras starting with his first recital in Hong Kong in 1991. Importantly, I was to help set up and manage the last three public concerts Luciano was ever to sing before a paying public – in greater China during December 2005. Not only do all these concerts require a book virtually on their own, at the end of 2022 I did finally publish a book covering many of my experiences with these and several other top international artists titled *Backstage with Pavarotti and Other Egos: Disasters on the High Cs*. Consequently I will only repeat here a few of those experiences.

Needless perhaps to say, however, the disasters frequently did not always involve the tenors themselves, for the entourages that surrounded them were responsible for a great many: several instant cancellations, frequent postponements, over-protective managers and promoters whose vocabulary and outbursts would make even hardened blue-collar workers blush. First there was Pavarotti's personal manager, Herbert Breslin. The British conductor Brian Priestman, who worked twice with the Philharmonic during my years with the orchestra, told me that

Herbert was known in the music business as "the biggest barracuda in the fish tank!"[1] For Herbert, a spade was always a spade! I had first been introduced to him when having breakfast with Tibor Rudas, the craggy-faced concert promoter with a contract to arrange up to 20 arena concerts each year for Luciano. Some weeks before my concert in Hong Kong, we had all attended a Pavarotti concert in Osaka. When Breslin was introduced to me the morning following the concert, he looked me straight in the eye.

"Mr. Duffus, are you arranging the orchestra for the concert in Hong Kong?"

"Yes I am, Mr Breslin."

"Well, I trust they will play better than the shit lot we heard last night. They were fucking awful!"[2]

Then there was Tibor Rudas. A former member of the Boys Chorus at the Hungarian State Opera, he was in love with opera. After his voice broke he concentrated on acrobatics in addition to his studies. When the Second World War erupted, he managed to avoid the Nazi round-up of Jews until near its end when he was consigned to the Bergen Belsen concentration camp. After gaining his freedom, he emigrated to Australia where he worked on entertainment projects. So successful was he that he was lured to run the entertainment at the Tropicana Casino in Las Vegas. His casino enterprise soon added entertainments for casinos in the Bahamas and then Atlantic City.

But catering to the needs of the artists he presented, headliners like Frank Sinatra, Dean Martin, Diana Ross and Dolly Parton, was one thing. He still desperately wanted to become involved in classical music. He spent many months persuading his casino bosses that there was a market for classical music, as he was soon to prove with concerts in Atlantic City by the likes of soprano Dame Joan Sutherland and violin virtuoso Itzhak Perlman. But Tibor always wanted the biggest and the best. There was only one artist at that time who filled that bill: Luciano Pavarotti. Although it took three years, he finally managed to persuade Breslin that Pavarotti would present one concert in Atlantic City for an agreed fee that had finally been negotiated of around US$100,000. This was for just two days' work. To earn a sum of that magnitude, he would almost certainly have had to sing in many performances at New York's Metropolitan Opera covering the better part of several months!

The relationship that was to develop between Pavarotti and Rudas was virtually a marriage made in heaven. Rudas was thrilled that he built a strong friendship and trust with Pavarotti. Luciano thrived on large audiences; 8,000 filled that first Atlantic City concert. These would soon increase to 12,000, 15,000 and even occasionally up to 250,000 in London's Hyde Park or New York's Central Park. Luciano embraced those audiences as though in love with them. And they embraced him back. He became the biggest, richest and most adored superstar in the history of classical music.

In his wake, though, he and Rudas left behind a string of promoters, many of whom suffered from his seemingly casual approach to contracts and performance dates. My two Hong Kong concerts were to result in major postponements. The first, originally scheduled for December 9, 1989, was to have taken place in the Hong Kong Coliseum and should have seen my company make a very substantial profit. Unfortunately, even though tickets had gone on sale months in advance, this concert was postponed not once but twice, before we ended up with a third take-it-or-leave-it date on February 11, 1990. After being informed of the second postponement, I made a quick trip to California for an urgent meeting with Rudas in a vain attempt to renegotiate the contract, for the Coliseum was not available for that February date. Only the new Exhibition Centre in Wanchai was free, and it could only hold 8,000 seats. The loss of 4,000 seats was a crippling blow. Any level of profit would be hard to achieve. I managed a slight degree of renegotiation but little more. By 5:00pm at the meeting with Rudas we all shook hands when suddenly the office on the first floor of a small two-storey largely wooden building in Pacific Grove started to shake. I assumed it was merely a heavy lorry passing outside. It was a great deal worse. The strongest earthquake to hit the San Francisco area in 83 years had just struck. Measuring 6.9 on the Richter scale and located only 35 miles away in the Santa Cruz Mountains, it was the most damaging quake to hit the area since that disastrous one in 1906. I felt Pavarotti's Hong Kong concert was definitely jinxed.

By this time in his career, Luciano had been cancelling and postponing too many concerts and performances. Earlier in 1989 the Chicago Lyric Opera had banned him from further appearances with the company on the grounds that he had cancelled, often at the last minute, 26 of his last scheduled 41 performances. He did finally come to sing in Hong Kong. Although the Exhibition Centre was not a good venue, the audience seemed to enjoy the concert and pleaded for encore after encore. Before then, there were times during the concert when I felt the applause after arias bordered on the lukewarm. Sitting in the front row next to Herbert Breslin, I became nervous when Herbert turned to me and said –

"I must congratulate you, Mr. Duffus. You are the only promoter I know who has managed to get an audience out of a graveyard!"[3]

As I was to learn, it was a typical Breslin comment. Fortunately, at the end of the concert the audience cheered and cheered.

While he also caused havoc by postponing my second Hong Kong concert scheduled for June 2001, I will highlight here just one other concert in which I was heavily involved: a *Three Tenors* concert featuring Pavarotti, Domingo and Carreras. It illustrates the difficulties – some might suggest near-impossibilities – of doing business with Tibor Rudas.

The request for a *Three Tenors* concert had come from a concert promoter in Taipei with whom I had been working for more than a decade. He was aware of my involvement with Pavarotti's Asian concerts and that I had a direct line to Tibor Rudas. One of his regular sponsors, a prominent television station, was soon to be launching a new free-to-air satellite television service from Hong Kong for all of China. This company was keen to curry favour with the Beijing municipal government and the Chinese ministry dealing with telecommunications. It had decided the best way would be to present a really big event in Beijing to coincide with the final visit of the Olympics Bidding Committee to Beijing the following summer, some three weeks before the full committee selected the city to host the 2008 Summer Games. Beijing had declared Saturday June 23 as "Olympics Day" and the event had to take place on that date. If there was a big enough event, the Beijing authorities had promised it would be possible to hold it in the Forbidden City. I was asked to sound Tibor out about a *Three Tenors* concert.

This was never going to happen! It was a fool's errand! How could anyone be given the rights to host any 'live' arts event in such an historically unique venue as the extraordinary Forbidden City? It was true that three years earlier the Italian film director, Bernardo Bertolucci, had produced his Oscar-winning movie *The Last Emperor* with many exterior scenes being shot within the City's courtyards and palaces. I was aware, too, that a number of concerts and operas had been presented in a smaller palace adjacent to the main complex. But that location could only accommodate around 6,000 seats. A *Three Tenors* concert would need at least 20,000 mostly high-priced tickets at a minimum.

I almost never made that call to California. What was the point of the cost of even a phone call when the chance of the tenors and their large retinues being available on one specific day less than nine months away was as close to zero as you can get? Yet after I thought about it, I just decided to get it over and done with.

When I got through to Tibor, I outlined the request. Impossible! He had another city already booked on that date and was awaiting the deposit. But he might be able to offer me a date three days before or after, provided the fee was high enough. I was quickly able to get back to him with the information that the only possible date for Beijing had to be June 23. He expressed his regret and wished me luck finding another mega-event. And that, I believed, was the end of that!

Even at the start of the new millennium, Tibor never used emails. It was always either phone calls or fax. So it was no surprise that I was awoken early on a Wednesday morning several weeks later.

"John! Do your clients still want a Beijing concert on June 23 next year? If so, tell them urgently I have worked wonders to make sure the tenors can now be available for them. But time is extremely short and I have another city ready to pay.

"Here's the deal. I need your client to remit $400,000 to my Swiss account by the close of business on Friday. No paperwork. This is not a deposit. It is a goodwill gesture to show they are genuine. Provided they do that, I will eventually send you a draft contract and give you one week in which to agree the fee and finalise all the details. Assuming it is signed, I will deduct the goodwill payment from the deposit. If they fail to sign the contract by the deadline, the negotiations are at an end and they lose their money."[4]

No-one likes seemingly impossible deadlines, and the television company on whose behalf I was ultimately working was a public company. It was not going to deposit such a large sum into a stranger's account without at least knowing the final fee and having some backup paperwork.

I was still sure nothing would come of the idea, but I was pressed by my client to try and obtain Tibor's signature on a one-page memorandum of agreement. This would at least enable the client to remit the goodwill payment. As usual with Tibor, the answer was 'no'. But by then I had learned how to work with him. By the following morning he had reviewed a relatively simple memorandum I had drafted. Having cleared the wording with the sponsors, I faxed it to Tibor – and waited. By that evening I had his agreement and the following morning a faxed copy of the document with his signature. The goodwill payment was remitted later that afternoon.

Before then, we knew that the total fee would be in the region of US$3.1 million – plus all expenses. Luciano and José would require private jets to get them to international gateways before flying first class on an international airline to Beijing. Tibor wanted me to know this would not work for Plácido. At that time he would be in the middle of a series of performances at the Mariinsky Opera in St. Petersburg. He would therefore require a private jet to fly him to and from Beijing at a cost Tibor estimated at around $500,000. I assumed this would be a deal breaker. Not at all! My client was desperate for this concert actually to take place.

I had informed Tibor we would need about a month to get all the paperwork prepared. Thereafter we could receive his contract and the clock could start for signature. We required that extra time for, in addition to Tibor's master contract, several other contracts were required. Not only was it essential for the sponsor to have a partner in Beijing, that partner would need a raft of contracts with the Beijing municipal government and various national government departments for all the permits required before any concert could proceed, especially the agreement to hold the concert in the Forbidden City.

A month later I spent an entire week in the offices of a top law firm in Hong Kong. Before then I had been through Tibor's draft in detail and knew there were several issues I could negotiate down on the sponsor's behalf. Additionally I had spent a lot of time tweaking the wording since staging the event in the Forbidden City was hardly like working in other cities where there had been *Three Tenors* concerts.

As we approached Tibor's deadline, we had cleared all the hurdles in the master agreement. But the sponsor still had several major items to finalise with its partner in Beijing. To expedite signature of the master, one of the company's executives got on a plane to Beijing for a series of hastily arranged meetings. Then at virtually the last minute, one key issue remained outstanding. We simply would not be able to get the Beijing contract signed off in time to get Tibor's master contract over to Miami where he was presenting another of his Pavarotti arena concerts. Aware of his temper and the likelihood that he did indeed have another city ready to take over the date, I called him at his hotel.

I begged for an additional 12 hours and explained why. Predictably he was irate, but soon calmed down when I reminded him that with a 12-hour time difference the signed contract would still be on his fax machine early in the morning. Our extra hours would be when he was mostly asleep. Finally he agreed he would countersign the faxed draft and we could commence detailed planning. We made it with about three hours to spare.

We still had only fax copies of the signed agreement. Since the sponsor wished to make a big public relations splash about the event, it was agreed we would all fly with a television crew to Chicago shortly before Christmas where Tibor was presenting yet another *Three Tenors* concert. It would also provide an opportunity for the tenors to film a short 30-second promotion in Chinese for airing throughout China.

Chicago in mid-December is mind-numbingly cold. When I arrived, it was even too cold for me to walk outside our hotel. Presumably because no other was available, Tibor had booked – of all venues – an ice rink! As we arrived for the concert, whatever heat had built up in the arena during the day quickly evaporated, leaving an audience shivering in their seats. Far from conducive to an evening of pleasant music-making, the concert just seemed to drag on almost interminably. As usual, things livened up during the encores, but it was with some relief that I went to warm up backstage when it was all over.

Tibor told me the TV promotion commercial was just being filmed in one of the dressing rooms. As I sat in another dressing room, time dragged on with the approved version of this short clip taking well over 30 minutes. With filming complete, Tibor suggested I get a limousine over to the VIP dinner venue. He still had some other business with the tenors for he would not have an opportunity to see them all together again for some months. Heading for the exit, one thing surprised me: the presence of a large number of Koreans. I had no idea why they were there. I soon put them out of my mind.

The VIP dinner was in aid of the Chicago AIDS Foundation and held in an elegant function hall in the converted Chicago Union Station. Several hundred guests in black tie and their wives dolled up to the nines were seated at round tables anxiously awaiting the arrival of the tenors who would be seated at three tables set high on a smallish stage. I assumed I would be at a table on the floor of the hall. But no. I was ushered to the middle table on the stage where some other guests of Tibor's were already waiting.

With a further hour passing since my arrival, dinner had started and the patrons below were finishing their dessert when Pavarotti, Domingo and Carreras finally made their entrance. I felt this a disgraceful lack of courtesy on Tibor's part to have them arrive so late. As those of us on stage were finally able to start our meal, many of the patrons had trooped out to their waiting limousines, each collecting a goodie bag at the door with gifts from various sponsors. Not for the first time at one of Tibor's events, I felt more than a little embarrassed.

Three days before the *Three Tenors* concert in June the following year I arrived in Beijing. I had worked on several tours with José Carreras and we had become good friends. I hoped there would be time between rehearsals for us to have a quick cup of coffee. After dropping my bag at my hotel, I got a taxi over to the Beijing Hotel where the tenors, Rudas and the many other members of the party were staying. At the front desk I was told that Mr. Carreras was not staying there. It is not unusual for major artists to use different names in hotels so they will not be continually pestered by members of the public. But I could not recall José ever using an assumed name before. And I could not think what name he might be using apart from David Giménez, his conductor nephew, or Lorenzo Bavaj, the regular pianist for his recitals. No, neither a Mr. Giménez nor a Mr. Bavaj were guests. So I tried to contact Tibor. Oddly, he too was not staying there! Nor were any members of his technical and production team. Where were they? They should all have been working hard getting all the staging and lighting ready in the Forbidden City.

The following day I was met with the same stories. Neither the tenors nor anyone from the Rudas Organisation were in Beijing – allegedly. When I met up with the local Beijing presenters, all I got were blank faces. Surely there had to be rehearsals going on somewhere in Beijing? One of the biggest entertainment events in China's history, one that was being televised throughout China and recorded for DVD in two days' time, yet the participants were nowhere to be seen. Something was going on. Whatever it was, I was more than annoyed I had not been informed about it.

So I just waited for the concert. That evening I was seated in the front row next to Marta Domingo. My friends were in corporate seats which had cost US$2,000 each and were located about 20 rows behind me! It was only after chatting with Mrs. Domingo that the pieces began to fall into place about the mysterious disappearances. It had all been to do with the large number of Koreans I had seen backstage at the concert in Chicago the previous December.

When I had first contacted Tibor, he had been on the point of finalising a concert for Saturday June 23 in the huge Olympic Stadium in Seoul. After informing him Beijing had to be on that date, he started to work out how he could kill two very lucrative birds with one stone. The obvious course was to move Seoul forward or back by three days, but Plácido could not free up time due to his prior commitment in St. Petersburg. Besides, the Seoul organisers were only interested in a concert on a Friday, Saturday or Sunday evening. Since Seoul was probably paying Tibor slightly less than my client for Beijing, I suspect he then decided first to finalise the contract for Beijing.

Then at those extensive December backstage meetings in Chicago, the reason for the overlong delay in getting to the dinner venue became clear. Tibor was having difficult and no doubt heated negotiations with the tenors and the Koreans to find an alternative date for the Seoul concert. I suspect the Koreans had actually paid their deposit before I appeared on the scene and like others before them were now faced with a near impossibility of finding an alternate date very quickly or losing the deposit. After lengthy discussions a solution was reached. The Seoul concert would be presented not three nights before Beijing, not two nights beforehand – but on the previous evening. That this was an utterly staggering decision was made even more extraordinary by the fact that the tenors actually agreed to it.

The basis of the deal was that the tenors would first arrive in Beijing for two days during which there would be a large media conference and preliminary rehearsals with the orchestra. Private jets would then take them on the two-and-a-half-hour international flight to Seoul, followed by two more rehearsals with the Korean orchestra. Following the Friday evening concert before an audience of around 70,000 in the extreme heat and humidity of a summer evening in Seoul, the tenors were whisked to a hotel for a contractual appearance at the VIP dinner and a quick bite to eat. Then it was back to Seoul's private jet terminal, immigration and customs formalities, the flights to Beijing, more immigration and customs formalities followed by a fleet of limousines to the Beijing Hotel. I doubt if they reached their rooms before 4:00am at the earliest.

To make this all work, the Koreans were sworn to secrecy. They were permitted to market their concert but only in South Korea. International media exposure was strictly prohibited. If the world had got to know that three singers in their late 50s/mid 60s had agreed to such a mad schedule, accusations of their being totally money-grabbing would have been difficult to live down. As it turned out, Tibor had guessed correctly. Word did not get out. But singing two long open-air concerts in such enervating conditions with rehearsals and extensive travel in between added to insufficient rest took its toll, at least in Beijing. It was clear that José and Luciano were far from at their best throughout the evening. Only Plácido with his extraordinary stamina sounded vocally fresh. I felt for those sitting behind me who had paid so highly for their tickets. It was virtually a slap in the face.

At the end of the concert, I went backstage to chat with the tenors and congratulate them on the success of the concert. I did not believe it had been a success. Yet, as so often happened with concerts featuring the tenors, the audience had clearly loved it. They had purchased their expensive tickets to see three legends in the world of opera rather than to enjoy an artistic experience of the highest standard. At least it had all looked magnificent.

24

MUSICALS #1: MY FIRST ATTEMPT TO PRESENT *CATS*

As I was in the process of leaving the Philharmonic in the summer of 1986, I was so busy lining up classical music projects that I had little time to concentrate on my other objective for Pacific Images – commencing a series of Broadway musicals that I hoped could tour in the region in addition to long seasons in Hong Kong. Until the late 1980s, Hong Kong had seen very few musicals. There had been a week of performances of *Chicago* in the early 1980s and less than a handful of performances of 'bus and truck' versions. 'Bus and truck' refers to the cheapest form of production that depends mostly on cloth scenery. After a Saturday performance, the cast travel in a bus and the scenery is rolled up into a truck for the trip to the next town on the tour. The production is re-assembled in that town's theatre on the Sunday ready for an opening on the Monday for a run of seven or eight performances.

One of the few bus and truck productions I had attended was of Lerner and Loewe's *My Fair Lady*. Of all venues it was in Singapore's vast Indoor Stadium. A production intended for a small stage with an orchestra of only around nine musicians and mostly cloth scenery cannot – or at least should never – be mounted in a 12,000-seat stadium. The local producer had cut capacity to around 1,500 which meant all the audience was seated on ground level. In such a barn of a place, though, of atmosphere there was absolutely none. I walked out at the interval.

My ambition was to give Hong Kong and regional audiences the same level of staging experience they would gain from attending performances in London, New York, Sydney or other major capitals. Inevitably this would be vastly more expensive than my own company's resources could consider, and I was a virtual novice when it came to the financing of musicals. Equally, all my past experience had been based on marketing arts performances that would run for at most three nights. To make a musical work, it would be necessary to find audiences to fill the theatre for several weeks. That is a very different discipline.

I therefore decided to start in a small way and limit my ambition to Hong Kong. Even before I left the Philharmonic, I had decided that Andrew Lloyd Webber's *CATS* would be the ideal starter. With the combination of music, songs, a single fascinating set, stunning cats' costumes and, of course, the hit song "Memory", it would be, I assumed, relatively simple to present. So I wrote to Lloyd Webber's Company in London, The Really Useful Group (RUG), seeking a licence to present a version of the show in Cantonese. I received no reply. I wrote again – twice – before getting a response that basically stated, "No!"

Looking back, I am amazed at how naive I had been! How could I possibly have mounted a production requiring such fantastic singer-dancers? Who would have produced and choreographed it? Where would I have found the finance? How could I possibly translate it into Cantonese when Cantonese has nine tone levels and would be impossible to fit any of Lloyd Webber's melodies? It would almost certainly have completely changed their meaning! I quickly realised that if I was to make musicals work, I would need an experienced partner. But who?

Knowing of my background in opera, the Director of the Hong Kong Arts Festival, Keith Statham, asked if I would undertake the duties of Company Manager for the Festival production of Wagner's *The Flying Dutchman* he planned for the 1987 Festival. It was during one of the stage rehearsals that I met for the first time the production's costume supervisor, Sue Wilmington. Over drinks one evening I was lamenting my bad luck with RUG. What I did not know at that moment was that only a few months earlier Sue had been the assistant to the brilliant designer whom I had known well at Scottish Opera, Maria Björnson, and who had designed the sets and costumes for *The Phantom of the Opera* in London.

"Don't speak to Really Useful," was Sue's advice. "I'll talk to Cameron for you and see if I can set up a meeting when you are next in London."

Now I was again amazed! Cameron Mackintosh was arguably the world's most famous producer of musicals at that time. Sue was true to her word and within a few months I was having lunch with Martin McCallum, the managing director of Cameron's company. Martin explained they were anxious to find a way of extending the runs of their Australian productions and Asia seemed the obvious region. I left our meeting with an agreement that I undertake a tour of the capitals of most Asian countries researching the possibilities of mounting musicals that could run for at least three weeks or more in each. The one country of no interest to them was Japan, but only because they already had a very profitable joint venture there with a Japanese company.

Until Cameron started his collaboration with the Shiki Theatre Company, most Broadway musicals had been limited almost exclusively to versions in English straight from an American tour, performing for around four weeks in Tokyo and two in Osaka. When Cameron and Shiki wanted to produce *CATS* in Japan two years after its London opening, they needed more than the usual six weeks since *CATS* could not recoup its costs in just six weeks. They wanted an open-ended initial 12 weeks so that the production could run as long as there was public demand for tickets, as in the west. Open-ended runs were unheard of in Japan at the time. It was therefore little surprise that no theatre owners were interested.

Since *CATS* had a self-contained set that required no flying of scenery, Cameron and Shiki decided a formal theatre was not essential. So they rented a plot of land next to the Keio Plaza Hotel in the city's skyscraper district of Shinjuku and mounted a specially adapted version in a large tent. Most of Japan's theatre establishment will have been shocked when it ran for two whole years in that one location. With the landowner anxious to redevelop the site, Shiki took the production and the tent to Osaka for many more months. They then returned to another plot of land, this time on the eastern side of Shinjuku station. And again the production ran for years. The Japanese phenomenon of *CATS* continues and has totalled more than 10,000 performances. *CATS* is still being performed in Japan and was scheduled to run at least until May 2024. More than 10 million Japanese have now seen *CATS*. I sometimes wonder what the theatre owners who turned down the production in 1983 now think about all the massive profits they could have made!

For the other countries in the region, none of us expected more than a few weeks in each city, the more so given that the region had seen no musicals of that size and scale. But with many Asians having been educated in the west and accustomed to occasional visits to musicals, we were certain there was an audience and that we could attract them. Before I started my visits, I flew to Melbourne to see the 1,000th performance of *CATS* in Australia and to meet the directors of Cameron's Australian company, John Robertson and James Thane. Soon we were all considering a 16-week tour to take place in Kuala Lumpur, Singapore and Hong Kong for early 1990.

In July the year prior to the tour I was having a holiday in Penang when I received a most unwelcome fax. As with all their tours and productions, the Cameron Mackintosh company depended on investors to come up with the pre-production capital. Often called 'angels' in the business, they put up the initial investment and in return received a regular dividend when the show went into profit. Many angels invest primarily for the 'face' value of being associated with a show, for most accept that the chance of losing the entire investment is traditionally extremely high. One of the major investors for the *CATS* Asian tour had unexpectedly pulled out at the last minute, too late to find a similar amount elsewhere. So the tour had to be cancelled.

As I had negotiated my fee on the basis of weekly costs plus a small share of the profits, I suddenly found myself with a large hole in our budget for the first half of 1990. Added to the losses from the postponement of my Pavarotti concert, I became more than desperate about how Pacific

Images could find its way out of the sea of red ink that now threatened to engulf my small company. Very fortunately I would soon find myself working on a longer tour of *CATS* in the 1993/94 season, but this would be for Andrew Lloyd Webber's own company, RUG. And that truly is another story!

25

YET MORE OF THE CLASSICAL SUPERSTARS

That first Hong Kong concert with Pavarotti in February 1990 had been all but a financial disaster given the loss of revenue from 4,000 seats and about US$150,000 in additional costs. When I had first met with Tibor Rudas to discuss it a year in advance, it almost never got near a contract. Rudas made it clear that he would only operate on the basis of a partnership with him being the senior partner. Additionally, he had to receive an advance on his share of the profits of US$400,000 within one week of the contract being signed.

Pacific Images had absolutely no possibility of making that deposit. I had been very concerned that with my foot finally in the door, the deal itself would collapse. In order to find the funds, though, I had contacted the relatively new worldwide agency IMG Artists. Although the parent company International Management Group (IMG) was the world leader in sports event and athlete representation with offices in more than 40 cities around the world, it had recently taken over a small artists' agency in New York with a view to developing a new branch for its business. Six years later in 1990 it still only had a small dedicated staff to look after classical music events based in New York and London. Thanks to my knowing one of the senior artists' managers based in London, he had recommended I become an IMG Artists consultant and was already managing its arts events in Asia. In sport, IMG worked with many high-income-generating sports stars and also on managing much more lucrative sports events. It was keen to do the same in the arts for it believed there was unlocked earning potential in at least some of the big names. To achieve this, it would need to work more with superstars like Dame Kiri Te Kanawa and the three most famous tenors. It was therefore necessary that it go on the acquisition trail to find a manager for Asia. Fortunately for me, I was ideally placed.

After a series of meetings in London and Sydney, it offered me a very sweet deal. It would take over Pacific Images which then had considerable debts and repay to my business partner and me our initial capital investments. In return I would become the Director of IMG Artists for Asia and move to Tokyo which it felt was a more profitable location for its Asian base than Hong Kong. I was both surprised and thrilled with the offer. Having made around six annual trips to Tokyo during the previous nine years, I had fallen in love with the city and the country. I felt it was virtually my second home after Hong Kong. Not that I would be missing Hong Kong, for my role in charge of Asia would see me returning to Hong Kong for three or four days each month to continue overseeing recitals and concerts. The original Cartier Master Musician series was continuing but with YSL as the sponsor. These recitals included performances by Yo-Yo Ma, Isaac Stern, Alexis Weissenberg, Anne-Sophie Mutter and the Chung Trio. The latter included three members of the Korean Chung family – one of the world's great violinists Kyung-wha Chung, her sister the noted cellist Myung-wha Chung and their younger pianist/conductor brother Myung-whun, the same Myung-whun whom we had considered as a possible Music Director of the Philharmonic back in 1983.

Not all the recitals were without occasional hitches. The most difficult came in 1991 with the formidable Bulgarian virtuoso, Alexis Weissenberg. Despite an often icy demeanour when seated at the keyboard, he could produce electrifying and breathtaking performances. He worked regularly with virtually all the major conductors of his day. He was a particular favourite of Herbert von Karajan with whom he had recorded several concertos. Indeed von Karajan had said of him, "with his personality and remarkable insight, he is one of the key performers of the 20th century."[1]

I had contracted him for recitals in Hong Kong and in Taipei two evenings later. After his arrival he said he was most anxious to discuss something with me. Could he invite me for dinner that evening? We dined at the Mandarin Hotel's Man Wah Restaurant. Initially we made only small talk as he seemed reluctant to bring up the real reason for the dinner. So I broached the subject.

"Maestro, you said there is something urgent you would like to discuss."

He looked me directly in the eyes.

"I am sorry but I have to make a change in the recital programme."

"Which work would you like to replace?" I asked.

"All of them!"

That shook me! It was not unusual for an artist to seek to change one work in a programme, especially if it was one he had not performed complete before. Programmes are not just thrown together. Almost always they have a theme or the works have a specific coherence. As one who had been giving recitals since he was eight years old, more than half a century earlier, Weissenberg must surely have provided me with a recital programme that he knew would work, I had assumed. But no! He never gave me a reason. I was left with two recitals for which the programmes had already been printed and it was too late to do other than make an announcement prior to the recitals and provide a quickly photocopied sheet of basic information.

Outside the Cartier and YSL series, I did present other occasional recitals, especially with artists with whom I wished to work, artists like the wonderful Spanish pianist Alicia de Larrocha, violinists Pinchas Zukerman and Cho-liang Lin, guitarist Narciso Yepes and double bassist Gary Karr (referred to in Chapter 11). Although all were excellent, the most outstanding was undoubtedly one with another piano virtuoso, the amazing American Earl Wild whose memories of Rachmaninov I also recount in Chapter 11. He had additionally been friends with the conductor Arturo Toscanini for whom he worked for eight years and with whom he made the first-ever recording of Gershwin's *Rhapsody in*

Blue. At the start of the 1980s, the doyen of music critics in America was Harold Schoenberg who wrote for *The New York Times*. In a long two-page article, he bemoaned the dying art of the true piano virtuoso, those who were not only extraordinary performers but accomplished in the art of transcribing orchestral works for the piano. Only three remained alive, he maintained – Vladimir Horowitz, Shura Cherkassky and Earl Wild. Cherkassky had taken part in one of our Cartier recital series. A small and rather difficult man, he had played superbly.

I had first invited Earl Wild to perform the Grieg concerto just prior to the Philharmonic's Asian tour in 1983. I asked him back to the Philharmonic in 1985 and in 1990 for a recital in the HKCC of works by Chopin and Liszt, of whom he was one of the leading specialists. A tall, thick-set man with a shock of white hair, he strode on to the platform, sat gently down at the piano and without any of the histrionics that some pianists nowadays like to display, performed a programme the likes of which I have never again been privileged to witness. This was extraordinary playing of the highest possible standard.

At the stage rehearsal that morning, Earl had requested the piano tuner to bring a steam iron, in my experience before and since a unique request. He first asked the tuner to take out the 'action' of the piano – the full keyboard – to expose the hammers. He then had the tuner press the steam gently on to the felts of each hammer. This would give the instrument's keyboard action a slightly different sound, one that he believed more suitable for the works he was performing. After a short rehearsal basically to test the Concert Hall's acoustics, I took him and his manager, Michael Rolland Davis, over to Gaddi's in the Peninsula Hotel for an hilarious lunch. I knew from his earlier visits that Earl was one of the most amusing artists on the concert circuit. Our lunch was filled with much hilarity. And also many fascinating tales. His knowledge of music and musicians was encyclopaedic and his comments on the art of piano playing and some of his contemporaries stretching back to those he heard in the 1920s and 1930s, including Rachmaninov, Schnabel, Cortot, Iturbi, Rubinstein, Gieseking, Josef Lhevinne, Hofmann and others, up to then-present day including Brendel, Ashkenazy, de Larrocha, Argerich, Jorge Bolet and Cherkassky were utterly fascinating. What is even more fascinating is that many of the pianists and conductors Wild worked with had direct links to the composers themselves. Some of those earlier in the century had actually studied with students of the composers. Wild recalled in an interview that although not a pianist, in his mid-teens the great conductor Arturo Toscanini had met Richard Wagner. He then showed Wild the handkerchief Wagner had given him.

"It was a big handkerchief, a large one that looked like a lady's scarf, and was all covered with embroidery daisies. It was very beautiful," adding much to the mirth of the interviewer, "loud but beautiful!" He also relates that when he [Wild] was "in my early teens, I knew people who had played with Brahms."[2]

Anyone wishing to learn about the piano and the art of performance should immediately purchase Earl's autobiography, published after his death in 2010. At just over 800 pages, *A Walk On The Wild Side* is long but filled with so many wonderful insights and anecdotes from a true master of his craft. One pianist he did not admire was Alfred Brendel whom he describes with the nickname used by some in the music profession, 'Brendull'! He comments –

"I cannot fathom musicians such as Brendel who talk about the old composers as if he had lunch with them yesterday! He writes as though he was on intimate terms with composers such as Beethoven, Schubert and others. He portrays himself as though he knows exactly what their intentions were when writing a certain piece of music. Individuals like this are no better than cheap evangelists!" He later adds –

"I don't hear any imagination, drama or initiative in his performances. I find this type of approach to music undesirable because I believe that imagination, drama and elegance are what music is all about . . .Who wants to hear a literal facsimile of the printed page?"[3]

The parent company of IMG Artists had been founded as International Management Group (IMG) in 1960 by an American lawyer, Mark McCormack. McCormack knew the most popular golfer in the world,

Arnold Palmer, and it was a handshake deal that saw Palmer have McCormack become his manager. Although he probably did not know it at the time, McCormack was to create the totally new business of athlete representation and sports event management. He was soon managing many of the world's top sportsmen and women covering a wide array of sports including the young tennis star, Andre Agassi, and from the 1980s the extraordinary young golfer, Tiger Woods. IMG held a piece of the pie in many major sports events around the world, including the lucrative business of sponsorship and corporate hospitality. To ensure that profits from the increasing popularity of televised sports were not spread around the terrestrial networks, he founded IMG's own television network, Trans World International (TWI), which quickly became the world's largest distributor of sports programming. Within 30 years, IMG was a billion-dollar-a-year business and McCormack was titled the 'King of World Sports'.

I had twice briefly met McCormack. One group I had toured regionally on several occasions was the ever-popular Vienna Boys Choir. On one occasion in the late 1980s I was delighted we were invited to give a concert in Beijing in aid of the Soong Ching Ling Foundation in memory of that remarkable lady. Earlier I had been asked by American Express if once the choir reached Hong Kong it could sing three items at a special dinner event for their top clients. This agreed, I was then informed that Mark McCormack would also be giving an address at the dinner. Following the choir's performance, McCormack came over to me and said how much he had enjoyed the choir's singing.

When the colleagues I had made at IMG in London, New York and Sydney proposed that I be engaged as Director of IMG Artists' activities in Asia, I was informed I first had to have a one-on-one meeting with Mark. Early in 1990 he was in Hong Kong for a visit to his local office. He was also promoting his latest book, *The Terrible Truth About Lawyers*.

I had read McCormack's first book, *What They Don't Teach You At Harvard Business School*. In this he advises those interviewing candidates for a post in his company to ensure that the interviewee does most of the talking. I realised that mentioning our Vienna Boys Choir meeting would be a good way of starting the conversation but I felt I had to find some form of sporting link to get a conversation really going. My mother was a keen golfer. So I called her to ask if she had any anecdote that might impress McCormack.

"Why not mention that Stewart Lawson is my cousin?"

I had heard her occasionally mention a Stewart but had never met him and was not aware why mention of him might impress McCormack.

"He is Captain of the Royal and Ancient Golf Club in St. Andrews."

Mark was bound to know him well since IMG's golf division was heavily involved with the development of golf and Mark attended all major golfing tournaments. So, when I met with Mark, immediately I brought up the Vienna Boys Choir association and then mentioned I knew Stewart Lawson. That certainly got his attention and we got on famously. Within 24 hours I received a call from his office in Sydney (which held a watching brief over Asia) that my employment was confirmed. I was absolutely delighted.

My contract was initially for two years with an option on a third. The intention was that I would remain with the company for longer but events conspired – as they tended to do throughout my career – to ensure that I was destined for a very different form of employment, one not unrelated to my past experience.

With my work for IMG Artists and the joys and pitfalls of working on large-scale events when based in Tokyo, overall I loved my time there and had planned to take up the offer to extend my contract. Not that everything went smoothly. Being the first foreign Head of Department in a staff of just over 40, I was subjected to a number of small indicators making it clear that I was not Japanese and would always remain outside the group. Usually these would be quite irrelevant but they mounted up over time. As I was well aware, in Japan the group is far more important that the individual. As I describe later, others in more senior positions than I had similar problems.

Sometimes I would be taken aback by suggestions made by artists. When I went out to Narita airport to meet José Carreras for our first Japan tour, we were chatting in the limousine when he said there was one thing he really wanted to do once the official concerts and recitals were over.

"I want to sing in a karaoke bar!"

I could not believe that one of the world's greatest classical artists would wish to sing in a small, probably smoky karaoke bar. But he kept on about this so we decided to fulfil his wish. We talked with the owner of an elegant karaoke bar in Shinjuku, informed him that a famous singer would be coming to the bar and asked that he prohibit smoking until after José had left. Being the sakura season, the bar owner had decorated the bar with some branches of the delicate cherry blossoms. About ten of us joined José on that little excursion. When he went up to sing, he chose the popular Frank Sinatra classic "My Way". When he saw the visuals on the screen, he was delighted they were of his home town, Barcelona! In all he sang about ten songs, sometimes accompanying members of the IMG staff.

There was only one occasion when I became angry because it specifically affected me and an artist I had engaged. Prior to my arrival in Japan, Kazuo Kondo had managed the small number of recitals given by Dame Kiri Te Kanawa and a handful of other IMG artists. I had taken that 'perk' away from him. Some years earlier, Rolex in Japan had revived what was allegedly an old Japanese custom – Time Day. In early June each year, it worked with IMG to present a concert in Tokyo's Suntory Hall by a major artist. When I arrived, the head of Rolex, Chris MacDonald, said he would very much like to have the violinist Isaac Stern for the Time Day concert in 1991. I was touring Stern in Taipei and Hong Kong just before then but his manager, Lee Lamont at ICM Artists in New York, was never keen on her artists appearing in IMG Artists' events. Thankfully I knew Lee well and with the addition of an extra fee was able to negotiate a two-recital extension to my tour for two Time Day concerts in Osaka and Tokyo.

Stern was not the violinist he had been in his best years in the 1950s and 60s, but he was still a major draw. He was also well aware of events of local significance. Some days earlier there had been a major volcanic eruption at Mount Unzen near Nagasaki which killed 43 people. As he came offstage in Osaka, I had been searching for the bouquets of flowers to be presented to him and his pianist. I could not locate them. He, though, was not then concerned with concert protocol. He wanted to be reminded of the name of the volcano as he would inform the audience he was dedicating his first encore to those who had lost their lives. This was much appreciated by the packed audience.

Floral bouquets had always been the province of Kondo and his secretary. I located my assistant and asked where the bouquets were located as they would need to be presented in less than a minute. He said he had no idea, merely reminding me this was an issue for Kondo.

I have no doubt whatever that Kondo's failure to arrange bouquets that evening was deliberate. It was one way he could embarrass me without seeming to be responsible for it. When I went to Stern's dressing room to congratulate him on the recital, almost his first comment was, "No flowers?" I waffled about their having been sent to the wrong concert hall and would ensure they were delivered to his suite when we got to Tokyo the following day. But I was furious. Whatever Kondo's dislike of a foreigner being placed in his department, to embarrass one of the world's top musicians for such a petty reason was a disgrace.

For Time Day the following year we had engaged the Los Angeles Chamber Orchestra. I invited as my guests two old friends from Hong Kong, Tom and Marie Myerscough. Marie was a freelance journalist whom I had got to interview Pavarotti in New York prior to my 1990 Hong Kong concert with the great tenor. Tom had been the CEO of the British company Courtaulds, based in Tokyo for a spell in the 1980s and been recently posted back. He told me not to worry. Even as head of his company, he still found little niggling things going wrong, as if to make him remember he was a foreigner!

After much thought I left IMG Artists in Japan in 1994 to take up the post of Asian Director of Andrew Lloyd Webber's companies back in Hong Kong – as I describe in the following chapters. Thereafter I formed my second company, now much wiser and more experienced than I had been nearly a decade earlier, and I continued to be involved occasionally with Tibor Rudas and with IMGA.

In 2003, even after making Luciano Pavarotti into the most popular and wealthiest classical singer on earth, both Rudas and Breslin were fired by Pavarotti. I assumed this meant the 2001 *Three Tenors* concert in Beijing and solo concerts in Hong Kong and Shanghai later in 2001 would mark the end of my collaboration with Luciano. I was wrong.

Late in 2004, I received a call from an old friend, Harvey Goldsmith. I had known Harvey since the summer of 1989 when he presented a concert with Pavarotti in the ghastly London Docklands Arena. Harvey had immediately been in touch with Pavarotti after the ouster of Breslin and Rudas. He spoke to Luciano about mounting a Farewell World Tour in 2005. Luciano liked the idea and Harvey started working on planning. So great was demand that the tour was extended into 2006. His call to me was about my possible interest in presenting concerts in greater China towards the end of 2005 after a tour in Australia. I jumped at the chance. Although I was pipped to the post when bidding for the Hong Kong concert, we had no trouble arranging concerts in Shanghai, Beijing and Taichung in central Taiwan in December 2005. None of the 20,000 who turned up for the open-air concert in relatively cold conditions in the Taichung park had any idea at the time that this concert was to be the last Luciano was ever to sing before a paying public. By the following summer he was discovered to be suffering from pancreatic cancer. He died in October 2007. It is unlikely any of us will ever again hear in our lifetimes such an amazing voice attached to such an outgoing and loveable character. That I had had the pleasure (and sometimes the anguish!) of working with him over a dozen concerts is a joy I never expected and will never forget.

26

MUSICALS #2: THE DESIRE FOR A NEW ADVENTURE

It was when I was in Sydney for a meeting of IMG Artists' executives and to attend the first-ever arena concert given by IMG's latest client, José Carreras, that fate again conspired to change my career. Leaving the packed Sydney Entertainment Centre, I thought I heard my name being called above the babble. It was hard to look around in such a crush. Then I heard it again. Once out of the small entrance tunnel, I waited. I was delighted when a smiling James Thane came up to me. He informed me that since our last meetings over the aborted *CATS* tour of Asia in 1990, he had changed companies and now was in charge of the Australasian company of Andrew Lloyd Webber's RUG. With crowds milling all around us, he suggested we meet for tea the following afternoon at my hotel. IMG had a worldwide deal with the Hyatt group and IMG senior staff were accommodated in the luxurious Park Hyatt Hotel with a view of the Sydney Opera House from every window.

Over tea, I filled James in on my activities since that last meeting some 30 months earlier. He was not aware I worked in Japan for IMG Artists, nor understandably that I had been offered a contract extension. He then told me that in his discussions with the directors in London about joining Lloyd Webber's company, he informed them Asia would be a key part of his strategy. He even went as far as to predict that Australasia would be generating 20% of the group's profits within three years. That was a brave, if not outrageous, claim given that large-scale musicals had still not started touring Southeast Asia.

The problem, as he saw it, was that the main markets for Lloyd Webber musicals were becoming mature. In Europe and the USA profit growth would continue only as long as Lloyd Webber continued to churn out hit after hit. The view seemed to be that the hugely profitable string of long runs of musicals like *Evita*, *CATS*, *Phantom of the Opera* and possibly of the upcoming *Sunset Boulevard* due to open in the summer of 1993 were unlikely to continue.

The cost of mounting and then sustaining long runs had escalated dramatically. Even Lloyd Webber had suggested that in future musicals would be on a smaller and much less expensive scale. So James believed new markets would have to be found and nurtured. He then came round to the reason for wanting to meet so urgently. He needed someone as Managing Director for Asia. He would very much like to work with me again and felt we were both on the same wavelength. Would I be interested in the job?

Initially I really did not know how to respond! On the one hand I had enjoyed working with James. In a sense the failure to make the planned *CATS* tour happen in 1990 meant I had unfinished business. I also wanted to learn more about producing and marketing musicals. As noted, for most of my time in Asia I had been involved with concerts which were either one-offs or had at most two and three repeats. Marketing was a relatively simple matter, even in those days without mobile phones, the internet or social networking apps. Posters, flyers, occasional newspaper advertisements and media interviews were virtually the only tools available to us. If you run a musical for, say, ten weeks, how do you ensure that those wishing to purchase tickets do not all rush to get the first weeks of performances. If so, how do you fill the final weeks? In Southeast Asia there was no tradition of long-running musicals. It would be necessary to educate audiences as we were educating ourselves.

Even with unfulfilled dreams, I was still enjoying my time in Tokyo as the Asia Director of IMG Artists. It was not always easy, partly a result of the cultural conflicts. But my love for Japan had increased and I tried as often as I could to explore more of the country. For example, if there was a meeting in Kobe, I would try to set it up for a Monday morning. I could then leave Tokyo late on Friday and spend two days in the Kobe area before returning late on Monday. But that was never easy given the scope of my workload. The geographical spread of my responsibilities covered a huge area from Hokkaido in the north to Jakarta in the south. With the distance between Tokyo and Singapore being virtually identical to that between London and New York, it is hardly surprising that I was spending half of each year out of Japan. Hong Kong as noted earlier was a regular each month. Here, some of the work of the IMG Artists' Division was still directed from the IMG office where my two former colleagues from Pacific Images, K. C. Lee and Maria Tam, did much of the work. Seoul was another regular destination, as was Beijing. With the gradual development in all the arts in China and the planned construction of many new performing venues, an occasional visit was essential if only to develop the connections so essential to doing business.

I also found Tokyo an easy city to live in. I had a lovely small flat near the centre which IMG Artists paid for, I had a good salary and handsome allowances for travel and entertaining. Could I really give all that up?

My initial thought was perhaps I could. Since my move, it was clear that the big projects IMG Artists really wanted to develop were not going to happen. The spectacular bursting of the Japanese economic bubble of the 1980s had seen to that. We would still oversee various tours with artists like Joshua Bell, Itzhak Perlman, André Watts and José Carreras. These, though, hardly justified the expense of having me based in Tokyo and I knew some senior IMG staff in Head Office had started to consider returning me to Hong Kong once my initial contract had been completed. Not that that in any way concerned me, for I still enjoyed a love affair with the territory – apart from one difficulty. After I had moved to Tokyo, Mark McCormack's elder son Breck, who had started with IMG some years earlier as a lawyer in the London office, was put in charge of Asia and based in Hong Kong. He was clearly a go-getter and was quickly to open a dozen or so new IMG branch offices around the region. I got to know him reasonably well on my monthly trips back to

Hong Kong when it became obvious our chemistry was not working. I had huge admiration for his father, but when it came to the Artists Division, Breck knew little. He seemed to me someone who concentrated more on small detail than on the larger picture. No doubt he found me just as difficult to work with. I was certainly more of a maverick than he would have liked.

In Tokyo I had come to realise there were difficulties in being based on one of the geographical fringes of a major multinational company. On paper, I reported to John Webber in London, one of a group of about 16 senior executives who were particularly close to Mark. On the other hand, John knew little about classical music. His expertise within the company was corporate finance until 1984 when Mark had decided, persuaded in large part by Kiri Te Kanawa during a game of golf, that there were many similarities between managing the world's top athletes and the world's top musicians. Following discussions with another of his close friends, James Wolfensohn, a man who was passionately interested in music and was soon to become head of the World Bank, IMG had bought the small Hamlen/Landau boutique artists' management agency in New York. With no big name on its books – although the 17-year-old violinist Joshua Bell would soon become a world name – Mark and his colleagues saw it as a base from which it could expand into a major international agency. Since Charles Hamlen and Edna Landau had no major international corporate experience, John Webber was given oversight of their activities.

I found Charlie and Edna not only easy to work with, we had an immediate rapport and quickly became the best of friends. If I had only had to deal with them and Webber, life in Tokyo would have been all but a breeze. But I also had to report to Breck and to his immediate boss, James Erskine, who ran Australia with a watching brief over Asia. For the few major projects that materialised, I had to report to an old friend, Michael Storrs in London. As if keeping all these executives in touch with my activities and obtaining collective approval for some was not sufficient, I had to add a seventh to the mix. Peter Smith, the head of IMG's hugely profitable television arm TWI and a close associate of

Mark, had also to be kept in the loop. On top of all that, Kondo as head of administration in Tokyo had to be briefed on what was going on in his patch. The reporting structure and the difficulty in getting everyone to agree on decisions had become increasingly frustrating.

It was not part of my job description to talk with artists about programming. Usually this did not present much of a problem. But there was one occasion when planning a Japan and Korea tour for José Carreras almost came to a dead stop. I just could get no information from Michael Storrs about the programme José was to sing. Finally I fired off a round-robin fax basically implying that unless we got a programme within about a week, we would not have time to publicise the recital tour and might have to consider calling it off. Michael was quickly on the phone to tell me he was far too busy and that I should just call José myself. I managed to reach him in Dusseldorf. José always liked to pack his programmes with relatively unknown art songs by composers like Paolo Tosti when what the audiences basically wanted were operatic arias and perhaps a song or two from musicals. He seemed perfectly happy when I queried his choices and agreed his planned programme needed some changes. After considerable toing and froing, we finally had a programme. Yet deep down he was not really happy with my changes. In Seoul for the first recital in the 3,700-seat Sejong Cultural Centre, we were going down in the hotel lift before getting the limousine to the venue when he said he was still not convinced about the programme.

"Let's see how it goes this evening," I suggested. "If at the end you are still not happy with it, we have time to make some changes before we get to Japan."

Six encores and over 30 minutes of applause at the end convinced him that I had been right!

In the eight years since the founding of IMG Artists, that department of IMG had grown very considerably. It had added a number of major artists to its books including arguably the most famous violinist of the day, Itzhak Perlman. But the decision-making structure remained weak with basically too many people involved and too often I found this frustrating.

One example concerned the Vienna Boys Choir and my meeting with Mark at the American Express dinner in Hong Kong.

If that had helped start my association with IMG, it also played a part in my departure. The choir was not expensive and invariably popular, so I did further tours in 1990 and 1992. I was aware the choir's 500th anniversary would take place in July 1998. At one of our half-yearly meetings of the IMG Artists worldwide personnel in London I proposed that we should consider capitalising on this unique anniversary by contracting the choir for a series of special worldwide events, these to include a major television documentary which I believed could easily be sold to all the many countries in which it regularly gave concerts. I was certain the basic investment required would be small and the sponsorship potential high.

Each year the choir was split into four smaller ensembles. One would remain in Vienna for its regular Sunday concerts. The other three would tour to various parts of the globe. It was therefore one of the best known and best loved ensembles worldwide. It was also relatively inexpensive for concert presenters. By the start of the 1990s the per concert fee was US$5,000. Additionally presenters had to pay for local hotels, meals and transport plus a pro rata share on the international air travel.

Although the choir then had different managements in different countries, I felt that if we made a success in managing a series of special 500th anniversary events, there had to be at least a possibility of IMG Artists taking over the rights to many of these countries, if not worldwide. The choir would then become a very lucrative addition to the IMGA roster.

Everyone at the London meeting was enthusiastic, the more so since Mark had several times expressed his desire that IMGA work with the choir. So I was quickly despatched to Vienna for a meeting with the choir's director, Dr. Walter Tautschnig, who rather surprised me by mirroring Mark's enthusiasm. He added there would certainly be competing 500th anniversary offers from Austria and other countries. But if we were the first to make a formal bid, our offer would be considered promptly.

On my return, I circulated a report on my Vienna meeting. I outlined various touring options, ways in which representation could be acquired around the world and a series of possible highlights for the 500th anniversary documentary. The documentary film and resultant DVD would surely become particularly profitable given that an audience numbering probably more than a million heard the choir on tour each year. Many audience members would be interested in a souvenir DVD.

I awaited reactions. Mark had always claimed that one of IMG's great advantages was the synergy between its various departments. I assumed that at least the sponsorship departments around the world would come up with some possible leads to approach for such an important Vienna Boys Choir anniversary. Absolutely nothing! Occasionally I would bring the issue up at other meetings, but I was always told a decision was far from pressing. That was no doubt true. But other companies were bound quite soon to become interested in developing deals for the 500th anniversary. Although we should have been the first, no deal ever materialised.

This reinforced the opinion I had formed earlier that there was in fact very little synergy between IMG Sport and IMG Artists. It reminded me of another London meeting at IMG's Chiswick offices. After having avoided the Championships for three years, tennis great and IMG client Andre Agassi, then aged 21,was to be appearing at Wimbledon in 1991. With his long blond hair and film-star good looks, Agassi by then was a huge media star. No one in the Artists division commanded that sort of world attention. Edna made a suggestion. Hamlen/Landau had taken on a young American violinist soon after he made his debut with Riccardo Muti and the Philadelphia Orchestra at the age of 14 and he was beginning to develop a major reputation. Would it not make sense for IMG to help Joshua Bell's career by capitalising on the popularity of both IMG clients with a joint photo session?

It was a simple and obvious request that would have taken perhaps an hour of Agassi's time. It was met with an audible hush! Ian Todd, an extremely bright senior executive in the London office and one of the circle of 16 or so very close to Mark, quickly dismissed the idea. Agassi was a huge star. His schedule was already over-full. Apart from playing in Wimbledon, all his time would be taken up with practising, media interviews, sponsor receptions and other official activities. The message was clear. Once the Artists division had made Josh Bell a star at a similar level, they could perhaps discuss joint photo ops. Until then, get on with developing Bell's career! So much for the much-vaunted synergy between sports and arts!

Although the Vienna Boys Choir issue was still in the future, with IMGA I had already branched into more popular entertainment. On one of my monthly visits to the Hong Kong office, I noticed that one of the legal team was obviously having a problem judging by all the exasperated "Oh nos!" I heard him utter.

"Can I help?" I asked.

He was trying to get to grips with a 30-page closely typed American entertainment industry contract sent for the participation of one of the most popular internationally acclaimed singers of the 1960s and 70s, Dionne Warwick, for a dinner during a major golf tournament being held in Thailand at the start of the year. The annual Johnnie Walker Asian Classic brought many of the world's top golfers for a four-day event. Organised by IMG for the drinks company United Distillers, a major pop star had been requested for the gala dinner on one of the evenings and Dionne Warwick engaged. With a typical entertainment contract drawn up by a specialist American law firm, though, Graham was totally confused as to the meaning of many of the terms.

"What's a top hat?" he asked.

"A percussion instrument," I told him.

I then suggested he give me the contract to review and pass him my comments. The end result was that Graham was very happy to hand the whole project over to me. So it was that I found myself in Thailand with one of the great names of popular music. In 1971 Warwick had been signed to a US$5 million recording contract, the most lucrative for any female performing artist up till then. But all was not easy! The main problem we had with her contract was that it called for bottles of the finest Cristal champagne to be in her suite and her dressing room at all times. That was only a problem because there was no distributor of Cristal in Thailand in 1992. I therefore had to have all the IMG executives flying in from Hong Kong bring a bottle.

The following year the Classic dinner was held at the Shangri-La Hotel in Singapore when we had engaged the gospel singer Gloria Gaynor, best known for her mega-hits "I Will Survive" and "I Am What I Am" at the turn of the decade in 1980. The problem she presented was that her contract called for her to arrive in Singapore from New York a minimum of 24 hours before the start of her performance. Her agent and musicians arrived on time, but she had decided to fit in a concert in Las Vegas immediately prior to Singapore. The following morning I was going near crazy wondering what I would do if her flight from the US West Coast failed to arrive at midday on the performance day as we had been advised only two days beforehand. Thankfully it was on time. She had brought her 21-year-old nephew George who was obviously a bit new to the business. When I gave him the cue to have Gloria start the performance, as stage manager he gingerly went up to her and asked –

"Aunt Gloria, are you ready to start now?"

For some reason I found that very funny!

Near the end of the century I received a panic call from Dick Kaufman who ran a small Hong Kong advertising and PR company. He had organised an outdoor Christmas fair and had been trying for months to get Pavarotti! Could I help? By now it was late October. I scolded Dick as he must have known that I had excellent contacts with Pavarotti's concert promoter and could have checked his availability with one phone call earlier in the year. Not that I would have been successful, though, as Pavarotti would never fly thousands of miles for a one-off event like this. Besides, Dick could never have afforded anything like his fee!

Through my agent friend in Los Angeles, Merv Goldstein, in spite of the very short lead time I was able to get Dick the wonderful Olivia Newton-John. Meeting her, watching her rehearsal and performance which included a duet with one of the four Canto-pop kings, Jacky

Cheung, and having the luxury of spending some time with her was a total joy.

These concerts, though, were one-offs. At our Sydney meeting James Thane was talking about a full-time position as RUG's managing director for Asia. I told him I was certainly interested in working for RUG and would think about it. He said there was no urgency. He would be in Hong Kong a couple of months later and hoped our trips would coincide so we could chat further there. We did, and I confirmed my enthusiasm to become the first managing director of RUG's Asian operations. He asked me to meet with the RUG directors in London.

On my next visit I was pleasantly surprised when meeting the Chairman, Patrick McKenna, Finance Director, Bill Taylor, and the Business and Legal Affairs Director, Keith Turner. They seemed genuinely delighted that I was considering joining the group and the outline of an offer was made. I made only one point. James as the Regional Director was vastly more experienced in producing and marketing musicals than I. On the other hand I had far more experience of Asia. I wanted their assurance that I would not end up being simply a personal assistant, a general dogsbody type of job that is ideal at the start of a career – but I had ceased in that role almost 20 years earlier. They agreed. They added that in between seasons of the blockbuster musicals which James would originate, they wanted the Asian office to originate its own productions of smaller musicals like Andrew's delightful *Song & Dance*. London would send out the production team and we would cast mostly from local sources. It did not take me long to confirm my agreement.

How to tell IMG Artists that I wanted to leave at the end of my three-year contract, the more so as they had generously taken over the struggling Pacific Images? I decided merely to put on paper some of the frustrations I was encountering and had decided my future lay elsewhere. As IMG had an option period for a further year and my contract had a non-compete clause, the company could have made life difficult. John Webber was clearly upset. There was no long-term bad feeling, though, and in the future I would return to work for IMG Artists in Hong Kong as a consultant on a number of projects, including more tours by Dame Kiri Te Kanawa, The Kings Singers and José Carreras.

27

MUSICALS #3: CATS AND BROKEN PROMISES

And so at the end of 1992 I returned from Tokyo and found a small flat in Hong Kong's New Territories. With RUG I no longer had a housing allowance. Paying my own rent with Hong Kong property prices soaring was not easy. My salary was also considerably below what I had been earning. Against that, RUG permitted its regional directors the perks of first-class intercontinental travel and first-class hotels!

James Thane had just one agenda: getting the Andrew Lloyd Webber brand known. We were both aware that some people in Hong Kong would have heard of *CATS*, *Jesus Christ Superstar*, *Evita* and *Phantom of the Opera*. Most would know the hit songs "Don't Cry for Me Argentina" and "Memory". A few would actually have seen the shows somewhere in the world. James believed we had to link all three under an ALW brand. To achieve this, he wanted a production of *CATS* into the region as fast as possible and then immediately follow it with another.

We had soon planned a seven-week run in Singapore followed by ten in Hong Kong. Only a month after that tour was to have ended, he wanted to bring in a production of *Phantom of the Opera* for 16 weeks in Hong Kong and then 12 weeks in Singapore. Virtually an entire year devoted to just two productions in just two cities! I felt it was far too much too soon. How would our small office cope even with lots of assistance from James and his staff in Sydney? I kept getting the same refrain from James: he had made a huge success of *CATS* and *Les Misérables* in Australia against all the odds. He would achieve the same results in Asia.

I learned a lot during the two-year contract with Andrew Lloyd Webber and RUG and for some of the time I enjoyed it immensely. I was amazed at the enormous talent and energy of the young Australian cast of *CATS*. After seeing the production, even Andrew Lloyd Webber said he felt it was the best of the eight productions then playing around the world. Some of the characters I met were fascinating. And there were some moments that were hilarious. I was asked to attend the premiere of *Phantom of the Opera* in a new theatre that had been constructed bang in the middle of the main railway station in Sapporo. As usual in Japan, a vast array of merchandise attached to the show was on offer. About to buy a sweatshirt with the show's three main visual images on the front – the *Phantom* mask, the rose and the shards of glass – I dropped it. Picking it up I noticed on the back a short sentence typical on many such items in Japan to describe a show. This had clearly been thought up in Japanese and then translated into English. And as was quite common, the English was either not quite accurate or contained double entendres. This one said simply –

She chased him around the Opera House and finally caught him by the organ!

I thought this fun, but when news filtered back to London, instructions were given for all that merchandise to be destroyed and a new batch without the seemingly offensive slogan produced!

Overall, though, when working for RUG I found little of the sense of personal satisfaction I had hoped I would experience. And whilst it was the intention of everyone that I remain for longer than my two-year contract and a second contract had been negotiated, it did not work out that way. Rather than start at the beginning, I will begin at its end.

My last day as Managing Director of RUG Asia was a Monday. I was at home in my New Territories flat about to set off for a meeting with executives of American Express. The tour of *CATS* had recently ended and James, Julie Brookes, his Australian production administrator, and Fiona Thomas who handled marketing in Australia had just arrived in Hong Kong to join me for the meeting. Our earlier deal whereby Amex had been the "official card" for *CATS* had been hugely successful with more than 30% of all the tickets sold in advance through the cards. I had already negotiated a similar deal for *Phantom of the Opera* and the point of the meeting was merely to dot i's and cross t's prior to a contract being signed. James had a second reason for coming to Hong Kong. He planned to spend a week making pitches for the above-the-title sponsorship of *Phantom*. This would require one company contributing in excess of US$1 million plus a lot more in marketing support.

As I was grabbing the keys of the car, the phone rang. It was Sarah, James's secretary in Sydney. James had decided to postpone the American Express meeting and first fine-tune a few details in the office. I should meet him there. I was confused, but then James always kept some cards close to his chest. I drove to the office completely unaware he might have a very different agenda in mind. Nor did it strike me as odd that Sarah should have called from Sydney when James was by that time in his Hong Kong hotel. He could easily have called himself.

Being fired is not a pleasant experience! This is especially true when it comes completely out of the blue. After I had been in the office for about 30 minutes, James, Julie and Fiona arrived. James asked if we could chat privately. He looked almost grey as if from a total lack of sleep. Without preamble he informed me he had spoken with Patrick and the board. It had been decided that with *Phantom* delayed a year till 1995 – that struck me as weak given that he had actually made this decision five months earlier, finally recognising what should have been perfectly obvious at the outset that running two shows so close together was wholly impractical – and *CATS* having returned minimal profits from its Singapore and Hong Kong seasons – true, but he omitted to mention that Singapore which he had been supervising had lost money whereas Hong Kong which I looked after had turned a profit – cuts had to be made in the Asian office costs. The board could no longer justify a managing director in the region when it could be looked after from Sydney. He therefore wished me to resign with immediate effect. Without even looking at me, he took from his briefcase two sets of papers requiring my signature: one to resign all my directorships, another confirming I would no longer be a signatory to bank documents.

It was all so clinical. You're out! Effectively fired! Only it was not technically being fired as I was at the end of a contract. The parallel between the Philharmonic musicians whose contracts had not been renewed 15 years earlier was eerily similar. And the very real fact was that my immediate resignation was a fait accompli. As a friend for several years James clearly found the whole business distasteful and said so more than once. So many thoughts flashed through my mind, the most immediate being how to tell K. C. Lee and Maria, both of whom had given up their IMG Artists jobs to join RUG out of loyalty to me.

I asked James for an hour's recess. I was too angry to hold an intelligent conversation. I needed to clear my head. I also had to shake off a major sense of disbelief. So I walked out of the office. I wandered aimlessly around Causeway Bay, that same district where I had spent my first years in Hong Kong. Here I was at the age of 48 with a very successful career behind me and an enviable resume. Yet I was now out of a job and had no idea where the next one would be coming from. To my thinking, I had done little wrong. I believed James and his team were merely pissed off that I did not do everything they wanted of me as though I were a slave. What I had feared, despite having received Patrick and the board's confirmation that I would be a director making decisions in my own right and not always subservient to the wishes of Sydney, had come true.

It was also only little more than six months since Patrick had told me over dinner at the Shangri-La Hotel in Hong Kong that RUG valued my services highly and of his hope I would stay on after the end of my contract. Only two months later, following the hugely successful Hong Kong premiere of *CATS*, James had taken me to lunch in the Grand Hyatt's Grissini Restaurant to praise the work I had done and to confirm that for my new contract starting mid-year, London had finally agreed a housing allowance. My basic salary would remain the same, but that allowance would be US$4,000 per month, effectively enabling a move into an apartment near the city centre by giving me a very handsome raise.

My mind wandered. I thought about the recent disagreements that had arisen between me and the office in Sydney. They were, I felt, largely a result of the Australians being determined that they would run the RUG productions exactly as they did in Australia despite there being major differences in Asia's theatre-going habits and experience. I was the managing director for Asia. When unable to get James for whatever reason, I had made decisions based on my extensive experience and knowledge of working in the region – the very reason I had been hired in the first place.

The biggest issue we had faced and which was eventually to cause the biggest rift between us only days after that Grand Hyatt lunch had actually been known to us all almost as soon as I started working with the company well over a year earlier. James still believed *CATS* should be the first musical to tour and that it would need a minimum ten-week season in Hong Kong. Scheduling any tour at relatively short notice was always going to prove difficult because there was only one acceptable theatre in Singapore and two in Hong Kong. All three got booked up far in advance. After checking availabilities, it had been decided to open in Singapore and run for seven weeks during the last two months of 1993. Allowing for the time taken to transfer the show between the two cities, it would be ready to open in Hong Kong's Lyric Theatre in mid-January 1994. Since *CATS* was no longer in production in Australia, James would remount a special four-week season in Adelaide prior to its being flown up to Singapore and ready to open about a week later. I arranged for Singapore Airlines to divert one of its 747 freighters from its normal Sydney/Singapore route to Adelaide to fly all the scenery, costumes and equipment, generally named the "physical production", to Singapore.

The crux of the problem was that Hong Kong's splendid 1,200-seat Lyric Theatre was not available for four weeks bang in the middle of our planned season. It was blocked every year for a month devoted to performances during the Hong Kong Arts Festival. The season would therefore have to be split into two parts. What did James plan to do with the production during the month-long gap?

No need to worry, was always James's reply. We'll find a solution. If not, he would close the show and send the company back to Australia for a few weeks' break. He then surprised me by adding –

"If we're really stuck, we can always speak with Patrick and get him to play the Patten card."

The Patten card? During the 1992 general election in the United Kingdom, the ruling Conservative Party had been expected to lose. The campaign to have Prime Minister John Major's government re-elected was headed by the chairman of the party, Christopher Patten. In doing so, Patten arranged for Andrew Lloyd Webber to write the party's election song. To everyone's surprise, the Conservative Party won with a small majority, but Patten lost his seat in his constituency of Bath. In gratitude, Major offered him a senior government position. He declined. He asked to be named as the last Governor of Hong Kong, the first time the post had ever been given to a politician rather than as traditionally to a senior civil servant. The Patten card was therefore effectively calling in a favour to Lloyd Webber. Now that Patten was installed in Hong Kong, James was convinced he would ensure the freeing-up of the Lyric Theatre. I was absolutely astonished. I knew this just could never happen. The Arts Festival had a very high-powered committee structure. No governor had the authority to impose major Festival changes. I told James of my serious concerns. They were dismissed.

Not knowing what was to happen during this period created all manner of difficulties. One was with the hotel for the company members. I had negotiated a deal with the city's Century Hotel within walking distance of the theatre. This allowed for 70 hotel rooms for arrival a few days prior to the start of performances, four weeks for the first part of the season and then six weeks after the month's break. That totalled almost 5,400 room nights. But we also had to include a 'hold' on 2,000 room nights over that February/March 'break' period just in case the Patten card actually worked.

As we got closer to the time when tickets had to be put on sale several months in advance, I still had no decision on what was to happen about that four-week gap. James insisted that we had to go and talk with the director of the Festival before Patrick in London rang Patten. When I asked James for a convenient time for him to meet the Festival director, he decided this was a job for me and that I had to go on my own. If necessary I was to 'threaten' the Festival. That was an idiotic idea that was never going to work, but that is what I had to do. Since the Festival's executive director, Sun Man Tseng, was a former colleague who had worked for me as the highly successful marketing manager at the Philharmonic and whom in a small way I had helped persuade to take the job of running the Festival, I was in a very difficult position. But I now ran RUG Asia. I accepted my personal feelings were irrelevant.

Sun Man was politely firm. Patten card or no, he would not recommend to his board they release the dates we wanted for there was no alternative theatre for the international ballet and dance companies he had already contracted. James now had to talk with Patrick. But when push finally came to shove, James then was clearly annoyed when he informed me that Patrick had refused to raise the issue with Patten. Patrick's view was this was a problem we had to solve, not London, although why we had had to wait the better part of an entire year before getting round to attempting any other solution was the real question that was neither asked nor answered!

James then took the decision he would not close the show. Instead, he would find somewhere else in Asia. That in itself was a big gamble at so late a stage, for who would take a very expensive production of a major musical with the possibility of only three full performing weeks to recoup such a major investment?

Without any reference to me, when we met up some days later in Singapore where *CATS* was now halfway through its season, he said he had the answer. The company would play in a casino in the Genting Highlands Resort south of Kuala Lumpur. I was stupefied! How, I asked, did he propose to get the physical production there? In container trucks was his response.

"By road? Taking which route?" I asked.

"Through China, Vietnam, Thailand and down to Malaysia."

I suppressed a laugh. It was a totally ridiculous suggestion. There simply were no roads in southwest China capable of taking 40-foot containers quickly through to Vietnam. As bad, there were so many border crossings the journey to Malaysia and back would probably take a good 10 days driving around the clock. The only possible way to make it work would be chartering a 747 freighter, and that would result in a three-week season being financial madness.

For his next idea, I was again not consulted. Eventually I was told by his general manager in Australia, Brian Barnes, that James had contacted one of the promoters he had met whilst setting up the auditions in Manila for the hugely successful Cameron Mackintosh London production of *Miss Saigon* some years earlier. Manila would take *CATS*. Being relatively close to Hong Kong, that certainly seemed much more feasible. And that is how the matter was left for several more weeks.

I was in Singapore for the last night of *CATS* at the end of December. I then flew to Hua Hin in Thailand for a short break. No sooner had I entered my hotel room than I received a message that Brian needed to speak to me urgently. The Manila season had fallen through! Oh well, I thought, that means the company has to go back to Australia. Wrong! Brian wanted me to talk to other promoters who might be able to take the show. If so, James had said the contract conditions would be the same as those he had negotiated for Manila. This was another completely mad idea! There were just six weeks before the first four-week run would finish in Hong Kong. Who would be crazy enough to find financing and a theatre, finalise contracts, get a huge marketing and PR campaign underway and tickets put on sale – all in a couple of weeks?

As I thought about it, though, I realised one colleague might just have access to the required finance and be crazy enough to try and make it work. Michael Chung belonged to one of Korea's most important international classical music families. The businessman brother of conductor Myung-whun Chung and violin superstar Kyung-wha Chung, Michael had recently set up a promotion company with backing from Samsung. Before I called him, I asked Brian to reconfirm in precise detail the main points of the Manila contract. Since transportation of the physical production to and from Manila was not mentioned, I queried its absence. James had informed Manila that RUG would absorb these, I was told. I wanted this made absolutely clear so there could be no subsequent dispute. I spelled it out. Did he mean that Michael would only have to pay for the flights for the cast and crew between Hong Kong and Seoul, not the physical production? Correct? Correct!

Michael loved the idea, despite all the horrendous time issues. Within a couple of days, I was both surprised and delighted we had the basis of the contract agreed. At the very least I had proved my value to the company. Brian informed me James was very pleased and the Sydney office would get the contract out once the New Year holiday was over. No, I said. This would clearly be too late. Due to the urgency of time, I begged Brian to fax the contract to Michael within 24 hours. It was not done. Why any company would delay sending such a vital contract given the enormous time constraints on both parties, New Year or no, I never found out. When it did arrive, Michael exploded. He immediately called me. The contract he had received, contrary to everything he had been repeatedly told, stipulated he would indeed have to pay for transportation of the physical production. This would make his season impossible. By this stage, though, he had already signed the contract for the new Seoul Opera House and his PR and marketing campaigns would be launched in a couple of days. Not going ahead would result in his incurring massive irrecoverable losses.

James was adamant. Freight costs for the physical production had to be part of the contract. I countered as best I could, reminding him time and again of his agreement with the Manila promoter and the cast-iron guarantees I had been given by Brian about Seoul. I further reminded him he had told me many months earlier that any performances in this period would be infinitely preferable to sending the company back to Australia, that his Genting Highlands idea would have lost vast amounts of more money, that Brian had gone through every iota of the agreement with Manila more than once and had confirmed each and every time that freight was not part of any deal with a promoter. I added the obvious: that pulling out now would probably result in Michael taking legal action on the basis of breach of verbal agreements. At about the same time, Michael called me urgently. He had contacted Korean Air. A round trip 747 freighter would add about US$180,000 to his costs. It was far too late for him to recoup any of this from sponsors or by increasing ticket prices.

Soon James was sending me faxes copied to Patrick in London. Normally he merely sent faxes to me with copies only to Brian when required. With hindsight I was soon certain he had just assumed he could sell the deal to London. But London had not agreed. The last of the series was one from Patrick to James stating angrily that he would never allow anyone to make money by giving them *CATS* without their paying the full costs of the performances in their entirety. He would rather cancel the rest of the *CATS* tour. That had to be a bluff, for the losses from Seoul and the remaining six weeks in Hong Kong would end up being humongous at a time when RUG was desperately trying to boost revenue from all sources. For whatever reason, James just did not attempt to fight the decision. And neither he nor Brian ever apologised to me for providing totally incorrect information about freight costs being an integral part of the deal. It was cover-up time.

I felt desperately sorry for Michael. I had merely relayed the specific instructions provided to me, and in good faith he had agreed. Faced with this new fait accompli about the freight, he generously agreed to go part of the way to meeting the freight costs. He would do his best to find up to an additional $100,000. He would not, however, put that in any contract. With time running out for both parties, James finally gave in and signed the altered contracts.

The short Seoul season was an even more remarkable sold-out and artistic success than anyone could have expected. Neither James nor Brian bothered to turn up. The dress rehearsal was held on the afternoon of the first performance. Michael had asked if some performer friends could attend, telling me they would be no more than a few dozen. At lunchtime we were faced with a queue of over 800, all desperate to get into the theatre. We had no option but let them in. As it turned out, this was the most extraordinarily enthusiastic audience any performance of *CATS* anywhere could have had. There were three standing ovations – and that was just during the overture as the cast entered the auditorium through the stalls' aisles.

This whole problem had arisen exclusively as a result of a serious lack of communication. The office in Sydney was directing all operations without keeping the Asian office in the loop. They were also relaying information back to London, again without any of that information first being cleared with me in Hong Kong. They merely assumed they had the answers, despite not having nearly enough knowledge of the region. I knew well that the way a written communication is drafted can be interpreted in a variety of ways. Had Australia really been totally honest with London over the cavalier way in which it had waited for the better part of a year before trying to find a solution to the four-week gap in the middle of the Hong Kong season? Had part of that blame been placed at my door? If so, and not having seen the correspondence, I have no idea how true or otherwise this might be. For all I knew it could have conveyed a wholly inaccurate picture, given that I had been pressing for many months for Australia to concentrate on a solution.

Having been dropped well and truly in the shit over Korea, I was soon to attract the ire of Julie and Fiona regarding the Hong Kong hotel. Once the move to Seoul was finalised, I was able to cancel the four 'held' February/March weeks at the Century Hotel without penalty. We then took out an additional option for a further three weeks at the end of the scheduled season in May just in case we quickly sold out the remaining six weeks of performances. These ended up selling well, but not as well as in the first four weeks. For this was another consequence of closing the show for a month. When you split a season, there is always the danger that many potential audience members will just assume the show has ended – unless you have a large amount in the budget for a lot more advertising and promotion. We did not have that luxury.

When it came to the contractual deadline to exercise that final three-week hotel option, I pressed Sydney to make a decision. I kept being told: just give us another couple of days. This greatly annoyed the hotel management. May was peak season for hotel occupancy and understandably it did not wish to have almost 1,500 room nights become available at virtually the last minute. The more I pressed, the more Sydney stalled and the more times I had to go and almost beg the hotel manager to keep holding the rooms. As it turned out, *CATS* closed on the originally scheduled date and there was no need to exercise the option, but that decision came well after the contracted date. The hotel was unhappy, Sydney was unhappy, and I was mightily pissed off.

By this time, both Julie and Fiona were in touch regularly about my setting up meetings with potential sponsors for the long 16-week *Phantom* season now scheduled for the summer of the following year. James's masterstroke, as outlined earlier, was to have *Phantom* play for four months in Hong Kong immediately after *CATS* had closed. In addition to the Lyric Theatre for *CATS*, he had booked the larger Grand Theatre in the HKCC for four months commencing in June 1994. Despite the enormity of the challenges, James pressed ahead. But then all the various difficulties in getting *CATS* mounted began to surface and it was finally realised we just did not have the qualified manpower to make two productions work one after the other. James had also finally realised that there was no physical production available to bring into the region in the summer of 1994.

By the time *CATS* had moved up to Hong Kong at the start of the year, James broke the news that *Phantom* would be delayed for a year and he would have to cancel that four-month booking RUG had made for the Grand Theatre in the HKCC. Did he go to inform the theatre management to tell them they would now have an empty theatre for a continuous four-month period at just five months' notice? Brian and I had to do this one. Of course theatres have cancellations all the time. But four consecutive months at such desperately short notice? That was unheard of in Hong Kong. Still, cancellations were permitted in the Grand Theatre's contract provided all deposits were forfeited. Thus James ensured that RUG lost in excess of US$130,000 on what had with hindsight been merely a whim rather than a well-researched plan.

Once the idea of having *Phantom* follow *CATS* fell through, James negotiated a deal with the Canadian producers of *Phantom*. Live Entertainment (Livent) in Canada had two productions, one playing permanently in Toronto and the other which toured. That touring production was scheduled to finish in Honolulu in the spring of 1995. It could easily be shipped over to Hong Kong.

Livent was to be a joint venture partner in the Asian season. So we all met up in Vancouver for a preliminary series of meetings to flesh out a deal. Walking with a limp, Garth Drabinsky, the CEO of Livent, seemed more of a mafia-type figure than a theatrical producer. Outwardly he was extremely successful, running a chain of cinema and theatre venues in Canada and a series of well-reviewed musicals. At one time, Livent was Canada's most prolific producer of entertainment. It had branched out into the USA where its presentations included the Hal Prince-directed production of *Show Boat* on Broadway. Although that ran for three years, its huge cast and physical production drained massive amounts of cash. Livent Canada eventually went bankrupt in 1998. In 2009 Drabinsky and his co-founder in Livent were convicted in Toronto of accounting fraud for overstating their business finances by millions of dollars for years. Drabinsky was sentenced to seven years in jail, a term reduced to five years on appeal.

In 1994, though, he acted the role of the big producer. When he made his first visits to Singapore and Hong Kong to view the theatres and start working on marketing plans, the first thing he did in each city was hire a helicopter to get a better idea of the layout of each territory. I was surprised and delighted that he had some new marketing ideas. As going to cinemas was a popular leisure activity in both cities, he planned to spend large amounts in cinema advertising during the main holiday periods of Christmas and Chinese New Year. To start the campaigns, one full quarter of each season's marketing budget would be splashed on double-page full colour advertisements in several major newspapers in each city. Such a massive initial spend had never been heard of before.

Soon contracts were signed and a start made to a major sponsorship drive. Ever since presenting Luciano Pavarotti in Hong Kong in early 1990, I had kept in close contact with that concert's sponsors, Philip Morris (Asia). I knew that its corporate affairs manager, Don Harris, was extremely anxious for another one-off mega-event. It only took a couple of meetings with him and his colleagues for me to convince him that a 16-week run of *Phantom* could bring the company very substantial sponsorship benefits. A formal deal was just a signature away.

But this was not sufficient for Sydney. They wanted a series of meetings with several potential sponsors. With the amount of the title sponsorship in excess of US$1 million plus a lot of additional marketing support, not many companies would be interested. I had great difficulty arranging more than a handful of meetings with corporate executives. As always in Hong Kong, I arranged for these to be held in conference rooms at the relevant corporate headquarters, along with the various visual aids James would need.

In the week prior to James's arrival for that first meeting with American Express, I reminded everyone in the Sydney office that the very first meeting with Philip Morris was 99.9% certain to result in a contract. The others were largely superfluous. I went through all the various details of the companies we would be visiting with Julie and Fiona in Sydney. It was only at the end of that week that they decided to inform me that James would not go to the companies' offices. They asked why had I not arranged for the senior executives to come to the large presidential suite he would be staying in at the Grand Hyatt where they could be properly entertained before and during the presentation? Yet again, there had been a total lack of any communication. I told them there was a very good reason! James and I had made all the presentations for *CATS* by visiting corporate offices, and that had worked extremely well. More importantly, no one in the Sydney office had thought to tell me that James wanted a different arrangement on this visit nor where he planned to stay. I quickly pointed out that a couple of the companies were based in the New Territories and thus quite far from the central location of the Grand Hyatt. I knew there was no possibility of their CEOs having time at short notice to come in to the city merely for a sponsorship presentation.

Why anyone in any company like RUG, which was making every effort to increase profits at every turn, would require – and could afford what was then upwards of US$3,000 a night – an enormous 400-square-metre two-bedroom presidential suite in the Grand Hyatt with living room, dining room, kitchen, jacuzzi, sauna and amazing harbour views merely to make sponsorship presentations totally defeated me. Yet again my advice was not heeded. I had no option. I then had to spend that Friday afternoon on the phone doing my best to persuade these corporate CEOs and marketing managers to agree to change the venue for the presentations. The Australians were not happy.

Mulling over all this, I also thought back to another key mistake on James's part, one which had certainly had a very negative effect on ticket sales for *CATS* in Singapore.

On one of our early trips to the city-state, we talked a lot about the entertainment buying habits of Singaporeans and how best *CATS* should be marketed. Singapore is a city with many wealthy people who tend not to show their wealth, unlike their counterparts in Hong Kong. How could they be persuaded to purchase top-price tickets that had to be some of the most expensive ever sold in Singapore at over US$100? How could the younger generation of newly affluent citizens who were adopting a very Singaporean identity be persuaded that *CATS* was the show they had to see?

James had heard about a cabaret show with Singapore's own brand of stand-up comedy that was risqué, caustic and provocative. The Boom

Boom Room[1] had opened the previous year and was attracting a large, enthusiastic and young crowd. He had the concierge book us a table. The show was certainly fun, although with much of the dialogue in Singlish[2] we could not fully understand it. The audience though lapped it up. As the enthusiasm increased, James turned to me and shouted above the noise –

"This is the audience we must attract for *CATS*. We have to find a way of getting them in to the show."

In due course he decided how to make that happen. Some years earlier, when doing an initial round of casting during auditions for Cameron Mackintosh in Southeast Asia for *Miss Saigon*, he had heard a Singaporean singer and model named Jacintha. Although she had not been ideal for that particular production, James now felt she might be perfect for the role of Grizabella in *CATS*. Trevor Nunn's assistant on the original *CATS* productions, Jo-Anne Robinson, who would be mounting the Asia tour production, came to Singapore to work with Jacintha for several days to help decide if she could fit the part. It was agreed that with more work she could. James was certain he now had his ace card. He would reveal it at the major press conference to announce the *CATS* season a few weeks later. At the same time he wrote to Andrew Lloyd Webber about scoring a new version of the hit song "Memory" in an Asian style to be issued on CD in advance of the performances.

James was jumping far too quickly into what were to prove muddy waters. I knew well that Singaporeans were proud of their nation's achievements. Many had been educated overseas. I did not see how we could square the promise of the highest standard of production as seen on Broadway when one key member of the cast was a local Singaporean who had never been near Broadway. Whenever I aired my concerns, though, James kept stressing that he had succeeded in selling *Les Misérables* in Australia and having it run for three years, when most commentators felt it would only run for a few months. He knew how to sell shows. He would make his ideas for Singapore work. I had made my point. Again I could not argue it further.

The press conference in Singapore's Hyatt Hotel attracted a large group of journalists, writers and representatives from sponsors. None had been let in on the secret and so the reception given to Jacintha when she came into the darkened room and sang "Memory" would give us a clue about whether or not James's idea was going to work. James gave the 'unknown' guest a huge build-up. Then as the lights darkened, as the music for "Memory" started and Jacintha appeared, there was an audible sigh of disbelief. Far from helping to market the Singapore season, this move had at a stroke now made it much more difficult.

The Asian version of "Memory" scored by Andrew Lloyd Webber's long-time collaborator, David Cullen, was another error. Again it just weakened the key selling point of *CATS* being a truly international production. When the show opened with a largely invited first night audience, Jacintha's supporters and detractors were out in force. Some cheered. Others greeted her performance with mild jeers. This was hugely unfair on her. Yet she was a trooper and continued performing, each night growing more into the role. A couple of weeks into the Singapore run, we brought her to Hong Kong to attend a special press briefing where we could build up her presence there. Sadly for her, though, it was never to happen. Casting her had been a gamble. It had not paid off.

By the time the cast had moved to Hong Kong, they had a few days off before a dress rehearsal in the Lyric. The early-January weather was gloriously sunny and so I took the company out for lunch on a junk tour around the Island. It was only at a meeting chaired by James the next morning I was informed that Jacintha's contract had been terminated. Her 22-year-old Australian understudy would be taking her place. I told James I would issue a brief media release. No! No release! There would be no announcement! This was another decision I failed to grasp. I reminded James that we had 'blown-up' Jacintha in the Hong Kong media. If she failed to appear, the gossip columnists would immediately be on the phone. Again I was told: no release! They never did this in Australia. There would be no need to do so in Hong Kong. Again he was wrong!

After *CATS* had opened to very enthusiastic audiences, John Dykes, who ran the society gossip column in the *South China Morning Post*, called to ask what had happened to Jacintha. Why was she not in the show? I played for time and promised to call him in an hour or so. By this time James had flown back to Sydney. He had a house in the Blue Mountains which was in danger from serious bush fires and he could not be contacted. Brian advised me to stick to the advice I had been given. I told him I could not. I had no doubt John Dykes was already talking to staff at the theatre. If I did not get back to him with a plausible story, John would run one of his own. Since it involved Jacintha, it would hit both the Singapore and Hong Kong media and could cast a negative light not just on Jacintha but also on the production of *CATS* and on RUG's Asian operations.

Having consulted a throat specialist and agreed with Jacintha's manager a plausible story about ill health affecting the vocal cords, I decided to call John and give him the story. I doubt if he "bought" it, but as it was the official RUG Hong Kong line, he had no option but to print it. The story ran over a couple of short paragraphs – and then died. Exactly the effect I wanted.

James, though, was near apoplectic! I had gone against his decision. I had not consulted him. I had been wrong to even talk to the media! To this day I have not the faintest idea why this issue had such a dramatic effect on him. It was a storm in the tiniest of teacups. Yet for days he harped on angrily about it.

As I wandered slowly back to the office that hot and sticky June morning, I remembered another series of incidents. At a meeting of worldwide directors in London in mid-1993, we had learned of the company's urgent need to maximise profits. In early 1986 Lloyd Webber had placed 60% of the company's shares on the London Stock Exchange. A few years later, unhappy with the expectations of investors seeking steady returns in a business notorious for its financial and artistic peaks and troughs, the accounting firm of Deloittes was engaged to re-privatise the company. So successful was this that Lloyd Webber installed two Deloittes executives in the company's most senior positions. Patrick McKenna became the CEO and Bill Taylor its CFO. Patrick thereafter arranged a placement of 30% of the company's shares with the recording and entertainment conglomerate Polygram. More importantly, the price paid by Polygram covered most of the total cost of the buy-back. And better still, part of the deal involved Polygram paying even more if RUG's profits in the first three full years of the association exceeded certain agreed levels. Thus there was intense pressure on all divisions to maximise profits.

RUG's first dip into Asian waters had not been anything like the financial success James had forecast. *CATS* had lost money in Singapore and made only a small profit in Hong Kong. Add to that the US$130,000 lost theatre deposit with the cancellation of *Phantom* in Hong Kong for mid-1994 and the near $100,000 that RUG had had to pay as its share of air-freighting *CATS* to and from Korea, it was clear that James must have been under intense pressure from head office. After all, he had advised he could generate up to 20% of the group's profits from Australasia. Getting rid of my salary and cutting back on the Hong Kong office costs no doubt seemed a good idea to the bean counters in London.

I reflected also on Lloyd Webber's visits to Singapore and Hong Kong three months earlier when he attended the first Hong Kong performance after the show had returned from its huge success in Seoul. James had decided he would look after Andrew in Singapore and I would host him in Hong Kong. Had I actually ended up with those responsibilities, many of the problems that arose and angered Andrew would not have happened.

They started with a stream of requests from Andrew's PA Sarah Snow. One was that we organise at short notice a cocktail party for Andrew and his wife Madeleine to meet some of Hong Kong's movers and shakers. Totally against my advice, the date was set for a Wednesday. This happens to be the evening when horse racing takes place and racing in Hong Kong was virtually a religion as well as a major social event. Even so, we managed to assemble an interesting cross-section of Hong Kong personalities from the arts, entertainment, society and politics.

Only later was I informed that the one person Andrew really wished to see was prominent businessman and socialite, David Tang. Founder of the Shanghai Tang chain of stores, David had an extensive group of international friends who included Princess Diana and the Duchess of York in London. I called David. He said he'd be delighted to attend.

Working out where to dine after the cocktail party was not difficult. One of David's very successful ventures was the China Club in the old Bank of China Building in Central. He suggested that I take Andrew and his party to the club for dinner. I had reluctantly to point out that I was not a member. Very generously he arranged a week's complimentary membership for me with his picking up the tab for my visits.

Mid-way through the cocktail party at the Grand Hyatt, the captain informed me I was wanted on the phone. It was David. He asked me to convey to Andrew and Madeleine his sincere regrets. He was in the midst of a complicated negotiation at the China Club with some Japanese clients and could not get away. However, he asked me to assure Andrew that once we had all arrived for dinner, he would come to our table and have a drink with us. Andrew appeared only slightly annoyed.

Following cocktails, three limousines took us the short distance over to the China Club. As we entered, I reminded the captain that David Tang was to be joining us for drinks. He would inform David's assistant that we had arrived. Madeleine asked me to order. After purveying the menu, I asked about Andrew's likes and dislikes. Adventurous, I was told. So, in consultation with Madeleine I ordered a mix of items such as ducks' tongues for starters along with more standard fare.

Still David had not joined us. I went back over to the captain. David would be down shortly. When our food started to arrive, I was horrified to see that Andrew instantly disliked the ducks' tongues and the more adventurous dishes. Then the captain came over to the table. Unfortunately, I was informed, David had had to leave rather suddenly with his guests. He asked me to extend his deepest regrets to Andrew and Madeleine. When I informed Andrew, the entire table froze.

James had arrived from Singapore in time for the cocktail party and dinner and had witnessed the events of the evening. He had known Andrew would not be in the best of moods for he had had to handle a difficult problem on the final evening in Singapore. As he told me, he had taken Andrew and the party for a Chinese dinner in the famous Raffles Hotel. For some reason, Andrew had been unhappy at some of the arrangements for his visit and laid into James. He kept on and on, his voice gaining in intensity to the point where other diners were starting to look over to their table. James then asked the captain to bring a carving knife.

"But sir," he was told, "you have no dishes that require a carving knife."

James all but shouted –

"Bring me a carving knife!"

When one arrived, he opened his shirt front, handed the knife to Andrew and suggested he use it quickly so that the other diners could get back to enjoying their dinner in peace. No doubt shocked, Andrew ceased his criticisms.

The next morning, James called me, relayed the story and asked me to ensure that everything ran like clockwork in Hong Kong because Andrew was "on the warpath". David Tang's absence had ensured that this evening had not been a success. As we got out of the limousines at the Grand Hyatt, instead of turning left to the elevators, Andrew turned right to make his way to the Champagne Bar. As I started to follow, my arm was yanked by James. Time for us to disappear, he said. What was about to happen would not be pretty. From what I learned the next morning, there had been much cursing and swearing in the bar that evening.

The most embarrassing incident was a direct result of me and my team having absolutely no other responsibility for Andrew's schedule in Hong Kong as promised. It was James and Julie who decided that the after-show party would be held at a restaurant way up in The Peak complex. This made absolutely no sense whatsoever! Apart from it being a bus and limousine trek up the hill for the cast, crew and VIPs, the view which the

Australians were certain would impress Andrew so much could only be imagined. Humidity in Hong Kong starts to rise dramatically by mid-March. Consequently the picture windows in the restaurant were totally steamed up for the entirety of the event!

Worse, while the complex had various entrances during the day and evening, only one exit was open after midnight. And of course the Australians had failed to make an advance walk-through. They had zero idea where that exit was. So when Andrew and Madeleine decided to call it a night, I bade my farewells as Julie escorted them to their limousines. I then waited a good ten minutes before leaving to find my own limousine. Unfortunately, Julie had taken the party to several "exits", each of which she discovered to be closed. Understandably Andrew was becoming very far from pleased.

I also got lost and happened upon the single exit just as Julie had finally managed to locate it. Andrew by then was furious. At the sight of me he launched into a vicious verbal attack about how badly he had been treated in Hong Kong. When I tried to interject that my team and I had had absolutely no decision whatever on the planning and detail of the evening, for a moment he directed his ire at James. He was left with no alternative but to fire James in the morning, he said. He would probably also close the Hong Kong office and never have his shows return.

Slowly I managed to steer the party to the two waiting limousines, got him into his car, apologised as best I could and wished them all goodnight. When I returned to go back into the building for the stiff drink I felt I deserved, there was Julie staring at me. Once Andrew's tirade had started, she had conveniently eased herself away from the group and out of vision. Now she laid into me.

"Why did you put up with all that foul crap?" she asked.

I was staggered. I was also deeply angry.

"He is my employer," I shouted. "What was I supposed to do? Shout back and tell him that the one responsible for this disaster was standing right behind me – you? And you did absolutely nothing to ensure this disaster never happened. You insisted that you organise the party, you chose the venue, you chose the menu, you arranged the transport. Yet you never once considered bringing my team into the discussions, you never did a night-time walk-through and then you just stood idly by whilst I had to absorb all that abuse!"

When I got home, I called and woke James. I told him what had occurred. I said we should both meet Andrew in the hotel lobby as he had brought forward the departure of their private jet from the following evening to the morning. I wanted to ensure the bad feelings had not lingered. Whilst I had been insulted, I knew an apology would not be forthcoming. But I was about to get a contract to work for this man for another couple of years and I wanted us to part amicably.

James had no intention of getting up early. No doubt he had been through it all before. I could do as I wished, he said. So it was that just a few hours later I sat in the hotel lobby waiting for the party to appear. As they did so, it was obvious Andrew was surprised to see me. Madeleine was carrying what seemed like quite a heavy bag and so I went up and took it gently from her. She smiled and thanked me. As we walked to the front of the lobby, Andrew put his arm around my shoulders.

"This is very kind of you to come and see us off. Really very kind."

There was then a short pause. Almost conspiratorially, he leaned towards me and said quietly –

"I hope I did not say anything last night. I was tired and had perhaps a little too much to drink. I do hope you understand."

It was not an apology, but it was more than I expected. I thanked him for coming and wished them all a safe trip back to London. When I arrived in my office after grabbing a quick breakfast in the hotel, there on my desk was a large bouquet of spring flowers and a bottle of Dom Perignon beautifully wrapped. The accompanying note thanked me and my team for looking after them so admirably! Since we had done so little, I felt like sending them over to Ms. Brookes. But I like Dom Perignon too much!

All this flashed through my mind as I wandered back to the RUG office that June morning. I knew by then I had no choice but to accept reality.

I was determined to be courteous to James, but also firm. For a brief moment I had considered suing. Yet who sues Andrew Lloyd Webber unless they are prepared to bankrupt themselves before getting anywhere near a courtroom? I had no options but bite the bullet and negotiate the best possible settlement. The basic severance package was generous and quickly agreed. The other smaller issues were settled at a meeting in James's palatial suite in the Grand Hyatt the following morning when the resignation agreement I had drafted and typed up was signed. I actually felt sorry for James. We had been good friends for several years. I know he felt relieved I had not made his life more difficult.

And so I walked out of the company for which I had abandoned my well-paid job at IMG Artists in Japan, the country I loved. Did I regret the outcome? In some ways, of course, especially being effectively just a personal assistant with no real authority. On the other hand I had gained a great deal of very useful experience in the production, budgeting and marketing of musicals and the management of tours.

If my departure from RUG Asia was unexpected and the financial reasons spurious in the context of the company's own profligacy over which I had had zero control, I simply had to accept I did not fit in with a corporate culture I found difficult, no matter the many enjoyable times. My one sadness was that the company's dream of opening a theatre school in China to train some of the huge talent pool available in the country and then mount several concurrent tours to the hundreds of thousands waiting for all forms of entertainment failed to materialise. Some Lloyd Webber musicals have since made it to China but almost all have been touring productions with overseas casts.

Although I was certainly no harbinger, my departure was in some ways a sign of things to come for the parent RUG worldwide. James's prediction of 20% of group profits accruing from Australasia was never more than a mirage. After the *Phantom* run in Singapore and Hong Kong in 1995, the Asian office in Hong Kong was closed. Soon James was moved from Australia to the London office.

In June 1997 the *Wall Street Journal* quoted an entertainment analyst at Paine Webber in New York –

"Lord Webber (sic) and his group are going to have to totally rethink the way they approach the business."[3]

By that time James, Patrick McKenna and 16 other staff were no longer with the company.

Lloyd Webber himself was to find himself far from immune to the downward spiral being felt in the corridors of the RUG offices in central London. As he said to a *Telegraph* reporter in early 2014 before his latest musical *Stephen Ward* posted closing notices –

"I haven't had a hit in 20 years. I've written six musicals in that time."[4]

After I had left the employ of RUG I formed another arts and entertainment promotion company based again in Hong Kong and this was to take me to the end of my career in arts promotion and administration in 2017. In addition to brokering *CATS* into Bangkok, my only other success with musicals had been to mount a touring production in greater China of Rodgers and Hammerstein's *The Sound of Music* in association with the Chinese arm of a company based in New York. Before that could be agreed, I had to meet with and be approved by the composer's daughter, Mary Rodgers, and the head of the Rodgers and Hammerstein Organisation, Ted Chapin, son of a former general manager of New York's Metropolitan Opera. This took place over a perfectly lovely dinner in New York. Mary was such fun to be with. I was not surprised that our partnership for the tour was quickly agreed. That Mary herself joined us for the premiere at the Shanghai Grand Theatre was the icing on the cake.

28

ABJECT FAILURES AT THE HONG KONG TOURIST ASSOCIATION

As summer gave way to autumn in 1997, Asia was consumed by the disastrous effects of the economic recession which quickly developed into a regional financial meltdown. This had started in Thailand when the Thai government was forced by speculators to free the exchange rate of the baht. Since the mid-1950s the baht had been pegged to the US dollar, initially at 20 baht and then since the mid-1980s adjusted to 25 baht. As the Thai economy boomed in the 1980s and into the early 1990s, it had not been difficult to maintain that peg, although a largely uncontrolled financial market coupled with a generally unrestricted property boom had resulted in interest rates rising steeply. With rates in other parts of the world considerably lower, there was an influx of hot money into the country. Given the ever-larger difference in interest rates, many Thai companies and individuals then borrowed in overseas currencies in the belief that the baht/US$ peg would never change. After speculators mounted an unsuccessful attack on the currency early in 1997, interest rates had to rise further. Few seemed to realise that in fending off that attack, the government had had to spend virtually all of its foreign exchange reserves. When the next attack came on July 1st, there was no possibility of the government again defending the peg. The Bank of Thailand abandoned the link and allowed the baht to float.

Within a day the baht had fallen to 30 against the US$. By the end of the year it was down to 53. In large measure Asia's crony capitalism led to other countries following suit. With the exception of Hong Kong's dollar and China's RMB, all currencies fell sharply and all economies contracted. This was to have a major impact on a project I had started early the previous year.

In 1998, Shanghai opened the first of the modern large-scale theatres in China, the Shanghai Grand Theatre. This was to be managed by my old friend Qian Shi-jin whom I had met when he ran the Shanghai Symphony Orchestra a decade earlier. Designed by the French architect Jean-Marie Charpentier, it was capable of accommodating virtually the world's largest theatrical and operatic companies. Through a friend of Qian's, I was asked if could assist him in two ways: helping to train up his staff and devising a month-long programme of events for the opening two years later.

I thoroughly enjoyed my regular trips up to Shanghai and doing my best to help. The city had developed almost unbelievably since my last visit with the Philharmonic in February 1986. For programming I had contacted many colleagues in the music business around the world and had provisionally planned concerts with several top international artists like José Carreras, Dame Kiri Te Kanawa, Anne-Sophie Mutter and a week of concerts and master classes with Isaac Stern. Stern was revered in China for the visit in 1979 which resulted in the documentary *From Mao to Mozart* and won the Oscar for Best Documentary in 1981.

Qian had made it clear from the outset that he could not pay fees for such major musicians. We therefore agreed a deal whereby my company would assemble a mutually agreed programme and then go out and find sponsorship to cover both the artists' fees and our commissions. Such an arrangement always has a risk element attached for it depends very much on corporations with sufficient funds in marketing budgets prepared to devote some to an arts project. In Shanghai I remained convinced the risk was low. Shanghai was attracting many major international companies as their base in China. For these, sponsorship of such a countrywide event as the opening of the Grand Theatre would provide an opportunity not only to cement ties with the city government but also representatives from central government ministries in Beijing.

So it proved – in the initial stages.

Then the Asian economic crisis hit. Initially it did not seem to have much effect on China. But it had a big effect on many of the companies which were based there. Whereas General Motors was a virtual shoo-in for sponsorship of one of the major international artists, by the time we met with them for a second time in September 1997 they apologised that they had had to redirect a considerable amount of their marketing budget to other countries in the region. The company suggested it would be impossible for it to proceed with any major arts sponsorship in the next financial year. Soon other dominoes began to fall. In October I held a meeting with Qian to inform him of the near certainty we would be unable to proceed with sponsorship for the programmes we had lined up. I still remained hopeful that we might rescue perhaps one or two. However, with just a year to go before opening and having had the agents hold the dates for their artists for many months, it was only a matter of weeks before I would have to release them.

By late November I was left with no option. I called Lee Lamont at ICM Artists. She had called me many weeks earlier begging for the contract for Isaac Stern which we could not send. She had asked for my word that the opening festival would definitely go ahead. I promised her it would. I then had to eat my words. She was understandably very upset. Very angry would be a better description of Anne-Sophie Mutter's agent at Columbia Artists Management also in New York. I soon had an email stating he would be taking legal action against me and my company. Obviously I felt very upset about the way everything had worked out, but I certainly was not concerned about legal action, the more so in the absence of a legal contract. Having warned Qian earlier that events were no longer in our control, in November I had to tell him the worst had happened. We had no other course of action than to pull out of work on the opening festival. If he felt he and the mayor could exert pressure on Chinese companies, I confirmed I would happily do my best to keep some of the artists we had asked to hold dates (as we did with José Carreras who eventually opened the festival with sponsorship from a local Chinese company). I liked Qian and had enjoyed working with him. I felt miserable that I had been unable to fulfil the promises I had made to him 18 months earlier.

It was late on a Thursday evening, my last in Shanghai, following very difficult meetings with Qian that I was lying on my bed in the Westin Hotel bemoaning my failure to make any profits from the Shanghai venture. The phone rang. It was a call from Hong Kong, the wife of an old friend who had arrived in Hong Kong shortly after me in 1979. Douglas Gautier had come to work for the administration's radio station, RTHK. In succeeding years he had become an executive with Rupert Murdoch's Star TV, executive director of the Arts Festival, managing director of the PR company Hill & Knowlton and then deputy chief executive of the Hong Kong Tourist Association (HKTA).

Yvonne Gautier was organising a major fundraiser the following February for the flying eye hospital, Project Orbis. We had been discussing a possible engagement for the popular singer Gloria Gaynor with whom I had worked at the dinner event in Singapore for United Distillers some years earlier. Yvonne had been very keen in our earlier discussions but the call was to tell me that her board found the fee too expensive and so they would be looking for a cheaper alternative. Not for the first time, I found myself wishing that for events like this I could charge an initial basic fee to be deducted from the final commission assuming the event went ahead. That was just not the way the business operated.

Yvonne did say, though, that Douglas wanted a word with me. I was aware he had moved to the HKTA. He asked if I had heard of the HKTA's initiative to attract more international events to Hong Kong through a new grant fund being set up by the government. I had vaguely heard of the International Events Fund (IEF) but paid little attention to it. He explained that the HKTA had advertised for someone to oversee this new fund and go out and obtain more events for Hong Kong. He asked if I might be interested, adding he knew of no-one better qualified. I said I would be returning to Hong Kong on an evening flight the following day. I would certainly be happy to learn more about the detail of the job and suggested we meet for lunch the following week.

This posed a problem. As he explained, the post had been advertised and the closing date was less than 24 hours after our call. He suggested that if I had a serious interest, he would send me the paperwork first thing in the morning so that I could complete the application form and fax it back to him prior to the deadline. We would still meet for lunch on my return. If I had then decided not to be considered, I could still withdraw at that point. All that seemed reasonable.

Having read through the information, I decided this could well be an interesting job. Besides, with the Shanghai venture having all but collapsed, I had urgent need for paid employment. Lunch with Douglas became breakfast at the Park Lane Hotel, the sort of meeting I always dislike because having spent my life working in the arts and entertainment business I was used to late nights and later mornings. Douglas informed me that a concentration on international events was part of the HKTA's new post-1997 strategy to attract more visitors. The HKTA had been extremely successful prior to July 1997 in persuading a much larger number of tourists to see Hong Kong under its existing administration. By early 1997, though, projections showed that future tourism was likely to fall off dramatically. In an effort to turn this around, one executive had come up with the idea of taking over the vacant Tamar site (where the Hong Kong Government Offices are now located) and mounting three months of open-air concerts. Many of the planned artists would be selected to appeal to a Japanese audience for the Japan tourist market looked like it would all but collapse. Someone should have realised that the HKTA was not a concert organiser and experts should have been brought in right from the start. As a result, what was billed *100 Days of Wonders* was quickly being talked about as the *100 Days of Blunders*!

It was an Australian promoter, Patrick Condon, in consultation with the HKTA who had come up with the idea of an IEF. Patrick had not worked in Hong Kong other than presenting a short season of ballet with *Stars of the Bolshoi*. But he saw an opportunity. He got to know people at the HKTA and was commissioned to write a report about bringing events to Hong Kong. The problem for any promoter, his report pointed out, was twofold. Firstly the Grand Theatre in the Cultural Centre had become the most popular venue in the territory. Consequently, it was very difficult to book dates at any time, let alone specific dates to tie in with a longer tour of a major production to Japan or Australia, for example. For an events strategy to work, Hong Kong desperately needed another venue.

The more important issue was that Hong Kong arts and entertainment venues could only be booked on what is termed a 'four walls contract'. In other words, booking gave a presenter the right to use the theatre or concert hall. But no assistance would be provided in terms of advice, publicity and marketing, event management and other issues vital to a successful performance. Event promoters with little or no experience of Hong Kong had to start by assembling a local team from scratch which inevitably involved considerable initial investment. Until the late 1990s, promoters could offset some of their early investment costs by obtaining advances on ticket sales from their chosen ticketing company. Then an event promoter pitched a large marquee in Victoria Park for a popular entertainment show. When a typhoon zipped through Hong Kong, shredding the tent and destroying the production's equipment, advances from ticket sales were stopped because it took many months if not longer to recoup the advances given to the promoter of that show and repay ticket holders.

With a producer required not merely to gain a detailed knowledge of Hong Kong audience habits and Hong Kong's event history before considering bringing an event to Hong Kong but also to put up in advance the venue's large deposit and all the pre-production costs which could involve several hundred thousand US dollars, there was obviously little incentive to encourage overseas producers new to Hong Kong. The IEF was modelled on the States' Events Funds in Australia where a large amount of the initial investment would be provided by the funds.

The HKTA's events strategy included heavy promotion of Hong Kong as *The Events Capital of Asia*. Hong Kong was not and had never been anywhere near an events capital in the region. Tokyo was streets ahead in all manner of sporting and cultural events. But what did an inaccurate slogan matter? Few in the general public knew. As long as Hong Kong lacked venues and impresarios, it could never compete. Worse, Singapore was pushing ahead with its own events strategy. There was always intense competition between the two cities.

I applied for the post as advertised and was appointed Head of International Events. Almost as soon as I started work, I was surprised to learn from Douglas that after civil service pressure it had been decided that the IEF would be a loan fund and not, as I had been informed up till then and as proposed by Condon, a grant fund. This was bound to lessen the impact of the fund for any producers who might be interested in presenting events. But it was still workable. I then learned that the fund itself had only been proposed to the government and not actually approved. So Douglas and I along with the Executive Director of the HKTA, Amy Chan, attended a meeting of the Legislative Council to propose agreement to the fund. As we waited in an ante-room, the Secretary for Economic Affairs came in and had a word with Amy Chan. I was then staggered to learn that the civil servants had decided it would be difficult to get a zero-interest loan fund approved. Accordingly, the department had put forward a scheme similar to that used by the Housing Department – a loan fund with the principal and 5% interest repayable.

This was ridiculous! Yet neither Amy Chan nor Douglas Gautier put up any objection. It was a fait accompli. Quite why, I never discovered. The ensuing meeting was to result in spirited debate. One member complained about the lack of background given in the paper for consideration by members. Another suggested that as loans were to be repaid, events provided with loans would presumably be profitable and there was therefore little justification for providing any loan at all. Another member proposed that it was event organisers whose events might otherwise run into financial difficulties who should be provided with cash grants rather than loans.

After all was said and done, the Legco Finance Committee voted on a motion on March 27, 1998 to approve item 11 which stated –

"HKTA will pay a simple interest at 5% per annum on the outstanding amount of the loan."[1]

Only it seems this was not a fait accompli. On February 7, 2001, when questioned by Dr. Hon. David Lee in the Legislative Council, the then Secretary for Economic Services, Ms. Sandra Lee, stated –

"The loans may attract interest at a commercial rate, a concessionary rate *or be interest-free.* In addition, the IEF can provide assistance in kind, such as publicity and marketing programmes overseas and in Hong Kong to help enhance the events' publicity and ticket sales."

The loans may be interest-free? That was neither acknowledged nor approved during my tenure with the HKTA. Whether the regulations had changed over the 20 months following my departure, Ms. Lee added later in her answer –

"To date, the IEF has extended support to 12 events of a wide variety covering sports, entertainment and exhibitions. A cumulative total of HK$24.7 million *interest-bearing loans* has been granted."[2]

In other words, absolutely no events had ever been offered interest-free loans!

Worse was to come. I had been informed that I would work with a new sub-committee of the HKTA on which I would have input. There were two individuals with a great deal of experience in event management I particularly wanted on the committee – legislative councillor Selina Chow, who years earlier had persuaded me to allow the Philharmonic to perform in arenas, and Canadian businessman Allan Zeman, who had been heavily involved in promotions by pop impresario Andrew Bull. Both kindly accepted invitations. Another who did was Dick Kaufman. Although then running his own PR company, Dick was better known for having rescued Allan Zeman's restaurant *California* and as a result helped create what was to become the hugely popular Lan Kwai Fong dining and entertainment district in the centre of Hong Kong Island.

Chaired by the Chairman of the HKTA, Y. S. Lo, I felt the committee had a useful mix of international and local experience. At the first meeting, though, I all but fell off my seat. I had assumed Allan Zeman would be a major ally. Almost his first question was to the chairman.

"Why is the HKTA spending large sums of government money on events? The HKTA should be nowhere near the funding of events. Having worked on various events for many years, I can tell you that 90% lose money. How are you going to ensure that this large loan will be repaid – and repaid with interest?"

I could not believe I was hearing this. Appointed to help make the IEF work, Allan had virtually sabotaged it before it was even up and running. Given his experience, most members clearly did not wish to disagree with him. Selina Chow put up a good case and Dick Kaufman agreed. Y. S. Lo was very clearly alarmed, though. How on earth do we recover from this, I wondered. Then Allan made it all even worse.

"Since we have to repay the government, it is important that we get from those who receive IEF funding the full amount of the investment returned to us from the initial receipts of these events."

I have to use that word again – this was total 'madness'. The whole point of the fund was to help promoters with their up-front costs. It was fact that profit from most events would come not from the initial ticket sales but from the last of such sales. When I had been running Andrew Lloyd Webber's RUG in the planning for the 16-week season of *Phantom of the Opera*, we were well aware that the profit would only start after about the 13th week. Pulling an investment in an event from the first batch of ticket sales would merely render every event far more risky – and might kill it altogether.

Of the many issues that arose from the HKTA and its IEF, three stand out. In late 1998, Dick Kaufman enthusiastically proposed that the fund invest in Andrew Bull's upcoming concert with one of the most popular singers of the day, Celine Dion. Bull had negotiated for it to be the only concert in Asia outside Japan. He claimed it would therefore bring in a very large number of tourists. What was not reported at the time was that Dick's company had been engaged to do the PR and marketing for the concert. He therefore had a direct interest in the event.

According to Dick, the concert would be held at the now unused Kai Tak Airport with seating for around 36,000. I cannot now recall how much was agreed as the fund contribution but believe it was not less than HK$500,000. As soon as tickets went on sale, it was clear the concert faced difficulties. Once the stage was erected, the Environmental Protection Department was called in because there would be considerable noise pollution above permissible limits for the nearby apartments. So Andrew had to turn his amphitheatre 180 degrees. Then tickets did not sell nearly as well as anticipated. By the day of the concert, it is understood little more than 12,000 had been sold and the concert lost a great deal of money.

When the sluggish ticket sales were reported to the IEF committee, Allan Zeman again asked why the HKTA was involved in funding events. He insisted that someone from the HKTA had to go to the ticket agency to collect the first instalment of the ticket sales due to the promoter. My colleague K. C. Lee stood at the ticket agency to receive the cheque alongside a very unhappy representative from Andrew Bull's company.

The Environmental Protection Department had become much more active following the 1994 renovation of the Hong Kong Stadium in Happy Valley. With the intention of hosting large-scale pop concerts for an audience of around 40,000 in addition to major sporting events like the hugely successful annual Rugby Sevens tournament, the main stands on both sides of the stadium had incorporated several dozen corporate boxes for rental to companies on an annual basis. I understand most if not all were snapped up. What the developers had failed to realise was that above a cliff at the south end of the stadium were apartment blocks. After the first pop concert, there were many complaints about noise pollution. When the Environmental Protection Department officials inspected the site, it was agreed that the maximum decibel level for future concerts had to be at such a low level it completely ruled out the possibility of any pop concerts. Many were furious about this, but there was nothing to be done. One senior civil servant ridiculously went to the media and suggested there was a way around the regulations. Concerts could in future just not feature amplification. Instead the unamplified sound should be relayed to headphones handed out to each member of the audience, and gloves used to avoid noise from applause. How any senior official could come out with such nonsense still beats me!

A second issue concerned the executive to whom I reported. I had been told from the very first discussion right up to my interview that I would report to Douglas. I was perfectly happy with that. After all, we were friends. As soon as I started working, however, I was informed I would have to report to a lesser executive, Stanley Yip. What his full responsibilities were I was never sure apart from overseeing the HKTA's initiative to promote country parks. No doubt he brought his own particular expertise to the HKTA but as far as the IEF was concerned his singular motivation was in finding the funds to guarantee that the HKTA repay the interest on the HK$100 million loan. After reviewing a number of options, he decided to lease part of the still-vacant Tamar site for use as a car park. This seemed very much a case of putting some sort of tiny cart before a vastly larger horse! Why would I report to a man whose sole desire was to achieve that 5% interest? It was clear he had little interest in any of the events I submitted or indeed any desire to become involved in them. This was perfectly illustrated little more than six months into my job.

As the Head of International Events and in charge of the IEF, I had my own annual budget which had been earlier approved by the CEO. This included a line item for travel as it was always assumed I would have to travel both to see events and to negotiate with presenters. In September, Patrick Condon, who had been bitterly disappointed that his proposal for a grant fund had quickly been watered down to a loan fund with interest, called to say it was vital that I visit Australia. I should see how each state's event fund was managed and liaise with them about possible future events which could take part in both Australia and Hong Kong. He even arranged for me to attend an Indy Car motor race on the Gold Coast which had received funding from the Queensland Event Fund. I would sit with the chairman in his box.

The HKTA had a travel office. Each executive had a level of hotel in which he or she was permitted to stay. I contacted the office and asked them to arrange my travel for the week's trip. At the same time I was duty-bound to inform Stanley. The following day he asked me to visit his office. He would prefer me not to travel at that time. What? He gave no specific reason but indicated that I should not question his authority. I went straight to Douglas's office and told him about this directive. He said he would deal with it. The following day he came to my office. This is a sensitive time for the HKTA, he told me, and it would be best to postpone my trip. I was furious. No-one gave me any valid reason why I had to be in Hong Kong at that particular time. If I had been requesting additional funds, I would have understood. But I was perfectly within my rights to make the trip had I been inclined to reject the advice. I finally agreed to their wishes, believing it was a battle not worth winning. There would be more.

Some months prior to this episode, Douglas had asked me to bring with me to the following day's heads of department meeting a list of 10 major events I was working on for possible IEF funding. As this was just two months after I had joined the Association, I had hardly had enough time to discuss even five events seriously with producers. Following the success in Hong Kong earlier in the 1990s of large-scale Broadway musicals starting with *CATS*, top of my list was the one major blockbuster which had not been able to visit Hong Kong due to the complexity of its staging. This was the Cameron Mackintosh production of *Miss Saigon* which now seemed much more of a possibility. Second was an event which Patrick Condon planned to bring – a major exhibition of *Treasures from the Kremlin* that would feature a number of stunning artefacts including several priceless Fabergé eggs.

Armed with my draft list, at the meeting the HKTA CEO Amy Chan, whom I had never met on a one-on-one basis even though I was one of her senior executives, dropped her bombshell. Why was I talking about *Miss Saigon*? She did not think it should be on any list. I was staggered! I gave the meeting all the reasons, including the fact that other large-scale blockbuster musicals had resulted in well over ten thousand visitors from Taipei alone and many more from elsewhere. This was not sufficient reason, she informed the meeting. What sort of crazy notion was this, I wondered? The CEO of Hong Kong's main tourism organisation not prepared even to consider an event likely to bring tens of thousands of tourists?

"I saw *Miss Saigon* and I didn't like it. It demeans Asian women. I don't think we should be funding its coming to Hong Kong," she stated.

Mrs. Chan then repeated this comment, seeking approval from her deputy, Ellen, sitting on her right. I was incredulous. Any responsible CEO would surely have had meetings with senior executives at least on a monthly basis when this and other issues could have been discussed in detail. Mrs. Chan seemed to feel such meetings were irrelevant. She was perfectly happy to demean a senior executive in front of all his colleagues. That such a petty individual view should have such an effect on general policy was in my eyes extremely unprofessional. Indeed, after Mrs. Chan's employment ceased, it was not long before *Miss Saigon* finally came to Hong Kong. It was a major success.

It was of little compensation at the meeting that everyone was in favour of the *Treasures from the Kremlin* exhibition. This was a project included in Patrick Condon's November 1997 consultancy report. It had advanced to a degree following meetings between Patrick and the director of the Kremlin Museum, Irina Rodimtseva, held in Hong Kong three months earlier. The memo in Russian and English exchanged after the meeting did indeed confirm the museum's "interest" in bringing the exhibition to Hong Kong and that the most convenient time would be between February and May 1999. Tellingly, no fee was mentioned. Point 8 of the agreement merely stipulated that "all sides agreed that the Museum will be paid a compensation," although Patrick stated elsewhere in his report that he had negotiated this down by 50% to US$500,000.

In discussions I had with Patrick, it was understandably obvious that he, as a promoter, saw the IEF and the association with the HKTA's events strategy as an excellent opportunity to expand his Australian business.

His report had included a considerable number of international events, along with dates when they would be visiting Hong Kong. These included performances by the famous Kirov Ballet (renamed the Mariinsky after the fall of the Soviet Union) for the Regional Council in December 1998, a rare concert by Barbra (misspelled as Barbara!) Streisand being "held" for a period after May 1998, the musicals *Crazy for You* and *The King & I*, *Nutcracker on Ice* in August-September 1998, the Dance Theater of Harlem for mid-1998 . . . and a host of others. For sports, he proposed a Formula 1 Grand Prix for 1999. If negotiations for that failed, then an Indy Car Race could take its place. Art exhibitions to complement the *Treasures from the Kremlin* included traditional costumes from St. Petersburg's Hermitage Museum and works from the New York Museum of Modern Art, the Smithsonian Institute and Moscow's Tretyakov Gallery. To these were added a host of other events including orchestras, ballet companies, fashion shows, international musicians and sports events. In effect, most could have been merely drawn out of a hat.

As with the Kremlin memorandum, Condon's report was very long on generalities and very short on specifics. It was certainly accepted by the HKTA with undue haste. After it was presented in November 1997, the HKTA very soon advertised for its Head of International Events. Little, if any, due diligence had been done on any aspects presented in Condon's report. Nor was it ever suggested that other promoters or impresarios in Hong Kong and other countries be asked to make their own reports. With the HKTA having blessed his ideas, Patrick set up a small office in Hong Kong that November which, as claimed in his report, would include a "team of entertainment specialists, experienced in all facets of the sponsorship, promotion, logistics, operation and marketing of large-scale events." On the one occasion I visited the office in early 1998, I saw just one relatively junior secretary in addition to Patrick. Apart from *Treasures from the Kremlin*, they seemed to be working on no other events. With the exception of the Mariinsky Ballet, not one of those proposed in his report actually materialised.

It also turned out that Patrick had not done his sums correctly. He had estimated US$100,000 for insurance of the Kremlin exhibition. I have no idea how he arrived at that figure or if he had consulted any specialist art exhibition insurers. The result was *Treasures from the Kremlin* never happened. The insurance bill for so many near-priceless artefacts was vastly in excess of his estimate and he had to pull out of the project. By then, though, another problem had arisen. The relevant LCSD committee responsible for the art gallery outright refused to accommodate any visiting exhibition unless the gallery's usual top entrance price of HK$50 (US$6.35) was not exceeded. This was another act of collective madness. Did these people not realise that galleries all over the world regularly house specially-curated top international visiting exhibitions with entrance prices considerably higher than normal admission prices for the standard collection? Clearly not.

When I went before them, I made two basic points.

Many international visitors to Hong Kong would happily pay much more than the regular top price just for a glimpse of some of the utterly unique Fabergé eggs. This would still be less than the international average. Secondly, unless the gallery's regular top price was raised, there was no possibility of the exhibition even coming to Hong Kong.

I was met with a group of stony faces. Not one committee member wanted to know. Rules were rules! The HK$50 maximum entrance fee had to be maintained. Allied to the insurance issue, it was then certain the project would die. Patrick's office in Hong Kong also died. He no longer saw any benefit from trying to work with the HKTA and the IEF.

In the evening following the hugely embarrassing heads of department meeting, I wrote a letter of resignation to Douglas. There seemed no point in working with the HKTA if I was to be treated in such a cavalier manner. Around 5:00pm Douglas came into my office and closed the door. He did not intend to accept my resignation. He was sorry about what had occurred earlier in the day and he realised that I was not enjoying the work I was doing. He himself was leaving for a two-week vacation in Australia that evening. He asked me to take back the letter and hold it until his return. In the meantime, he hoped I would write him a bullet point letter to inform him how I saw my responsibilities being revised in such a way that I would stay with the HKTA. He did add he was not sure how far the HKTA would be able to go in agreeing to my "demands", but he would try his best. This seemed a not unreasonable suggestion. I agreed.

After Douglas's return and his promise to go as far as possible with the revisions I had requested, absolutely nothing changed! Whenever I raised the issues, he would merely say he was working on them. Still nothing changed. My reporting directly to him rather than Stanley was one of my key requests. It did not happen and Stanley became an increasingly annoying thorn in my side. After vetoing my planned trip to Australia, he then vetoed a trip I wanted to make to Beijing to see the spectacular production of Puccini's *Turandot* in a part of the Forbidden City conducted by Zubin Mehta and directed by one of China's great directors, Zhang Yimou. After all, large-scale opera had already been mounted in Hong Kong. I wanted to meet and discuss this with Zhang. This time I took no notice of Stanley's veto. I carried on with the trip to Beijing.

After two vetoes, I was surprised when Douglas came into my office at the end of November. There was pressure to fund more events. He wanted me to do a round-the-world trip as quickly as possible to discuss events with many overseas promoters. One he specifically wanted me to meet was the department in Disney responsible for their musicals. *The Lion King* had recently become the hottest ticket on Broadway. The Disney movie studio had made an animated version of the Chinese tale *Mulan*. He wanted me to get Disney to create a stage musical from the film and then premiere it in Hong Kong. He wanted exclusivity for Hong Kong as long as it could possibly run – maybe one or two years before it toured elsewhere in the region. This would ensure a huge regular inflow of tourists.

Having known Douglas for 20 years and despite our friendship during that time, this was yet more madness! Sheer madness! I asked who was going to pay Disney to make this happen. Disney, he replied! I reminded him that creating a musical could take up to a year and involve dozens of talented individuals to work on the book, the lyrics, the songs and the orchestrations. All these people had to be paid. A producer/director, casting director, choreographer, set, costume and lighting designers had then to be contracted long before a period of at least three months of rehearsals commenced. Even before the show was ready, Disney would also have to cough up a huge deposit for an open-ended run in a theatre. But Hong Kong had no theatre which could be hired on an open-ended basis. Indeed, following complaints from the local performing companies who were locked out of its largest theatre, the Grand Theatre in the HKCC, during the 18 weeks when *Phantom of the Opera* had rented it in 1995, the relevant committee of the old Urban Council had placed a ban on any hire in excess of 11 weeks. I knew I would be laughed out of the Disney office unless I had arrived bearing many millions of US dollars as a down-payment and a guarantee of a working theatre.

Douglas got angry. Go!, he said again. Persuade them! I have no idea what planet he thought he was living on by that stage. But it was certainly some sort of cloud cuckoo land.

Finally I said I would undertake the trip with stops in London, New York and Los Angeles. I would take my faithful assistant K. C. Lee with me and we'd arrange it in January. No, said Douglas. You must go now! I was incredulous. This was more madness.

"Don't you realise," I said, "that December is the busiest month for almost all event promoters? With the Christmas holidays, there are more events than ever and all promoters will be working overtime to maximise attendances. In London alone, Raymond Gubbay, whom I do wish to meet and who could bring several concert tours and events to Hong Kong, has nightly different concerts in the Royal Albert Hall with over 150,000 tickets to sell. Broadway shows are packed. It's the worst possible month to spend money on such a trip."

Nothing would dissuade him. Since it was an order, I could not decline. I therefore spoke to K. C. to work out a schedule of possible meetings. I also sent a detailed memo to the travel office copied to Douglas requesting flights and hotels. It soon came back with flights. But the head of the office apologised. There were so many tourists in those cities in December she could not obtain any hotels for us!

Rather than take this up with Douglas, I first spoke to the HKTA offices in each of the cities. They would find hotels for us, I was informed. Yet two days prior to our departure from Hong Kong, London had still been unable to find any hotel. New York had been unable to find any hotel. Los Angeles was the same. I wrote memos to each pointing out this was an "emergency trip" authorised at the highest level and we had to find accommodation.

On the morning of the day we left, there was a memo saying the London office had found two rooms in the centrally located five-star Churchill Hotel. The rooms would not be available until 3:00pm. Since we were arriving at 6:00am, they would allow us complimentary use of the presidential suite to freshen up and change as they would not require it till the evening. In New York we had to go through the same nonsense with no hotel possible even by the time we had arrived for our three nights in London. Eventually that office did find us rooms in a W Hotel which had just been taken over from another hotel chain. Off mid-Park Avenue, the rooms felt cramped and tired but the location ideal. As we still did not have any accommodation in Los Angeles, I called the agent friend with whom I had worked on a number of projects in Asia, Merv Goldstein. I explained we were on a limited budget but were now desperate. He called back later in the evening to say he had got us two rooms at the Regent Beverly Wilshire Hotel. I knew this would be well above the budget we were permitted, but he quickly added he had got a friend to arrange a 50% discount for us. Surely this would be acceptable to the HKTA mandarins?

I need only add here that Disney did not laugh when I mentioned the *Mulan* suggestion. They thought it a good idea. As I had not only expected but knew perfectly well, they asked how many millions we would put on the table to make it happen. I played dumb and said I would check on this and get back to them after Christmas.

The whole trip was virtually an unmitigated disaster. We came back with some ideas, including the hosting of a Seniors' World Cup just prior to the 2002 Soccer World Cup in Japan and South Korea. It did, though, have one unusual and very unexpected result. A couple of weeks after our return, K. C. and I received formal memos from the head of administration. These stated we had not paid attention to HKTA regulations by staying in hotels that were above the grade permitted by our level of responsibility. We were asked for an explanation before being given a formal slap on the wrists: we must not do this again.

Had I not become used to the level of incompetence and the lack of communication between departments and individuals in the HKTA, I would have stormed into the office of the CEO. Instead I went into K. C.'s office and we just laughed. I then went into the office of Grace who headed administration and lost my temper. By now it was becoming abundantly clear that I just could not work for much longer in this organisation which was totally incompetent when it came to the matter of events.

If the first two problems were infuriating, the next was by far the most difficult, most complex and was ultimately to result in extremely serious repercussions for the IEF and the HKTA. It stemmed innocently enough from a request to the HKTA chairman. Y. S. Lo knew a German businessman in Hong Kong who was starting to pester him about the value to Hong Kong of hosting a Formula 1 Grand Prix race. There was no doubt that a race similar to the annual Monaco Grand Prix street circuit would do wonders for the image of Hong Kong, the more so with the city's skyline and harbour prominently seen in so many worldwide television images.

Formula 1 had never seriously been on the HKTA radar until soon after that meeting. In the late 1990s, the city of Zhuhai just north of Macao had built a circuit with the intention of hosting China's first Formula 1 race. F1 officials visited Zhuhai several times and a race was placed on the provisional F1 calendar for the year 2000. The world champion in 1998 and 1999 was the Finnish driver Mika Häkkinen. The first green flag to be waved was a request to the HKTA hotels department requesting a hold on 10,000 rooms over the weekend of the F1 Zhuhai race.

Few events at any time required 10,000 rooms for four consecutive nights. I then received a memo asking me what was Formula 1 (!) and why would a Finland travel agency seek so many rooms. The HKTA executive was clearly unaware that F1 races have a huge travelling spectator base. One of Zhuhai's problems was lack of hotels. The city could only accommodate the racing teams, all their travelling personnel and F1 officials. That was no real problem with Macao just a few kilometres away. But Macao's hotel building boom was still only in the planning stage. With many hundreds of journalists and broadcasters from all over the world there would be little possibility of accommodating up to 100,000 non-Chinese spectators who would also descend on our part of Asia. So the travel agent in Finland had assumed Hong Kong would be the next best bet. Analysing the travel requirements, though, it was obvious that transporting perhaps around 80,000 daily between Hong Kong and Zhuhai would be a logistical nightmare since most would wish to travel at roughly the same times each day. Apart from the lack of sea transport, the immigration officers in Zhuhai would certainly be overwhelmed and unable to cope with such numbers. Unsurprisingly, Zhuhai's F1 Grand Prix never happened. China would have to wait until the opening of the Shanghai circuit in 2004. But interest in having so many visitors to Hong Kong if a race could be held in the territory suddenly became of great interest.

As a result the HKTA chairman asked me to take his German friend for lunch, which I did at the Foreign Correspondents' Club. He explained he was a friend of the former F1 driver Gerhard Berger. As a fan of F1, I knew of Berger and had seen him race. Since retiring as a driver he had become a consultant. He was very keen to come to Hong Kong and undertake a study on the feasibility of a race. I asked how much such a study would cost. I was informed he had done a similar study which resulted in the Austrian Grand Prix being reinstated in the annual F1 calendar. This went into all manner of detail. He would arrange for it to be sent to me. He then informed me a study for Hong Kong would cost US$50,000.

That seemed a huge amount of money given all the problems we would face with the Environment Protection Department regulations alone. With the noise of just one F1 car revving around the north shore of the Island emitting around 150 decibels in 1999, this would easily break the maximum decibel level for those living and working nearby. I suspected with between 20 and 24 cars the noise would be heard throughout Kowloon as far as the Lion Rock Tunnel. Developing a circuit on Hong Kong Island had to be out of the question. There would be a need to repave many of the roads and find locations for huge public grandstands. An extensive pit area for the teams plus the space above it for the very large corporate hospitality facilities which form a part of every F1 Grand Prix were also vital. Where could that be located?

I asked Patrick Condon how Australia handled the noise factor given that the country had similarly effective noise pollution legislation. He told me the organisers of the Australian F1 Grand Prix in Melbourne merely negotiated a fine which was then paid to the state of Victoria for breaking the regulations. Initial discussions with the Hong Kong Environmental Protection Department got nowhere. The response was a simple 'No'!

Reading through Berger's report on the Austrian Grand Prix, it quickly became obvious the financial arguments also meant little for Hong Kong. The basic fee payable to the F1 organisation was then in excess of US$25 million. The local infrastructure costs would add at least 100% more. Provided they could be accommodated beside the racetrack, the entrance ticket prices for the 100,000 or so who would be expected to watch the race would go some way to offsetting this expenditure. But by far the largest financial argument in Berger's report for Austria was in the amount of VAT gained by the government on overseas visitors' tickets, accommodation and other local expenditure. Hong Kong only had a small tax on hotels. It had no VAT. At a stroke it was obvious an F1 race would be an impossible drain on the public purse.

It so happened that around this time I met a man named Peter Wearing-Smith. An Australian, Wearing-Smith was heavily involved with the annual Macao Formula 3 race meeting where he was a consultant to the Watson's Racing Team from Hong Kong. He had come to my office to introduce me to two Australians who had previously done considerable work for Hong Kong's Museum of History. They informed me they were working on an event titled *The Spirit of Flight* which was scheduled to open in San Francisco 18 months later. It would include large models of many historical aircraft. The *pièce de resistance* was a walk-through model of the Concorde. It occurred to me that rather than spend US$50,000 on a report by Gerhard Berger, we could instead spend US$2,500 or thereabouts on getting Wearing-Smith to write one.

After discussions with Douglas, this was agreed. After presentation, it was obvious an F1 race was simply not possible. It must have been galling for those in charge of tourism to learn that in 2008 Hong Kong's rival city of Singapore would be awarded the world's first night race thanks to a partnership between the private and public sectors. It was a huge success and has been part of the F1 calendar ever since. The total cost of that first race was just over US$100 million.

Wearing-Smith was very keen that we become involved financially with *The Spirit of Flight* project. He later flew to Australia and reported back on progress. On the Australia autumn trip that I had been forced to cancel, I had planned to visit the Australians' studio to satisfy myself on early design progress. Eventually the Australians came to Hong Kong to show us a portfolio of large-scale drawings on the various exhibits. These certainly looked impressive.

Nothing more about it was heard until K. C. and I were in Los Angeles. Before going out to attend a morning meeting, I received a call from a man who said he was an independent event financier. I can no longer recall his name and believe he said he was based in Arizona. Here I shall merely here call him 'the financier'. He said he had recently met the two Australians and had decided to invest in *The Spirit of Flight* project. So much interest had been expressed by cities in the USA and in Asia that he would be investing in the project on the basis that two identical exhibitions would be created. That would enable an exhibition to open in Hong Kong earlier than originally thought. Singapore's events fund would also be providing financing.

He then steered the conversation around to the IEF. Realistically, how much did I think the Hong Kong exhibition could apply for? I informed him the rules established by the committee stipulated that the maximum amount for any one event would be US$1 million. But this would only be for a particularly attractive event. Like all IEF-funded events, it would also have to go through the extensive vetting process before funding was approved. I added I felt $500,000 would be a certainty but he should not bank on more. He then informed me that he would be going to Australia in the spring. On that trip he would return via Hong Kong to meet with me and my colleagues on his way back to the USA.

Prior to that meeting we learned from Peter Wearing-Smith that he would be involved in the event by chairing the Hong Kong company being set up to oversee the exhibition. All involved were aware that funds from the IEF could only be provided to a Hong Kong registered company, not one based overseas. Applications for funding would be made by that company and first reviewed by myself and K. C. If we found merit in the project, the application would then be sent to the HKTA hierarchy before being vetted by the full IEF committee, the one with Allan Zeman and Selina Chow among its membership. Subject to approval by the committee along with a final recommendation for the amount of funding to be awarded, the papers would go through to the HKTA's head of administration for a final review and thereafter approval to release the funds after discussion with the CEO.

There was one flaw in the decision about funds being remitted only to a Hong Kong-registered company. Once these funds had been awarded and remitted to the company, there was no procedure for tracking how the funds were thereafter spent. Nor was there any provision preventing the company from remitting the funding overseas, even though one primary objective of the IEF was to assist promoters with the extra costs they would have to incur specifically within Hong Kong.

The financier duly arrived in Hong Kong and took several officials from the HKTA along with Wearing-Smith out for a very pleasant dinner on a junk in the harbour. He made it clear to Douglas and me that Wearing-Smith would be applying for the maximum US$1 million. We would receive the application within a matter of days. Just as it arrived, Douglas came to my office for another of his little chats. There was now greater urgency in approving *The Spirit of Flight* application, he told me. Amy Chan had been informed that a top civil servant had become aware of the event and was very keen that the IEF be seen to fund at least one mega-event prior to the millennium. *The Spirit of Flight* application then became fast-tracked. It sailed through the IEF committee and was sent through to Administration. The full US$1 million was then remitted to the new company headed by Wearing-Smith.

As earlier noted, for many months I had become increasingly frustrated and not a little angry at the way I was treated at the HKTA. I determined there was no possibility I could see the end of my three-year contract. By leaving early, I realised I would lose my 15% end-of-contract bonus in lieu of a pension. But I had not taken the job primarily for the money. I even found the friendship I had enjoyed with Douglas for nearly two decades had soured so badly to the point where I no longer trusted him. This saddened me. Accordingly, I consulted my lawyer about getting out of the contract early. Going through the full details of my appointment, my contract and the promises made, he felt there were certainly grounds for leaving as the HKTA was in breach of three contractual items. In accordance with the terms of the contract, I would have to give the HKTA two weeks in which to make good the broken promises. If thereafter nothing had been done, I could legally depart.

I first told K. C. Lee, who had worked with me over many of the previous 15 years, of my plans. He said he not only perfectly understood, he too would leave soon after. As I placed little trust in what anyone told me any more, I spent part of a week going through files and making photocopies of several documents which proved many of the points I have written here. Two weeks before my monthly salary was due, I handed the head of administration my resignation letter. Surprisingly, at least so I thought, I received no reply until 13 days later. It was then a brief letter informing me the HKTA had taken note of my complaints and would give them due consideration. They would eventually give me a reply. I do not know if they wished me to leave or if they assumed I was bluffing. The following afternoon they realised I was not bluffing. As soon as I had notification from the bank about my monthly fee having been deposited, I said goodbye to K. C. and walked out of the office. Immediately I drove to the General Post Office in Central and posted letters to each of the IEF committee members informing them of my action and the reasons behind it.

The relief I felt by not having to be in that HKTA office before 9:00 every morning was a huge weight off my mind. I decided I was just going to spend two months relaxing before looking for another job. What I was not in any way prepared for was a request to report to the Hong Kong Police Headquarters in Admiralty. An investigation had been opened into *The Spirit of Flight* exhibition. As I later discovered, the financier who had been so keen on developing a second exhibition had disappeared with the $1 million loan from the IEF. What Peter Wearing-Smith had done on receipt of the funds, I can only surmise. Almost certainly he must have remitted most if not all to the USA or Australia whereupon it disappeared. Soon, though, I was to learn that Douglas had put two and two together and made 26. He jumped to the assumption that my departure was linked to the loss of those funds! The HKTA's expensive lawyers were instructed to investigate everything thoroughly and then to take action against me if they found any evidence whatever.

Given all the hurdles that had to be overcome before loan funding from the IEF could be provided, the idea that I might have benefitted from *The Spirit of Flight* exhibition in any way was ridiculous. It would have meant I had to be in bed in some way with Wearing-Smith, the

American financier and the two Australians. When I attended the Police Headquarters to make a formal statement, it was abundantly clear to the police that I had no relationship with any involved in the exhibition. I never found out what evidence Wearing-Smith had provided, nor what the Australians had provided – assuming they had indeed been contacted, or to find out how they had become involved with the financier. Nor did I have a clue how what had been presented as a very valid project from a pair of Australians who had already worked very satisfactorily on other projects in Hong Kong had become wrapped up in what was clearly a scam.

Thereafter, I heard nothing more. I never heard of any court case that materialised nor read anything in the media about how the HKTA had been scammed out of a very large sum. All I learned from an insider was that the prospect of legal proceedings against me had been initiated by Douglas. Little more than a year later Douglas had left along with his fat end-of-contract bonus. Even before then it was announced that Amy Chan, a 29-year veteran with the Association, was taking early retirement and would leave the HKTA. Many asked –

"Did she resign or was she pushed?"

Regularly critical of her, the *South China Morning Post* "made it clear that Chan was pushed out." As bad, the government's first Commissioner for Tourism, civil servant Mike Rowse, also left his post in 2000 after less than a year in the job. Hong Kong tourism had lost its three key players in remarkably quick succession.[3]

The future would soon see the HKTA abolished and replaced by a new Hong Kong Tourism Board. This is also tasked with sourcing events. Frankly, civil servants and tourism bodies have their own very specific areas of expertise. Sourcing, negotiating with event producers and then organising the events themselves desperately requires a private sector of experts and impresarios. Yet why Hong Kong continues on this road, I just do not know.

The friendship I had enjoyed with Douglas over two decades had not only gone downhill badly during my time at the HKTA. After I left, it died. When I met him some years later at a reception following a Hong Kong Philharmonic concert, I acknowledged his presence by politely saying "hello". I refused to shake his hand.

29

WEST KOWLOON: A GREAT IDEA DRAMATICALLY WATERED DOWN

Near the end of my refreshing two-month break from the HKTA, I was extremely surprised to receive a call from Johnny Chin of Sun Hung Kai Properties (SHKP). I only knew Johnny because he had been the SHKP executive with whom Stanley Yip had negotiated the rental for use of part of the Tamar site as a car park. Johnny asked to meet. He wanted me to join a team of architects, engineers and other experts being assembled by SHKP to make a bid for what had been termed the West Kowloon Cultural District. I would be the team's artistic consultant. Although it was not known how long the employment would last, I jumped at the opportunity, for I had been involved in this project almost since my first day working at the HKTA 18 months earlier.

For several years, those living and working on Hong Kong Island had looked over to Kowloon and seen a plot of highly desirable reclaimed land still undeveloped. During the Chief Executive's annual address to Legco in October 1998, the public learned that the site had been earmarked as the West Kowloon Cultural District. The first of its several international quality cultural venues, an impressive and large opera house, was due to open as part of the celebrations marking the 10th anniversary of the return of Hong Kong to China in 2007. The opera house would be comparable in size and quality to many then being designed and constructed for major cities in China. As discussed earlier, this would enable Hong Kong to become part of a natural Chinese touring circuit for the best international performing events.

By 2008 and a vast array of changes later, little was happening on the site. Indeed, as I write in 2022, there is still very little happening as originally planned. Ten years after the announcement to Legco, the government decided to form the West Kowloon Cultural District Authority (WKCDA) led by an executive committee to oversee the planning. As with many government bodies involving the arts, the WKCDA comprised few who had any practical professional experience in the performing arts. This body was then especially unfortunate in having to appoint three CEOs in the space of just one year after two quickly departed. Overall, the project which held out so much initial promise has, in my view, very sadly become a hugely wasted opportunity to create a Hong Kong that would have been much closer to becoming at least one of the "events capitals of Asia". To discover the reason why that has not happened, it is necessary to go back and review how the whole West Kowloon project was botched from the outset, a result of continual alterations to the plans due primarily to interference from parties who seemingly refused to take any specialised international advice on how to proceed.

When the HKTA had come up with its plan to make Hong Kong the *Events Capital of Asia*, it fully accepted that there were two parts of the jigsaw missing. One was the relative lack of private-sector local impresarios and the funding needed to assist overseas promoters in the administration of their projects; the other was what was becoming a quite serious lack of suitable performing venues. It was partly to overcome the first that the IEF had been established. The fact that no-one had ever taken time to consider why Hong Kong had hardly any private-sector arts impresarios by the late 1990s seems not to have been considered, when it certainly should have been. Tokyo was the true events capital of Asia in large measure because of its thriving and very diverse private sector. Seoul was quickly following behind for the same reason. That major international companies like those run by Cameron Mackintosh, Andrew Lloyd Webber and International Management Group's Asian Artists' Division (IMGA) had opened up companies in Hong Kong had been encouraging, but all quickly closed them. It must have been somewhat galling when IMGA moved its base to Hong Kong's rival Singapore.

Throughout 1998, within the HKTA I led a committee considering the second issue: the need for a major new arts/entertainment venue. This working group had received a grant of HK$3 million from the government. The project team included experts in architecture, theatre and more general performance-based events, other event production, tourism and estate management. By year's end our group of professionals had put together the drafts of two large volumes of a report.

I led the presentation to a meeting of representatives from about 20 government departments early in 1999. The basic proposals outlined a consortium of facilities to include a new opera house-type theatre capable of the largest theatrical productions, and a second even larger arena approximately mid-way in size between the Queen Elizabeth Stadium in Wanchai and the Hong Kong Coliseum. What happened thereafter during the internal discussions at both the HKTA and government level, I am not aware since I had ceased my activities with the HKTA early that summer.

For the location of the facilities, our group identified four possible sites. The most desired was closest to the city centre – the vacant Tamar site. Just as New York's theatre and entertainment facilities are clustered around Broadway going up as far as the Lincoln Center with its home for many art forms including the Metropolitan Opera and the New York Philharmonic Orchestra, and London theatres are clustered around the West End, the Tamar site's central location and proximity to the City Hall and Academy for Performing Arts complexes made it by far the most ideal. The West Kowloon reclamation, the newly vacant Kai Tak airport site and one on Lantau were the other very much secondary options. Unfortunately, the government already had its eye on the Tamar site as the location for new government offices. Why government offices have to occupy prime harbour sites has always seemed more than strange to me. These could surely have been located elsewhere rather than on an expensive piece of harbourfront real estate, especially one which could have been a natural gathering place for entertainment events.

In October 1999, after I had started working for SHKP, the government called a meeting of all local property developers. This was held in the Concert Hall of the HKCC. As everyone entered, they were handed a photocopied three-sheet summary. These were the basic requirements for those entering the competition for development of West Kowloon.

The paper was long on generalities; very short on specifics. A detailed design competition for the entire site would be held. Rather surprisingly it would be open only to local developers. Requirements included the large lyric theatre/opera house, a medium-sized theatre, and what is known as a small black-box theatre – an infinitely variable space that is often used for experimental works. At that stage the facilities seemed almost a mirror image of those in the HKCC. Detail and size were to be up to each competition entrant. An art gallery/museum and venues for other more entertainment-based productions like the hugely popular *Cirque du Soleil* were also to be incorporated. Opening date for the large lyric theatre had to be the summer of 2007 in time to celebrate the 10th anniversary of the return of Hong Kong to China. For the remainder of the complex, opening dates would be at some time still then to be determined in the mid-2010s.

A key item concerned the land itself. The West Kowloon site covered approximately 80 acres partially split in the middle by ventilation shafts for the cross-harbour tunnels for road and MTR transport. The winning developer would be awarded the entire area for 30 years. The 40 acres closest to the built-up Kowloon area could be used by the developer for profit-generating commercial purposes like office blocks, upmarket housing, retail and other commercial activities. The western half was earmarked for the Cultural District.

Even more significant were those paragraphs dealing with financing. The successful developer would not only have to plan, design and construct all the cultural facilities; it would be required to run them for the period of the lease. In other words, much of the profit from the commercial developments would need to be ploughed into financing the new cultural facilities and their offerings. The intention was that the Cultural District be run very much along the lines of the multi-venue Lincoln Center in New York – a completely new departure for Hong Kong. For the first time in Hong Kong's history, a large part of the territory's arts, culture and entertainment would be in private rather than government hands. Many believed this marked an excellent new development that would lead to enhanced competition between civil service-run venues and private-sector venues. The citizens of Hong Kong could only benefit as a result.

At the end of the meeting, the government representatives asked for the return of their document. In the light of future events, this proved an eminently sensible decision. If you cannot be proved to have stated something, it becomes easy to deny it was ever said in the first place! Someone in SHKP had, however, arranged for the document to be taken out and copied during the meeting!

Only a few property developers immediately plunged into their planning for the new Cultural District. Within SHKP we were given very tight deadlines for each phase of the planning. To understand what makes ideal theatres and event spaces, our project team travelled all over the world from Tokyo and Osaka to Las Vegas and New York, London to Sydney. Amongst others, we looked at good opera houses and bad ones, good theatres and less good theatres, superb large museums and more boutique, excellently run smaller galleries. At each venue, a film crew recorded my comments on the facilities and general reasons why the venue worked well or not.

In addition to the hardware, we met with a large number of software providers, from event and theatrical producers like those from *Cirque du Soleil* and the Cameron Mackintosh companies to directors of the world's most famous entertainment conglomerates as with those from Disney musicals and top international museums and galleries like the Guggenheim in Los Angeles and New York. At the same time I was heavily involved in estimating details of all the staffing that would be required. Preparation of budgets covering the first five years of actual performances was another of my responsibilities.

One event already creeping up fast on Hong Kong was the Asian economic crisis that had started in Thailand in July 1997. Hong Kong had largely dodged the initial financial recession that had impacted the economies of all other Asian countries. That finally hit Hong Kong hard in 2000. The recession that ensued was the worst since World War II. One of the first sectors to feel the pinch was the property market. By the end of the millennium, demand had collapsed and land values were plummeting. Developers had little interest in new projects. The prospect of having to develop a 40-acre site on West Kowloon and diverting a large chunk of the profits into cultural facilities and presentations in the adjoining 40 acres was far from appealing to most. Few had any interest whatever in West Kowloon.

Aware of this lack of enthusiasm, the government made the first of what was to become a series of major U-turns. First it changed the terms of the competition. No longer would proposals be expected to present full details of the various cultural components, the type of shows, events and exhibitions to be presented, along with specific details of staffing and budgeting. Instead, the competition would be severely restricted to very basic components such as overall layout and town planning. For those of us who had spent so much time on the detail, this was a massive disappointment. Most of our extremely detailed work would at best have to be put on to the back burner. Many of us then found ourselves out of a job. Still, though, less than a handful of developers entered the competition.

A winner was eventually announced. Having submitted three entries, SHKP perhaps unsurprisingly won with a general design concept whose primary feature was a monster undulating canopy covering much of the site designed by the celebrated architect Norman Foster. Public debate was totally split on such a massive structure dominating the West Kowloon skyline. So much so that the government was forced to call yet another time-out.

After the passage of yet another 18 months, it finally announced the next phase. It intended to keep the canopy structure. All the other facilities would have to be accommodated underneath. That drew yet more criticism. But it was not the only outcry facing the government. During the multi-year delay since the initial announcement of the project, two other groups had since had time to rethink their views.

With the local economy recovering from the recession, several developers now cried "Foul!" The essence of this claim was that by awarding one developer the entire West Kowloon site, the government was effectively doing a land deal. Whereas they had shown absolutely no interest three years earlier, with land prices on the rise, these developers now wanted a piece of the action. And they used all their government contacts and PR resources to press their claim.

After further heated debate, even after the government had revised the competition guidelines, to calm the storm it once again changed tack. So yet another design competition was announced. The entries of the three winners were exhibited in detail and public comments invited. It was now fast becoming a typical government fudge. How could any government expect members of the general public to comment on aspects of what are extremely technical and specialised arts facilities?

Within government circles, though, a second storm was brewing. Some senior civil servants working in the field of arts and culture were by now lobbying hard behind the scenes. Their concern? A privatised West Kowloon would almost certainly steal away some of those civil servants with the most experience in the management of existing arts, culture and entertainment facilities. After all, the government's LCSD by now not only planned and managed most of Hong Kong's venues, it was Hong Kong's biggest and virtually exclusive arts impresario. If it were to lose its key civil servants, would there be enough expertise left within LCSD? Unlikely, was the view increasingly promoted by those special interests within the administration.

This was all so extremely narrow-minded. There are many thousands of highly experienced managers and technical personnel around the world, including more than a few in greater China, who would have loved the chance of working in Hong Kong. That, though, proved of little consequence. The fudge was now complete. Internal pressures won the day.

As noted, the government-approved WKCDA was finally put in place to oversee the future of the project. How many, I wonder, realised that its creation came about a year after the Opera House on West Kowloon was supposed to have opened its doors to the public? The WKCDA appointed its first executive director in mid-2009, a former executive from Hong Kong's small and hurriedly conceived Disneyland. He lasted only a fortnight before resigning. Future appointments were hardly more successful. After it was announced in the spring of 2010 that Graham Sheffield, the artistic director of London's Barbican Centre, had been appointed, I met with Graham in his London office before he left for Hong Kong. My hope was that perhaps there might be projects we could work on together. It was an extremely affable meeting that went on for much longer than the allotted 30 minutes. It was quickly obvious that Sheffield knew little about Hong Kong. Indeed, he seemed to use the meeting to find out a lot more on what he should really have been briefed prior to his appointment. I also left that meeting wondering how it was that a man whose experience was in organising arts performances (i.e. performance software) had been appointed to a post when there was absolutely no possibility of any performances taking place for close to a decade. What that job required was a professional much more experienced in the performance hardware of venue design and putting bricks and mortar together, skilled also in persuading often reluctant officials that his way was the right way in giving Hong Kong the best physical facilities possible. I was not at all surprised when Graham walked out of his highly paid job within about four months. That another two CEOs were eventually to resign or were forced to resign surely indicates that the committee's appointment procedures were flawed.

I should add here that I have a great deal of respect for LCSD and its predecessors, the CSDs of the Urban and Regional Councils. Without their work, Hong Kong could well have remained a cultural desert. Like Topsy, though, they had just grown and grown to an immense size. And with hardly any member of the Legislative Council having any experience of the arts and entertainment business (with the honourable exception of Selina Chow), there was the impression given that the blind were all but leading the blind. Thus, quite unusually – and unlike most other major international cities – Hong Kong's arts, entertainment and culture had come to be largely provided and financed by the public purse.

Under the WKCDA, staffing would not be civil servants. But the government was still supplying all the funding. Thus instead of the fully private sector-driven enterprise on West Kowloon that I remain convinced would have revitalised the sector with a wide variety of new and original venues providing new and original offerings, someone or some group within the administration had decided the management of the West Kowloon facilities be taken out of private hands and, like almost all other venues, be overseen effectively by the civil service. In 2011 the cost to the public purse of the entire West Kowloon project was announced as over HK$29 billion. And even though the initial completion date of the entire complex has now been delayed by over a decade and a half, it will likely end up not only as a great deal longer, it will also be even more expensive. Few today realise the cost could have – and in my view should have – been much closer to $0! Further, the land and the cultural facilities would have reverted to the government after 30 years! In many respects it could surely have been a total win-win situation for Hong Kong.

Finance and the type and quality of performances are just two issues. Developers who had taken part in the various competitions had brought in a number of the world's most renowned architects. These included Frank Gehry and Cesar Pelli. For the third design competition I was engaged by Swire Properties (SP) which had been a silent partner with SHKP in 1999/2000. Aware of the increasing land value of the West Kowloon site, SP decided that rather than locate so many facilities and venues in one relatively small area with what could well result in consequent problems of access and egress if all venues had performances at the same time, SP decided its submission would be based on Hong Kong as a whole being a 'cultural harbour'. This would complement the existing facilities on both sides: the City Hall complex, the Academy for Performing Arts venues, the smaller Arts Centre, the notoriously ugly HKCC and the undistinguished exterior of the Art Gallery. SP's plan was to locate a Frank Gehry-designed museum between the two Island complexes. For Kowloon the plans involved stripping the HKCC of its entire windowless, featureless façade and replacing it with an all-glass exterior providing stunning views from inside its public spaces. The Art Gallery would be deconstructed and moved elsewhere to provide room for a world-class opera house that would be directly linked to and complement the HKCC.

Since any deviation from the West Kowloon reclamation was not part of the competition, it was no surprise to any on the team that SP's submission was rejected outright. Stupidly so, in my view. Although I gave the impression earlier that there is a benefit from clustering performance venues as in New York and London, not all such venues are included in those clusters. This is particularly true of concert halls, galleries and museums. So I still believe today that spreading the new arts venues around the harbour rather than concentrating them all in one location was a superb solution on the part of SP. But that surely is part of the problem when civil servants take control of what was intended as a purely private-sector enterprise. Rules are rules and must be followed however frequently they change, no matter that without independent outside expert consultants there could surely have been room for a degree of flexibility and variety with the final design being more dependent on its overall benefit to Hong Kong.

Even so, having had the opportunity of meeting Frank Gehry was certainly one of the highlights for me. Who knows? Perhaps Hong Kong could have ended up with at least one building as iconic as the Gehry-designed Guggenheim Museum in Bilbao or the Walt Disney Concert Hall in Los Angeles. We can only hope that nowhere on West Kowloon will Hong Kong once again end up with another government architectural design disaster like the windowless, soulless exterior of the Hong Kong Cultural Centre.

30

SUMMARY: HOW MUCH AND WHO PAID?

Having spent most of my career in various branches of the performing arts in Hong Kong over several decades and having voiced both plaudits and criticisms about the manner in which the arts were managed, I cannot end this series of reminiscences without looking in some detail at the funding element.

By the mid-1990s and with the return of administration back to Beijing just two years away, the disbandment of the Urban and Regional Councils became an issue of concern. Both looked after the management of almost all the major performing venues and arts galleries in addition to the Urban Council providing large annual subsidies to many of Hong Kong's performing ensembles. With the government also providing some direct financing to some performing companies, an overriding question at the time was: did anyone in government have any real clue of the true cost of this annual contribution to the arts in Hong Kong?

How the arts are funded by governments is always a thorny issue, the more so when taxpayer funding is also required for hospitals, schools and other community services. There will always be some who argue that arts should be an integral part of our lives, just as there are some who advocate they are a waste of precious resources. In March 2022, arts managers in England and Wales (which have a separate funding formula from Scotland and Northern Ireland) were in uproar about funding cuts which would see a dramatic fall off in opera touring. The national broadcaster, the BBC, soon faced unprecedented opposition to its plans to disband the professional chorus it has maintained for almost 50 years, the excellent

BBC Singers. So strong has been the strength of public feeling that the BBC has been forced to reverse course, at least for the time being. Other proposed cuts to the strength of the BBC's three English-based symphony orchestras remain after the suggestion that replacements be found from freelance players has drawn equal derision.

Part of the problem in England and Wales lies in the appointment of arts ministers in the Westminster government with little knowledge and understanding of the arts. In addition, those who are appointed to the Arts Council of England and Wales, the arms-length body established to receive funding from the government and then decide how it is to be allocated, are frequently criticised for being incompetent in more than a few disciplines. In its 2022 review, it argued for the move of the English National Opera (ENO) from the large Coliseum Opera House in the centre of London, where it has been based since 1968, to Manchester. Unless the company did so, funding would cease. In other words, the company would be killed off. This more than cavalier decision totally failed to consider the costs of moving for a company comprising several hundred people, most with mortgages in London, children in schools – and so on. Since that decision was announced, the Arts Council has backtracked, if only slightly. Where the ENO will finally be based remains unknown as I write.

Perhaps with a similar desire to set itself to a certain extent at arms-length from at least some arts funding, the Hong Kong administration decided to establish the Arts Development Council (ADC) in 1995. Rather like the Arts Councils in Great Britain, this body would be provided with annual grants. It would then decide how that funding was to be allocated, but only to five of Hong Kong's performing companies – the City Contemporary Dance Company, Hong Kong Ballet, the Hong Kong Sinfonietta, Chung Ying Theatre Company and Exploration Theatre. Some larger 'national' performing companies would soon cease being funded in whole or in part by the Urban Council and had that funding responsibility taken over by LCSD. These were the the Hong Kong Philharmonic Orchestra, the Hong Kong Arts Festival, the Hong

Kong Chinese Orchestra, the Hong Kong Dance Company and the Hong Kong Repertory Theatre.

Still no one knew how much was actually being spent. Even more crucially, was it being spent wisely? After all, the Hong Kong Philharmonic had become the first effective local professional performing company in 1974, a mere 21 years earlier. (The Arts Festival had been inaugurated a year beforehand but management and almost the entire programmes for the first few years were of artists and performances from overseas. It could not till later be regarded as local). Since then, as described earlier, the creation and financing of performing companies and the development of the arts infrastructure in general had grown like Topsy.

In an effort to get some handle on the total level of funding – and especially its relationship to the funding of similar organisations in other countries – at the start of 1997 the ADC commissioned an in-depth study from the accounting firm Coopers & Lybrand. Its report, titled *Hong Kong Arts Development Council: Review of General Support Grant,* was submitted in October 1997. The report itself runs to 62 pages with 1,308 paragraphs to which are added several long appendices. Yet the bulk of the report only considers the five performing companies in receipt of subventions from the ADC. Given that the government's subvention to the Philharmonic alone was higher than that given to all five ADC subvented companies put together, how much use the report turned out to be has to be somewhat questionable.

In summary, the report highlights the ad hoc historical nature of the development of the performing arts in Hong Kong with companies being formed, or turned from amateur to professional bodies, as a result primarily of administration decisions. It congratulates the various governing bodies on having the "most developed arts infrastructure in the region with the probable exception of Japan" but adds not only that the level of public subsidy provided by government sources is "substantial", when looked at in the context of international performing companies "public subsidy of the arts in Hong Kong is high".

I take issue with these comments about Hong Kong in the regional context. As I mention above, by 1995 Japan and Tokyo in particular was so far ahead of Hong Kong that the use of the adjective "probable" was ridiculous. Further, South Korea as a whole and Seoul in particular had the second most developed arts infrastructure in Asia. Although these are perhaps basically irrelevant to the overall argument, they unfortunately gave the lie to the HKTA's soon to be announced slogan of Hong Kong being the *Events Capital of Asia*!

The issue of total arts subsidies being just "high" is also questionable. One of several confusing elements in the report regards the figures in Table 3.3. This provides detail of the annual per capita government spend on the arts in various countries. Germany comes top with US$311; Hong Kong second at US$288. In comparison, the average spend in the UK was only US$132. When we note that the population in Germany in 1995 was 81.86 million and that in Hong Kong 6.156 million, comparisons become easier. Germany thus spent US$25.458 billion on the arts whereas Hong Kong was spending US$1.773 billion. On that basis at least, the Hong Kong total seems far from unreasonable.

There is a vital – and vast – difference, though. If we take into consideration the fact that both national subsidies relate to the number of performing companies and the running and maintenance of buildings for the arts and culture, it becomes very obvious that the report completely fails in attempting to compare like with like. For example, as pointed out in a Goethe-Institut paper written by the journalist Nadine Berghausen[1], by 2019 the subsidy provided by Germany's federal government and its individual states covered roughly 140 theatres, each with professional performing ensembles. These included major international opera companies like those in Munich, Berlin (three separate houses – the Deutsche Oper Berlin, the Komische Oper and the Staatsoper Unter den Linden), Hamburg, Dusseldorf, Cologne, Dresden and Stuttgart. All employ their own full-time orchestras, singers, choruses, ballet companies, specialist technicians, scenery and costume workshops, and smaller theatre companies. Accordingly, it is likely that each has a full-time permanent staff of an average of somewhere between 700 and 2,000 employees. As I write, the Berlin Staatsoper Unter den Linden alone has roughly 200 permanent staff purely in the various technical departments.

Subsidy is also provided to around 70 other smaller opera companies[2]. Then add in to the mix symphony orchestras. These include large world-class ensembles like the Berlin Philharmonic, the Staatskapelle Dresden, the Leipzig Gewandhausorchester, the Bavarian Radio Symphony as well as more than 120 others (which include some smaller chamber orchestras like the Stuttgart Chamber Orchestra). Then add in more than 7,000 art galleries and museums, as well as 70 music festivals held each year. Although there is a 24-year difference in the comparative figures in these reports, the total number of companies in Germany did not increase by any measurable degree between 1995 and 2019.

We can therefore quickly see that official subsidies to the arts in Germany were not only vastly more efficient than those in Hong Kong: they were humongously so. It is not only the number of companies and management of buildings for the arts that the subsidy covers, it is also employment. Approximately 1.8 million full-time professionals are employed in the performing arts and other creative industries in Germany. With Hong Kong's total subsidy being roughly 7% that of Germany, a comparison of the total per capita subsidy should result in Hong Kong employing about 126,000 professionals. According to the website statista.com, the number of professionals similarly employed in the performing arts in Hong Kong in 2020 was just 5,280.[3] Even if those figures fail to include civil servants managing the performing arts and those involved in music education at, for example, the HKAPA, they are staggeringly below the total employment created as a result of the subsidy in Germany.

The Hong Kong government does publish a paper titled *Hong Kong: The Facts – Creative Industries*. This indicates that in July 2022, Hong Kong had 29,420 creative industry-related establishments and the sector employed 136,470. Look more closely, however, and this paper is not involved with the professional performing arts. It deals almost exclusively with several initiatives covering design, fashion and film. In no way, therefore, can that figure of 136,470 compare with employment in Germany's professional performing arts companies.[4]

The issue is further confused by another paper issued by the Research Office of the Legislative Council Secretariat titled *Statistical Highlights: Art Sector in Hong Kong*.[5] This claims that 29,000 jobs were created in the sector in 2020. But yet again the word "Art" can be confusing for this paper primarily deals not with the performing arts but with the market for international art and art sales in the HKSAR.

Very simply put, therefore, by the mid-1990s Hong Kong was spending a great deal more to generate a great deal less than the other countries in the Coopers & Lybrand report. In terms of value for money, the report highlights some other major issues. For example, the companies exclusively funded by the Urban Council had phenomenally high levels of subsidy. Figure 3.6 in the report shows that in 1996/97 the subsidy as a percentage of total expenditure for the HK Chinese Orchestra and the HK Dance Company respectively was 94% and 97%. This amounted to a cash subsidy for every performance of HK$337,333 and HK$393,529. With average paid attendance at their main performances of only around 300, those subsidies were valued at around US$100 and US$150 per seat sold respectively. Think about this for a moment. No matter the quality of the performances, can such a staggeringly high level of per-seat-sold subsidy really be justified? The answer has to be a resounding 'No'!

The huge subsidies are partly explained in the report as a result of the attitudes of some performing companies giving a near-total lack of importance to anything more than very basic marketing. To a certain extent this is perhaps not really surprising. I agree it is unreasonable to expect civil servants who are rotated between jobs on a regular basis and who happen temporarily to manage a performing company to have much if any expertise in specialist arts marketing. Yet when public performances continue to require subsidies well in excess of 90%, clearly something had to be more than just wrong; it was very wrong.

The last point I will make here is that the report highlights how extremely unusual it is in international terms for any government department responsible for subsidising the performing arts companies also having near-total responsibility for the management of the venues in which they perform AND the finding of external arts events for the majority of these arts venues AND having to make these stages available for most local professional companies. Such had been the case in Hong Kong from the moment the decision was made to construct the City Hall Concert Hall complex in the 1950s. No doubt this continued largely on the basis of precedent. No alternative specific examples are cited in the report and I was not one of those consulted in its preparation. Yet as noted in these pages, even just in my own capacity as a small-time impresario I have provided examples where this near-monopoly acted knowingly against private-sector interests. The far more obvious recent example has been outlined in detail in the previous chapter dealing with the West Kowloon Cultural District.

One result of the report was to make the incoming SAR government realise that changes had to be made both in terms of how grants were allocated and indeed how the arts in general should be managed in Hong Kong in the future. Internally it was agreed that overall the administration was spending far too much on arts funding and that improved assessment methods of determining the value of annual subventions in performance terms had to be implemented.

The change of administration in 1997 provided an excellent timing for change. With there now being no Urban or Regional Councils, it could have been an ideal time to reconsider all aspects of government arts policy and the provision of funding to all the many separate departments. That would certainly have been a major upheaval. Instead, everything was brought under the wing of the new mega LCSD. Little changed in the initial years. The LCSD become a behemoth of massive size whose remit also covered libraries, art galleries and museums, beaches and swimming pools, parks, zoos and gardens, and sports venues in addition to its responsibilities for managing performance venues and spending vast sums on subsidising local performing arts companies and importing many such companies and individual artists from overseas. Taking into account the point acknowledged above about the multiple roles required of the LCSD in the performing arts, there was the clear implication, while not stated, that breaking up the near-total monopoly of functions into separate entities would certainly be beneficial. It seems this has not happened.

The continuing control of LCSD over arts venues like the HKCC Concert Hall in particular and the way it conducts some of its business has drawn criticism from several quarters, not least the Philharmonic's former Music Director, Edo de Waart. In the Philharmonic's annual report for his final season in 2011/12, he points out not only the deficiencies of the Concert Hall but the orchestra's lack of access to the venue.

"Without a true home in which we could be allowed to grow to our full potential, the orchestra offers only as much musical activity as our main venue will allow us. Since confirmation that we have the venue is provided on a short timeline, it is difficult to negotiate with and secure the upper range of international artists, whose diaries stretch years in advance. These issues will continue to hamper the growth of the orchestra and what it can offer to the city and people of Hong Kong."[6]

He ends with the hope that the new Concert Hall on West Kowloon will solve the Philharmonic's problems. Yet, as I write, while there is evidence that a major new Concert Hall for West Kowloon is being considered, nothing has definitely been planned, no finance has been set aside and no timetable has been set. The new Concert Hall remains little more than a mirage that may or may not become fact at some time in the future.

Another result of the report was the realisation that in general too much public money was being provided to performing companies and some would have to endure ongoing cuts. Initially cuts were indeed imposed. In the 10 years between 1998/99 and 2007/08 the annual subsidy to the Hong Kong Philharmonic was actually reduced by a total 18% to HK$56.538 million.[7]

The Philharmonic's annual report for the 2019/2020 year, however, shows that these cuts had not only ceased but substantial increases thereafter been awarded. That year government subsidy had ballooned to HK$94.79 million plus an additional HK$10 million through the government's relatively new Art Development Matching Grant Scheme[8]. This represented a doubling in just 10 years at a time when general worldwide inflation was at historic lows.

To be fair, artistically under its Music Director since 2012, Jaap van Zweden, the Philharmonic has reached an extraordinarily high international standard and received the most prestigious accolade of *Orchestra Of The Year* award for 2019 from Britain's *Gramophone* magazine. Considering it gained this award in competition with such illustrious international ensembles as the London, Boston and San Francisco Symphonies, the Orchestra dell'Accademia Nazionale di Santa Cecilia and the Staatskapelle Berlin, this achievement was nothing short of spectacular. The Hong Kong Philharmonic thus became the first Asian-based orchestra to receive the award.

That van Zweden is responsible for the orchestra's current international standing is no subject for debate. The fact that he has announced his departure during the 2023/2024 season is much more a matter of concern. After all, he had earlier stated his objective to make the Hong Kong Philharmonic the New York Philharmonic of Asia (the NYPO then being his other major international orchestra). Some assumed this might in part be due to the long commute between New York, his home in Holland and Hong Kong. He will certainly also be giving up his Music Directorship of the NYPO at around the same time. But Asia will remain very much on his schedules as at the end of 2022 his appointment as Music Director of the Seoul Philharmonic with effect from 2024 was announced. There he will certainly find a very fine orchestra. Perhaps as importantly the orchestra's concert hall is vastly superior in every respect to that in the HKCC. In 2011 the Music Director of the Seoul Orchestra from 2005 to 2015, Myung-whun Chung, had arranged a long-term recording contract for the orchestra with the world's most prestigious international recording label, Deutsche Grammophon (DGG). There is discussion in musical circles that perhaps DGG might have expressed interest in returning to Seoul to record with van Zweden. But as I write, that remains pure speculation.

And so we come full circle. In many much lesser respects, some of these were relatively similar issues to those I faced in March 1979 when I arrived as General Manager. The Philharmonic then was understandably a completely different and very young organisation. Despite all the problems, we were fortunate to start the development of the orchestra to becoming a true community orchestra and to ascend at least to the first rung or two on the ladder of international recognition. How much further Jaap van Zweden's successor can take the orchestra may well, at least in part, depend on the orchestra's political masters finding two vital requirements: a permanent purpose-built home for rehearsals, and a new concert venue that is a vast improvement over the HKCC Concert Hall.

AFTERWORD

As far as I am aware, in historical terms there has been no blueprint for creating the hardware and software for an arts infrastructure in any city or country. The classical arts in Europe were encouraged and financed primarily in the multitude of princely courts dotted around the continent and the Catholic and Protestant churches. This was particularly true in the development of what we regard as classical music. Opera, theatre and painting also depended on a large degree of private patronage. As the smaller states were over time gobbled up to become larger countries more similar to those in existence today, in many cases the larger national governments took over responsibility for the subsidies to arts organisations.

The model in the United States emerged very differently. During the 19th century, it was private individuals in each community, frequently immigrants and almost exclusively rich, who determined that like Europe their societies should also have symphony orchestras, opera companies and other arts organisations. As had been the case in Europe prior to that time, attending arts performances was very much a desirable leisure activity. Indeed in American cities many soon saw it as a duty to be seen as regular attenders. If their absence was noted in the boxes they paid for on an annual basis, it became a matter for much discussion in the society of the day. It was, though, very much an activity for the upper echelons of society. To that extent, the major arts organisations usually had very closed subscription audiences.

And so it remains today. European governments believe they have an obligation, to a greater or lesser extent, to fund arts performances that are available to a very wide section of the public. Hence high levels of public subsidy. In the United States, where the federal government and the individual states contribute little, private funding remains essential and those elected to the various boards of arts companies are expected to make substantial individual financial contributions as well as soliciting from others. While the USA continues to go its own way, in Europe there has been strong pressure in several countries for arts organisations to follow their US counterparts in finding additional sources of financing from the private sector. This has worked to a certain extent, but tends to be limited either to major corporations contributing to large companies like the Royal Opera or the Royal Shakespeare Company which have a major public following and a high level of international visibility, or to local businesses providing far smaller levels of support to much more local organisations serving their specific area.

With little professional arts management expertise and virtually no professional arts environment back in the 1950s, Hong Kong had little option but to follow the early European model. If the administration and the Urban Council had not taken the initiative, Hong Kong would have remained the 'cultural desert' many continued to call it long after it had ceased to suggest that bleak outlook. The real problem for Hong Kong was that with its monopoly over venues and most performances, it failed to realise that the arts overall in terms of both buildings and performances soon came to be identified as a government project.

Obtaining support from the corporate and private sector therefore faced an uphill PR battle. It was not just that Hong Kong tax rates were very low, thereby rendering tax advantages given for arts philanthropy in the US and the UK, for example, a virtual non-starter. There were other largely unconsidered effects. As Hong Kong grew into a wealthy centre of finance with many Chinese businessmen taking over companies and some becoming extremely rich, philanthropy was not absent from their individual and companies' portfolios. But since the arts were viewed almost exclusively as a government responsibility, that philanthropy came to be increasingly geared towards China in general and education in particular.

I recall a meeting with Sir Run Run Shaw in 1997 when I had hoped to persuade him to become chairman of a Friends of the Shanghai Grand Theatre that could become a primary fundraising committee. He was generous in his praise of the idea but pointed out that all his philanthropic activities in the future were geared towards educational projects like schools and universities in China.

Across People's Square from the Shanghai Grand Theatre is the hugely impressive Shanghai Museum. Look above the entrance to each of its permanent galleries and you see the names of the donors who provided the financing for that particular gallery. Most are Hong Kong billionaires. As Deng Xiaoping had immediately realised when it came to finding initial financing for modernising China, Chinese roots wherever they may be found remain particularly strong.

It is not only in China that art and the arts in general have been the recipient of benefactors who spent most of their time or whose recent ancestors lived in Hong Kong. Anyone visiting the British Museum in London will be aware of the Sir Joseph Hotung Gallery of China and South Asia. The grandson of Hong Kong's richest man, Sir Robert Hotung, Sir Joseph was passionately interested in the arts. In Hong Kong, though, he is much more known for his educational philanthropy.

Hong Kong's "textile tycoon" Tang Ping-yuan had made many major philanthropic contributions in Hong Kong between the end of World War II and his death in 1971, including being a co-founder and the first president of the Community Chest. In 2023 his son Oscar and daughter-in-law Agnes made a US$40 million gift to the New York Philharmonic Orchestra, the largest-ever in the orchestra's history. In total the couple's philanthropic donations are estimated to be considerably in excess of US$250 million. Where, we should wonder, are similar magnificent individual donations to the performing arts now in Hong Kong? We then should ask: does Hong Kong really want private individual donations to the arts? If so, what incentives does the administration provide to encourage them?

And so it remains that the performing arts in Hong Kong, a territory once spoken of as the last bastion of true capitalism, depends today as it has done since the City Hall Concert Hall opened its doors in the 1960s – on public funding. There are a few private-sector charitable foundations like the Swire Trust which do provide a degree of funding, but overall it is very small in comparison to a massive total. Arts entrepreneurs in classical music like Harry O'Dell and Harry Weinrebe no longer exist. I fully accept that my first private-sector company, Pacific Images, failed in the late 1980s due in large part to a lack of sound business practice on my part. As also noted, a number of much more experienced and major international entertainment companies have set up shop in Hong Kong only thereafter to close down relatively quickly.

The question therefore remains: why is it that if Tokyo, Seoul, Taipei and Singapore, as examples, have a private sector much more heavily involved in the arts and entertainment, yet after so many years Hong Kong is all but totally reliant on government – and therefore taxpayer – financing? Why did it put in place limitations, some of which I have outlined herein, seemingly to stifle the growth of a private sector? Did no senior member of the administration accept Sir Cameron Mackintosh's view that a thriving private sector can actually complement what a government itself is providing? And perhaps if anyone examines the history of what past administrations have done over the decades, will they realise that some, at least, was under-thought and very considerably over-expensive?

Having raised the question, I then have to ask myself: is this fair comment? To a certain extent the answer has obviously to be 'no'. Economists and knowledgeable observers have been predicting problems for not merely orchestras but almost all arts-related companies for the better part of 60 years. The performing arts are essentially a people business and therefore not amenable to economies of scale or increases in productivity as would be the case with the use of robots in a manufacturing enterprise, for example. You need a certain number of players for a work by Mozart or Wagner or a play by Shakespeare. Costs are basically fixed and inevitably rise annually to take into account inflation, pension increases and, in certain countries, the ever-increasing cost of medical insurance. Audience sizes are necessarily limited by the size of the performing venues which in turn have to be tailored to the art form.

It is not so long ago that many felt halls with a larger number of seats would at least help that income gap. But as we already noted in reference to the HKCC Concert Hall, Alvar Aalto's Finlandia Concert Hall and the concert hall in the Sydney Opera House, the vital factor in any concert hall for symphonic concerts and the musical performing arts is the acoustics. Size can and must come second. In New York we have the perfect examples. In 1966 the Metropolitan Opera moved into its new purpose-built home in the Lincoln Center, next door to a cluster of several other arts venues. With 3,800 seats, it is not only the largest opera house in the United States, it is the largest in the world. Today many consider it far too large for much of the operatic repertoire. There have even been calls for a new house to be built with a smaller capacity. Yet the opera house it replaced, located on Broadway at 39th Street, had a roughly similar capacity with seating for 3,625. When compared with the world's other top opera houses, this is a massive auditorium. London's Royal Opera has 2,256 seats, Milan's La Scala has 2,030 seats, and the Vienna State Opera even less at 1,709.

Reducing the audience capacity of large arts venues is not a new phenomenon. When the new Metropolitan Opera opened, it was located next door to the home of the New York Philharmonic Orchestra, then named the Avery Fisher Hall. That was also on the large side for orchestra halls with 2,738 seats. Acoustically it was a near-disaster and many blamed its size. Despite two very expensive renovations, the acoustics remained problematic. Now renamed the David Geffen Hall it has recently undergone yet another multi-year renovation costing US$500 million, part of which has been to remodel the interior including a downsizing of seating capacity by 500. This has finally and dramatically improved the acoustics and offers the audience a much enhanced performance experience. In this sense it is very similar to the effect of the renovations in Sydney.

Given the constraints on seating capacities, arts practitioners and indeed governments have no choice but to accept that revenues from the sale of tickets will never increase by as much as overall expenditure. Ticket prices can only be raised so far before resistance becomes apparent and audiences contract. Additional forms of funding are therefore essential to cover the resultant income gap, a gap that will only increase over the years. In the USA this has proved increasingly problematic with the performing arts being traditionally funded by private patronage and grants from business foundations. That model has also changed in recent decades with requests for donations increasing greater than the available funds.

Then there is the fact that the individual members of most urban societies who used to provide the backbone of audiences and private donations tended to come from a better-off immigrant community, largely from Europe where classical music and the arts were often part of the fabric of community life. Recent decades have seen far greater immigration from Hispanic, Asian and peoples from other parts of the world, most of whom do not have that tradition. As problematic, few individuals have been willing to set aside part of their income to make up for a fall off in traditional subscription audiences whose continued regular attendances were vital to the financial health of orchestras in particular.

This situation has been made worse in more than some cases by ineptitude at board level. That may seem unfair to those who sit on boards and who willingly contribute their time and sometimes their cash. Sadly it is proven fact in too many cases worldwide and has resulted in the collapse or near-collapse of once-proud performing companies. One of the most prominent in recent years has been the New York City Opera. The company which for years boasted America's favourite soprano, Beverly Sills, and with a home for half each year in the initially named State Theater in the Lincoln Center, came to an inglorious end after many years of deficits, arrogant chairpersons who thought they knew best and discarded collegiality in favour of selfish personal opinions, CEOs who were just not up to the job given the company's many difficulties, and as often desperately poorly thought-through artistic decisions.

Other countries have other problems to face, problems that in some cases threaten the very existence of some of their performing arts companies. Orchestras in the US and the UK have had to close down. Some others are teetering on a financial precipice. Despite my earlier comments, the people of Hong Kong can therefore count themselves lucky that the performing arts have a more benevolent paymaster, one that is likely to continue well into the future.

In that future, though, I sincerely hope that more attention will be given to some of the main points discussed within these pages: a new concert hall designed by experts from the inside out with an iconic exterior that enhances its surroundings and interior spaces that give audiences and visitors several dining options with great views; privatisation of the management of major performing arts venues; providing greater incentives to make the funding of the performing arts much more appealing to business and commerce as well as to private individuals; and the opening of the design of important performing arts venues to international experts, as has been illustrated recently in many other cities in China.

Thanks in large part to the international success of the Hong Kong Philharmonic Orchestra and the regular international touring by other companies like the Hong Kong Sinfonietta and the City Contemporary Dance Company, Hong Kong now has a reputation as a centre for quality in at least some of the performing arts. Yet for over two decades, the administration has branded Hong Kong with the slogan *Asia's World City*. In its website, under the Arts & Culture section, it states –

"From Canto-pop to Broadway musicals and acclaimed international dance troupes, orchestras and art fairs, Hong Kong's vibrant arts scene echoes the city's East-meets-West culture."[1]

Strictly speaking, all that is only partly true. If you take away the performances as part of the international Arts Festival near the start of each year, the overall picture is not quite so rosy. Whereas there had been a major large-scale Broadway musical presented almost each year in the 1990s, there were estimated to be less than a handful in the decade from 2013. Visiting international dance troupes and international orchestras at other times of the year are also relatively rare. Shanghai, Beijing and some other Chinese cities offer more of all three. Leaving the Covid years aside, one reason is because in addition to national and local government financial support, China has its own private-sector impresarios going out into the international marketplace to contract artists and ensembles to tour in China, the very type of private sector so long lacking in Hong Kong.

And with that comment, I shall finally draw the curtain on this series of experiences during my decades working in the arts in Hong Kong. I will very happily be the first to acknowledge that Hong Kong has enabled me to live out many of my dreams. For that I am full of gratitude. If I am certain of one thing in my life, when I look back it is that moving to Hong Kong in early 1979 was the best decision I was ever to make in my long career.

FOOTNOTES

Websites are accurate at the time of writing but may have changed since then. Some may also now be behind a paywall.

Chapter 4

1 Basil Tschaikov: The Music Goes Round and Around – page 28

2 https://music.newcity.com/2022/10/21/remarkable-return-a-conversation-with-maestro-christian-thielemann-upon-his-return-to-chicago-after-more-than-twenty-years/

3 Basil Tschaikov: The Music Goes Round and Around – page 285. 287

4 www.jhnewsandguide.com/news/cops_courts/walk-family-lawsuit-says-funds-diverted/article_41b6eeef-6d55-5844-ba6e-c704c49f0fb7.html

5 Norman Lebrecht: Who Killed Classical Music? – pages 303-304

6 Basil Tschaikov: The Music Goes Round and Around – page 284

Chapter 6

1 Basil Tschaikov: The Music Goes Round and Around – page 286

Chapter 11

1 www.bruceduffie.com/karr.html

2 Earl Wild: A Walk on the Wild Side – page 56

Chapter 15

1 www.youtube.com/watch?v=Yfj0HbIi1i8

Chapter 16

1 https://time.com/4705809/first-aids-drug-azt/

2 www.who.int/news-room/fact-sheets/detail/hiv-aids

3 Linda Esther Gray: A Life Behind Curtains page 258

Chapter 17

1 Martha Ingram: Kenneth Schermerhorn: He Will Always Be The Music – pages 206-207

Chapter 22

1 www.legco.gov.hk/yr08-09/english/panels/wkcd/papers/wkcdcb2-1302-17-e.pdf

2 www.amscan.org/wp-content/uploads/2015/10/SR.Fall12_Finally-a-Concert-Hall.pdf
3 www.sydneyoperahouse.com/our-story/sydney-opera-house-history.html
4 www.theguardian.com/australia-news/2022/jul/02/better-than-we-dared-imagine-sydney-opera-house-unveils-its-miracle-new-concert-hall
5 www.themonthly.com.au/issue/2017/october/1506780000/darryn-king/not-opera-house
6 www.researchgate.net/publication/12672197_Acoustical_design_of_the_Tokyo_Opera_City_TOC_concert_hall_Japan
7 www.scmp.com/article/497040/developers-not-hub-job-says-cultural-centre-architect
8 www.thelocal.de/20171026/visitors-to-the-elbphilharmonie-hit-4-million-already
9 www.legco.gov.hk/1952/h520220.pdf
10 www.interlude.hk/front/hong-kong-philharmonics-gotterdammerung-dawn-wagnerian-orchestra/

Chapter 24

1 John Duffus: Backstage With Pavarotti And Other Egos – page 3
2 John Duffus: Backstage With Pavarotti And Other Egos – page 32
3 John Duffus: Backstage With Pavarotti And Other Egos – page 39
4 John Duffus: Backstage With Pavarotti And Other Egos – page 165

Chapter 26

1 https://interlude.hk/on-this-day-8-january-alexis-weissenberg-died/
2 www.bruceduffie.com/wild.html
3 Earl Wild: A Walk on the Wild Side – pages 581/582

Chapter 28

1 https://the-singapore-lgbt-encyclopaedia.fandom.com/wiki/Boom_Boom_Room
2 www.bbc.com/news/magazine-33809914
3 www.wsj.com/articles/SB866404207275292500
4 www.bbc.com/news/entertainment-arts-26336382

Chapter 29

1 www.legco.gov.hk/yr97-98/english/fc/fc/papers/f2703113.htm
2 www.info.gov.hk/gia/general/200102/07/0207224.htm
3 www.travelweekly-asia.com/Travel-News/Amy-Chan-leaves-HKTA

Chapter 31

1 www.goethe.de/en/kul/tut/21506299.html

2 https://australien.ahk.de/en/media/news-details/how-germany-is-helping-opera-to-survive-around-the-world

3 www.statista.com/statistics/631635/hong-kong-performing-arts-industry-workforce/

4 www.legco.gov.hk/research-publications/english/2022issh27-art-sector-in-hong-kong-20221107-e.pdf

5 www.gov.hk/en/about/abouthk/factsheets/docs/creative_industries.pdf

6 www.hkphil.org/f/documentary/11009/HK_Phil_annual_report_1112.pdf

7 www.legco.gov.hk/yr07-08/english/panels/ha/papers/ha0215cb2-1053-4-e.pdf]

8 www.hkphil.org/f/documentary/22236/hkphil-ar1920-web.pdf

Afterword

1 www.brandhk.gov.hk/en/live-and-work/cosmopolitan-lifestyle#arts_culture

Much of the content in paragraphs 25 and 27 comes directly from my book *Backstage with Pavarotti and Other Egos: Disasters on the High Cs.*

Photo credits

Rhinegold Publishing p177; John Duffus p178 top, p181 top and bottom, p184 top and bottom left, 189 top and bottom, p190 top, p194, p196 top and bottom, p197 top and bottom, p198 top and bottom, p199 top and bottom; Grand Teton Music Festival p179 top and bottom; Pacific Images p180; Hong Kong Philharmonic Society p185, p186, p187 top; Ivory Classics Foundation p185 bottom right; Leisure and Cultural Services Department, Hong Kong SAR Government 康樂及文化事務署 p190 bottom; Christchurch Town Hall, New Zealand p191 top and bottom; Tibor Rudas Productions and Pacific Images p195.

SELECTED BIBLIOGRAPHY

(in alphabetical order)

A Life Behind the Curtains – Linda Esther Gray, Green Oak Publishing

A Walk on the Wild Side – Earl Wild, The Ivory Classics Foundation

Alex: The Authorised Biography of Sir Alexander Gibson – Conrad Wilson, Mainstream Publishing

Anatomy of the Orchestra – Norman del Mar, University of California Press

Backstage with Pavarotti and Other Egos: Disasters on the High Cs – John Duffus, New Generation Publishing

Corresponding with Carlos: A Biography of Carlos Kleiber – Christopher Barber, Rowman and Littlefield Publishers

Distant Archipelago: Memories of Malaya – Peter Moss, iUniverse

Foreign Mud – Maurice Collis, Faber & Faber

Herbert von Karajan: A Life in Music – Richard Osborne, Pimlico

Hong Kong: Another City Another Age – Peter Moss, Formasia Books

Hong Kong: The Classic Age – Peter Moss, Formasia Books

Ibbs & Tillett: The Rise and Fall of a Musical Empire – Christopher Fifield, Ashgate Publishing

Kenneth Schermerhorn: He Will Always Be the Music – Martha Rivers Ingram with D. B. Kellogg, Nashville Symphony Orchestra Association

Mad Scenes and Exit Arias: The Death of the New York City Opera and the Future of Opera in America – Heidi Waleson, Metropolitan Books

Musical Heroes – Robert Ponsonby, Giles de la Mer Publishers

No Babylon: A Hong Kong Scrapbook – Peter Moss, iUniverse

Orchestra (with introduction by Andre Previn) – Macdonald and Jane's

Rhapsody in Red – Sheila Melvin and Jindong Cai, Algora Publishing

The Art of the Turnaround: Creating and Maintaining Healthy Arts Organisations – Michael M. Kaiser, Brandeis University Press

The Honourable Schoolboy – John Le Carré, Hodder & Stoughton

The King & I: The Uncensored Tale of Luciano Pavarotti's Rise to Fame by his Manager, Friend, and Sometime Adversary – Herbert Breslin & Anne Midgette, Doubleday

The Maestro Myth: Great Conductors in Pursuit of Power – Norman Lebrecht, Simon & Schuster

The Malayan Trilogy – Anthony Burgess, Vintage (Rand)

The Music Goes Round and Around – Basil Tschaikov, Fastprint Publishing

Who Killed Classical Music? Maestros, Managers and Corporate Politics – Norman Lebrecht, Birch Lane Press

ACKNOWLEDGEMENTS

Although based on my own diaries, notes and memories of events, I have been helped by many in the preparation of this book. I particularly wish to express my gratitude to Professor Sun Man Tseng who gave of his extremely valuable time to read through the manuscript and make a number of suggestions, some major. I first had the pleasure of working with Sun Man when he was marketing manager at the Hong Kong Philharmonic. He was of particular help to me during our few years together with the orchestra and it was no surprise that his career thereafter blossomed spectacularly in both the management of the arts and in academia. There will be many now working and soon to start working in arts management as a result of his ground-breaking work in establishing the Arts Administration Department at the Shanghai Conservatory of Music and becoming its first chair and professor in 2005. His other arts and academic activities are far too numerous to mention here. Suffice to say I can think of no-one with his depth of knowledge and expertise in arts management in China and elsewhere in Asia.

K. C. Lee is another former colleague from my final years at the Hong Kong Philharmonic. He then became a loyal ally and friend by joining me to work in almost all the companies I have both founded and for which I have worked. He was project director at Pacific Images, an executive at IMG Artists looking after operations in Hong Kong when I was based in Tokyo, joined me when I returned to Hong Kong as the Asian managing director of Andrew Lloyd Webber's Really Useful Company, and assisted me on various other projects in a freelance capacity including the final tour by Luciano Pavarotti in December 2005. K. C. generously read through and commented on some of the draft.

Yet another Philharmonic colleague was Lee Bo-luen, our highly effective orchestra manager. He kindly read through other sections and filled me in on details of which I had not been aware. Although he and his family moved to Toronto soon after he left the Philharmonic, we spent a very happy day together on a quick trip I made to Toronto in late 2005, concluding with a dinner at which we were joined by some former Philharmonic musicians.

Vennie Ho was a staunch ally during all my years at the Philharmonic. Although we have met occasionally since those times, it was only when we had meetings in 2023 that we were able to review a number of issues which I had largely forgotten. Life would also have been far more difficult without the constant assistance of my secretaries, first Vivien and then Maria.

I also extend my gratitude to another unsung group so essential to managing a symphony orchestra and other arts events – the artists' agents, especially those based in Japan who became increasingly important in my career, both in engaging artists, providing advice and assisting in my capacity as secretary general of the Federation for Asian Cultural Promotion. In Tokyo I was always treated with the utmost courtesy and respect by Naoyasu Kajimoto and later his son Masahide in the Kajimoto Music Office, the late Yoshiro Kambara and his small agency staff, Yasuo Nakato, Masayuki Sekita and all their colleagues at Japan Arts, along with several others.

Finally no book about a career in the performing arts can omit mention of the musicians and artists. Some with whom I worked have become dear friends and provided insights incorporated in these pages. To all of those with whom I had the pleasure of working over more than four decades in Hong Kong, you made my life (mostly!) one of near utter joy. Thank you all from the bottom of my heart.